BASIC ELECTRONIC DISCOVERY

a casebook approach

Practicum Press

© 2021 by Antony P. Ng

No part of this publication may be reproduced or distributed in any form or by any means, electronic or mechanical, without written permission from the author or the publisher.

Practicum Press
Austin, Texas

Printed in the United States of America

ISBN: 979-8-5117425-8-8

Acknowledgments

I would like to thank Craig Ball, Reginald Hirsch, and Dana Huebner for their time and effort in reading the manuscript as well as adding valuable insights.

TABLE OF CONTENTS

Forward v

Introduction 1

Chapter 1

E-Discovery Rules 3

    Federal Rules of Civil Procedure 3
    Federal Rules of Evidence 21

Chapter 2

Electronic Discovery Reference Model 23

    Stages of EDRM 23
    Limitations of EDRM 26
    E-discovery Process 26

Chapter 3

Scope and Limits 27

    Proportionality 27
    Accessibility 47

Chapter 4

Conference and Cooperation 53

    Rule 26(f) Conference 53
    Cooperation 57

CHAPTER 5

PRESERVATION OF ELECTRONICALLY STORED INFORMATION ... 65

- Litigation Hold ... 65
- Other Preservation Methods ... 70
- Duty to Preserve ... 72
- Possession, Custody or Control ... 77

CHAPTER 6

SPOLIATION AND SANCTIONS ... 85

- Finding Spoliation ... 85
- Type of Sanctions ... 116

CHAPTER 7

COLLECTION OF ELECTRONICALLY STORED INFORMATION ... 175

- Locations where ESI Resides ... 175
- Entities that Perform Collection ... 183
- Collection Strategy ... 190
- Data Collection Tools ... 192
- Ensuring Data Integrity ... 194

CHAPTER 8

TECHNOLOGY-ASSISTED DOCUMENT REVIEW ... 195

- Predictive Coding ... 195
- Court's View on Technology-Assisted Review ... 200

CHAPTER 9

PRODUCTION OF ELECTRONICALLY STORED INFORMATION 223

    Forms of Production 223
    Compel Production 236
    Privacy 248

CHAPTER 10

PRIVILEGE ISSUES IN E-DISCOVERY 271

    Burden of Proving Inadvertent Disclosure 271
    Reasonable Steps to Prevent Disclosure 279
    Reasonable Steps to Rectify Error 289
    Clawback Agreements 299

CHAPTER 11

COST SHIFTING AND COST SHARING 327

    Cost Shifting under Statutes 327
    Cost Shifting under Judicial Rules 315

CHAPTER 12

ELECTRONICALLY STORED INFORMATION 333

    Analog and Digital ESI 333
    Numbering Systems 337
    Encoding Schemes 339
    File Extensions 341
    Metadata 342

Chapter 13

Information Processing Machines 343

Hardware 343
Software 346

Chapter 14

Mobile Devices 349

Chapter 15

Encryption and Hashing 353

Encryption 353
Hashing 355

Glossary 359

FORWARD

As a special master for the courts, I believe law students who plans to do litigation (and lawyers who are doing litigation) should learn electronic discovery, or at least should have a good understanding of it.

I first met Antony at a State Bar meeting over 25 years ago. It was a time when people still talk to each other instead of texting because smart phones had not even come into existence yet. It was a time when only a handful of lawyers had laptop computers, and lawsuit discoveries were mostly related to boxes and boxes of papers.

Many things have changed since then, and so is the practice of law. Paper discovery has been rapidly replaced by electronic discovery. Since electronic discovery tends to require legal as well as technical knowledge, today's and future lawyers need to have a certain level of technical competency in addition to their legal skills.

Unlike other areas of substantive law, electronic discovery is a difficult subject to explain via a casebook. However, this book has provided a clear framework on many major electronic discovery concepts illustrated by relevant cases accordingly. In addition, this book also provides its readers a basic rundown of some technical subject matters that are related to electronic discovery. I also find it delightful to see drawings and flowcharts are used to illustrate certain important technical and legal concepts.

This book serves as a good introduction of the ever changing world of electronic discovery to a new generation of law students and lawyers.

Gale "Pete" Peterson

Introduction

Electronic discovery (e-discovery) is a process to preserve, collect, review, and exchange electronically stored information (ESI) for the purpose of using ESI as evidence in a lawsuit. There are many different types of ESI that may be sought in e-discovery, ranging from traditional data, such as word-processed documents and emails, to non-traditional data, such as text messages and social media postings.

E-discovery begins when litigation is reasonably foreseeable and last until the case is settled or goes to trial. After the scope of e-discovery has been determined by opposing parties, potential litigants have the legal duty to preserve potentially relevant ESI. After the parameters have been defined, ESI is then collected, analyzed, and formatted for presentation in court.

In general, only active data are collected, which are easily available through file storage and programs utilized by businesses or individuals. Attorneys typically work with IT professionals, with IT professionals collecting data, and attorneys performing review on the collected data.

In conjunction, digital forensics (or computer forensics) is a scientific method for extracting data from a digital device. A forensic analysis of data is needed when a litigation requires a deeper look at the data. It is carried out by digital forensic experts who are specialize in computer hardware and software. Digital forensic experts are brought in to produce more than data for a case. They sort through data in search of hidden files or deleted data to help provide more-reliable evidence that can be used in a case. They can be called on in legal proceedings to defend their claims about the information.

Electronic discovery is useful when the only information needed involves easily accessible files such as documents, spreadsheets, emails, databases, etc. Digital forensics is needed to further analyze the data if it has been deleted or if someone has tampered with it.

E-discovery rules for civil cases were initially codified in the Federal Rules of Civil Procedure (FRCP) in 2006. The e-discovery rules in the FRCP were amended in 2015 to curb the excesses and legal gamesmanship.

E-discovery is a complex process that combines both legal and technical disciplines. In addition, technical competency is increasingly viewed as part of a lawyer's ethical duty to provide competent representation. For example, under Rule 1.1, the Model Rules of Professional Conduct now include that attorneys should "keep abreast of changes in the law and its practice, including the benefits and risks associated with relevant technology." Many states also include a technical competent requirement in their respective rules of professional conduct. Thus, it is important for attorneys to be able to understand and speak legal as well as technical during the e-discovery process.

The first part of this book provides an outline of the e-discovery process and the relevant laws. The second part of this book provides explanations on various technical concepts that are germane to the e-discovery process.

Chapter 1

E-Discovery Rules

The Federal Rules of Civil Procedure (FRCP) was amended in 2006 to address electronic discovery (e-discovery) as a distinct element of civil procedure. The FRCP was amended again in 2015. The 2015 amendments were intended to provide new guidelines on the scope of discovery and the spoliation of electronically stored information (ESI) while emphasizing the need for proportionality and cooperation between parties.

In addition to the FRCP, the Federal Rules of Evidence (FRE) also includes some rules that are relevant to e-discovery.

A. Federal Rules of Civil Procedure

Rule 1

Although not an e-discovery rule specifically, Rule 1 governs the entire FRCP, and it makes clear that the FRCP should be construed and administered by both the court and the parties to ensure a just and speedy determination of every action and proceeding without incurring exorbitant costs. With the esculating e-discovery costs and the potential for e-discovery costs being grown out of control, many courts use Rule 1 to push for cooperation between opposing parties as a means to expedite fair and efficient e-discovery.

Rule 1. Scope and Purpose

These rules govern the procedure in all civil actions and proceedings in the United States district courts, except as stated in Rule 81. They should be construed, administered, and employed by the court and the parties to secure the just, speedy, and inexpensive determination of every action and proceeding.

Rule 16

Active case management is the theme of Rule 16. The relatively short time frame for courts to issue a scheduling order and the bolstering of the Rule 26(f) conference are intended to reduce delays at the outset of litigation, which tends to make early case assessment even more important. Parties should know what types of data are implicated, where the data reside, and how the data will be reviewed and produced.

Rule 16 also permits scheduling orders to address the preservation of ESI, and clawback agreements under FRE Rule 502 to protect privilege work-products between parties. Under Rule 16, a Rule 26(f) conference needs to take place before any party can move for a discovery order.

Rule 16 requires attorneys coming into pretrial conferences informed and prepared to discuss their client's information technology (IT) and data environment in order for them to properly access the process of e-discovery. The setting of a timeline for pretrial matters helps controlling the cost of e-discovery.

Rule 16. Pretrial Conferences; Scheduling; Management

(a) Purposes of a Pretrial Conference. In any action, the court may order the attorneys and any unrepresented parties to appear for one or more pretrial conferences for such purposes as:

    (1) expediting disposition of the action;
    (2) establishing early and continuing control so that the case will not be protracted because of lack of management;
    (3) discouraging wasteful pretrial activities;
    (4) improving the quality of the trial through more thorough preparation; and
    (5) facilitating settlement.

(b) Scheduling.

    (1) Scheduling Order. Except in categories of actions exempted by local rule, the district judge, or a magistrate judge when authorized by local rule, must issue a scheduling order:
        (A) after receiving the parties' report under Rule 26(f); or
        (B) after consulting with the parties' attorneys and any unrepresented parties at a scheduling conference.

    (2) Time to Issue. The judge must issue the scheduling order as soon as practicable, but unless the judge finds good cause for delay, the judge must issue it within the earlier of 90 days after any defendant has been served with the complaint or 60 days after any defendant has appeared.

(3) Contents of the Order.

(A) Required Contents. The scheduling order must limit the time to join other parties, amend the pleadings, complete discovery, and file motions.

(B) Permitted Contents. The scheduling order may:
- (i) modify the timing of disclosures under Rules 26(a) and 26(e)(1);
- (ii) modify the extent of discovery;
- (iii) provide for disclosure, discovery, or preservation of electronically stored information;
- (iv) include any agreements the parties reach for asserting claims of privilege or of protection as trial-preparation material after information is produced, including agreements reached under Federal Rule of Evidence 502;
- (v) direct that before moving for an order relating to discovery, the movant must request a conference with the court;
- (vi) set dates for pretrial conferences and for trial; and
- (vii) include other appropriate matters.

(4) Modifying a Schedule. A schedule may be modified only for good cause and with the judge's consent.

(c) Attendance and Matters for Consideration at a Pretrial Conference.

(1) Attendance. A represented party must authorize at least one of its attorneys to make stipulations and admissions about all matters that can reasonably be anticipated for discussion at a pretrial conference. If appropriate, the court may require that a party or its representative be present or reasonably available by other means to consider possible settlement.

(2) Matters for Consideration. At any pretrial conference, the court may consider and take appropriate action on the following matters:

(A) formulating and simplifying the issues, and eliminating frivolous claims or defenses;
(B) amending the pleadings if necessary or desirable;
(C) obtaining admissions and stipulations about facts and documents to avoid unnecessary proof, and ruling in advance on the admissibility of evidence;
(D) avoiding unnecessary proof and cumulative evidence, and limiting the use of testimony under Federal Rule of Evidence 702;
(E) determining the appropriateness and timing of summary adjudication under Rule 56;
(F) controlling and scheduling discovery, including orders affecting disclosures and discovery under Rule 26 and Rules 29 through 37;
(G) identifying witnesses and documents, scheduling the filing and exchange of any pretrial briefs, and setting dates for further conferences and for trial;
(H) referring matters to a magistrate judge or a master;
(I) settling the case and using special procedures to assist in resolving the dispute when authorized by statute or local rule;
(J) determining the form and content of the pretrial order;
(K) disposing of pending motions;
(L) adopting special procedures for managing potentially difficult or protracted actions that may involve complex issues, multiple parties, difficult legal questions, or unusual proof problems;

(M) ordering a separate trial under Rule 42(b) of a claim, counterclaim, crossclaim, third-party claim, or particular issue;

(N) ordering the presentation of evidence early in the trial on a manageable issue that might, on the evidence, be the basis for a judgment as a matter of law under Rule 50(a) or a judgment on partial findings under Rule 52(c);

(O) establishing a reasonable limit on the time allowed to present evidence; and

(P) facilitating in other ways the just, speedy, and inexpensive disposition of the action.

(d) Pretrial Orders. After any conference under this rule, the court should issue an order reciting the action taken. This order controls the course of the action unless the court modifies it.

(e) Final Pretrial Conference and Orders. The court may hold a final pretrial conference to formulate a trial plan, including a plan to facilitate the admission of evidence. The conference must be held as close to the start of trial as is reasonable, and must be attended by at least one attorney who will conduct the trial for each party and by any unrepresented party. The court may modify the order issued after a final pretrial conference only to prevent manifest injustice.

(f) Sanctions.

(1) In General. On motion or on its own, the court may issue any just orders, including those authorized by Rule 37(b)(2)(A)(ii)-(vii), if a party or its attorney:

(A) fails to appear at a scheduling or other pretrial conference;

(B) is substantially unprepared to participate, or does not participate in good faith, in the conference; or

(C) fails to obey a scheduling or other pretrial order.

(2) Imposing Fees and Costs. Instead of or in addition to any other sanction, the court must order the party, its attorney, or both to pay the reasonable expenses, including attorney's fees, incurred because of any noncompliance with this rule, unless the noncompliance was substantially justified or other circumstances make an award of expenses unjust.

Rules 26

Rule 26 mandates that discovery be reasonable, relevant to any party's claim or defense, and proportional to the needs of the case. Rule 26 requires attorneys to understand the ESI that is relevant to the case early in the process in order to create and share discovery plans at a Rule 26(f) conference, in the hope of saving time and money. Rule 26(a) permits equests for production to be sent before the Rule 26(f) conference. Rule 26(c) requires that before filing a motion for a protective order, the movant must confer with the other affected parties in a good faith effort to resolve the discovery dispute. Rule 26(d) provides that formal discovery not to be commenced before the Rule 26(f) conference.

Rule 26. Duty to Disclose; General Provisions Governing Discovery

(a) Required Disclosures.

   (1) Initial Disclosure.

      (A) In General. Except as exempted by Rule 26(a)(1)(B) or as otherwise stipulated or ordered by the court, a party must, without awaiting a discovery request, provide to the other parties:

         (i) the name and, if known, the address and telephone number of each individual likely to have discoverable information—along with the subjects of that information—that the disclosing party may use to support its claims or defenses, unless the use would be solely for impeachment;

         (ii) a copy—or a description by category and location—of all documents, electronically stored information, and tangible things that the disclosing party has in its possession, custody, or control and may use to support its claims or defenses, unless the use would be solely for impeachment;

         (iii) a computation of each category of damages claimed by the disclosing party—who must also make available for inspection and copying as under Rule 34 the documents or other evidentiary material, unless privileged or protected from disclosure, on which each computation is based, including materials bearing on the nature and extent of injuries suffered; and

         (iv) for inspection and copying as under Rule 34, any insurance agreement under which an insurance business may be liable to satisfy all or part of a possible judgment in the action or to indemnify or reimburse for payments made to satisfy the judgment.

      (B) Proceedings Exempt from Initial Disclosure. The following proceedings are exempt from initial disclosure:

         (i) an action for review on an administrative record;

         (ii) a forfeiture action in rem arising from a federal statute;

         (iii) a petition for habeas corpus or any other proceeding to challenge a criminal conviction or sentence;

(iv) an action brought without an attorney by a person in the custody of the United States, a state, or a state subdivision;
(v) an action to enforce or quash an administrative summons or subpoena;
(vi) an action by the United States to recover benefit payments;
(vii) an action by the United States to collect on a student loan guaranteed by the United States;
(viii) a proceeding ancillary to a proceeding in another court; and
(ix) an action to enforce an arbitration award.

(C) Time for Initial Disclosures—In General. A party must make the initial disclosures at or within 14 days after the parties' Rule 26(f) conference unless a different time is set by stipulation or court order, or unless a party objects during the conference that initial disclosures are not appropriate in this action and states the objection in the proposed discovery plan. In ruling on the objection, the court must determine what disclosures, if any, are to be made and must set the time for disclosure.

(D) Time for Initial Disclosures—For Parties Served or Joined Later. A party that is first served or otherwise joined after the Rule 26(f) conference must make the initial disclosures within 30 days after being served or joined, unless a different time is set by stipulation or court order.

(E) Basis for Initial Disclosure; Unacceptable Excuses. A party must make its initial disclosures based on the information then reasonably available to it. A party is not excused from making its disclosures because it has not fully investigated the case or because it challenges the sufficiency of another party's disclosures or because another party has not made its disclosures.

(2) Disclosure of Expert Testimony.

(A) In General. In addition to the disclosures required by Rule 26(a)(1), a party must disclose to the other parties the identity of any witness it may use at trial to present evidence under Federal Rule of Evidence 702, 703, or 705.

(B) Witnesses Who Must Provide a Written Report. Unless otherwise stipulated or ordered by the court, this disclosure must be accompanied by a written report—prepared and signed by the witness—if the witness is one retained or specially employed to provide expert testimony in the case or one whose duties as the party's employee regularly involve giving expert testimony. The report must contain:
(i) a complete statement of all opinions the witness will express and the basis and reasons for them;
(ii) the facts or data considered by the witness in forming them;
(iii) any exhibits that will be used to summarize or support them;
(iv) the witness's qualifications, including a list of all publications authored in the previous 10 years;
(v) a list of all other cases in which, during the previous 4 years, the witness testified as an expert at trial or by deposition; and
(vi) a statement of the compensation to be paid for the study and testimony in the case.

(C) Witnesses Who Do Not Provide a Written Report. Unless otherwise stipulated or ordered by the court, if the witness is not required to provide a written report, this disclosure must state:

(i) the subject matter on which the witness is expected to present evidence under Federal Rule of Evidence 702, 703, or 705; and
(ii) a summary of the facts and opinions to which the witness is expected to testify.

(D) Time to Disclose Expert Testimony. A party must make these disclosures at the times and in the sequence that the court orders. Absent a stipulation or a court order, the disclosures must be made:
(i) at least 90 days before the date set for trial or for the case to be ready for trial; or
(ii) if the evidence is intended solely to contradict or rebut evidence on the same subject matter identified by another party under Rule 26(a)(2)(B) or (C), within 30 days after the other party's disclosure.

(E) Supplementing the Disclosure. The parties must supplement these disclosures when required under Rule 26(e).

(3) Pretrial Disclosures.

(A) In General. In addition to the disclosures required by Rule 26(a)(1) and (2), a party must provide to the other parties and promptly file the following information about the evidence that it may present at trial other than solely for impeachment:
(i) the name and, if not previously provided, the address and telephone number of each witness—separately identifying those the party expects to present and those it may call if the need arises;
(ii) the designation of those witnesses whose testimony the party expects to present by deposition and, if not taken stenographically, a transcript of the pertinent parts of the deposition; and
(iii) an identification of each document or other exhibit, including summaries of other evidence—separately identifying those items the party expects to offer and those it may offer if the need arises.

(B) Time for Pretrial Disclosures; Objections. Unless the court orders otherwise, these disclosures must be made at least 30 days before trial. Within 14 days after they are made, unless the court sets a different time, a party may serve and promptly file a list of the following objections: any objections to the use under Rule 32(a) of a deposition designated by another party under Rule 26(a)(3)(A)(ii); and any objection, together with the grounds for it, that may be made to the admissibility of materials identified under Rule 26(a)(3)(A)(iii). An objection not so made—except for one under Federal Rule of Evidence 402 or 403—is waived unless excused by the court for good cause.

(4) Form of Disclosures. Unless the court orders otherwise, all disclosures under Rule 26(a) must be in writing, signed, and served.

(b) Discovery Scope and Limits.

(1) Scope in General. Unless otherwise limited by court order, the scope of discovery is as follows: Parties may obtain discovery regarding any nonprivileged matter that is relevant to any party's claim or defense and proportional to the needs of the case, considering the importance of the issues at stake in the action, the amount in controversy, the parties' relative access to relevant information, the parties' resources, the importance of the discovery in resolving the issues, and whether the burden or expense of the proposed discovery outweighs its likely benefit. Information within this scope of discovery need not be admissible in evidence to be discoverable.

(2) Limitations on Frequency and Extent.

(A) When Permitted. By order, the court may alter the limits in these rules on the number of depositions and interrogatories or on the length of depositions under Rule 30. By order or local rule, the court may also limit the number of requests under Rule 36.

(B) Specific Limitations on Electronically Stored Information. A party need not provide discovery of electronically stored information from sources that the party identifies as not reasonably accessible because of undue burden or cost. On motion to compel discovery or for a protective order, the party from whom discovery is sought must show that the information is not reasonably accessible because of undue burden or cost. If that showing is made, the court may nonetheless order discovery from such sources if the requesting party shows good cause, considering the limitations of Rule 26(b)(2)(C). The court may specify conditions for the discovery.

(C) When Required. On motion or on its own, the court must limit the frequency or extent of discovery otherwise allowed by these rules or by local rule if it determines that:
- (i) the discovery sought is unreasonably cumulative or duplicative, or can be obtained from some other source that is more convenient, less burdensome, or less expensive;
- (ii) the party seeking discovery has had ample opportunity to obtain the information by discovery in the action; or
- (iii) the proposed discovery is outside the scope permitted by Rule 26(b)(1).

(3) Trial Preparation: Materials.

(A) Documents and Tangible Things. Ordinarily, a party may not discover documents and tangible things that are prepared in anticipation of litigation or for trial by or for another party or its representative (including the other party's attorney, consultant, surety, indemnitor, insurer, or agent). But, subject to Rule 26(b)(4), those materials may be discovered if:
- (i) they are otherwise discoverable under Rule 26(b)(1); and
- (ii) the party shows that it has substantial need for the materials to prepare its case and cannot, without undue hardship, obtain their substantial equivalent by other means.

(B) Protection Against Disclosure. If the court orders discovery of those materials, it must protect against disclosure of the mental impressions, conclusions, opinions, or legal theories of a party's attorney or other representative concerning the litigation.

(C) Previous Statement. Any party or other person may, on request and without the required showing, obtain the person's own previous statement about the action or its subject matter. If the request is refused, the person may move for a court order, and Rule 37(a)(5) applies to the award of expenses. A previous statement is either:
- (I) a written statement that the person has signed or otherwise adopted or approved; or
- (ii) a contemporaneous stenographic, mechanical, electrical, or other recording, or a transcription of it, that recites substantially verbatim the person's oral statement.

(4) Trial Preparation: Experts.

(A) Deposition of an Expert Who May Testify. A party may depose any person who has been identified as an expert whose opinions may be presented at trial. If Rule 26(a)(2)(B) requires a report from the expert, the deposition may be conducted only after the report is provided.

(B) Trial-Preparation Protection for Draft Reports or Disclosures. Rules 26(b)(3)(A) and (B) protect drafts of any report or disclosure required under Rule 26(a)(2), regardless of the form in which the draft is recorded.

(C) Trial-Preparation Protection for Communications Between a Party's Attorney and Expert Witnesses. Rules 26(b)(3)(A) and (B) protect communications between the party's attorney and any witness required to provide a report under Rule 26(a)(2)(B), regardless of the form of the communications, except to the extent that the communications:
- (i) relate to compensation for the expert's study or testimony;
- (ii) identify facts or data that the party's attorney provided and that the expert considered in forming the opinions to be expressed; or
- (iii) identify assumptions that the party's attorney provided and that the expert relied on in forming the opinions to be expressed.

(D) Expert Employed Only for Trial Preparation. Ordinarily, a party may not, by interrogatories or deposition, discover facts known or opinions held by an expert who has been retained or specially employed by another party in anticipation of litigation or to prepare for trial and who is not expected to be called as a witness at trial. But a party may do so only:
- (i) as provided in Rule 35(b); or
- (ii) on showing exceptional circumstances under which it is impracticable for the party to obtain facts or opinions on the same subject by other means.

(E) Payment. Unless manifest injustice would result, the court must require that the party seeking discovery:
- (i) pay the expert a reasonable fee for time spent in responding to discovery under Rule 26(b)(4)(A) or (D); and
- (ii) for discovery under (D), also pay the other party a fair portion of the fees and expenses it reasonably incurred in obtaining the expert's facts and opinions.

(5) Claiming Privilege or Protecting Trial-Preparation Materials.

(A) Information Withheld. When a party withholds information otherwise discoverable by claiming that the information is privileged or subject to protection as trial-preparation material, the party must:
- (i) expressly make the claim; and
- (ii) describe the nature of the documents, communications, or tangible things not produced or disclosed, and do so in a manner that, without revealing information itself privileged or protected, will enable other parties to assess the claim.

(B) Information Produced. If information produced in discovery is subject to a claim of privilege or of protection as trial-preparation material, the party making the claim may notify any party that received the information of the claim and the basis for it. After being notified, a party must promptly return, sequester, or destroy the specified information and any copies it has; must not use or disclose the information until the claim is resolved; must take reasonable steps to retrieve the information if the party disclosed it before being notified; and may promptly present the information to the court under seal for a determination of the claim. The producing party must preserve the information until the claim is resolved.

(c) Protective Orders.

(1) In General. A party or any person from whom discovery is sought may move for a protective order in the court where the action is pending, or as an alternative on matters relating to a deposition, in the court for the district where the deposition will be taken. The motion must include a certification that the movant has in good faith conferred or attempted to confer with other affected parties in an effort to resolve the dispute without court action. The court may, for good cause, issue an order to protect a party or person from annoyance, embarrassment, oppression, or undue burden or expense, including one or more of the following:

(A) forbidding the disclosure or discovery;
(B) specifying terms, including time and place or the allocation of expenses, for the disclosure or discovery;
(C) prescribing a discovery method other than the one selected by the party seeking discovery;
(D) forbidding inquiry into certain matters, or limiting the scope of disclosure or discovery to certain matters;
(E) designating the persons who may be present while the discovery is conducted;
(F) requiring that a deposition be sealed and opened only on court order;
(G) requiring that a trade secret or other confidential research, development, or commercial information not be revealed or be revealed only in a specified way; and
(H) requiring that the parties simultaneously file specified documents or information in sealed envelopes, to be opened as the court directs.

(2) Ordering Discovery. If a motion for a protective order is wholly or partly denied, the court may, on just terms, order that any party or person provide or permit discovery.

(3) Awarding Expenses. Rule 37(a)(5) applies to the award of expenses.

(d) Timing and Sequence of Discovery.

(1) Timing. A party may not seek discovery from any source before the parties have conferred as required by Rule 26(f), except in a proceeding exempted from initial disclosure under Rule 26(a)(1)(B), or when authorized by these rules, by stipulation, or by court order.

(2) Early Rule 34 Requests.

(A) Time to Deliver. More than 21 days after the summons and complaint are served on a party, a request under Rule 34 may be delivered:
(i) to that party by any other party, and
(ii) by that party to any plaintiff or to any other party that has been served.
(B) When Considered Served. The request is considered to have been served at the first Rule 26(f) conference.

(3) Sequence. Unless the parties stipulate or the court orders otherwise for the parties' and witnesses' convenience and in the interests of justice:

      (A) methods of discovery may be used in any sequence; and
      (B) discovery by one party does not require any other party to delay its discovery.

(e) Supplementing Disclosures and Responses.

    (1) In General. A party who has made a disclosure under Rule 26(a)—or who has responded to an interrogatory, request for production, or request for admission—must supplement or correct its disclosure or response:

      (A) in a timely manner if the party learns that in some material respect the disclosure or response is incomplete or incorrect, and if the additional or corrective information has not otherwise been made known to the other parties during the discovery process or in writing; or
      (B) as ordered by the court.

    (2) Expert Witness. For an expert whose report must be disclosed under Rule 26(a)(2)(B), the party's duty to supplement extends both to information included in the report and to information given during the expert's deposition. Any additions or changes to this information must be disclosed by the time the party's pretrial disclosures under Rule 26(a)(3) are due.

(f) Conference of the Parties; Planning for Discovery.

    (1) Conference Timing. Except in a proceeding exempted from initial disclosure under Rule 26(a)(1)(B) or when the court orders otherwise, the parties must confer as soon as practicable, and in any event at least 21 days before a scheduling conference is to be held or a scheduling order is due under Rule 16(b).

    (2) Conference Content; Parties' Responsibilities. In conferring, the parties must consider the nature and basis of their claims and defenses and the possibilities for promptly settling or resolving the case; make or arrange for the disclosures required by Rule 26(a)(1); discuss any issues about preserving discoverable information; and develop a proposed discovery plan. The attorneys of record and all unrepresented parties that have appeared in the case are jointly responsible for arranging the conference, for attempting in good faith to agree on the proposed discovery plan, and for submitting to the court within 14 days after the conference a written report outlining the plan. The court may order the parties or attorneys to attend the conference in person.

    (3) Discovery Plan. A discovery plan must state the parties' views and proposals on:
      (A) what changes should be made in the timing, form, or requirement for disclosures under Rule 26(a), including a statement of when initial disclosures were made or will be made;
      (B) the subjects on which discovery may be needed, when discovery should be completed, and whether discovery should be conducted in phases or be limited to or focused on particular issues;
      (C) any issues about disclosure, discovery, or preservation of electronically stored information, including the form or forms in which it should be produced;
      (D) any issues about claims of privilege or of protection as trial-preparation materials, including, if the parties agree on a procedure to assert these claims after production, whether to ask the court to include their agreement in an order under Federal Rule of Evidence 502;
      (E) what changes should be made in the limitations on discovery imposed under these rules or by local rule, and what other limitations should be imposed; and

(F) any other orders that the court should issue under Rule 26(c) or under Rule 16(b) and (c).

(4) Expedited Schedule. If necessary to comply with its expedited schedule for Rule 16(b) conferences, a court may by local rule:
    (A) require the parties' conference to occur less than 21 days before the scheduling conference is held or a scheduling order is due under Rule 16(b); and
    (B) require the written report outlining the discovery plan to be filed less than 14 days after the parties' conference, or excuse the parties from submitting a written report and permit them to report orally on their discovery plan at the Rule 16(b) conference.

(g) Signing Disclosures and Discovery Requests, Responses, and Objections.

(1) Signature Required; Effect of Signature. Every disclosure under Rule 26(a)(1) or (a)(3) and every discovery request, response, or objection must be signed by at least one attorney of record in the attorney's own name, or by the party personally, if unrepresented, and must state the signer's address, e-mail address, and telephone number. By signing, an attorney or party certifies that to the best of the person's knowledge, information, and belief formed after a reasonable inquiry:
    (A) with respect to a disclosure, it is complete and correct as of the time it is made; and
    (B) with respect to a discovery request, response, or objection, it is:
        (i) consistent with these rules and warranted by existing law or by a nonfrivolous argument for extending, modifying, or reversing existing law, or for establishing new law;
        (ii) not interposed for any improper purpose, such as to harass, cause unnecessary delay, or needlessly increase the cost of litigation; and
        (iii) neither unreasonable nor unduly burdensome or expensive, considering the needs of the case, prior discovery in the case, the amount in controversy, and the importance of the issues at stake in the action.

(2) Failure to Sign. Other parties have no duty to act on an unsigned disclosure, request, response, or objection until it is signed, and the court must strike it unless a signature is promptly supplied after the omission is called to the attorney's or party's attention.

(3) Sanction for Improper Certification. If a certification violates this rule without substantial justification, the court, on motion or on its own, must impose an appropriate sanction on the signer, the party on whose behalf the signer was acting, or both. The sanction may include an order to pay the reasonable expenses, including attorney's fees, caused by the violation.

Rule 34

Rule 34 is intended to limit any confusion regarding production obligations and objections to requests for production. Rule 34 aligns with Rule 26 to deliver early discovery requests. In addition, Rule 34 governs the form of production and requires specificity and timeliness in requests (and objections), which intends to force parties to understand the matters at hand and not to rely on boilerplate language.

Rule 34 requires that an objection must also include whether any responsive materials are withheld on the basis of that objection, with the intent to prevent misleading objections that leave the requesting party in the dark about whether or not information is being withheld after a partial production.

Rule 34. Producing Documents, Electronically Stored Information, and Tangible Things, or Entering onto Land, for Inspection and Other Purposes

(a) In General. A party may serve on any other party a request within the scope of Rule 26(b):

(1) to produce and permit the requesting party or its representative to inspect, copy, test, or sample the following items in the responding party's possession, custody, or control:

(A) any designated documents or electronically stored information—including writings, drawings, graphs, charts, photographs, sound recordings, images, and other data or data compilations—stored in any medium from which information can be obtained either directly or, if necessary, after translation by the responding party into a reasonably usable form; or

(B) any designated tangible things; or

(2) to permit entry onto designated land or other property possessed or controlled by the responding party, so that the requesting party may inspect, measure, survey, photograph, test, or sample the property or any designated object or operation on it.

(b) Procedure.

(1) Contents of the Request. The request:

(A) must describe with reasonable particularity each item or category of items to be inspected;

(B) must specify a reasonable time, place, and manner for the inspection and for performing the related acts; and

(C) may specify the form or forms in which electronically stored information is to be produced.

(2) Responses and Objections.

(A) Time to Respond. The party to whom the request is directed must respond in writing within 30 days after being served or if the request was delivered under Rule 26(d)(2) within 30 days after the parties' first Rule 26(f) conference. A shorter or longer time may be stipulated to under Rule 29 or be ordered by the court.

(B) Responding to Each Item. For each item or category, the response must either state that inspection and related activities will be permitted as requested or state with specificity the grounds for objecting to the request, including the reasons. The responding party may state that it will produce copies of documents or of electronically stored information instead of permitting inspection. The production must then be completed no later than the time for inspection specified in the request or another reasonable time specified in the response.

(C) Objections. An objection must state whether any responsive materials are being withheld on the basis of that objection. An objection to part of a request must specify the part and permit inspection of the rest.

(D) Responding to a Request for Production of Electronically Stored Information. The response may state an objection to a requested form for producing electronically stored information. If the responding party objects to a requested form, or if no form was specified in the request, the party must state the form or forms it intends to use.

(E) Producing the Documents or Electronically Stored Information. Unless otherwise stipulated or ordered by the court, these procedures apply to producing documents or electronically stored information:

- (i) A party must produce documents as they are kept in the usual course of business or must organize and label them to correspond to the categories in the request;
- (ii) If a request does not specify a form for producing electronically stored information, a party must produce it in a form or forms in which it is ordinarily maintained or in a reasonably usable form or forms; and
- (iii) A party need not produce the same electronically stored information in more than one form.

(c) Nonparties. As provided in Rule 45, a nonparty may be compelled to produce documents and tangible things or to permit an inspection.

Rule 37

Rule 37 is directed to the preservation and loss of ESI by outlining considerations of whether information should have been preserved, and specifying measures a court may employ if information that should have been preserved is lost and cannot be restored or replaced. Rule 37 gives judges the power to sanction parties for failing to produce relevant documents.

Under Rule 37, reasonableness, not perfection, is expected in preserving ESI. The most serious sanctions will only be issued when there is proof of "intent to deprive" a party of the use of ESI in the course of the matter. The Committee Note clarifies that "easonable steps to preserve suffice; it does not call for perfection," but mentions that proportionality, including consideration of the parties' resources, will be a factor when evaluating the reasonableness of preservation efforts. The "reasonable steps" language is designed to encourage responsible and targeted preservation and retention efforts.

Rule 37(e) provides when duty to preserve arises, reasonable steps to preserve, the extent of duty to preserve, the consequences of failure to take reasonable steps to preserve, and specific measures addressing failure to preserve,

---

Rule 37. Failure to Make Disclosures or to Cooperate in Discovery; Sanctions

(a) Motion for an Order Compelling Disclosure or Discovery.

(1) In General. On notice to other parties and all affected persons, a party may move for an order compelling disclosure or discovery. The motion must include a certification that the movant has in good faith conferred or attempted to confer with the person or party failing to make disclosure or discovery in an effort to obtain it without court action.

(2) Appropriate Court. A motion for an order to a party must be made in the court where the action is pending. A motion for an order to a nonparty must be made in the court where the discovery is or will be taken.

(3) Specific Motions.

(A) To Compel Disclosure. If a party fails to make a disclosure required by Rule 26(a), any other party may move to compel disclosure and for appropriate sanctions.

(B) To Compel a Discovery Response. A party seeking discovery may move for an order compelling an answer, designation, production, or inspection. This motion may be made if:
- (i) a deponent fails to answer a question asked under Rule 30 or 31;
- (ii) a corporation or other entity fails to make a designation under Rule 30(b)(6) or 31(a)(4);

(iii) a party fails to answer an interrogatory submitted under Rule 33; or
(iv) a party fails to produce documents or fails to respond that inspection will be permitted, or fails to permit inspection, as requested under Rule 34.

(C) Related to a Deposition. When taking an oral deposition, the party asking a question may complete or adjourn the examination before moving for an order.

(4) Evasive or Incomplete Disclosure, Answer, or Response. For purposes of this subdivision (a), an evasive or incomplete disclosure, answer, or response must be treated as a failure to disclose, answer, or respond.

(5) Payment of Expenses; Protective Orders.

(A) If the Motion Is Granted (or Disclosure or Discovery Is Provided After Filing). If the motion is granted, or if the disclosure or requested discovery is provided after the motion was filed, the court must, after giving an opportunity to be heard, require the party or deponent whose conduct necessitated the motion, the party or attorney advising that conduct, or both to pay the movant's reasonable expenses incurred in making the motion, including attorney's fees. But the court must not order this payment if:
(i) the movant filed the motion before attempting in good faith to obtain the disclosure or discovery without court action;
(ii) the opposing party's nondisclosure, response, or objection was substantially justified; or
(iii) other circumstances make an award of expenses unjust.

(B) If the Motion Is Denied. If the motion is denied, the court may issue any protective order authorized under Rule 26(c) and must, after giving an opportunity to be heard, require the movant, the attorney filing the motion, or both to pay the party or deponent who opposed the motion its reasonable expenses incurred in opposing the motion, including attorney's fees. But the court must not order this payment if the motion was substantially justified or other circumstances make an award of expenses unjust.

(C) If the Motion Is Granted in Part and Denied in Part. If the motion is granted in part and denied in part, the court may issue any protective order authorized under Rule 26(c) and may, after giving an opportunity to be heard, apportion the reasonable expenses for the motion.

(b) Failure to Comply with a Court Order.

(1) Sanctions Sought in the District Where the Deposition Is Taken. If the court where the discovery is taken orders a deponent to be sworn or to answer a question and the deponent fails to obey, the failure may be treated as contempt of court. If a deposition-related motion is transferred to the court where the action is pending, and that court orders a deponent to be sworn or to answer a question and the deponent fails to obey, the failure may be treated as contempt of either the court where the discovery is taken or the court where the action is pending.

(2) Sanctions Sought in the District Where the Action Is Pending.

(A) For Not Obeying a Discovery Order. If a party or a party's officer, director, or managing agent, or a witness designated under Rule 30(b)(6) or 31(a)(4), fails to obey an order to provide or permit discovery, including an order under Rule 26(f), 35, or 37(a), the court where the action is pending may issue further just orders. They may include the following:
- (i) directing that the matters embraced in the order or other designated facts be taken as established for purposes of the action, as the prevailing party claims;
- (ii) prohibiting the disobedient party from supporting or opposing designated claims or defenses, or from introducing designated matters in evidence;
- (iii) striking pleadings in whole or in part;
- (iv) staying further proceedings until the order is obeyed;
- (v) dismissing the action or proceeding in whole or in part;
- (vi) rendering a default judgment against the disobedient party; or
- (vii) treating as contempt of court the failure to obey any order except an order to submit to a physical or mental examination.

(B) For Not Producing a Person for Examination. If a party fails to comply with an order under Rule 35(a) requiring it to produce another person for examination, the court may issue any of the orders listed in Rule 37(b)(2)(A)(i)-(vi), unless the disobedient party shows that it cannot produce the other person.

(C) Payment of Expenses. Instead of or in addition to the orders above, the court must order the disobedient party, the attorney advising that party, or both to pay the reasonable expenses, including attorney's fees, caused by the failure, unless the failure was substantially justified or other circumstances make an award of expenses unjust.

(c) Failure to Disclose, to Supplement an Earlier Response, or to Admit.

(1) Failure to Disclose or Supplement. If a party fails to provide information or identify a witness as required by Rule 26(a) or (e), the party is not allowed to use that information or witness to supply evidence on a motion, at a hearing, or at a trial, unless the failure was substantially justified or is harmless. In addition to or instead of this sanction, the court, on motion and after giving an opportunity to be heard:
(A) may order payment of the reasonable expenses, including attorney's fees, caused by the failure;
(B) may inform the jury of the party's failure; and
(C) may impose other appropriate sanctions, including any of the orders listed in Rule 37(b)(2)(A)(i)-(vi).

(2) Failure to Admit. If a party fails to admit what is requested under Rule 36 and if the requesting party later proves a document to be genuine or the matter true, the requesting party may move that the party who failed to admit pay the reasonable expenses, including attorney's fees, incurred in making that proof. The court must so order unless:
(A) the request was held objectionable under Rule 36(a);
(B) the admission sought was of no substantial importance;
(C) the party failing to admit had a reasonable ground to believe that it might prevail on the matter; or
(D) there was other good reason for the failure to admit.

(d) Party's Failure to Attend Its Own Deposition, Serve Answers to Interrogatories, or Respond to a Request for Inspection.

   (1) In General.

      (A) Motion; Grounds for Sanctions. The court where the action is pending may, on motion, order sanctions if:

         (i) a party or a party's officer, director, or managing agent, or a person designated under Rule 30(b)(6) or 31(a)(4), fails, after being served with proper notice, to appear for that person's deposition; or

         (ii) a party, after being properly served with interrogatories under Rule 33 or a request for inspection under Rule 34, fails to serve its answers, objections, or written response.

      (B) Certification. A motion for sanctions for failing to answer or respond must include a certification that the movant has in good faith conferred or attempted to confer with the party failing to act in an effort to obtain the answer or response without court action.

   (2) Unacceptable Excuse for Failing to Act. A failure described in Rule 37(d)(1)(A) is not excused on the ground that the discovery sought was objectionable, unless the party failing to act has a pending motion for a protective order under Rule 26(c).

   (3) Types of Sanctions. Sanctions may include any of the orders listed in Rule 37(b)(2)(A)(i)-(vi). Instead of or in addition to these sanctions, the court must require the party failing to act, the attorney advising that party, or both to pay the reasonable expenses, including attorney's fees, caused by the failure, unless the failure was substantially justified or other circumstances make an award of expenses unjust.

(e) Failure to Preserve Electronically Stored Information. If electronically stored information that should have been preserved in the anticipation or conduct of litigation is lost because a party failed to take reasonable steps to preserve it, and it cannot be restored or replaced through additional discovery, the court:

   (1) upon finding prejudice to another party from loss of the information, may order measures no greater than necessary to cure the prejudice; or

   (2) only upon finding that the party acted with the intent to deprive another party of the information's use in the litigation may:

      (A) presume that the lost information was unfavorable to the party;
      (B) instruct the jury that it may or must presume the information was unfavorable to the party; or
      (C) dismiss the action or enter a default judgment.

(f) Failure to Participate in Framing a Discovery Plan. If a party or its attorney fails to participate in good faith in developing and submitting a proposed discovery plan as required by Rule 26(f), the court may, after giving an opportunity to be heard, require that party or attorney to pay to any other party the reasonable expenses, including attorney's fees, caused by the failure.

B. Federal Rules of Evidence

In light of the vast amount of ESI, FRE Rule 502 seeks to protect attorney-client privilege and provides some protection against inadvertent disclosure of ESI by creating a uniform and predictable standard for inadvertent disclosure.

FRE Rule 502 is intended to reduce the costs of pre-production privilege review by reducing the fear that even a minimal or inadvertent production of privileged documents would be deemed a waiver of privilege for all communications on similar subject matter.

FRE Rule 502(b)

If attorney-client privileged or work product protected material is inadvertently disclosed, FRE Rule 502(b) allows an attorney to get it back if the attorney has taken reasonable steps to prevent the error and responded promptly to fix the error.

Rule 502(b) Inadvertent Disclosure.

When made in a federal proceeding or to a federal office or agency, the disclosure does not operate as a waiver in a federal or state proceeding if:

(1) the disclosure is inadvertent;

(2) the holder of the privilege or protection took reasonable steps to prevent disclosure; and

(3) the holder promptly took reasonable steps to rectify the error, including (if applicable) following Federal Rule of Civil Procedure 26(b)(5)(B)

FRE Rule 502(d)

FRE Rule 502(d) allows opposing parties to enter clawback agreements during discovery so that if privileged information is unintentionally revealed during e-discovery, it cannot be used against either party. It also eliminates the needs for opposing parties from having to engage in filing motions in order to get privileged information returned.

Rule 502(d) Controlling Effect of a Court Order.

A federal court may order that the privilege or protection is not waived by disclosure connected with the litigation pending before the court in which event the disclosure is also not a waiver in any other federal or state proceeding.

FRE Rule 902

Under FRE Rule 902(13)-14), two categories of ESI are qualified as self-authenticating evidence. In other words, FRE Rule 902(13)-(14) make it easier for attorneys to authenticate ESI using hashtags or hash codes.

Rule 902. Evidence that is self-authenticating

...

(13) Certified Records Generated by an Electronic Process or System. A record generated by an electronic process or system that produces an accurate result, as shown by a certification of a qualified person that complies with the certification requirements of Rule 902(11) or (12). The proponent must also meet the notice requirements of Rule 902(11).

(14) Certified Data Copied from an Electronic Device, Storage Medium, or File. Data copied from an electronic device, storage medium, or file, if authenticated by a process of digital identification, as shown by a certification of a qualified person that complies with the certification requirements of Rule 902(11) or (12). The proponent also must meet the notice requirements of Rule 902(11).

CHAPTER 2

ELECTRONIC DISCOVERY REFERENCE MODEL

In order to address the lack of e-discovery standards, George Socha and Tom Gelbmann created the Electronic Discovery Reference Model (EDRM) back in 2005. The EDRM provides a visual framework for the e-discovery process, and it is still considered as relevant today.

A. Stages of EDRM

The EDRM features nine distinct e-discovery stages connected by arrows to indicate the sequential and iterative nature of e-discovery stages, as shown in Figure 2.1. The first four stages are information governance, identification, preservation, and collection. The remaining five stages are processing, review, analysis, production, and presentation.

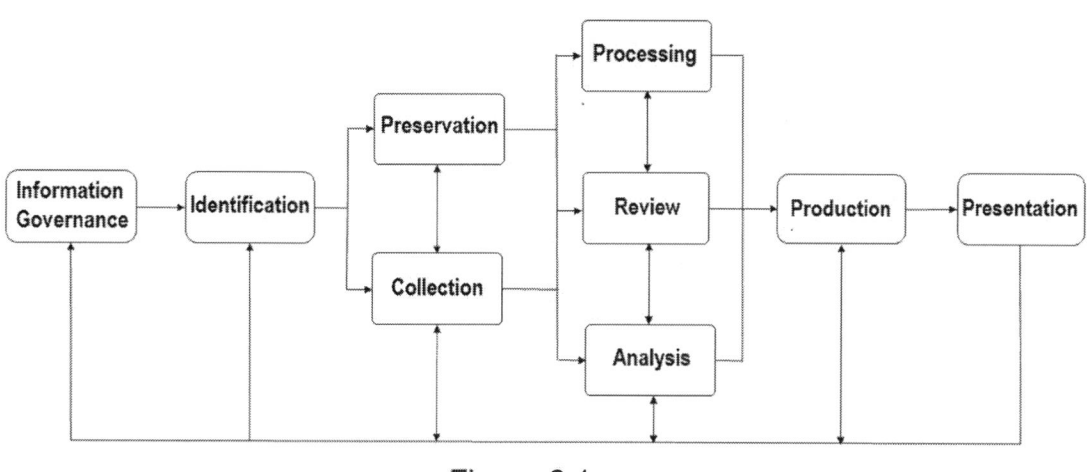

Figure 2.1

1. Information Governance

Information Governance (or Information Management) refers to the set of policies, procedures, processes, and controls implemented to manage a company's information required during the course of business. In essence, information governance is performed in anticipation of future litigation.

2. Identification

A legal duty to preserve relevant electronically stored information (ESI) arises when litigation becomes reasonably foreseeable. But someone needs to determine what the relevant ESI is before the relevant ESI can be preserved. A variety of methods can be utilized to identify sources of potentially relevant ESI, such as reviewing case facts, interviewing key players, and understanding the data environment in which ESI resides.

3. Preservation

After relevant ESI has been identified, it needs to be protected from any inappropriate alteration or destruction (*i.e.*, spoliation). While there are different methods to preserve relevant ESI, the most common legal method is to issue a litigation hold. A litigation hold is a formal communication sent from attorneys to relevant data owners (known as custodians), instructing them not to delete certain ESI.

4. Collection

Relevant ESI are then collected and centralized for further processing during the e-discovery process. It is important to ensure that the contents of the relevant ESI are not altered as a result of the collection process regardless of the chosen method(s) of collection.

There is a tendency for some people to conflate the Collection stage with the Preservation stage. Preservation is simply ensuring potentially relevant data not to be deleted, while Collection is the first step towards producing information. Even though collection can be viewed as a way to preserve, but collection is also a very expensive and inefficient way to preserve.

5. Processing

Processing involves the preparation of the collected ESI, the reduction of its size, and the conversion of its format, if necessary, to a format that is more suitable for review and analysis. The processing stage is typically performed by specialized software, which may entail extracting files from folders, removing meaningless data, converting file formats, etc.

6. Review

The processed ESI needs to be reviewed and evaluated for relevance and attorney-client privilege. The Review stage is by far the most expensive of all the ediscovery stages. However, the cost can be somewhat reduced by employing proper software tools to separate the relevant ESI from the non-relevant ones, and to identify privileged documents from the relevant ESI.

7. Analysis

Analysis deals with evaluating ESI for content and context, including key patterns, topics, people and discussions. Even though the Analysis stage appears after the Review stage, in practice, it is deployed in many stages throughout the e-discovery process.

8. Production

ESI that has been determined to be relevant must be produced for use as potential evidence. E-discovery rules address how ESI must be produced, such as delivering ESI to opposing party in appropriate forms and using appropriate delivery mechanisms.

9. Presentation

Presentation involves the display of ESI before an audience at depositions, hearings, trials, etc. to elicit further information, validate existing facts, and/or persuade the audience.

B. Limitations of EDRM

While the EDRM is widely used and referenced, it also has some limitations. The EDRM is essentially a framework that represents a conceptual view of e-discovery and not a workflow or process. Thus, it should be viewed as a guide than processing stages that can be followed in a linear fashion.

In addition, the EDRM represents an old paradigm. When the EDRM was first created in 2005, only point tools (*i.e.*, specialized software tools that served specific purposes) were available for performing e-discovery. But now there are integrated software tools that can address multiple ERDM stages in a concurrent fashion.

Another limitation of the EDRM is its exclusion of several key e-discovery processes. For example, the concept of early case assessment (ECA) to perform a preliminary analysis of the ESI in the early stage of a matter is not represented.

C. E-discovery Workflow

E-discovery is different from paper discovery because of the large amount of digital data involved. For example, while it may be easy to request every single document from 2010-2020, but that's 10 years' worth of data. Thus, a different thought process and approach are needed. As a starter, it is important to have a broad understanding of the case from the beginning in order to capture the relevant ESI, and it is also crucial to be cognizant about the scope of discovery requests in order to avoid time and money being wasted.

After all potentially discoverable ESI (such as text messages, emails, voicemails, scanned paper documents, etc.) have been preserved, they are then collected and uploaded to a central location where the ESI can be processed either manually or via specialized e-discovery software. Depending on the amount of ESI, processing ESI manually can be cumbersome, but specialized e-discovery software designed for processing ESI tends to quite expensive.

During review, certain files can be tagged for relevant keywords, and some documents can be marked for privilege, and/or redacted as necessary.

Finally, the discoverable ESI will be produced to opposing counsel in format(s) previously agreed with the opposing counsel.

Chapter 3

Scope and Limits

FRCP Rule 26(b) governs the scope and limits of discovery. Under FRCP Rule 26(b)(2)(B), a responding party does not need not produce ESI from sources that the responding party identifies as not reasonably accessible because of undue burden or cost. If the requesting party moves to compel discovery of such information, the responding party must show that the information is not reasonably accessible because of undue burden or cost. Once that showing has been made, a court may order discovery only for good cause, subject to the provisions of FRCP Rule 26(b)(2)(C).

A. Proportionality

Proportionality defines the scope of discovery via a cost-benefit analysis. The intent of proportionality is to guard against over-discovery that can be costly. Prior to the 2015 FRCP amendments, FRCP Rule 26(b)(1) did not specifically impose a proportionality limit on the scope of discovery. However, with the ever increasing amount of ESI, the costs of e-discovery become overwhelming. Thus, one of the purposes of the 2015 FRCP amendments was to curtail overreaching e-discovery. A court considers the needs of a case and weighs the importance of ESI against the burden of producing it.

FRCP Rule 26(b)(1) lists six factors that courts can use to balance the costs of producing information against its benefits, and they are:

- importance of the issues at stake in the action
- amount in controversy
- parties' relative access to relevant information
- parties' resources
- importance of the discovery in resolving the issues
- whether the burden/expense of the proposed discovery outweighs its likely benefit

Both monetary and non-monetary considerations are included in the FRCP Rule 26(b)(1) proportionality factors. Sometimes even relevant and nonprivileged ESI may not be discoverable when the effort to produce those ESI is not proportional to the needs of the case.

Balancing Cost and Burden

The party requesting discovery must establish that the information sought is relevant and important to the case. On the other hand, the party objecting on proportionality grounds must establish that the burden or expense of producing information outweighs its benefit. Parties are encouraged to leverage technology for the purpose of limiting the cost of discovery, and if possible, parties should obtain discovery from the most convenient and least burdensome sources.

If a request from opposing parties is determined to be overly burdersome, a judge may order a requesting party to pay for part of the e-discoery costs.

Requesting the right data can maximize the ability of a requesting party to advance agruments. Basically, e-discovery competency can win or lose cases.

The following is a set of tips for meeting proportionality:

* Tips for meeting proportionality *

- understand what are relevant ESI that needs to be collected
- control the method of collection
- agree on key terms with opposing parties regarding searching and culling data
- discuss methods to share data amongst multiple parties and eliminate duplicative data in the case
- define a production specification early on in the case so that each party only delivers relevant ESI
- provide an estimate cost of the suggesting e-discovery method can help a requesting party win a propoertionality argument

Gilead Sciences, Inc. v. Merck & Co., Inc.
No. 5:13-cv-04057-BLF, 2016 WL 146574 (N.D. Cal. 2016)

GREWAL, Magistrate Judge

Proportionality in discovery under the Federal Rules is nothing new. Old Rule 26(b)(2)(C)(iii) was clear that a court could limit discovery when burden outweighed benefit, and old Rule 26(g)(1)(B)(iii) was clear that a lawyer was obligated to certify that discovery served was not unduly burdensome. New Rule 26(b)(1), implemented by the December 1, 2015 amendments, simply takes the factors explicit or implicit in these old requirements to fix the scope of all discovery demands in the first instance.

What will change—hopefully—is mindset. No longer is it good enough to hope that the information sought might lead to the discovery of admissible evidence. In fact, the old language to that effect is gone. Instead, a party seeking discovery of relevant, non-privileged information must show, before anything else, that the discovery sought is proportional to the needs of the case. The present dispute offers a good example of the wisdom of the Advisory Committee on Civil Rules in elevating proportionality in defining the scope of permissible discovery.

Merck asserts that Gilead infringes two of its patents to a certain kind of nucleoside analog. Among other things, Gilead says it was the one to conceive and reduce to practice the inventions, in 2003, in a compound named PSI-6130. And so a key issue in this case is what did Gilead synthesize and when did it know it.

As part of a related litigation in Canada, Gilead's expert Dr. Christopher Seeger produced a photograph of various tubes of compounds. At least one of the tube labels lists a molecular weight of 259.2, the weight of PSI-6130. In a later deposition in this case, Seeger testified that he got the compounds before 2003 from the founder of an entity later acquired by Gilead. Given the importance of figuring out when Gilead first synthesized the disputed compound, Merck immediately demanded further production of further information about the tubes and their contents, including the tubes themselves. At this point, Merck would seem to be on solid ground in making its demands.

But lots of compounds share the same molecular weight. In fact, Merck's own patents list different nucleosides that share the same molecular weight. Most importantly, Merck has long had information from Gilead that confirms that the tubes in question held PSI-0194 and PSI-1834, two entirely different nucleosides from PSI-6130. This information includes the laboratory notebook from the chemist at the Gilead acquisition that identifies the compounds as PSI-0194 and not PSI-6130. Gilead also provided a further letter from Seeger's source that confirmed that the compounds were not PSI-6130, the compound Merck sought. Not satisfied, Merck presses on, protesting that it should not have to take Gilead's word as to what exactly is in those tubes.

Merck's demands are exactly the type of disproportionate demands that Rule 26(b)(1) proscribes. Sure, it's possible that Gilead's evidence confirming the compounds are not PSI-6130 is false and even concocted. But Merck offers no real evidence that this is the case, and as the court recently explained in denying a motion to compel by Gilead, "[w]ithout more specific information triggering some reason for doubt, the Court must take the producing party ... at its word."

And so that leaves Gilead in the position of having to produce discovery on all sorts of compounds that bear no indication of any nexus to the disputes in this case. This is untenable. It would be like requiring GM to produce discovery on Buicks and Chevys in a patent case about Cadillacs simply because all three happen to be cars. In the absence of any reason to doubt the proof Gilead has tendered about the identity of the disputed compounds, and given the cost and potential delay introduced by the requested production, Merck's request is precisely the kind of disproportionate discovery that Rule 26—old or new—was intended to preclude.

Merck's motion to compel is DENIED.

***

SANTANA V. MKA2 ENTERPRISES, INC.
No. 18-2094-DDC-TJJ (D. Kan. 2019)

JAMES, Magistrate Judge

This is an employment discrimination case. Plaintiff alleges he was discriminated against, retaliated against, and terminated because of his race, in violation of Title VII of the Civil Rights Act and 42 U.S.C. § 1981. Defendant has filed a Motion to Compel Discovery Requests. Plaintiff opposes the motion. For the reasons set forth below, the Court denies the motion.

On June 26, 2018, Defendant served its First Request for Production of Documents on Plaintiff. On August 8, 2018, Plaintiff served his responses and objections on Defendant. After conferring, the parties were unable to resolve their disputes as to Request for Production No. 21. That request states:

> Produce all cellular telephones used by you from the date your employment with Defendant started to the present for purposes of inspection and copying.

Plaintiff's response states:

> Plaintiff objects because this request seeks irrelevant information and is not proportional to the needs of this case. The request is unduly burdensome and

invasive in light of the nature of the case—Defendant has shown no need for the production of Plaintiff's cell phone. Further, the majority, if not all, of the information contained on said device is entirely irrelevant to the present cause of action and any request for relevant nonprivileged information can be made through less invasive means.

Although not the subject of the motion to compel, Defendant also requested that Plaintiff "produce a full and complete copy of all text messages between (Plaintiff) and Defendant and between (Plaintiff) and current or former employees of Defendant." Plaintiff's response stated "Plaintiff objects to the extent this request seeks irrelevant information and is not proportional to the needs of this case. Subject to and without waiving said objections, see SANTANA 000007-000010."

The parties agree that the relevancy of a discovery request is governed by Fed. R. Civ. P. 26(b). That rule states "[p]arties may obtain discovery regarding any nonprivileged matter that is relevant to any party's claim or defense and proportional to the needs of the case ..." The rule goes on to say that the Court must limit discovery if it determines that the discovery sought is unreasonably cumulative or duplicative; can be obtained from a more convenient, less burdensome, or less expensive source; or is outside the scope permitted by Fed. R. Civ. P. 26(b)(1).

Defendant argues its request is relevant on its face because Plaintiff's cell phone contains information relevant to his claims and Defendant's defenses, specifically in the form of "texts, other messages, and phone calls to co-workers, former co-workers, and current employees of Defendant." Plaintiff argues that even if the request is relevant, Defendant's motion to compel should be denied pursuant to Fed. R. Civ. P. 26(b)(2) because the request is unduly burdensome and invasive and is not proportional to the needs of this case. The Court agrees.

Defendant's RFP No. 21 is broad in scope, requesting production of all Plaintiff's cell phones for inspection and copying, without any limitation on the data ultimately to be produced from the copy or image of the phone(s). Defendant in its briefing attempts to limit the request to "texts, other messages, and phone calls to co-workers, former co-workers, and current employees of Defendant." But, on its face the request is not so limited and Defendant sets out no protocol or process through which the data it deems responsive would be culled from the copy or image of the phone(s) and any unresponsive and/or privileged data removed or protected.

In any event, Plaintiff's cell phone likely contains a tremendous volume of information, including possibly text messages, email messages, phone logs, and photographs that are not at all relevant to the claims or defenses in this case. Even many or most of those texts and messages between Plaintiff and his co-workers or former co-workers may have no relevance to the claims and defenses in this case. Further, Defendant does not define what it means by "other messages," or explain how phone calls are relevant. It is not readily apparent how the mere fact that a phone call to a co-worker, former co-worker, or current employee of Defendant was made could be relevant to this employment discrimination case. Even if Plaintiff did call a coworker, there would be no way to tell what was discussed, or whether the phone call had anything to do with Plaintiff's allegations. Any relevant information concerning phone calls Plaintiff made to or received from coworkers and former co-workers could be more easily and less invasively obtained by asking Plaintiff about the calls during his deposition. As noted in the Advisory Committee Notes to Fed. R. Civ. P. 34(a):

> Inspection or testing of certain types of electronically stored information or of a responding party's electronic information system may raise issues of confidentiality or privacy. The addition of testing and sampling to Rule 34(a) with regard to documents and electronically stored information is not meant to create a routine right of direct access to a party's electronic information system, although such access might be justified in some circumstances. Courts should guard against undue intrusiveness resulting from inspecting or testing such systems.

Defendant cites no cases involving the imaging of a cell phone and only one case in which a computer inspection and imaging was ordered. However, in Jacobson, the Court noted that it was "unusual" to order production of a computer for inspection, but that it did so because the record in that case reflected a history of Starbucks providing incomplete and inconsistent responses to Jacobson's production requests (Starbucks had failed to have three key employees search their computers for documents responsive to plaintiff's discovery requests). As will be discussed in greater detail below, there is no evidence of such a history on the part of Plaintiff in this case. Defendant has never explained why it is necessary for it to conduct a physical inspection and copying of Plaintiff's cell phone(s), and its mere skepticism regarding whether Plaintiff has produced complete copies of all responsive text messages from the phone(s) does not warrant such a "drastic discovery measure."

The Court finds that Defendant's RFP No. 21 is overly broad, unduly burdensome and not proportional to the needs and issues of this case. Defendant's separate request for the narrowed scope of text messages also illustrates that Defendant has the ability to obtain relevant cell phone data through less invasive means. In accordance with Rule 34(a), the Court must guard against the undue intrusiveness that would result from the requested inspection and copying of Plaintiff's cell phone(s). The Court will therefore sustain Plaintiff's objections to RFP No. 21.

***

IT IS THEREFORE ORDERED BY THE COURT that Defendant's Motion to Compel Discovery Requests is denied.

***

OXBOW CARBON & MINERALS LLC V. UNION PACIFIC RAILROAD CO.

No. 11-cv-1049 (PLF/GMH) (D. D.C. 2017)

HARVEY, Magistrate Judge

This matter was referred to the undersigned for the resolution of all discovery disputes. Presently ripe for resolution is Defendants' motion to compel, requesting that the Court order Plaintiffs to produce all documents belonging to their CEO, the production of which Plaintiffs, in turn, argue would be unduly burdensome and disproportionate to any value the documents might possess to Defendants in this litigation. ***

BACKGROUND

Plaintiffs are five related companies (collectively, "Oxbow") that mine and sell coal and petroleum coke ("petcoke"). They allege in the Amended Complaint that Union Pacific ("UP") and BNSF Railway Company ("BNSF")—both railroad companies with which Oxbow contracts to ship coal and petcoke—conspired to engage in anticompetitive conduct from 2004 to 2012 in violation of the Sherman Antitrust Act, codified at 15 U.S.C. §§ 1 and 2, that forced Oxbow to pay higher prices to ship coal and petcoke. Specifically, Oxbow believes that UP and BNSF conspired to (1) fix fuel rates applied to commercial rail freight service above competitive levels through a uniform fuel surcharge and (2) allocate certain markets for coal shipment to each other, granting UP a monopoly in at least one region of the country. Oxbow claims it paid Defendants more than $50,000,000 in illegal fuel surcharges as a result of the conspiracy. Oxbow seeks to recover treble damages under 15 U.S.C. § 15, as well as its "lost business and profits" that proximately resulted from the conspiracy.

In their motion, Defendants request that the Court compel Oxbow to add William I. Koch ("Koch"), Oxbow's founder, CEO, and principle owner as a document custodian whose records will be searched for material responsive to Plaintiffs' discovery requests. Defendants maintain that Koch indisputably possesses relevant, unique information responsive to their requests, and argue that Oxbow has improperly refused to produce this information based on the unsupported theory that production of his documents would be disproportionately burdensome and duplicative of the documents produced from the search of the nineteen other Oxbow document custodians' files. Based upon its review of the documents already produced from the other Oxbow custodians, Defendants believe that Koch's records contain information that would, among other things, reveal that market forces—as opposed to Defendants' alleged collusion—contributed to the increasing rail freight costs and any of Oxbow's lost profits. Relatedly, Defendants assert that their discovery request is proportionate and reasonable in light of the facts of this case, including the tens of millions of dollars that Oxbow seeks in damages.

In their opposition, Oxbow argues that Defendants have failed to satisfy their burden of demonstrating that the discovery they seek is responsive and not unduly burdensome. Based on their calculations, Oxbow estimated that adding Koch as a document custodian would result in roughly 130 gigabytes of additional documents to be filtered through the parties' previously agreed-upon search terms, a process that Oxbow initially estimated would cost $250,000. Oxbow further contends that many of Koch's documents would likely be duplicative of the other custodians' documents or only marginally responsive given Koch's senior position over a conglomerate of Oxbow companies, only some of which are involved in the coal and petcoke businesses. Despite these arguments, Oxbow represented at the first hearing on Defendants' motion that it was open to analyzing a random sample of Koch's records using the agreed-upon search terms to provide the parties with concrete numbers regarding the responsiveness of Koch's documents to the terms and with a basis to negotiate new search terms if necessary. Accordingly, the undersigned held Defendants' motion in abeyance pending the analysis of a sample of Koch's documents and the parties' attempt to negotiate a resolution of the dispute themselves.

Following the hearing, Oxbow collected a total of 467,614 documents from Koch's electronic and physical files and provided them to a vendor for processing. After removing any duplicative records, the vendor searched Koch's documents using the previously agreed-upon search terms, which yielded 45,639 document hits—82,600 documents in total when including "families" of documents. The vendor collected a random sample of ten percent of these hits and any associated families—12,074 documents in total—and provided them to Oxbow for review for privilege and responsiveness. Of these 12,074 documents, Oxbow determined that approximately 1,300 documents—11.67 percent of them--were actually responsive to the search terms and produced them to Defendants. In total, the initial processing of Koch's records and review of the sample documents cost Oxbow $57,197.95. Based on its experience reviewing the sample documents, Oxbow now estimates that it will cost approximately $85,000 to process, review, and produce the remainder of Koch's documents to the Defendants, bringing the total cost of the effort, including the review of the sample documents, to approximately $142,000—significantly less than Oxbow's original estimate of $250,000. Oxbow's initial estimate was based on its prediction that, after processing, searching, and filtering Koch's documents through the agreed-upon search terms, it would have to review approximately 214,000 documents for false positives and privileged information before producing the responsive documents to Defendants. In reality, applying the agreed-upon search terms yielded only 45,639 hits on Koch's documents—82,600 documents when including document families.

Unfortunately, the sampling effort did not result in the parties resolving the dispute without further intervention of the Court. In their August 2, 2017 Joint Status Report, the parties advance dramatically different interpretations of the significance of the sampling's results. Despite the lower-than-expected cost of the analysis, Oxbow believes that the results confirm that a complete production of Koch's documents would be an unnecessary burden and expense, particularly in light of the documents' low responsiveness rate to the search terms. Further, following its sampling of Koch's documents, Oxbow refused to negotiate with Defendants over the agreed-upon search terms, or to provide Defendants with the data from the sampling necessary to evaluate the effectiveness of the terms. According to Oxbow, the only purpose for doing so would be to negotiate narrower search terms, an effort that Oxbow deemed not worth the attorney time it would take to accomplish because it was unlikely "to dramatically reduce the number of hits Oxbow will ultimately need to review." Accordingly, Plaintiffs asked again for the Court to deny the motion to compel or, in the alternative, order Defendants to bear the cost of the production of the documents it seeks. Defendants, in turn, view the results of the sampling as proof of the existence of relevant and unique documents in Koch's records. While acknowledging that Koch's records are less responsive to the search terms than the other Oxbow custodians' files, Defendants note that such a result is to be expected because the other custodians deal more exclusively with Oxbow's coal and petcoke business than Koch, Oxbow's CEO. Moreover, the lower-than expected number of hits in Koch's records confirms to Defendants that the search terms effectively narrowed the universe of documents that Oxbow must review for production. Further, Defendants contend that the total number of responsive documents likely in Koch's possession—approximately 10,000, based on Defendants' extrapolation from the results of the sampling effort—is significant and roughly equivalent to the total number of documents produced by each of Oxbow's other custodians. And while Defendants represent that they were willing to renegotiate the agreed-upon search terms to tailor future searches following the sampling, Oxbow's refusal to do so, or to even share the data from the sampling necessary to have an informed discussion of the effectiveness of the search terms, has dampened its enthusiasm for the task. Given Oxbow's refusal and the large amount of money at stake in the litigation, Defendants oppose Oxbow's request for cost-sharing and seek a ruling on their motion to compel now.

The Court's ruling follows below.

LEGAL STANDARD
Rule 37 of the Federal Rules of Civil Procedure provides that, "[o]n notice to other parties and all affected persons, a party may move for an order compelling disclosure of discovery" from a party who fails to comply with its discovery obligations. Fed. R. Civ. P. 37(a). The party that brings the motion to compel bears the initial burden of "proving that the opposing party's answers were incomplete," If the movant satisfies this burden, the burden then shifts to the non-movant "to explain why discovery should not be permitted."

As for the scope of discovery, it has long been recognized that "[u]nder the broad sweep of Rule 26(b)(1) of the Federal Rules of Civil Procedure, a party 'may obtain discovery regarding any matter, not privileged, which is relevant to the subject matter involved.'" The broad presumption in favor of discovery of relevant information embodied in Rule 26 is not without limits, however. Instead, under the amended Rule 26, discovery must be relevant and "proportional to the needs of the case." Fed. R. Civ. P. 26(b)(1). To determine whether a discovery request is proportional, courts weigh the following six factors: "(1) the importance of the issues at stake in this action; (2) the amount in controversy; (3) the parties' relative access to relevant information; (4) the parties' resources; (5) the importance of the discovery in resolving the issues; and (6) whether the burden or expense of the proposed discovery outweighs its likely benefit." "[N]o single factor is designed to outweigh the other factors in determining whether the discovery sought is proportional," and all proportionality determinations must be made on a case-by-case basis. To be sure, however, "the amendments to Rule 26(b) do not alter the basic allocation of the burden on the party resisting discovery to--in order to successfully resist a motion to compel—specifically object and show that ... a discovery request would impose an undue burden or expense or is otherwise objectionable."

DISCUSSION

Oxbow ultimately does not dispute that Koch's records contain documents that are responsive to the parties' negotiated search terms and relevant to this litigation. In fact, Oxbow has already produced approximately 1,300 such documents as a result of the sampling of Koch's records. Instead, Oxbow objects to Defendants' request that it be compelled to review and produce discovery from Koch's remaining documents because doing so would be unduly burdensome and because the benefit to Defendants would not justify that effort and expense. Indeed, Oxbow argues that the cost of complying with Defendants' request is so unreasonable that, if the undersigned is inclined to order such discovery, the Court should ignore the long-standing presumption that a "responding party must bear the expense of complying with discovery requests," and order Defendants to cover the costs of the production. *Oppenheimer Fund, Inc. v. Sanders*, 437 U.S. 340, 358 (1978). The Court is unpersuaded by Oxbow's arguments. In its briefing, Oxbow declines to address any of the other proportionality factors highlighted in Rule 26--namely, the importance of the issues at stake in this action, the amount in controversy, the parties' relative access to relevant information, the parties' resources, or the importance of the discovery in resolving the issues in this case, *see* Fed. R. Civ. P. 26(b)(1)—stressing only that the burden and cost of complying with Defendants' request would outweigh its likely benefit. Weighing the six Rule 26 proportionality factors, however, demonstrates that adding Koch as a custodian of documents to be searched for material responsive to Defendants' discovery requests in this matter will be neither unduly burdensome nor unreasonably expensive in light of the facts of this case. Likewise, the Court finds that the instant circumstances do not warrant shifting the costs of doing so to Defendants. Accordingly, Defendants' motion to compel will be granted and Plaintiffs shall be ordered to produce all remaining responsive documents from Koch's file, the cost of which Plaintiffs shall bear.

A. The Proportionality of Defendants' Discovery Request

1. The Importance of the Issues at Stake

This first Rule 26 factor calls for the Court to "examine[] 'the significance of the substantive issues [at stake in the litigation], as measured in philosophic, social, or institutional terms.'" For example, courts should carefully scrutinize discovery requests in "cases in public policy spheres, such as employment practices, free speech, and other matters," which often "seek[] to vindicate vitally important personal and public values" and "may have importance far beyond the monetary amount involved." Fed. R. Civ. P. 26 advisory committee's note. By Oxbow's own suggestion, the instant case involves important issues and has the potential to broadly impact a wide range of third-parties not involved in the litigation. Oxbow has stated that a favorable ruling from this Court "could benefit all of America's shippers and consumers, saving billions of dollars a year in reduced rail freight charges in the United States." What is more, Koch himself has publicly accused Defendants of long relying on "overreaching and abusive behavior" to "shortchange[] the American consumer," and of "using aggressive tactics to prevent competition and intimidate customers," including "American farmers, miners[,] and shippers[.]"

Defendants, for their part, do not disagree with Oxbow's estimation of the significance of this case, noting that Oxbow has made serious allegations against Defendants that have the potential to impact many people. Accordingly, the undersigned finds that the importance of the issues at stake here weighs in favor of granting Defendants' discovery request, which Oxbow concedes will produce documents that are relevant to the resolution of this case's claims. *See BlueAlly*, 2017 WL 876266, at *4 (finding that this factor weighs against allowing discovery where the issues at stake in the case would not "have an impact beyond the parties involved").

2. The Amount in Controversy

Under the second proportionality factor, courts should "compare[] the cost of discovery to the amount in controversy to determine [the proposed discovery's] proportionality." Here, Oxbow seeks to recover the more than $50,000,000 in illegal fuel surcharges it alleges were the result of the Defendants' collusion. It also seeks recovery of its "lost business and profits," and a trebling of its damages under 15 U.S.C. § 15. While Oxbow does not specifically quantify these damages in its Amended Complaint, Defendants have suggested that Oxbow seeks to recover over $150 million--a figure that Defendants do not appear to dispute. Meanwhile, Oxbow's estimated cost of complying with Defendants' proposed discovery is approximately $140,000, including the $57,197.95 that Oxbow has already spent on sampling Koch's documents. Given the very substantial amount of damages that Oxbow seeks to recover in this case, its cost of complying with the discovery request to produce information relevant to Defendants' defense of Oxbow's claims does not strike the undersigned as excessive. Accordingly, the Court finds that this factor, too, favors granting Defendants' discovery request.

3. The Parties' Relative Access to the Relevant Information

In considering this factor, courts look for "information asymmetry"—a circumstance in which one party has very little discoverable information while the other party has vast amounts of discoverable information. In such a case, "the burden of responding to discovery lies heavier on the party who has more information, and properly so." To the extent this factor is applicable here, any informational asymmetry favors Oxbow. Indeed, neither party disputes that Koch is in possession of relevant, unique information, and there appears to be no other way for Defendants to obtain this information than moving to compel Oxbow to produce it. Accordingly, the Court finds that this factor militates in favor of granting Defendants' request.

4. The Parties' Resources

Taking into account the parties' resources, the Court again concludes that this factor weighs in favor of granting Defendants' request. While discovery should not be used to "wage a war of attrition or as a device to coerce a party," regardless of whether the party is "financially weak or affluent," Oxbow represented at the hearing in this matter that it does not object to Defendants' request based on an inability to pay for it. Accordingly, the undersigned sees no reason to deny Defendants' request on this basis.

5. The Importance of the Discovery in Resolving the Issues

This fifth factor requires courts to determine whether "[t]he issues at stake are at the very heart of [the] litigation." Though Oxbow initially objected to the relevance of any documents in Koch's possession, it has since acknowledged that Koch's records contain relevant and unique documents, although not in the same ratio as other Oxbow custodians' records, and has produced a portion of these documents to Defendants. The Court appreciates that Koch's files do not appear to contain as a high a proportion of responsive documents as the files of custodians who dealt exclusively with Oxbow's coal and petcoke business, but it strains reason to suggest that the principal owner and CEO of a company, who has publicly commented on the importance and magnitude of litigation to which his company is a party and in which the financial health of his company is at issue, would have no unique information relevant to that litigation in his possession. While it may be too early in the production process to determine exactly how significant Koch's records are, the categories of relevant documents identified by Defendants after reviewing the approximately 1,300 documents produced from Koch's files indicates to the Court that Defendants' discovery request has merit and is not intended to be the first strike in a war of attrition or a coercion tactic. Accordingly, the Court concludes that this factor favors granting Defendants' proposed discovery.

6. Whether the Burden or Expense of the Proposed Discovery Outweighs its Likely Benefit

Oxbow rests its argument entirely on this final factor, asserting that it is the most important of the Rule 26 proportionality factors and counsels against granting Defendants' proposed discovery. In support of its argument, Oxbow contends that its random sampling analysis suggests that approximately half of the agreed-upon search terms' hits on Koch's documents are false positives with no or only marginal relevance to the litigation. To be sure, Oxbow also concedes that the cost of processing Koch's records for discovery is far less than it originally estimated and that the search terms narrowed the scope of Koch's responsive documents far more than it originally anticipated. Nevertheless, it asserts that the $85,000 that it estimates it will take to review and produce the remaining responsive documents from Koch's files is prohibitively burdensome. The Court disagrees. The cost of reviewing and producing Koch's documents does not strike the undersigned as unduly burdensome or disproportionate, especially given the discovery conducted to date and the damages that Oxbow seeks in this action. Plaintiffs' counsel explained at the second hearing in this matter that Oxbow has spent $1.391 million to date on reviewing and producing approximately 584,000 documents from its nineteen other custodians and Oxbow's email archive. And again, Oxbow seeks tens of millions of dollars from Defendants. Through that lens, the estimated cost of reviewing and producing Koch's responsive documents—even considering the total approximate cost of $142,000 for that effort, which includes the expense of the sampling effort--while certainly high, is not so unreasonably high as to warrant rejecting Defendants' request out of hand. *See Zubulake v. UBS Warburg, LLC*, 217 F.R.D. 309, 321 (S.D.N.Y. 2003) (explaining, in the context of a cost-shifting request, that "[a] response to a discovery request costing $100,000 sounds (and is) costly, but in a case potentially worth millions of dollars, the cost of responding may not be unduly burdensome"); *Xpedior Creditor Trust v. Credit Suisse First Boston (USA), Inc.*, 309 F. Supp. 2d 459, 466 (S.D.N.Y. 2003) (finding no "undue burden or expense" to justify cost-shifting where the requested discovery cost approximately $400,000 but the litigation involved at least $68.7 million in damages). Moreover, based on the parties' representations at the second hearing in this matter, the projected number of responsive and unique documents in Koch's files--approximately 10,000--is largely consistent with the number of responsive and unique documents produced by the other Oxbow custodians, and the responsiveness rate of Koch's documents—11.67 percent—while low, is not the lowest among Oxbow's custodians. In light of the above analysis—including the undersigned's assessment of each of the Rule 26 proportionality factors, all of which weigh in favor of granting Defendants' motion—the Court is unwilling to find that the burden of reviewing the remaining 65,000 responsive documents for a fraction of the cost of discovery to date should preclude Defendants' proposed request. *** For all of the reasons stated above, and absent any evidence establishing that Defendants are using the discovery of Koch's records to wage a war of attrition or as a device to coerce Oxbow, the Court finds that Defendants' motion must be granted.

CONCLUSION

For the foregoing reasons, Defendants' motion to compel the production of documents from Koch's records is GRANTED.

***

GORDON V. T.G.R. LOGISTICS, INC.
No. 16-cv-00238-NDF, 2017 WL 1947537 (D. Wy. 2017)

CARMAN, Magistrate Judge

This comes before the Court on the Defendant T.G.R. Logistics, Inc.'s motion to compel discovery production. ***

BACKGROUND

Defendant filed its Combined Motion and Brief to Compel Discovery Production from Plaintiff Brenda Gordon on April 21, 2017. Defendant seeks an order requiring Plaintiff to produce an electronic copy of her entire Facebook account history for the two Facebook accounts she has identified.

Defendant served the following Request for Production on Plaintiff on January 25, 2017:

REQUEST NO. 11: Utilizing the instructions attached hereto, download and produce an electronic copy of your Facebook account history to the enclosed flash drive.

Neither party provided Plaintiffs response to this request for production, but from the arguments of the parties it is clear that the Plaintiff has not, and will not, voluntarily produce the Plaintiffs entire Facebook history. Nevertheless, this Court is not aware of the specific objections Plaintiff presented in her response to the discovery request.

The parties have conferred and complied with the January 24, 2014 General Order and conducted an informal hearing with this Court on April 10, 2017. After hearing the nature of the pending motion the Court granted Defendant leave to file its motion to compel with briefing.

Plaintiff was driving her motor vehicle on June 28, 2015 on US Highway 309 in Lincoln County, Wyoming. As she was executing a left-hand turn she was struck by a tractor-trailer unit owned and operated by Defendant T.G.R. Logistics, Inc. and driven by Defendant Varga which was attempting to execute a pass in the left lane. As a result of this collision Plaintiff alleges numerous physical injuries, pain (back, neck and jaw), traumatic brain injury, posttraumatic stress disorder, anxiety and depression. Defendant asserts that Plaintiff's Facebook account history is relevant and necessary to its defense of the damages claimed by Plaintiff.

The Plaintiff responds that the request for the Facebook account history exceeds the permissible discovery limits of Federal Rules of Civil Procedure 26. Plaintiff further asserts that the request is unduly burdensome, lacks relevance and is overly invasive of Plaintiffs' privacy. Plaintiff emphasizes that she has downloaded and produced the information from her Facebook accounts that references the accident or her injuries. Further the Plaintiff has provided the Facebook information for the following keywords as set forth by Defendant in its request for production number 12. Those keywords are: accident; attorney; TGR; Igor Varga; Kemmerer; Lincoln County, Wyoming; brain injury; concussion; posttraumatic stress disorder; and PTSD.

Discussion

The scope of discovery is defined in Federal Rules of Civil Procedure 26(b)(1):

> *Scope in General.* Unless otherwise limited by court order, the scope of discovery is as follows: Parties may obtain discovery regarding any nonprivileged matter that is relevant to any party's claim or defense and proportional to the needs of the case, considering the importance of the issues at stake in the action, the amount in controversy, the parties' relative access to relevant information, the parties' resources, the importance of the discovery in resolving the issues, and whether the burden or expense of the proposed discovery outweighs its likely benefit. Information within this scope of discovery need not be admissible in evidence to be discoverable.

There are three basic steps for the court to consider when determining the appropriate scope of discovery under Rule 26(b)(1). Those steps are: (1) is the information privileged; (2) is it relevant to a claim or defense; and (3) is it proportional to the needs of the case. There being no claim of privilege asserted herein, this matter will resolve with a review of the final two criteria.

The courts have a long history of attempting to define the proper scope of discovery. The federal discovery rules were initially adopted in 1938 and have been described as a striking and imaginative departure from tradition. Advisory Committees Explanation Statement Concerning 1970 Amendments to Discovery Rules. In the 1980s it became apparent that excessive discovery was becoming a problem.

> Excessive discovery innovation or resistance to reasonable discovery requests pose significant problems.... The purpose of discovery is to provide a mechanism for making relevant information available to the litigants. "Mutual knowledge of all the relevant facts gathered by both parties is essential to proper litigation." *Hickman v. Taylor*, 329 U.S. 495, 507 (1947). Thus the spirit of the rules is violated when advocates attempt to use discovery tools as tactical weapons rather than to expose the facts and illuminate the issues by overuse of discovery or unnecessary use of defensive weapons or evasive responses. All of this results in excessively costly and

time-consuming activities that are disproportionate to the nature of the case, the amount involved, or the issues or values at stake.

Advisory Committee Notes 1983 Amendment Federal Rules of Civil Procedure 26.

With the amendments of the Rules beginning in 1983, the issue of proportionality was introduced into scope of discovery evaluations.

This effort to properly limit the scope of discovery comes at a time when the amount of available data for discovery is growing exponentially. More data has been created in the last two years than in the entire previous history of the human race and the amount of data is predicted to grow 10-fold by 2020. *Data set to grow 10-fold by 2020 as internet of things takes off*, Antony Adshead, ComputerWeekly.com/news/2240217788. A great deal of that data will involve social media.

Social media presents some unique challenges to courts tn their efforts to determine the proper scope of discovery of relevant information and maintaining proportionality. While it is conceivable that almost any post to social media will provide some relevant information concerning a person's physical and/or emotional health, it also has the potential to disclose more information than has historically occurred in civil litigation. While we can debate the wisdom of individuals posting information which has historically been considered private, we must recognize people are providing a great deal of personal information publicly to a very loosely defined group of "friends," or even the entire public internet. People have always shared thoughts and feelings, but typically not in such a permanent and easily retrievable format. No court would have allowed unlimited depositions of every friend, social acquaintance, co-employee or relative of a plaintiff to inquire as to all disclosures, conversations or observations. Now far more reliable disclosures can be obtained with a simple download of a social media history. A few clicks on the computer and you shortly have what can consist of hundreds of pages of recorded postings and conversations of a party. There can be little doubt that within those postings there will be information which is relevant to some issue in the litigation. It is equally clear that much of the information will be irrelevant.

Just because the information can be retrieved quickly and inexpensively does not resolve the issue. Discovery can be burdensome even as it is inexpensive. Courts have long denied discovery of information which was easy to obtain, but which was not discoverable. "The court may, for good cause, issue an order to protect a party or person from annoyance, embarrassment, oppression, or undue burden or expense." Fed.R.Civ.P. 26(c)(1). Upon a finding of good cause a court may prohibit the production of relevant information. The recent inclusion of proportionality within Fed.R.Civ.P. 26(b)(l) further emphasizes this point.

The Defendant correctly observes that there would be very little time or expense involved in the initial production of Plaintiff's Facebook history. That's true on the front end. The problem is that such vast information has the potential to generate additional discovery or impact trial testimony. It's not difficult to imagine a plaintiff being required to explain every statement contained within a lengthy Facebook history in which he or she expressed some degree of angst or emotional distress or discussing life events which could be conceived to cause emotion upset, but which is extremely personal and embarrassing. There is also substantial risk that the fear of humiliation and embarrassment will dissuade injured plaintiffs from seeking recovery for legitimate damages or abandon legitimate claims. That being said, Defendant has a legitimate interest in discovery which is important to the claims and damages it is being asked to pay. Information in social media which reveals that the plaintiff is lying or exaggerating his or her injuries should not be protected from disclosure. Courts must balance these realities regarding discovery of social media and that is what most of the courts which have addressed this issue have done.

In *Equal Employment Opportunity Commission v. Simply Storage Management, LLC*, 270 F.R.D. 430 (S.D. Ind. 2010), the court denied a request for production of a claimant's entire Facebook and MySpace accounts. Even where the claimant alleges emotional injuries disclosure of their entire social media history is not required.

> [T]he simple fact that a claimant has had social communications is not necessarily probative of the particular mental and emotional health matters at issue in the case. Rather it must be the substance of the communication that determines relevance. *See Rozell v. Ross-Holst*, 2006 WL 163143 (S.D.N.Y. Jan. 20, 2006). As the *Rozell* court put it,

> > To be sure, anything that a person says or does might in some theoretical sense be reflective of her emotional state. But that is hardly justification for requiring the production of every thought she may have reduced to writing or, indeed, the deposition of everyone she may have talked to.

In *Simply Storage*, the court ultimately allowed discovery of the claimant's communications which related any emotion, feelings or mental state or referenced events which could reasonably be expected to produce significant emotion responses. In issuing this order the court recognized that such discovery was appropriate for alleged severe emotion distress, as opposed to "garden variety" emotional distress.

Similar reasoning has been expressed by other courts. In *Holter v. Wells Fargo and Co.*, 281 F.R.D. 340 (D.Minn. 2011), a former employer sought the entire Facebook history of the claimant.

> While everything that is posted on a social media website is arguably reflective of a person's emotional state, this court would not allow depositions of every friend and

acquaintance to inquire about every conversation and interaction with plaintiff. So too, the court will not require plaintiff to produce all information from all her social media websites to obtain similar information.

On the other hand, given the plaintiff has placed her employment with and termination of employment from defendant, along with her mental disability and emotional state in issue, the defendant is entitled to information from her social media websites that bear on these topics, including other stressors in plaintiff's life that could account for the emotional distress she is now claiming was due to her treatment at and termination of employment from defendant.

The United States District Court for the District of Kansas reminded us that our discovery rules provide the guidance to address social media discovery. While the medium of social media is relatively new, the principals of discovery remain the same.

As it currently stands, the record does not support defendant's extremely broad discovery request for all-inclusive access to plaintiff's social media accounts. As plaintiff notes, such access could reveal highly personal information—such as plaintiff's private sexual conduct—that is unlikely to lead to admissible evidence in this case. Information on social networking sites is not entitled to special protection, but a discovery request seeking it nevertheless must meet Fed.R.Civ.P 26's requirement that it be tailored "so that it appears reasonably calculated to lead to the discovery of admissible evidence." "Otherwise, the defendant would be allowed to engage in the proverbial fishing expedition, in the hope that there might be something of relevance in Plaintiff's [social networking] account[s]." The court agrees with courts that have recognized that a discovery request for unfettered access to social networking accounts—even when temporally limited-I would permit defendant "to cast too wide a net" for relevant information. As the court reasoned in *Ogden v. All-Star Career School*, [2014 WL 164-6934 (W.D.Penn. 2014) at 4]:

> Ordering plaintiff to permit access to or produce complete copies of his social networking accounts would permit defendant to cast too wide a net and sanction an inquiry into scores of quasi-personal information that would be irrelevant and non-discoverable. Defendants are no more entitled to such unfettered access to plaintiff's personal email and social networking communications than it is to rummage through the desk drawers and closets in plaintiff's home.

Admittedly, there are cases which have allowed broader discovery of social media accounts. Defendant relies upon *Held v. Ferrellgas, Inc.*, 2011 WL 3896513 (Kan. 2011). With little discussion the Court found that a request for Facebook information during a specified time period of employment was discoverable when Plaintiff could not recall if he posted anything relevant to the case on Facebook. The court did not share its analysis or what factors the court considered or what guided it in allowing the discovery. This case was later distinguished by *Smith v. Hillshire Brands*. Citing to *Held*, the court in *Moore v. Miller*, 2013 WL 2456114 at 2 (D. Colo. 2013), granted discovery of Facebook history during the period of plaintiff's employment based upon the finding that the plaintiff "has chosen to share his version of events online often and in many different forums, including detailed and specific descriptions of what he alleges happened to him on March 25, 2008, as well as the injuries he allegedly suffers to this day."

The Defendant further relies upon *Appler v. Mead Johnson & Co. LLC*, 2015 WL 5615038 (S.Ind. 2015). Appler differs from the other cases cited by Defendant. Appler recognizes and discusses at some length the reasons why discovery of social media is not unlimited. Ultimately the court granted broad access to the plaintiff's Facebook account due to the unique factual circumstances of the case. A critical issue involved the plaintiff's ability to work during earlier portions of the day as a result of her narcolepsy. A review of her entire Facebook activity history was relevant regarding her ability to work at different times of the day. The court made it clear that had the only issue been emotional damages, that the Facebook discovery would have been more limited.

The cases discussed have arisen in the context of employment related claims. Such claims are substantially driven by claims of emotional distress and the justification for discovery of social media histories is greater. Nevertheless, the general concepts would be applicable to a personal injury claim in which cognitive and emotional damages are claimed. Defendant, in apparent recognition that its initial request was overly broad, has offered to limit its request for social media temporally for three years prior to the motor vehicle accident to present. Defendant asserts that it will be unable to defend Plaintiff's damage claims without access to information regarding Plaintiff's emotional state prior to the accident. Defendant still seeks the entirety of the Facebook activity from three years prior to the accident to present. In this Court's opinion that is casting the net too wide. In determining the appropriate scope of allowable discovery, it is important to consider that the Plaintiff seeks damages for physical injuries as well as damages for posttraumatic stress disorder, anxiety and depression. From what has been presented this case is more of the "garden variety" emotion distress claim as mentioned in *Simply Storage*. Granting access to Plaintiff's entire Facebook history would provide minimal relevant information while exposing substantial irrelevant information. As such the discovery would exceed the proper limits of proportionality.

The Defendant's claim that it would be unable to challenge Plaintiff's damage claims is exaggerated. Defendants have been effectively defending such garden variety emotional distress claims for many years and such claims typically make up a small part of the damages in physical injury cases. The Plaintiff also alleges a traumatic brain injury. Such damages have long been a subject of the evaluation and diagnosis by experts using proven testing protocols. This Court has not been provided any authority for the proposition that access to social media prior to the date of the accident would significantly contribute to the evaluation and diagnosis of these conditions. Therefore, the Court will deny Defendant's request for social media discovery prior to the date of the accident of June 28, 2015. Nevertheless, the Court is not convinced that all relevant social media subsequent to that date has been produced. The Plaintiff will be required to produce all relevant history which addresses Plaintiff's <u>significant</u> emotional turmoil, any mental disability or ability, or relate <u>significant</u> events which could reasonably be expected to result in emotional distress. Plaintiff will also be required to produce all Facebook postings which reference the accident, its aftermath, and any of her physical injuries related thereto, insofar as such has not already been produced by Plaintiff. In its reply brief Defendant discusses the impact of Plaintiffs injuries on activities she enjoyed before the accident. The Court has not been provided any guidance as to what activities of the Plaintiff may have been impacted by this accident. The Court will order the production of Facebook history and photos which relate or show the Plaintiffs level of activity after the accident.

The Defendant's Motion to Compel Discovery is GRANTED in the following respects:

1. The Plaintiff is ordered to produce all post-June 28, 2015 Facebook history and photos which relate to Plaintiffs significant emotional turmoil, any mental disability or ability, or relate significant events which could reasonably be expected to result in emotional distress.

2. The Plaintiff is ordered to produce all post-June 28, 2015 Facebook history and photos which address or relate to the accident and its aftermath or any of her resulting physical or emotional injuries.

3. The Plaintiff is ordered to produce all post-June 28, 2015 Facebook history and photos which relate or show the Plaintiff's level of activity.

The Defendant's Motion to Compel Discovery is DENIED in all other respects.

***

B. Accessibility

In *Zubulake v. USB Warburg*, 217 F.R.D. 309 (S.D.N.Y. 2003) (*Zubulake I*), Judge Scheindlin determined whether the Federal Rules required the defendant to produce certain emails that the plaintiff had requested and which the defendant contended could be found only on backup tapes. According to the defendant, it would be burdensome and costly to retrieve these emails from the backup tapes. For the *Zubulake I* court, the determination of whether the requested discovery was unduly burdensome or expensive turned on whether the documents at issue (*i.e.*, ESI) were kept in an accessible or inaccessible format. Because the expense of production corresponded closely to the accessibility of the information, the *Zubulake I* court used accessibility as the test for the level of burden.

In order to evaluate accessibility, the *Zubulake I* court categorized different types of electronic data and placed them on a continuum of accessibility.

MOST ACCESSIBLE

1. Active, online data
   This includes data actively being created or received and processed. Access frequency and speed of access are both high. Examples include ESI on a hard drive.

2. Near line data
   This includes robotic storage systems that house removable media accessed remotely and automatically to store and retrieve records. A typical example of near line data is digital video discs (DVDs) and compact discs (CDs).

3. Offline storage/archives
   This includes removable optical disk or magnetic tape media used to make disaster copies of records and also for archival purposes where the likelihood of retrieval is minimal. The main difference between near line data and offline data is that offline data lacks the coordinated control of an intelligent disk subsystem.

> ### LEAST ACCESSIBLE
>
> 1. Backup tapes
>   Although tapes can store vast volumes of information, they are sequential access devices, meaning that to read any particular block of data, one must first read all of the preceding blocks of data. Data on backup tapes are not organized in a manner that would allow easy retrieval of individual documents and files.
>
> 2. Erased, fragmented, or damaged data
>   While electronic files are stored in contiguous clusters when a storage disk is new or has space available, electronic files are broken up and randomly placed throughout the disk when contiguous free space is no longer available. That non contiguous free space results from deletions of previously created files. Because the files are not active and are randomly placed, erased, fragmented, or damaged, data can only be retrieved after significant processing.

FRCP Rules 26 and 45 have essentially codified the *Zubulake I* decision regarding the obligation to produce reasonably accessible ESI.

In general, FRCP Rule 26 provides that parties may obtain discovery regarding any matter, not privileged, that is relevant to the claim or defense of any party. FRCP Rule 26(b)(2)(B), however, defines certain limits as follows:

> A party need not provide discovery of electronically stored information from sources that the party identifies as not reasonably accessible because of undue burden or cost.

Similarly, FRCP Rule 45(d) provides that persons responding to a subpoena need not provide discovery of ESI from sources that the responding person identifies as not reasonably accessible because of undue burden or cost.

In essence, under FRCP Rules 26 and 45, what is "reasonably accessible" is discoverable, and what is "not reasonably accessible" is presumed to be not discoverable. These rules create an obligation on a requesting party to identify the sources of ESI that a responding party considers not reasonably accessible.

ELKHARWILY V. FRANCISCAN HEALTH SYSTEM

No. 3:15 cv 05579 RJB, 2016 WL 4061575 (W.D. Wash. 2016)

BRYAN, District Judge

THIS MATTER comes before the Court on Plaintiff's Motion to Compel Discovery Responses.

A. Archived emails.

Plaintiff's motion requests, *inter alia*, that the Court compel Plaintiff's Request for Production #8 and Request for Production #9. The Court's Order on Plaintiff's Motion to Compel granted the request in part, as to the production of live emails, and continued the request in part, as to the production of archived emails, for Defendant to have the opportunity to file a surreply. According to the Order, Plaintiff's Reply introduced "new factual representations [that] could be grounds for a motion to strike ... [but] because of the burden shifting of Fed. R. Civ. P. 26(b)(2)(B), which allows Plaintiff to rebut Defendant's showing that electronic information is reasonably accessible, a surreply ... is appropriate." The Court now considers the merits of Plaintiff's motion to compel archived emails.

1. Factual background.

Discovery requests.

Plaintiff's Request for Production #8 seeks Defendant's "[production of] all emails and text messages concerning Plaintiff between employees, agents or attorneys of Defendant." Plaintiff's Request for Production #9 extends the same request to emails and messages between Defendant's employees, agents or attorneys and third parties: "(1) Plaintiff, (2) any employee, agent or attorney of Group Health, (3) any employee, agent or attorney of any former employer of Plaintiff and (4) any employee, agent or attorney of the National Practitioners Data Bank [NPDB]."

Defendant provided Plaintiff with the same response to both requests for production as follows:

Defendant objects to this request on the grounds that this request is overbroad and burdensome. Defendant further objects to the extent that this request seeks documents which are protected by the attorney client and/or work product privileges. Without waiving and subject to these objections, Defendant responds: Defendant does not have an email archiving system. This means there is no single location or application that can be queried for email matching specified criteria. Email can only be searched if it is maintained in a live email account. To locate documents responsive to this request, Defendant searched the live email accounts of the following custodians: Dr. Dennis deLeon, Dr. Tony Haftel, Dr. Mark Adams, Dr. William Cammarano, and Ms. Kim Nighswonger. Non privileged responsive documents are attached as FHS 000968 to FHS 000973. Defendant also refers to the emails previously produced with Defendant's initial disclosures as well as by Plaintiff in this matter.

Defendants email archiving system.

Defendant represents that it does not maintain an email archiving system, but rather archives emails on a monthly basis on physical backup tapes, as part of a disaster relief program.

Defendant represents that in order to retrieve all responsive discovery, Defendant would need to retrieve, restore, and review each backup tape, which at 14 hours per tape would require 1,400 hours in labor and $157,500 in costs.

Declarations of Plaintiff and Mr. Bruce Megard.

In a signed declaration, Plaintiff declares:

5. Right after the end of my last appeal in May 2013 I asked Mr. [Bruce] Megard [Defendant's lawyer] and Josh[ua Weaver] (the lawyer conducting my last hearing) if I could get copies of all emails (whether produced or not), minutes, documents, or any in writing note that was used in the process of my appeal or not produced for any reason. They both refused.

6. After [Defendant's] Board issued its final decision denying my application for privileges, which was July 2013, I called Mr. Megard immediately again and I asked him to send me copies of everything again and I told him at least I need copies of the emails and documents produced and were used in the entire privilege process. He refused and said Washington law does not allow him to send me any copies. He asked me why I needed those and I told him I am filing a law suit [sic]. Mr. Megard said, "I advise you not to. You are going to lose time and money and you will lose." I said, "Well, I will let the judge and jury decide that."

Mr. Bruce Megard, Defendant's lawyer, states in a signed declaration that he has no recollection of the telephone conferences referred to in Plaintiff's declaration, but that if Mr. Megard had been asked, he "would have informed [Plaintiff] that all discovery documents under FHS's Medical Staff Bylaws had already been produced during the course of the appeal process and that additional disclosures were not permitted under those same Bylaws.

Mr. Megard affirms that he keeps billing entries for teleconferences and has found no time entries for conversations with Plaintiff during the relevant timeframe.

While Mr. Megard did not find any emails directed to him, Mr. Megard was carbon copied in an email from Plaintiff to Joshua Weaver, attorney for FHS' Appellate Review Committee. The email, dated July 25, 2013, appears to be a response by Plaintiff to the Appellate Review Committee's Final Recommendation to deny Dr. Elkharily's request for Active Medical Staff membership and privileges. Dr. Elkharily writes, "Thank you Mr. Weaver for letting me know the decision. I guess there is nothing else I can do. Best wishes, Alaa[.]"

2. Discovery standard.

Fed. R. Civ. P. 26(b)(1) provides that "[p]arties may obtain discovery regarding any nonprivileged matter that is relevant ... and proportional[.]" The rule enumerates considerations when weighing proportionality: (1) the importance of the issues at stake in the action, (2) the amount in controversy, (3) the parties' relative access to relevant information, (4) the parties' resources, (5) the importance of the discovery in resolving the issues, and (6) whether the burden or expense of the proposed discovery outweighs its likely benefit. Fed. R. Civ. P. 26(b)(1). The discovery rule further provides that, on motion by a party or *sua sponte* courts must limit discovery that is unreasonably cumulative or duplicative, or can be obtained from a more convenient, less burdensome, or less expensive source. Fed.R.Civ.P. 26(b)(2)(C)(i). Specific to electronically stored information, a party "need not provide discovery ... [when] not reasonably accessible because of undue burden or cost." However, if that showing is made, "the court may nonetheless order discovery ... if the requesting party shows good cause[.]" Fed.R.Civ.P. 26(b)(2)(B).

3. Discussion.

Defendant argues that the archived emails are not readily accessible, costly to restore, and of only minimal discovery value. Defendant also argues that Plaintiff has not exhausted more easily accessible information and has not identified what kind of material Plaintiff believes will be found on the backup tapes, so compelling production of archived emails "amounts to an extremely expensive fishing expedition."

Plaintiff does not discredit Defendant's argument about the burden or cost of producing the archived emails, but, Plaintiff argues, Defendant is at fault. Defendant should have preserved emails in an accessible format, rather than archiving them, because around July of 2013 Plaintiff expressly requested them after his appeal was denied, and he warned Defendant of future litigation, which also triggered their preservation.

The emails that Plaintiff seeks to compel are discoverable under Fed. R. Civ. P. 26(b)(1), but Defendant has met its burden to show that retrieving the electronically stored information would result in an undue burden and cost to Defendant. Fed. R. Civ. P.

26(b)(2)(B). Defendant estimates $157,500 in costs to retrieve, restore, and review the backup tapes for responsive archived emails.

Because Defendant has met its burden, the Court considers whether Plaintiff has shown good cause, because if so, "the court may nonetheless order discovery[.]" Fed. P. Civ. P. 26(b)(2)(B). Plaintiff has not met his burden. Tellingly, Plaintiff does not name individuals that Plaintiff believes exchanged emails about Plaintiff, nor does Plaintiff describe suspected content of the emails. Plaintiff does not even represent with any surety that responsive emails exist. Because Plaintiff has not met his burden for good cause, compelling production of the discovery at expense to Defendant is not warranted.

Plaintiff's blame shifting is unpersuasive, because as between Mr. Megard's and Plaintiff's conflicting declarations, Mr. Megard's should be given more weight, for two reasons. First, Mr. Megard, who practices law and bills time to clients for telephone conferences, has no record of any phone calls from Plaintiff. Second, Mr. Megard's memory is consistent with the email exchange between Plaintiff and Mr. Weaver in July 2013, where Plaintiff stated that "I guess there is nothing else I can do [to appeal denial of privileges]."

Although Plaintiff has not met his burden to show good cause, which would overcome Defendant's showing that producing the archived emails is costly and burdensome, the archived emails are "discoverable" under Fed. R. Civ. P. 26(b)(1). Therefore, upon a request by Plaintiff, Defendant should facilitate access to the discovery, but should do so only at Plaintiff's expense, payable in advance. Plaintiff should be responsible for all costs, such as retrieving and restoring the backup tapes to an accessible format, except for costs relating to Defendant's review of the information for privileged material (which is like any other discovery request, e.g., the live emails).

Defendant should not otherwise be compelled to produce the archived emails, and to that extent Plaintiff's motion should be denied.

***

Therefore, it is HEREBY ORDERED that the remainder of Plaintiff's Motion to Compel *** is DENIED.

***

Chapter 4

Conference and Cooperation

A. Rule 26(f) Conference

A conference under FRCP Rule 26(f), commonly known as Rule 26(f) conference or "meet and confer," should take place as soon as practical and at least 21 days before a scheduling conference is to be held or a scheduling order is due under Rule 16(b). Under Rule 16(b), a judge must issue a scheduling order after receiving the parties' Rule 26(f) report or after consulting with the parties' attorneys and unrepresented parties. The scheduling order should reflect any agreements reached by the parties in the Rule 26(f) conference.

Rule 26(f) conference is not just meeting, it is more of a plan. The goal of a Rule 26(f) conference is to curtail discovery disputes and to avoid potential cost increase due to a failure to anticipate discovery problems. Parties can achieve this goal by adequately addressing and discussing the following three major topics:

1. preservation
2. production
3. privilege

Sometimes, multiple Rule 26(f) conferences may be necessary throughout a case in order to resolve various unforeseeable e-discovery problems.

Preservation

It is imperative to define the goals of preservation requests because preserving everything is usually not the right answer.

In order to avoid e-discovery disputes and ease the financial burden of preservation on the parties, it will be beneficial for the parties to agree on the scope of preservation. One way to limit the parties' duty to preserve is for the parties to agree on a date range for potentially relevant ESI based on the nature of claims and defenses. In other words, ESI beyond the agreed upon date range does not need to be preserved.

It would be helpful to understand the information technology (IT) structures of the parties, including data retention policies, if any.

If necessary, set up a Rule 30(b)(6) deposition for the opposing IT manager to inquire about:

    i. server structure and cloud storage
    ii. computer and mobile devices
    iii. software deployed
    iv. websites and/or social media
    v. data retention policy

It is important to define custodians who have access to discoverable ESI, to determine types of discoverable ESI that are available, and to define metadata field requirements.

Production

An essential component of a Rule 26(f) conference is that the parties should attempt to come to an agreement on the form of production. The form of production may refer to the file format (such as native format versus converted format) and the media (such as paper versus electronic) on which the documents are produced.

Before the parties can come to an agreement as to form(s) of production, the parties should have a reasonable idea of the subject matter of the discovery sought and the format in which the data is usually held in the ordinary course of business.

Rule 34(b) outlines a procedure for reaching agreement on the form(s) of production of ESI, and, if no agreement is specified, the responding party must produce ESI either in a format or formats in which it is ordinarily maintained or in a format or formats that are reasonably usable.

Some ESI, such as graphs, image files, etc., is more suitable for production in image formats. If this information is ordinarily maintained in a way that makes it searchable by electronic means, the parties should agree on a format that preserves the electronically searchable feature. These image formats are typically accompanied by load files, ancillary files containing textual content, and relevant metadata. Other ESI, such as databases, spreadsheets, etc., may require a form of production that is native, or near-native so that the receiving party can actually utilize the information. The parties should also work together to make sure that the form of production is compatible with the tools utilized to conduct the review.

The Advisory Committee Notes to Rule 34 contemplate that in some circumstances, the producing party may need to provide some "reasonable amount of technical support, information on application software, or other reasonable assistance to enable the requesting party to use the information."

Failure to communicate, and agree, early in the case on the appropriate form(s) of production may result in a party facing reproduction of discovery already reviewed and produced or further sanctions.

Privilege

The third major topic that must be addressed in a Rule 26(f) conference pertains to the assertions of privilege or work production protection. Parties should attempt to agree on a procedure for the assertion of these claims to encourage the efficacy of litigation and the discovery process.

One of the goals of a Rule 26(f) conference is to avoid the burden and expense of extensive and timely privilege review. According to the Advisory Committee Notes, "[f]requently parties find it necessary to spend large amounts of time reviewing materials requested through discovery to avoid waiving privilege ... [and] [p]arties may attempt to minimize these costs and delays by agreeing to protocols that minimize the risk of waiver." Thus, the Advisory Committee suggests two possible ways of minimizing this risk:

(1) the quick peek, in which the responding party provides requested materials for an initial examination without waiving any privilege or protection and the requesting party then designates the documents it wishes to actually have produced (which are then produced after privilege review); and

(2) clawback agreements in which inadvertent production does not result in a waiver as long as the responding party identifies the document mistakenly produced and the document is returned. To add some strength to the proposed anti-waiver agreement reached by the parties, Rule 26(f) permits the court to include any such agreement in a case management order.

Federal Rule of Evidence Rule 502 includes its own anti-waiver provision. If the disclosure is inadvertent, the holder takes reasonable steps to prevent disclosure and the holder takes reasonable steps to rectify the error. But parties to the Rule 26(f) conference can modify this rule 502 to fit the needs of their case by modifying or defining what is reasonable to prevent disclosure. Furthermore, parties could agree that if a receiving party obtains inadvertently produced information, it will notify the producing party of the inadvertent production.

The parties may also want to discuss methods for modifying production of a privilege log to ease the costs associated with its creation and how to redact privileged information from ESI and protect metadata that is to be produced.

The following is a sample checklist to help preparing for a Rule 26(f) conference:

Rule 26(f) Conference Checklist

1. determine what types of discoverable ESI are available in:

    a. local servers and/or cloud storage
    b. local computers and/or mobile devices
    c. emails and other productivity software
    d. websites and social media

2. understand parties' IT structure

    ♦ If necessary, set up a Rule 30(b)(6) deposition for the opposing party's IT manager to learn about their IT structure and data retention policy.

3. determine who has access to discoverable ESI (*i.e.*, custodians)

4. compile a list of keyword search terms and date ranges that may produce relevant ESI

5. draft a preservation request to define the scope of relevant ESI

    - Evaluate cost/burden vesus proportionality.

6. agree on metadata fields to be produced in a load file

7. determine format of production

    - Determine whether to include native files such as spreadsheets, databases, and audio/video files in the production, or if images of these files will be sufficient.

8. define what are privileged and confidential in the relevant ESI

    - Consider forming a clawback agreement.

B. Cooperation

One obvious reason for parties to cooperate throughout the discovery process is to avoid wasting time and money due to unnecessarily combative discovery actions.

Cooperation requires that an attorney adequately prepares prior to conferring with opposing counsel to identify custodians and the likely sources of relevant ESI, and the steps and costs required to access the relevant ESI. Preparation begins with a good understanding of the e-discovery requirements under the FRCP and the potential sources of ESI available. It requires disclosure and dialogue on the parameters of preservation.

Rule 26 imposes an obligation of good faith in attempting to agree on the proposed discovery plan, but it does not clarify the degree to which cooperation is required. Thus, setting a cooperative tone and decisions about the degree of disclosure a client is willing to make are strategies that should be discussed before attending a Rule 26(f) conference.

The Sedona Conference

The Sedona Conference is a non-profit research and educational institute dedicated to the advanced study of law and policy, including complex litigation and discovery of electronically stored information. The Sedona Conference has published the "Cooperation Proclamation" that calls for pre-trial discovery cooperation. The Cooperation Proclamation promotes open and forthright information sharing, dialogue (internal and external), training, and the development of practical tools to facilitate cooperative, collaborative, transparent discovery.

Many courts have invoked the principles of the Cooperation Proclamation in deciding discovery disputes. The authors of the Sedona Conference posit the well-founded argument that cooperation is required by the FRCP and by ethical rules, which includes the duties to expedite litigation and to provide competent representation, and the duty of candor to the tribunal and fairness to the opposing party. But beyond what legal and ethical rules require, there is a second level of cooperation promoted by the spirit of the e-discovery amendments to the FRCP and by the economics of e-discovery. Under this second level of cooperation, as envisioned by the authors of the Cooperation Proclamation, the parties should work together to develop, test and agree on the nature of information being sought. The parties should jointly explore the best method of solving discovery problems, especially those involving ESI. The parties should jointly address questions of burden and proportionality, seeking to narrow discovery requests and preservation requirements as much as reasonable.

The Cooperation Proclamation recognizes the following methods to act cooperatively:

1. Utilizing internal ESI discovery point persons to assist counsel in preparing requests and responses.

2. Exchanging information on relevant data sources, including those not being searched, or scheduling early disclosures on the topic of electronically stored information.

3. Jointly developing automated search and retrieval methodologies to cull relevant information.

4. Promoting early identification of form or forms of production.

5. Developing case-long discovery budgets based on proportionality principles.

6. Considering courtappointed experts, volunteer mediators, or formal ADR programs to resolve discovery disputes.

Cooperation must be tailored to the size, complexity, and players in the case. In essence, cooperation involves a mutually beneficial exchange of information that does not undermine the substantive positions of the parties and that preserves the assertion of privilege over such material

Many attorneys tend to resist the cooperative approach because they view giving information to opposing counsels is not pursing zealous advocacy. However, such thinking is resting on the misguided idea that adversarial conduct is part of advocacy. As the drafters of the Cooperation Proclamation recognize "[l]awyers have twin duties of loyalty: While they are retained to be zealous advocates for their clients, they bear a professional obligation to conduct discovery in a diligent and candid manner. Their combined duty is to strive in the best interests of their clients to achieve the best results at a reasonable cost, with integrity and candor as officers of the court. Cooperation does not conflict with the advancement of their clients' interests—it enhances it. Only when lawyers confuse advocacy with adversarial conduct are these twin duties in conflict."

ROMERO V. ALLSTATE INS. CO.
271 F.R.D. 96 (E.D. Pa. 2010)

BUCKWALTER, Senior District Judge

***

F. Disclosure of Prior and Current Search Methodology

Defendants also object to Plaintiffs' Request for the Production of Documents to the extent that Plaintiffs seek an order compelling Allstate to confer with Plaintiffs concerning additional relevant custodians and search terms, and what searches Allstate conducted in the past, "so that Plaintiffs receive all relevant documents concerning the Release." Defendants argue that "Allstate is under no obligation to provide plaintiffs with a list of the search terms Allstate has employed in the past or the method by which Allstate searched for responsive materials." *** Moreover, they claim that because such information is attorney work product, it need not be disclosed.

The Court agrees in part and disagrees in part. It is well-established that communication among counsel is crucial to a successful electronic discovery process:

> The Federal Rules of Civil Procedure, case law, and the Sedona Principles all further emphasize that electronic discovery should be a party-driven process. Indeed, HN9 Rule 26(f) requires that the parties meet and confer to develop a discovery plan. That discovery plan must discuss "any issues about disclosure or discovery of [ESI], including the form or forms in which it should be produced." Fed. R. Civ. P. 26(f)(3)(C) (emphasis added). In fact, the commentary to the rule specifically notes that whether metadata "should be produced may be among the topics discussed in the Rule 26(f) conference." Fed. R. Civ. P. 26(f) advisory committee's note, 2006 amendment.

*** Indeed, the Sedona Conference has advised that:

> Cooperation ... requires ... that counsel adequately prepare prior to conferring with opposing counsel to identify custodians and likely sources of relevant ESI, and the steps and costs required to access that information. It requires disclosure and dialogue on the parameters of preservation. It also requires forgoing the short term tactical advantages afforded one party to information asymmetry so that, rather than evading their production obligations, parties communicate candidly enough to identify the appropriate boundaries of discovery. Last, it requires that opposing parties evaluate discovery demands relative to the amount in controversy. In short, it forbids making overbroad discovery requests for purely oppressive, tactical reasons, discovery objections for evasive rather than legitimate reasons, and "document dumps" for obstructionist reasons. In place of gamesmanship, cooperation substitutes transparency and communication about the nature and

reasons for discovery requests and objections and the means of resolving disputes about them.

*** Among the items about which the court expects counsel to "reach practical agreement" without the court having to micro-manage e-discovery are "search terms, date ranges, key players and the like." (quoting 10 Sedona Conf. J. at 217 (footnote omitted)). "Moreover, '[t]he use of key words has been endorsed as a search method for reducing the need for human review of large volumes of ESI [,]' to be followed by 'a cooperative and informed process [which includes] sampling and other quality assurance techniques.'" (quoting 10 Sedona Conf. J. at 223 (alteration in original) (footnotes omitted)). Thus, HN11 counsel are generally directed to meet and confer to work in a cooperative, rather than an adversarial manner, to resolve discovery issues. ***

Considering these principles of cooperation, the Court deems it reasonable to compel the parties to confer and come to some agreement on the search terms that Defendants intend to use, the custodians they intend to search, the date ranges for their new searches, and any other essential details about the search methodology they intend to implement for the production of electronically-stored information concerning the Release. Such a process will eliminate duplicative discovery and help ensure that the searches remain narrowly focused on the core issues present in this case. Moreover, the Court does not find that such information is subject to any work product protection, as it goes to the underlying facts of what documents are responsive to Plaintiffs' document requests and does not delve into the thought processes of Defendants' counsel. ***

To the extent, however, that Plaintiffs seek a retrospective view of the searches Defendants have already conducted during the course of discovery over the past eight and half years, the Court is not inclined to compel such disclosures. To require Defendants to compile a list of all search terms, custodians, and other methods of searching used in the past would result in an undue burden on Defendants that is not justified by any potential benefit to Plaintiffs. Although Plaintiffs argue that "without knowing the search methodology for Defendants' previously-produced documents, [they] cannot evaluate the new searches that Defendants propose will result in the identification and production of electronic documents 'not previously produced,'" the Court is confident that the parties can coordinate their efforts on a forward-going basis to share information about what has already been completed and what needs to be done in order to avoid duplicative discovery. Thus, this portion of Plaintiffs' Motion is denied.

***

Ruiz-Bueno v. Scott
No. 12-cv-0809 2013 WL 6055402 (S.D. Ohio 2013)

KEMP, Magistrate Judge

***

III. When Discovery about Discovery is Permitted

Even in a case like this, questions can arise about the storage and retrieval of ESI. In fact, from the email chains and letters which both parties have attached to their memoranda, it appears that plaintiffs' distrust of the diligence with which defendants searched for ESI is at the heart of the current dispute. Because none of that information was properly authenticated or sworn to, however, the Court really does not have a record of what defendants did or did not do to find ESI, or what the actual state of defendants' ESI happens to be. *** Nonetheless, the Court infers that defendants resisted answering these two interrogatories not only because they believed that "discovery about discovery" was irrelevant, but because they believed that they had, through counsel's representations, satisfactorily addressed any concerns about whether they had made a good faith effort to locate and produce all relevant emails.

In an ideal world (a situation which apparently does not exist here), these types of disputes would never be presented to the Court because counsel would have recognized, early in the case, the potential for disagreements about proper search protocols, and would have actively sought to avoid such disagreements through collaboration. That concept appears in Fed.R.Civ.P. 26(f), which requires the parties to meet and confer early in the case about, among other matters, discovery, and, more specifically, to discuss "any issues about disclosure or discovery of electronically stored information, including the form or forms in which it should be produced...." Rule 26(f)(3)(C). That discussion can and should include cooperative planning, rather than unilateral decision-making, about matters such as "the sources of information to be preserved or searched; number and identities of custodians whose data will be preserved or collected ...; topics for discovery; [and] search terms and methodologies to be employed to identify responsive data...." Milberg LLP and Hausfeld LLP, "E-Discovery Today: The Fault Lies not in Our Rules...," 4 Fed. Cts. L. Rev. 131, 163 (2011). When that occurs, each party is able to exert some measure of control over the e-discovery process, and, in turn, to have some measure of confidence in its results.

Here, by contrast, it appears that defendants have been reluctant to share any of that information with plaintiffs. Although they have explained that the lack of ESI in this case is due to the relatively infrequent use of email within the Sheriff's office, they have not explained how they went about searching for such communications beyond the fact that each defendant was asked (twice, according to counsel's email) to produce his or her relevant emails. Perhaps that is a proper response to an opposing party's request for ESI; perhaps not. It certainly can be argued that either an organization like the Sheriff's office, which presumably has access to and control over the entirety of its ESI including employee-generated email, or that organization's litigation counsel, should undertake a more comprehensive search of the email database rather than simply relying on 50 different employees to search emails in some unspecified manner. How did the individual defendants do that here? Through keyword searches? Through searching by sender or recipient? Through searching emails sent or received in a specified time frame? Or going by memory? Did they all do it the same way, or were they left to pick among various methods? The record provides no answer to these questions.

What should have occurred here is that either as part of the Rule 26(f) planning process, or once it became apparent that a dispute was brewing over ESI, counsel should have engaged in a collaborative effort to solve the problem. That effort would require defendants' counsel to state explicitly how the search was constructed or organized. Plaintiffs' counsel would then have been given the chance to provide suggestions about making the search more thorough. That does not mean that all of plaintiffs' suggestions would have to be followed, but it would change the nature of dispute from one about whether plaintiffs are entitled to find out how defendants went about retrieving information to one about whether those efforts were reasonable. That issue cannot be discussed intelligently either between counsel or by the Court in the absence of shared information about the nature of the search.

Some attorneys may view this type of collaborative approach and sharing of information as an intrusion into privileged areas or as less than zealous advocacy for their clients. In fact, the defendants in this case have suggested, in a footnote (albeit without any cited support, and not in their objections to the interrogatories), that in order to answer the plaintiffs' interrogatories they would have to disclose privileged communications because "Defendants' discovery efforts involve communication with counsel ..." That may well be true in some broad sense, but there is a vast difference between describing, factually, what a party has done to comply with a document request, and revealing discussions between counsel and the client about that process. Simply put, discussing how to go about searching for and producing ESI does not ordinarily or necessarily entail revealing confidential client communications.

A collaborative discovery process is also completely consistent with the lawyer's duty to represent the client zealously. As one court has observed,

> It cannot seriously be disputed that compliance with the "spirit and purposes" of these discovery rules requires cooperation by counsel to identify and fulfill legitimate discovery needs, yet avoid seeking discovery the cost and burden of which is disproportionally large to what is at stake in the litigation. Counsel cannot "behave responsively" during discovery unless they do both, which requires cooperation rather than contrariety, communication rather than confrontation.

Mancia v. Mayflower Textile Servs. Co., 253 F.R.D. 354, 357-58 (D. Md. 2008).

The Rules of Civil Procedure, from the mandatory disclosure provisions of Rule 26(a) to the various "meet and confer" obligations imposed by Rule 26(f) and other portions of Rules 26 and 37, contain many such requirements that counsel approach discovery cooperatively. This area is no different.

Having said all that, the past is peculiarly unreceptive to change. Not so with the future. Simply put, when plaintiffs expressed some skepticism about the sufficiency of defendants' efforts to produce emails in this case based on the large number of parties and the small number of documents produced, defendants' counsel should have been forthcoming with information not only about why the results were as they were, but how defendants looked for responsive documents. That did not happen. The Court has the power, either by granting the motion to compel or in order to carry out its responsibility to ensure compliance with the Rules of Civil Procedure, to make that happen now. While the Court agrees that not every case will justify directing counsel or a party to provide "discovery about discovery," it appears to the Court that such an order is needed in this case. That is based, at least in part, on the fact that plaintiffs' concern about the volume of ESI appears to be reasonably grounded; the fact that defendants were less than forthcoming with information needed to make further discussion of the issue a collaborative rather than contrarian process; and the need to get this case moving toward resolution. Because, at this point, a statement made under oath would seem to have a greater potential to move the case along rather than a mere representation by counsel, the Court's order will take the form of an order compelling discovery.

**

CHAPTER 5

PRESERVATION OF ELECTRONICALLY STORED INFORMATION

Preservation involves taking steps to ensure that potentially relevant ESI is not destroyed during the pendency of a legal matter. Failure to preserve relevant ESI may lead to serious consequences such as sanctions. In order to avoid sanctions, deliberate steps must be taken to ensure that relevant ESI are preserved. Importantly, it is not a good idea to wait until or after a Rule 26(f) conference before dealing with preservation. Proportionality considerations also apply to preservation decisions, meaning that preserving everything is not a proper approach. Some ESI will be lost even with reasonable steps to preserve, so it is best practice to make a record of how things are done and why.

Preservation requires working with relevant data owners known as custodians. Preservation is not just a single step; it is an ongoing process.

A. Litigation Hold

The most common way to begin the preservation process is through a litigation hold. A litigation hold is a formal communication sent from attorneys to custodians, instructing them not to delete certain ESI.

The concept of litigation holds as a method for litigants to satisfy their preservation obligations was popularized by Judge Shira A. Scheindlin in her *Zubulake v. UBS Warburg LLC* (*Zubulake IV*) decision in 2003. Specifically, the court noted that once a party reasonably anticipates litigation, it must suspend its routine document retention/destruction policy and put in place a litigation hold.

In her *Pension Committee v. Banc of America Securities, LLC* decision in 2010, Judge Scheindlin held that "the failure to issue a written legal hold constitutes gross negligence because the failure is likely to result in the destruction of relevant information."

Begin Litigation Hold

Litigation hold may begin with the distribution of a litigation-hold memorandum that instructs, for example employees in a company, to preserve all relevant documents and to suspend document retention/destruction policies that may delete such documents. Litigation-hold memorandums must be in writing. It is imperative that attorneys advise their clients in their litigation-hold memorandum of the stakes involved in preserving all relevant records and obtain their clients' full cooperation in satisfying their preservation duties.

The purpose of a litigation-hold memorandum is to

(1) identify a litigation;
(2) specify parties to the litigation;
(3) explain the importance of complying with the litigation-hold memorandum;
(4) provide a point of contact within a company to answer questions;
(5) specifically identify the documents that need to be preserved;
(6) suspend document retention and destruction policies; and
(7) provide a formal tracking and verification process.

Identify documents that need to be preserved

A common problem regarding litigation holds cited by courts is the failure to adequately instruct employees what types of documents are relevant. Thus, in order to satisfy their preservation obligations, attorneys must tailor the contents of each litigation-hold memorandum to describe the specific issues and documents that are relevant to the case at hand.

In *Jones v. Bremen High School District 228*, No. 08-C-3548 (N.D. Ill. 2010), the court sanctioned the defendant for only instructing three individuals to cull through their personal documents and preserve anything related to the case, but did not provide any specific guidance on how to conduct their searches or how to determine what documents were relevant. Although there was no evidence of bad faith, the court sanctioned the defendant with an adverse jury instruction, and an order to pay plaintiff's costs and attorney's fees because there was a distinct possibility that emails relevant to plaintiff's case were destroyed.

Suspend document retention and destruction policies

Once litigation is anticipated, parties must suspend their routine document retention and destruction policies, and establish measures to ensure the preservation of relevant documents and information.

In *Pension Committee v. Banc of America Securities, LLC*, the court held that plaintiffs' continued deletion of ESI after the duty to preserve was triggered amounted to gross negligence and appropriate sanctions needed to be imposed.

The following is an example of a litigation-hold memorandum:

LITIGATION-HOLD MEMORANDUM

TO: Distribution
From: General Counsel

The Company has recently been sued by a former employee John Doe for alleged violations of the Fair Labor Standards Act (FLSA). Specifically, Mr. Doe alleges that he was required to work off-the-clock but was not paid wages and/or overtime for all hours worked.

We intend to defend this lawsuit. The law requires us to take immediate steps to preserve all paper records and electronic data that is relevant to the litigation. Paper records and electronic data (including duplicates) must be preserved at all storage locations including your office computer, home computers, and other portable electronic media such as thumb drives. Failure to preserve all paper records and electronic data may result in legal sanctions, including fines, instructions to the jury that any deleted data would have been harmful to our defense, and even a finding that the Company is precluded from defending Mr. Doe's case.

Please review the following list of preservation categories of documents (paper and electronic data) which must be preserved:

1. all notes, memoranda and documents related to Mr. Doe
2. all job descriptions for the positions held by Mr. Doe during his employment
3. all timesheets and other records reflecting the hours worked by Mr. Doe

All electronic data and paper documents including drafts, email negotiations and communications related to or about any of these categories must be preserved. Please determine immediately whether you have in your possession, custody, or control any paper or electronic data about, concerning, or related to any of the above preservation categories. Such paper documents or electronic data are called responsive paper documents or electronic data.

Please determine whether any responsive data is located on your laptop or office computer, home computer, iphone, ipad, thumbdrives, voicemail, or any other electronic storage locations. Please immediately suspend the deletion (manual or automatic) of relevant electronic data from any location where you believe responsive data may be found.

With respect to paper documents, please check all your office files and home files. Please immediately suspend the destruction of any responsive paper documents. This litigation hold should remain in place until you are notified otherwise by written correspondence from my office.

If you have any doubts about what paper or electronic data to preserve, please contact me. If you have any responsive paper documents, please immediately advise your supervisor. If you have any responsive electronic data held or stored at any location or on any media other than your office laptop, please immediately advise your supervisor.

Provide a formal tracking and verification process

While issuing a litigation-hold memorandum may be an important first step in the preservation process, the obligation to conduct a reasonable search for responsive documents continues through the litigation.

A litigation hold without more will not satisfy the "reasonable inquiry" requirement under Rule 26(b)(2). There is an on-going responsibility to take appropriate measures to ensure that a client has provided all available information and documents that are responsive to discovery requests.

One effective method of tracking and verifying litigation-hold memorandum is to require each custodian to sign an acknowledgment that the litigation-hold memorandum has been received, understood, and implemented. The following is an example of such acknowledgment:

<u>Acknowledgment</u>

I acknowledge I have read the above attached Litigation-hold memorandum. I will forthwith conduct a reasonable search for responsive documents and electronic data. I will preserve any such electronic data and paper documents. I will not delete any data from any locations that I believe may contain responsive electronic data. I understand that this preservation request is on=going and requests the continuing preservation of data, including data created or received both before and after receipt of the Notice.

> Employee Name
> Employee Signature and date

In addition to requiring that custodians sign acknowledgments that they have read, understood, and will comply with the litigation-hold memorandum, it is a good practice to schedule interviews with each custodian to review what data the custodian holds and how it must be preserved. This will create a document trail showing efforts to preserve all relevant documents, which will provide compelling evidence to defend any potential spoliation allegations.

A litigation-hold memorandum is generally not discoverable, especially when it is shown that the litigation-hold memorandum includes material protected by the attorney-client privilege or the work product exemption. However, the basic details surrounding the litigation hold are typically not privileged. A party is entitled to know what kinds and categories of ESI the opposing party was instructed to preserve and collect, and what specific actions they were instructed to take.

In addition, the prevailing view is that when spoliation occurs, litigation-hold memorandum becomes discoverable. For example, in *Major Tours, Inc. v. Colorel*, 720 F. Supp. 2d 587 (2010), the plaintiffs requested that the defendants produce their litigation-hold memorandum to allow an examination of the scope of the defendants' document production and whether they had spoliated relevant evidence. The plaintiffs claimed that the litigation-hold memorandum was no longer subject to the attorney-client privilege or the work-product exemption because they had made a preliminary showing of spoliation. The court denied the defendants' motion for protective order because there had been a "preliminary showing of spoliation of evidence."

End Litigation Hold

A litigation hold may be lifted after the litigation has finally been resolved, assuming that the preserved data is not required to be preserved for other existing or anticipated litigation. However, the decision to lift a litigation hold should be made only after conducting due diligence to ensure that the preserved data is not relevant to any claims or defense for other litigation matters, including audits and investigations.

Company-owned Devices and Personal Devices

Responsive ESI needs to be retained from company-owned, personally enabled (COPE) devices and from personal smart phones that company employees used under an *ad hoc* bring your own device (BYOD) policy. Unless appropriate steps are taken to preserve relevant ESI maintained on mobile devices, stored with cloud computing providers, or communicated through social networks, a company's litigation hold process may not be defensible. In addition, there is a need to develop mobile device use policies that protect the interests of a company. Whether it elects to use a COPE, BYOD, or a hybrid program, the policy should define the nature and extent of the company's right to access and preserve data on the employee device, particularly for use in litigation

B. Other Preservation Methods

1. Custodian Interview

Custodian interviews are extremely valuable, but they can also be very time-consuming and disruptive on employees. The following is an example of a custodian interview form.

Custodian Interview Form

GENERAL INFORMATION
   Case Name:
   Custodian Name:
   Current Title and Department:
   Contact phone and email:
   Date Range of Relevant Events:
   Date of Litigation Hold, if applicable:

EMAIL INFORMATION
   Identify all relevant email addresses and passwords for collection.
   Identify email folders that contain relevant information.

LOCATION OF DATA
   Do you have any files relevant to this case?
   Where are the relevant hard copy files maintained?
   Do you use a desktop computer, laptop, mobile devices, etc.?
   Identify all file paths for locations where you save documents locally on the desktop and/or laptop computers.
   Identify any external storage devices used to store information. (*e.g.*, flash drive).
   Identify software applications that you use that may contain information relevant to this case.
   What types of documents do you most often generate or receive?
   Where do you store your documents?
   Identify all company-issued laptop and mobile devices.
   Identify any non-company issued devices used for work.
   Has the device been set up/approved by the company?
   Do you have any relevant data stored on a external device, cloud storage, etc.?
   Do you use any cloud-based applications?
   Identify social media platforms or messaging applications you use for work.
   Identify the locations or folders where you save electronic documents, including network personnel directory, network department directory or other network shares/folders.
   Do you have any personal folders on a shared drive or network where you store data or information?
   Do you move messages to personal folders within your email?
   Have you moved email messages to an external storage device?
   Do you have any saved voicemails that contain relevant information?

Do you keep notes or calendar entries that contain any information relevant to the case?
Identify any instances where data was collected in the past that could relate to this case.
Identify any other information that could assist with locating relevant file materials.
Identify the names and contact information for anyone you believe may have access to or knowledge of information relevant to this case.

There are specialized interview tools that simplify the custodian interview process. They can be deployed to provide attorneys an access to configurable and reusable questionnaires, while also tracking and storing responses. Some systems allow custodian interviews to be appended to the litigation hold, which eliminates the need for custodians to respond to multiple communications.

2. ESI Data Mapping

Data mapping can be applied to preservation. Data mapping software helps attorneys create, update, and organize a complete directory of the data environment. Data maps support preservation by helping attorneys quickly connect key custodians with the data sources used by the attorneys in order to help focus the preservation efforts. Additionally, a comprehensive data map provides insight into the risk profile of certain data sources to help pinpoint what data should be targeted for preservation first.

3. In-Place Preservation

In-place preservation systems integrate with an attorney's data sources so the attorney can engage automatic preservation actions, such as suspending a delete function, without directly interacting with the data sources themselves. This capability is especially useful when the in-place preservation tool is integrated with the litigation hold application so that all preservation efforts can be consolidated into one centralized system of record for the client.

4. Employee Change Monitoring

An employee-change monitoring system can automatically detect when an employee leaves a company or changes departments and appropriate actions, such as sending an alert to the legal department or issuing a new litigation-hold memorandum, can be taken in order to ensure relevant ESI remains preserved.

C. Duty to Preserve

Under common law, the duty to preserve evidence begins when a party knows of or has a reasonable anticipation of future litigation. Specifically, the duty to preserve ESI is triggered when a party has notice that the evidence is relevant to litigation, or when a party should have known that the evidence may be relevant to future litigation. The duty to preserve evidence also extends to that period before the litigation when a party reasonably should know that the evidence may be relevant to anticipated litigation, but the duty to preserve evidence does not arise if there is merely a potential for litigation. Thus, the determination of when a party anticipates litigation requires a fact intensive inquiry.

ZUBULAKE V. UBS WARBURG LLC (ZUBULAKE IV)
220 F.R.D. 212 (S.D.N.Y. 2003)

SCHEINDLIN, District Judge

I. BACKGROUND

This is the fourth opinion resolving discovery disputes in this case. Familiarity with the prior opinions is presumed, and only background information relevant to the instant dispute is described here. In brief, Laura Zubulake, an equities trader who earned approximately $650,000 a year with UBS, is suing UBS for gender discrimination, failure to promote, and retaliation under federal, state, and city law. She has repeatedly maintained that the evidence she needs to prove her case exists in e-mail correspondence sent among various UBS employees and stored only on UBS's computer systems.

On July 24, 2003, I ordered the parties to share the cost of restoring certain UBS backup tapes that contained e-mails relevant to Zubulake's claims. In the restoration effort, the parties discovered that certain backup tapes are missing. In particular:

Individual Server	Missing Monthly Backup Tapes
Matthew Chapin (Zubulake's immediate supervisor)	April 2001
Jeremy Hardisty (Chapin's supervisor)	June 2001
Andrew Clarke and Vinay Datta (Zubulake's coworkers)	April 2001
Rose Tong (human resources)	Part of June 2001, July 2001, August 2001, and October 2001

In addition, certain isolated e-mails-created after UBS supposedly began retaining all relevant e-mails-were deleted from UBS's system, although they appear to have been saved on the backup tapes. As I explained in *Zubulake III*, "certain e-mails sent after the initial EEOC charge-and particularly relevant to Zubulake's retaliation claim-were apparently not saved at all. For example, [an] e-mail from Chapin to Joy Kim [another of Zubulake's coworkers] instructing her on how to file a complaint against Zubulake was not saved, and it bears the subject line æ UBS client attorney priviledge [sic] only," although no attorney is copied on the e-mail. This potentially useful e-mail was deleted and resided only on UBS's backup tapes."

Zubulake filed her EEOC charge on August 16, 2001; the instant action was filed on February 14, 2002. In August 2001, in an oral directive, UBS ordered its employees to retain all relevant documents. In August 2002, after Zubulake specifically requested e-mail stored on backup tapes, UBS's outside counsel orally instructed UBS's information technology personnel to stop recycling backup tapes.

Zubulake now seeks sanctions against UBS for its failure to preserve the missing backup tapes and deleted e-mails. ***

II. LEGAL STANDARD

Spoliation is "the destruction or significant alteration of evidence, or the failure to preserve property for another's use as evidence in pending or reasonably foreseeable litigation." The spoliation of evidence germane "to proof of an issue at trial can support an inference that the evidence would have been unfavorable to the party responsible for its destruction." However, "[t]he determination of an appropriate sanction for spoliation, if any, is confined to the sound discretion of the trial judge, and is assessed on a case-by-case basis." The authority to sanction litigants for spoliation arises jointly under the Federal Rules of Civil Procedure and the court's own inherent powers.

III. DISCUSSION

It goes without saying that a party can only be sanctioned for destroying evidence if it had a duty to preserve it. If UBS had no such duty, then UBS cannot be faulted. I begin, then, by discussing the extent of a party's duty to preserve evidence.

A. Duty to Preserve

"The obligation to preserve evidence arises when the party has notice that the evidence is relevant to litigation or when a party should have known that the evidence may be relevant to future litigation." Identifying the boundaries of the duty to preserve involves two related inquiries: when does the duty to preserve attach, and what evidence must be preserved?

1. The Trigger Date

In this case, the duty to preserve evidence arose, at the latest, on August 16, 2001, when Zubulake filed her EEOC charge. At that time, UBS's in-house attorneys cautioned employees to retain all documents, including e-mails and backup tapes, that could potentially be relevant to the litigation. In meetings with Chapin, Clarke, Kim, Hardisty, John Holland (Chapin's supervisor), and Dominic Vail (Zubulake's former supervisor) held on August 29-31, 2001, UBS's outside counsel reiterated the need to preserve documents.

But the duty to preserve may have arisen even before the EEOC complaint was filed. Zubulake argues that UBS "should have known that the evidence [was] relevant to future litigation," as early as April 2001, and thus had a duty to preserve it. She offers two pieces of evidence in support of this argument. First, certain UBS employees titled e-mails pertaining to Zubulake "UBS Attorney Client Privilege" starting in April 2001, notwithstanding the fact that no attorney was copied on the e-mail and the substance of the e-mail was not legal in nature. Second, Chapin admitted in his deposition that he feared litigation from as early as April 2001.

Merely because one or two employees contemplate the possibility that a fellow employee might sue does not generally impose a firm-wide duty to preserve. But in this case, it appears that almost everyone associated with Zubulake recognized the possibility that she might sue. For example, an e-mail authored by Zubulake's co-worker Vinnay Datta, concerning Zubulake and labeled "UBS attorney client priviladge [sic]," was distributed to Chapin (Zubulake's supervisor), Holland and Leland Tomblick (Chapin's supervisor), Vail (Zubulake's former supervisor), and Andrew Clarke (Zubulake's co-worker) in late April 2001. That e-mail, replying to one from Hardisty, essentially called for Zubulake's termination: "Our biggest strength as a firm and as a desk is our ability to share information and relationships. Any person who threatens this in any way should be firmly dealt with ... [B]elieve me that a lot of other [similar] instances have occurred earlier."

Thus, the relevant people at UBS anticipated litigation in April 2001. The duty to preserve attached at the time that litigation was reasonably anticipated.

2. Scope

The next question is: What is the scope of the duty to preserve? Must a corporation, upon recognizing the threat of litigation, preserve every shred of paper, every e-mail or electronic document, and every backup tape? The answer is clearly, "no." Such a rule would cripple large corporations, like UBS, that are almost always involved in litigation. As a general rule, then, a party need not preserve all backup tapes even when it reasonably anticipates litigation.

At the same time, anyone who anticipates being a party or is a party to a lawsuit must not destroy unique, relevant evidence that might be useful to an adversary. "While a litigant is under no duty to keep or retain every document in its possession ... it is under a duty to preserve what it knows, or reasonably should know, is relevant in the action, is reasonably calculated to lead to the discovery of admissible evidence, is reasonably likely to be requested during discovery and/or is the subject of a pending discovery request."

i. Whose Documents Must Be Retained?

The broad contours of the duty to preserve are relatively clear. That duty should certainly extend to any documents or tangible things (as defined by Rule 34(a)) made by individuals "likely to have discoverable information that the disclosing party may use to support its claims or defenses." The duty also includes documents prepared for those individuals, to the extent those documents can be readily identified (e.g., from the "to" field in e-mails). The duty also extends to information that is relevant to the claims or defenses of any party, or which is "relevant to the subject matter involved in the action." Thus, the duty to preserve extends to those employees likely to have relevant information-the "key players" in the case. In this case, all of the individuals whose backup tapes were lost (Chapin, Hardisty, Tong, Datta and Clarke) fall into this category.

ii. What Must Be Retained?

A party or anticipated party must retain all relevant documents (but not multiple identical copies) in existence at the time the duty to preserve attaches, and any relevant documents created thereafter. In recognition of the fact that there are many ways to manage electronic data, litigants are free to choose how this task is accomplished. For example, a litigant could choose to retain all then-existing backup tapes for the relevant personnel (if such tapes store data by individual or the contents can be identified in good faith and through reasonable effort), and to catalog any later-created documents in a separate electronic file. That, along with a mirror-image of the computer system taken at the time the duty to preserve attaches (to preserve documents in the state they existed at that time), creates a complete set of relevant documents. Presumably there are a multitude of other ways to achieve the same result.

iii. Summary of Preservation Obligations

The scope of a party's preservation obligation can be described as follows: Once a party reasonably anticipates litigation, it must suspend its routine document retention/destruction policy and put in place a "litigation hold" to ensure the preservation of relevant documents. As a general rule, that litigation hold does not apply to inaccessible backup tapes (e.g., those typically maintained solely for the purpose of disaster recovery), which may continue to be recycled on the schedule set forth in the company's policy. On the other hand, if backup tapes are accessible (i.e., actively used for information retrieval), then such tapes would likely be subject to the litigation hold.

However, it does make sense to create one exception to this general rule. If a company can identify where particular employee documents are stored on backup tapes, then the tapes storing the documents of "key players" to the existing or threatened litigation should be preserved if the information contained on those tapes is not otherwise available. This exception applies to all backup tapes.

iv. What Happened at UBS After August 2001?

By its attorney's directive in August 2002, UBS endeavored to preserve all backup tapes that existed in August 2001 (when Zubulake filed her EEOC charge) that captured data for employees identified by Zubulake in her document request, and all such monthly backup tapes generated thereafter. These backup tapes existed in August 2002, because of UBS's document retention policy, which required retention for three years. In August 2001, UBS employees were instructed to maintain active electronic documents pertaining to Zubulake in separate files. Had these directives been followed, UBS would have met its preservation obligations by preserving one copy of all relevant documents that existed at, or were created after, the time when the duty to preserve attached.

In fact, UBS employees did not comply with these directives. Three backup tapes containing the e-mail files of Chapin, Hardisty, Clarke and Datta created after April 2001 were lost, despite the August 2002 directive to maintain those tapes. According to the UBS document retention policy, these three monthly backup tapes from April and June 2001 should have been retained for three years.

The two remaining lost backup tapes were for the time period after Zubulake filed her EEOC complaint (Rose Tong's tapes for August and October 2001). UBS has offered no explanation for why these tapes are missing. UBS initially argued that Tong is a Hong Kong based UBS employee and thus her backup tapes "are not subject to any internal retention policy." However, UBS subsequently informed the Court that there was a document retention policy in place in Hong Kong starting in June 2001, although it only required that backup tapes be retained for one month. It also instructed employees "not [to] delete any emails if they are aware that ... litigation is pending or likely, or during ... a discovery process." In any event, it appears that UBS did not directly order the preservation of Tong's backup tapes until August 2002, when Zubulake made her discovery request.

In sum, UBS had a duty to preserve the six-plus backup tapes (that is, six complete backup tapes and part of a seventh) at issue here.

***

D. Possession, Custody, or Control

Under FRCP Rule 34, a party may serve on any other party a request to produce and permit the requesting party to inspect, copy, test, or sample certain items in the responding party's possession, custody, or control.

HUNTERS RUN GUN CLUB, LLC V. BAKER
No. 17-176-SDD-EWD (M.D. La. 2019)

WILDER-DOOMES, Magistrate Judge

Before the Court is a Motion to Compel Production from Keith Morris and Bridgeview Gun Club, LLC (the "Motion"), filed by Plaintiffs Hunters Run Gun Club, LLC ("Hunters Run") and The Great International Land Company, LLC (collectively, "Plaintiffs"). The Motion is opposed by Defendants Keith Morris ("Morris") and Bridgeview Gun Club, LLC ("Bridgeview") (collectively, "Defendants"). Plaintiffs have filed a reply.

***

I. Background

This litigation involves allegations that Defendants conspired with the Law Enforcement District of the Parish of West Baton Rouge (the "LED") by terminating the lease previously belonging to a Hunters Run affiliate for a shooting facility and gun club run by Hunter's Run and leasing the facility to Hunter's Run's competitor, Bridgeview, which is owned and controlled by Morris. Plaintiffs specifically allege that the LED notified Hunter's Run that it would not renew its lease with Hunter's Run as operator of the gun club shortly after Hunter's Run terminated the employment of its former manager, Defendant Eddie Baker ("Baker"), in August 2016. About three months after Baker's termination, in November 2016, Plaintiffs contend that the LED, a public entity, tried to lease the gun club to Morris, notwithstanding that Morris did not submit the highest bid to the LED for the lease. Plaintiffs successfully obtained injunctive relief against the LED in state court for the LED's failure to comply with Louisiana's bid law. Thereafter, the LED published a bid request, which resulted in lease of the gun club to Bridgeview. Plaintiffs allege that this conspiracy between Morris, Baker, Bridgeview and the LED resulted in damages to Plaintiffs.

Plaintiffs' Motion

In the course of discovery, Plaintiffs sought to obtain information in support of their conspiracy claims from Morris and Baker, including text messages and other communications between Morris and Baker "regarding any matter asserted in this litigation." Plaintiffs served Baker with discovery requests, but served a subpoena duces tecum ("subpoena") with an attached list of requests for production on Morris. The request at issue in the Motion states: "3. Please produce any and all correspondence, including but not limited to emails, text messages, facsimiles, voice mail message, and other communications, including correspondence referencing communications, by and/or between you and Eddie Baker from January 2015 through present, regarding any matter asserted in the instant litigation....)"

Defendants denied having possession of any responsive documents. However, Plaintiffs received Baker's AT&T cell phone records from January 2016 to February 2017, during the period of time encompassing Baker's termination through the LED's award of the lease to Bridgeview. Plaintiffs aver that these records, which identify participants to phone calls and text messages and the dates and times thereof but do not disclose the substance of text messages, show that Baker and Morris communicated immediately after Baker's termination. Plaintiffs contend that the records show that Baker also communicated with James Edgmon ("Edgmon"), the owner of R&R Trap Sales, a gun equipment vendor, just after Baker's termination, which is significant because Morris ordered equipment from Edgmon after the first LED lease was awarded to Bridgeview in December 2016. Plaintiffs further contend that the records show that Baker communicated with Morris and Edgmon earlier in 2016 while Baker was still employed by Plaintiffs. Thus, Plaintiffs contend that these phone records (and deposition testimony) establish that Defendants have responsive text messages that have not been produced.

On September 18, 2018, Plaintiffs filed the instant Motion, seeking to compel Defendants to produce the referenced communications because the information sought is relevant and supports Plaintiffs' conspiracy theory. Plaintiffs aver that they addressed Defendants' failure to produce with Defense counsel, but Plaintiffs have not received a substantive response from Defendants. Further, Plaintiffs contend that they suggested that Morris could authorize AT&T to release the contents of his text messages to Plaintiffs, rather than produce them himself. However, Morris has refused to provide the authorization. Plaintiffs argue that Morris' refusal to authorize the release shows that the requested information is damaging to Morris' case. Plaintiffs seek an order compelling Defendants to produce all responsive communications, including but not limited to the text messages shown on the AT&T records received by Plaintiffs, or in the alternative, compelling Defendants to produce them to the Court for an in camera review of their discoverability.

Defendants' Opposition

Defendants aver that they have communicated to Plaintiffs, on multiple occasions and in their discovery responses, that they are not in possession of the requested information. Defendants contend that Bridgeview does not own or maintain a cell phone and therefore cannot produce any records. With respect to Morris, Defendants contend that Morris disclosed to Plaintiffs that: Morris initially had service through AT&T until the August 2016 flood that occurred in East Baton Rouge Parish, Louisiana; since the flood, Morris has had service through Verizon; and, Morris no longer has the pre-flood phone or Verizon or AT&T billing records. Morris contends that he does not oppose Plaintiffs' subpoena to AT&T for the records, and Plaintiffs have not subpoenaed Verizon for records.

Defendants aver that Plaintiffs have no basis to accuse Morris of withholding information originating from Baker, when two digital forensic analysts retained by Plaintiffs analyzed Baker's personal computer and the Hunter's Run computers to which Baker had access at the time of his employment and failed to find anything of interest and/or worthy enough to be presented in an expert report. Defendants contend that they have devoted a substantial amount of time to responding to Plaintiffs' lengthy discovery requests and have fully responded that they are not in possession of the information requested.

Plaintiffs' Reply

Plaintiffs argue that even though Morris no longer has the AT&T phone and did not retain the records, he still has the ability to obtain the records, because, as set forth in this Court's Southern Filter Media, LLC v. Halter decision, "[d]ocuments are under the control of a party if the party 'has the legal right to obtain the documents on demand or has the practical ability to obtain the documents from a non-party to the action.'" Thus, according to Plaintiffs, Morris has control over his cell phone records, including the contents of the text messages, for the purposes of production under Fed. R. Civ. P. 34(a) since he can request that his service providers give him a copy of the records or produce the records to Plaintiffs.

Plaintiffs assert that there is additional evidence to show that Defendants have improperly withheld the requested information, in the form of a supplemental document production Plaintiffs received from the LED's counsel Christopher Whittington ("Whittington") on October 15, 2018. Whittington initially listed two documents (among others) on his privilege log in lieu of production, but ultimately withdrew the assertion of privilege as to two of the documents and produced them to Plaintiffs following the filing of Plaintiffs' Motion to Compel Production from Whittington. Plaintiffs aver that one of the documents contains "detailed technical discussions regarding the equipment and plans for operating the gun club [that] must have taken place between Eddie Baker and Morris in order for Morris' counsel or Morris (or Baker) to prepare [it]" and that both of the documents concern "negotiations between the LED and Keith Morris regarding the terms of the lease over a month before the bid process was even begun." Moreover and importantly, according to Plaintiffs, those two documents are still on the privilege log submitted by Matthew Green ("Green"), counsel for Defendants, in Green's responses to Plaintiffs' subpoena to Green. Plaintiffs argue that Green's objection to production of those documents, which is based on privilege pursuant to La. Code of Evidence art. 408, is inapplicable because this matter, and the two documents, are all unrelated to any potential settlement between the LED and Morris. Thus, Plaintiffs argue that Defendants have wrongly withheld production of these documents because they do not have a valid claim of privilege.

January 25, 2019 Telephone Conference

During the parties' January 25, 2019 telephone conference with the Court, the parties presented argument as to whether, under Fed. R. Civ. P. 34, Morris has possession, custody, or control of the cell phone records containing the contents of the text messages. Plaintiffs argued that, per Southern Filter Media, the text message records are in Morris' control because he has the right to obtain them, but he refuses to give his consent. Morris argued that Plaintiffs have obtained the records they sought from AT&T and Morris has no other responsive information in his control. Morris further argued that Southern Filter Media does not support Plaintiffs' position, and Morris is not aware of any cases that obligate him to either give his consent to release the records or to obtain the records from his provider(s).

II. Law and Analysis
A. Legal Standards and the Scope of the Motion

Under the Federal Rules of Civil Procedure, parties may obtain discovery regarding any nonprivileged matter that is relevant to any party's claim or defense and proportional to the needs of the case, considering the importance of the issues at stake in the action, the amount in controversy, the parties' relative access to relevant information, the parties' resources, the importance of the discovery in resolving the issues, and whether the burden or expense of the proposed discovery outweighs its likely benefit. The Court must additionally limit the frequency or extent of discovery if it determines that: "(i) the discovery sought is unreasonably cumulative or duplicative, or can be obtained from some other source that is more convenient, less burdensome, or less expensive; (ii) the party seeking discovery has had ample opportunity to obtain the information by discovery in the action; or (iii) the proposed discovery is outside the scope permitted by Rule 26(b)(1)."

Further, Rule 34 of the Federal Rules of Civil Procedure provides for the discovery of documents and tangible things:

> (a) In General. A party may serve on any other party a request within the scope of Rule 26(b):
> (1) to produce and permit the requesting party or its representative to inspect, copy, test, or sample the following items in the responding party's *possession, custody, or control*:
> > (A) any designated documents or electronically stored information--including writings, drawings, graphs, charts, photographs, sound recordings, images, and other data or data compilations--stored in any medium from which information can be obtained either directly or, if necessary, after translation by the responding party into a reasonably usable form; or
> > (B) any designated tangible things...(emphasis added).

"Once a party moving to compel discovery establishes that the materials and information it seeks are relevant or will lead to the discovery of admissible evidence, the burden rests upon the party resisting discovery to substantiate its objections." "A party objecting to discovery 'must state with specificity the objection and how it relates to the particular request being opposed, and not merely that it is 'overly broad and burdensome' or 'oppressive' or 'vexatious' or 'not reasonably calculated to lead to the discovery of admissible evidence.'"

The Court finds that Fed. R. Civ. P. 34 is applicable to Plaintiffs' claims herein, as the parties' arguments on the Motion, in brief and during the conference, were specifically premised upon the applicability of Fed. R. Civ. P. 34, and because Plaintiffs seek production of information from Morris, who was named Defendant in Plaintiff's First Amended Complaint about ten months ago.

Regarding the scope of the Motion, the Court has already granted Plaintiffs' Motion to Compel Production from Green and ordered Green to produce the documents responsive to Plaintiffs' subpoena previously withheld based on privilege. Therefore, to the extent the instant Motion raises production of those documents in Plaintiffs' Reply brief, that request is now moot. Plaintiffs otherwise seek production of the contents of text messages exchanged between Morris and Baker from January 1, 2015 through August 31, 2017, regarding "any matter asserted in the instant litigation," in order to support their conspiracy claims. The Court notes that Plaintiffs do not provide evidence of any other responsive information that is allegedly being withheld, and Plaintiffs' arguments are focused on the contents of text messages. Therefore, the Court considers the issue presented by the Motion to be limited a request for an order compelling production of Morris' cell phone records as described above.

B. The Requested Records are Responsive and Relevant

Plaintiffs argue that the requested text messages are responsive to Plaintiffs' request for production to Morris, and are relevant to Plaintiffs' conspiracy claims, particularly considering the timing of the texts and the participants thereto. Defendants offer no argument to the effect that the requested text messages are not responsive to Plaintiffs' document request or that they are irrelevant to Plaintiffs' claims herein. The Court finds that the contents of the text messages are responsive and relevant. First, they are within the scope of Plaintiffs' document request, as they constitute "...text messages...by and/or between [Morris] and Eddie Baker from January 2015 through present, regarding any matter asserted in the instant litigation...." Second, a discovery request is relevant when the request "seek[s] admissible evidence or 'is reasonably calculated to lead to the discovery of admissible evidence.'" Considering the participants to, and the timing of, these text messages, the Court finds that they could have bearing on Plaintiffs' claims herein, which is that Baker, Morris, and Bridgeview all allegedly conspired with the LED, during and after Baker's termination, to damage Plaintiffs' business and have Plaintiffs' lease canceled by the LED so that the lease could be awarded to Defendants.

C. The Requested Information is Within the Control of Morris

Plaintiffs contend that, per *Southern Filter Media, LLC v. Halter*, the requested text messages are within Morris' control because he has the ability to request that they be produced to him or be released to Plaintiffs by signing the release of the records required by his service provider(s). However, Morris contends that, while he has not opposed Plaintiffs' subpoena to AT&T, he has no obligation to execute a release, and the records are not in his "possession, custody, or control" as contemplated by Fed. R. Civ. P. 34.

The Court finds that *Southern Filter Media* is not controlling because it is factually distinguishable. In that case, the defendant requesting the documents sought to compel the plaintiff (SFM) to obtain information from two other non-party companies (Sun Minerals and Kinder Sand) that had the same management and ownership as the plaintiff. The Court granted the plaintiff's motion for a protective order on the basis that the defendant failed to show that the three companies were sibling companies, that they shared a parent company, that the plaintiff had any ownership interest in the other companies, that the companies exchanged any documents in the course of business, or that the plaintiff had any control over documents solely in the possession of the other two companies. Further, it was not enough that the three companies shared the same four owners because the owners were not parties to the case. In contrast, this case does not involve a request to a party-company to produce records in the possession of a related non-party company under common ownership. Rather, Plaintiffs herein seek to compel Morris to execute a release so that they can obtain records of his text messages from his cell phone service providers and/or to compel Morris to obtain the records himself and produce them to Plaintiffs.

The Court's research reveals several cases on point, none of which were cited by the parties. It is clear that the courts in this circuit (and nationwide) have different views on whether they are empowered under Fed. R. Civ. P. 34(a) to order a party to sign an authorization or release that permits the requesting party to obtain documents such as cell phone records from non-parties. *Vasquez v. Conquest Completion Services, LLC*, is factually similar in that it involves a request for a release of cell phone records and cogently addresses the circuit split. In *Vasquez*, the plaintiff claimed that the accident in which the plaintiff was injured may have been caused by the negligence of the defendant in using his cell phone. The *Vasquez* plaintiff thus sought an order compelling the driver defendant to execute an authorization to release his cell phone records upon his refusal to execute one. After finding that the cell phone records were relevant to the plaintiff's claims, the *Vasquez* court recognized that some courts in this circuit have held that they are not empowered by the Federal Rules of Civil Procedure to compel parties to sign authorizations so that the requesting party can obtain documents from a non-party.

The *Vasquez* court also noted, however, that other courts in this Circuit have reached the opposite conclusion. *See Mir v. L-3 Communications Integrated Systems, L.P.*, (ordering execution of a release of Social Security records on the basis that Fed. R. Civ. P. 34 and 37 empower the court to compel parties to sign written releases or authorization forms consenting to the production of various documents, and holding):

> The Court agrees with other courts' observations that a party can seek documents such as Social Security or health records directly from a non-party custodian through a Rule 45(a) subpoena—in response to which the non-party may or may not refuse to release records without the written authorization of the individual to whom such records pertain–and that a

party can, using Rule 34(a), request the records directly from the other party and thereby require that party to collect them from non-party custodians to the extent that the requested information is within the responding party's possession, custody, or control.

But those options' availability does not foreclose a party's using Rule 34(a) to seek a signed authorization or release from another party to facilitate disclosure by a non-party custodian of documents that are under the responding party's control but not within that party's possession or custody.

That is because requests for signing and executing written releases or authorizations may be properly made under Rule 34(a)–and then, if necessary, compelled under [] Rule 37(a)—insofar as they require a responding party to permit the requesting party or its representative to inspect or copy designated documents or electronically stored information in the responding party's control. See Fed. R. Civ. P. 34(a)(1). Reading Rule 34(a) to permissibly require parties to sign and execute written releases and authorization forms, so understood, does not amount to impermissibly requiring a responding party to create a new or non-existent document.

See also Lischka v. Tidewater Services, Inc., wherein the magistrate judge's order compelling plaintiffs to sign written authorizations for medical, tax, Social Security, and employment records was affirmed, and the Court squarely held:

> ... rule [34] allows for production of documents 'which are in the possession, custody, or control' of the party upon whom the request is served and that, for purposes of Rule 34, plaintiffs are in control of records that can be released via an authorization, 'because, by either granting or withholding [their] consent, [they] may determine who shall have access to them.'"(emphasis in original).

Further, *see Allen v. Indian Harbor Marine, Inc.*, which involved a factual scenario similar to the one herein in that the plaintiff contended that the documents requested were not under his possession, custody, or control and he was under no obligation to execute the requested Social Security and military records authorizations because the defendants had already subpoenaed those records pursuant to Fed. R. Civ. P. 45. Notably, the court rejected this argument, holding:

> Plaintiff's tortured argument regarding the availability of the requested documents pursuant to FRCP Rule 45 subpoena merits no discussion. The Court previously noted and any attorney who has ever handled even one case implicating records and documents in the physical possession of non-parties and particularly government entities, including medical records,

military records, social security disability records, tax records, and the like, will not be released without the written authorization of the individual to whom such records pertain.

Finally, *see Wymore v. Nail* (granting motion to compel and ordering plaintiff to execute HIPAA authorization release forms so that his medical records could be obtained by the defendants in response to plaintiff's damage claims involving a broken jaw).

The Court has already found that the requested records, including the content of the text messages, are relevant and discoverable. Because the records are relevant and discoverable, Morris cannot block production of a portion of the records, i.e., the contents of the text messages, simply by refusing to execute the required releases and/or refusing to request the records himself, particularly since Morris did not (and does not) object to Plaintiffs subpoenaing his service providers for the records in the first instance. See, e.g., Defendants' Opposition ("Mr. Morris does not oppose plaintiff's (sic) obtaining those records via subpoena...."). Therefore, the Court will grant the Motion to Compel as to Morris. While this Court generally agrees with the line of cases that have held that the Federal Rules empower courts to order parties to execute releases that direct non-parties to produce relevant information, particularly when the non-party has already been subpoenaed but refuses to release the requested information in the absence of such a release, the Court finds it appropriate in this case to order as follows, which is designed to effectuate the timely production of the requested information: Morris must either: 1) provide Plaintiffs with executed release forms/authorizations required by Morris' cellular phone service providers to facilitate release of Morris' cell phone records (including contents of messages) by and between Morris and Eddie Baker from January 1, 2015 through August 31, 2017 regarding any matter asserted in the instant litigation, or 2) Morris must obtain and produce the above-described cell-phone records. The Court additionally orders that all such records produced are subject to the parties' July 5, 2018 Stipulated Protective Order, and further, if the records ultimately received contain the contents of text messages that do not fall within the description set forth above, the contents of those nonresponsive text messages must be redacted.

D. There is No Evidence that Bridgeview Has Responsive Records

Defendants contend that Bridgeview does not have any records because it is a limited liability company that does not possess a cell phone. Plaintiffs did not address this argument. Moreover, Plaintiffs' subpoena and request for documents were directed to Morris, not Bridgeview. Plaintiffs' substantive argument is also directed to Morris, in that Plaintiffs seek for Morris to execute a release of the contents of the records. As there is no indication that Bridgeview has withheld any responsive records or persuasive argument or evidence from Plaintiffs that it does, there is no basis for Plaintiffs' Motion against Bridgeview and thus the Motion is DENIED as to Bridgeview.

***

CHAPTER 6

SPOLIATION AND SANCTIONS

Spoliation is the destruction or material alteration of evidence or the failure to preserve property for another's use as evidence in pending or reasonably foreseeable litigation. In essence, spoliation is the flip side of data preservation. It is relatively easy to secure paper documents such that they are not physically destroyed or thrown away. However, this is not the case with ESI.

A. Finding Spoliation

The determination of spoliation and the degree of sanctions that should be imposed by a court requires consideration of the following questions:

1. Was there a duty to preserve evidence?
2. Did the spoliator intentionally or negligently spoliate evidence?
3. Did the spoliator act in bad faith?
4. Did the spoliation prejudice the non-spoliator's ability to present its case or defense?
5. Did the spoliator intent to spoliate evidence?.

FRCP Rule 37(e)

(e) Failure to Preserve Electronically Stored Information. If electronically stored information that should have been preserved in the anticipation or conduct of litigation is lost because a party failed to take reasonable steps to preserve it, and it cannot be restored or replaced through additional discovery, the court:

(1) upon finding prejudice to another party from loss of the information, may order measures no greater than necessary to cure the prejudice; or

(2) only upon finding that the party acted with the intent to deprive another party of the information's use in the litigation may:
    (A) presume that the lost information was unfavorable to the party;
    (B) instruct the jury that it may or must presume the information was unfavorable to the party; or
    (C) dismiss the action or enter a default judgment.

The following flowchart graphically depicts FRCP Rule 37(e):

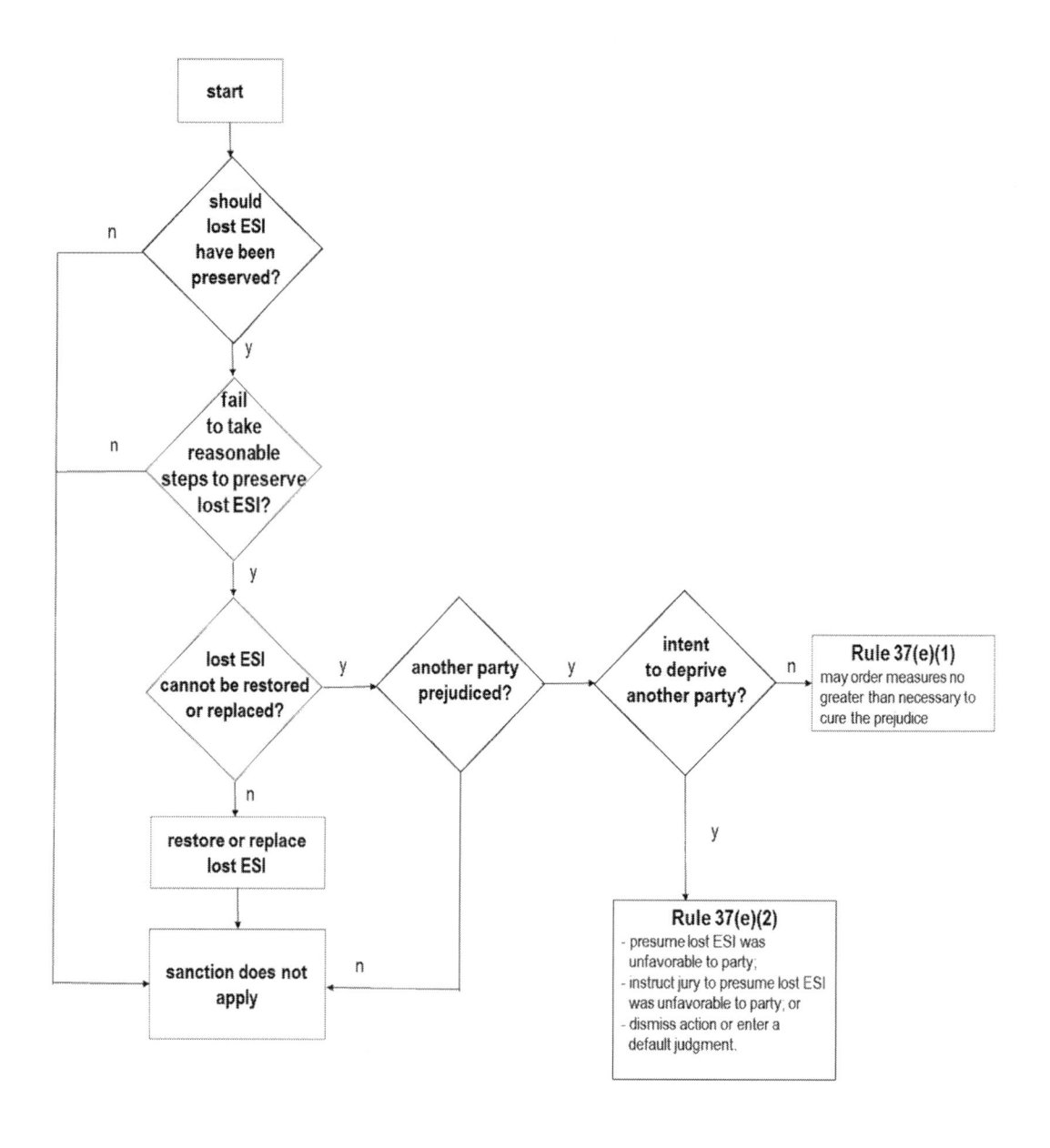

```
                    start
                      │
                      ▼
              ┌───────────────┐
         n    │  should lost  │
    ◄─────────│ ESI have been │
    │         │   preserved?  │
    │         └───────┬───────┘
    │                 │ y
    │                 ▼
    │         ┌───────────────┐
    │    n    │ fail to take  │
    ◄─────────│  reasonable   │
    │         │steps to preserve
    │         │   lost ESI?   │
    │         └───────┬───────┘
    │                 │ y
    │                 ▼
    │         ┌───────────────┐      ┌──────────────┐      ┌──────────────┐      ┌─────────────────────────┐
    │         │   lost ESI    │  y   │another party │  y   │  intent to   │  n   │ Rule 37(e)(1)           │
    │         │cannot be restored├──►│ prejudiced?  ├─────►│   deprive    ├─────►│ may order measures no   │
    │         │  or replaced? │      │              │      │another party?│      │ greater than necessary to│
    │         └───────┬───────┘      └──────┬───────┘      └──────┬───────┘      │ cure the prejudice      │
    │                 │ n                   │                     │ y            └─────────────────────────┘
    │                 ▼                     │                     ▼
    │         ┌───────────────┐             │             ┌─────────────────────────┐
    │         │restore or replace           │             │ Rule 37(e)(2)           │
    │         │   lost ESI    │             │             │ - presume lost ESI was  │
    │         └───────┬───────┘             │             │   unfavorable to party; │
    │                 │                     │             │ - instruct jury to presume lost ESI
    │                 ▼                     │             │   was unfavorable to party, or
    │         ┌───────────────┐    n        │             │ - dismiss action or enter a
    └────────►│ sanction does │◄────────────┘             │   default judgment.     │
              │   not apply   │                           └─────────────────────────┘
              └───────────────┘
```

STEVENS V. BRIGHAM YOUNG UNIV.-IDAHO
No. 4:16-CV-530-BLW (D. Id. 2019)

WINMILL, District Judge

***

LITIGATION BACKGROUND

Plaintiff Stevens, a former BYU-I student, alleges that Robert Stokes, a former BYU-I professor, initiated an unwanted relationship with her while she was a student and Stokes was a professor at BYU-I. Stevens alleges that this relationship ultimately became sexually and emotionally abusive. She further asserts that she, along with another student, Danielle Spencer, reported Stokes' inappropriate and abusive behavior to several BYU-I professors and officials, who failed to take any action. The relationship ended when Stokes died on July 1, 2016, from complications during heart surgery. Stevens originally sued BYU-I and the Stokes estate. She later settled her claims against the Stokes estate. The LDS Church intervened for "the limited purpose of protecting its claims of privilege ...."

There are now four claims in this case against BYU-I:

1. Teacher-on-student hostile environment/sexual harassment actionable under Title IX of the Education Amendments Act;
2. Teacher-on-student quid pro quo sexual harassment;
3. Hostile learning environment in violation of the Rehabilitation Act and the Americans with Disabilities Act; and
4. Violation of the Idaho Human Rights Act.

FACTUAL BACKGROUND

In this lawsuit, Stevens intends to introduce selected text messages between her and Stokes to describe that relationship and support her claim of harassment and abuse. It is undisputed, however, that Stevens selectively and intentionally deleted a large amount of texts between the two. BYU-I argues that Stevens' deletions warrant sanctions such as dismissal of this lawsuit or exclusion of the remaining texts from evidence. To resolve this motion, the Court must review what the record reveals about Stevens' deletions of the texts.

During her relationship with Stokes, and prior to his death, Stevens would selectively delete certain texts between the two, but stopped that practice after he died. So what did Stevens delete? She testified that she generally deleted "chitchat" such as her texts to Stokes that she "woke up at 5:00 this morning and I went and had breakfast." At other times, she randomly deleted texts with Stokes because she "was having a really bad day and my phone was clear full [and] I didn't even want to look at them, and I would just hit delete." But she kept Stokes' texts that reminded her that she was "a good person - because I need those reminders all of the time to function. If I looked at it, and it said, 'you're a good person,' then I saved it." She also saved text messages from Stokes where she questioned "whether he was telling me the truth or not." She kept those texts as a form of protection because "if it turns out he is lying to me, if I ever told anybody that he was having sex with me, nobody would believe me."

When asked if the number of texts she deleted prior to Stokes' death was "a huge number of texts," Stevens answered "yeah." At another point, when asked if she deleted texts before Stokes died, Stevens answered "[a]ll the time."

After Stokes died, Stevens testified that she took screen shots of the remaining text messages between her and Stokes and printed them out, resulting in 800 pages of texts. She did not at this time delete any of the remaining texts, so she had them both on her phone and in hard copy in six binders.

Stevens filed this lawsuit on December 9, 2016. About two or three months later - in February or March of 2017 - Stevens was using her phone when, she testified, her phone "froze" and quit working. To repair the phone, she took it to the AT&T store where she had purchased it, to have them restore the phones functionality. She told the clerk that "I had important things on there that I didn't want to lose." Nevertheless, the clerk did some type of factory reset that deleted all the text messages. When Stevens was asked why she did not take her phone to her attorneys for them to preserve the messages prior to it malfunctioning, Stevens explained that "I had all the text messages on the paper [and] ... I really didn't even realize how big of an issue it was going to be." Stevens testified that she did not tell her attorneys that she was taking her phone in for repairs and that her attorneys "didn't even know I went [to the AT&T store]."

This incident was described somewhat differently by Stevens' counsel Deann Casperson in her letter to defense counsel explaining the incident. Casperson wrote that,

> [w]e directed her [Stevens] to go to the Verizon store for professional assistance. We specifically instructed Ms. Stevens to inform the person assisting her that she absolutely could not lose the messages stored on her phone. She explained this to the clerk, but the clerk inadvertently reset Ms. Stevens' phone to its factory settings, deleting the text messages on her phone.

BYU-I argues that Stevens' intentional deletion of text messages is prejudicial to their defense of this case, and they seek sanctions under Rule 37(e), including a dismissal of this action or the exclusion of all remaining text messages from evidence.

LEGAL STANDARDS

The spoliation of electronic discovery is covered by Rule 37(e), "which essentially functions as a decision tree". *** Rule 37(e) states as follows:

> If electronically stored information that should have been preserved in the anticipation or conduct of litigation is lost because a party failed to take reasonable steps to preserve it, and it cannot be restored or replaced through additional discovery, the court:
> (1) upon finding prejudice to another party from loss of the information, may order measures no greater than necessary to cure the prejudice; or
> (2) only upon finding that the party acted with the intent to deprive another party of the information's use in the litigation may:
> (A) presume that the lost information was unfavorable to the party;
> (B) instruct the jury that it may or must presume the information was unfavorable to the party; or
> (C) dismiss the action or enter a default judgment.

See Rule 37(e) (emphasis added). The decision tree starts with an inquiry of whether the data is forever gone: The Court must consider three questions to determine whether ESI has been "lost" - (a) did the discoverable ESI exist at the time a duty to preserve arose, (b) did the party fail to take reasonable steps to preserve the ESI, and (c) is the evidence irreplaceably lost? If the answer to any of these questions is "no", then a motion for spoliation sanctions must be denied. If all the questions are answered "yes", then the Court proceeds to determine whether the moving party has been prejudiced and whether the party subject to potential sanctions had an intent to deprive.

The drafters of Rule 37(e) intended to preempt use of other sources of sanctions - such as state law or the long-established "inherent power" doctrine - and require findings consistent with Rule 37(e) as the only path to remedying the loss of electronically stored information. See Rule 37 Advisory Committee Notes to the 2015 Amendment (stating that Rule 37(e) "therefore forecloses reliance on inherent authority or state law to determine when certain measures should be used").

ANALYSIS

The Court begins its Rule 37(e) "decision tree" inquiry by determining whether the deleted texts are lost. They are. Stevens' phone cannot be used to recover any of the deleted texts because it was wiped clean by the AT&T clerk, according to Stevens. BYU-I subpoenaed records from AT&T but their records did not contain the contents of any texts. While Stokes' phone would have contained those texts, the phone he used was his personal phone and when counsel for BYU-I asked the Stokes Estate for the texts, they received only "a partial universe and did not include any of the missing texts or many of the texts that plaintiff did not produce." The requirement under Rule 37(e) that the texts be "lost" is therefore satisfied.

The next issues are whether the deletions were intentional and prejudicial. Stevens testified that her deletions during her relationship with Stokes were intentional - she meant to delete texts, as can be seen in the discussion above. Moreover, those deletions are prejudicial to BYU-I. Stevens intends to introduce the remaining texts to describe her relationship with Stokes. Stevens' expert, Anne Munch, will also use the texts to analyze the relationship. Stevens' selected texts may create a misleading description of their relationship but BYU-I is barred by her actions from challenging that narrative.

The next question is whether the texts were deleted at a time when the duty to preserve had arisen. That duty arises when "litigation is reasonably foreseeable." Both parties agree that this is an objective standard.

As discussed above, Stevens, during her relationship with Stokes and before his death, deleted texts at various times for various reasons as the relationship gradually progressed from platonic to sexual. With regard to deletions Stevens made early in the relationship, there is no indication that litigation was reasonably foreseeable at that time. But later in the relationship - when it turned sexual - Stevens testified that she felt manipulated and was sickened by the sex with Stokes.

At this point - when the relationship turned to manipulative sex - a reasonable person may have foreseen litigation. However, at the same time, there can be an immense difference between recognizing you are being manipulated by a sexual predator - a realization that may be slow to form, given the skill of the predator - and foreseeing that you could sue him. So even then, it is difficult to pin down the time when litigation became reasonably foreseeable.

But the real problem here is that the record does not reveal when the deletions occurred. That makes it impossible to rule as a matter of law that the deletions occurred at a time that the duty to preserve was in existence.

In contrast, the duty to preserve was clearly in place when Stevens took her phone to the AT&T store and the clerk deleted the texts, because this took place after Stevens filed this lawsuit. Rule 37(e) asks: Was that deletion intentional? According to Stevens, it was entirely unintentional. But there are substantial questions with her claim. Her account of the AT&T incident is inconsistent with that of her attorney's, as discussed above. Moreover, the AT&T deletion did not occur in a vacuum; it was preceded by Stevens' selective and substantial intentional deletions over a long period of time during the relationship - recall that she described the number of those deletions as "huge" because she was deleting texts "all the time" - raising a serious question whether she was deleting texts to create a fictional narrative of her relationship with Stokes. If there was any chance of challenging that narrative by recovering the deleted texts, that came to an end with the AT&T deletion. It threw such a protective shield over Stevens' narrative that it calls into question whether it was due merely to an errant AT&T clerk.

Further questions are raised by counsel's failure to preserve the phone texts, no matter which version of the AT&T incident is true. If counsel's version is correct, counsel allowed Stevens to retain possession of the phone without preserving the texts even after the lawsuit was filed, and then allowed Stevens to pursue repairs by an AT&T clerk without even attempting to take control of the phone and its repairs. Stevens' contrary version of the incident does nothing to exculpate counsel - even under this scenario, counsel failed to immediately preserve obviously crucial evidence at a time when the duty to preserve existed and instead allowed the phone to remain in Stevens' possession.

This cavalier attitude toward the preservation requirement adds another layer of doubt to the "errant clerk" story. These substantial issues regarding intent cannot be answered on this record. They must await trial. If intent is established at trial, the remedies listed in Rule 37(e)(2) come into play: "(A) presume that the lost information was unfavorable to the party; (B) instruct the jury that it may or must presume the information was unfavorable to the party; or (C) dismiss the action or enter a default judgment." Even if intent is not established, the Court is authorized, upon a finding of prejudice

> to allow the parties to present evidence to the jury concerning the loss and likely relevance of information and instructing the jury that it may consider that evidence, along with all other evidence in the case, in making a decision. ... In addition, [the Court may] give traditional missing evidence instructions based on a party's failure to present evidence it has in its possession at the time of trial.

See Rule 37 Advisory Committee Notes to the 2015 Amendment. BYU-I was prejudiced by the AT&T deletion because they cannot independently verify that Stevens' print-out captured all the remaining texts on her phone - they are forced to take her word for it. Stevens' other deletions - done during the relationship - are obviously prejudicial as discussed above.

Even if Rule 37(e) is inapplicable, Stevens' deletions of texts, including the AT&T incident, are relevant to her credibility. Thus, the Court will allow a full inquiry at trial into these matters. The Court is aware that this will increase the length of trial and create a "trial-within-a-trial" but it is the minimum necessary to ensure a fair opportunity for BYU-I to challenge the narrative created by Stevens' selective, intentional, and substantial deletions of text messages. More may be needed depending on the testimony at trial.

For these reasons, the Court will deny the motion for sanctions without prejudice to the right of BYU-I to raise the motion again at trial after admitting evidence and testimony concerning the issues raised in this decision.

* * *

SCHMIDT V. SHIFFLETT
No. CIV 18-0663 KBM/LF (D. Ct. N.M. 2019)

MOLZEN, Magistrate Judge

***

This case arises from a January 9, 2018 collision between Defendant Anthony Shifflett ("Defendant Shifflett") and Plaintiff John Carrillo. Plaintiff John Carrillo was installing striping on U.S. Highway 285, and Defendant Shifflett was driving a tractor trailer northbound on the same highway, when Defendant Shifflett's vehicle collided with Plaintiff John Carrillo, causing him to sustain severe injuries. Following the collision, Plaintiffs filed suit on June 5, 2018, in the First Judicial District Court of Santa Fe County, State of New Mexico, alleging negligence by Defendants. Plaintiffs now move for sanctions under Federal Rule of Civil Procedure 37(e), arguing that Defendants intentionally destroyed Defendant Shifflett's personal mobile device and failed to preserve the mobile phone data for the same device from the day of the collision.

I. Legal Standard

"Spoliation is the 'destruction or significant alteration of evidence, or the failure to preserve property for another's use as evidence in pending or reasonably foreseeable litigation.'" *** In order to prevent spoliation, litigants are under a duty to preserve evidence when they know, or should know, that it may be relevant to future litigation. *Zubulake v. UBS Warburg LLC*, 220 F.R.D. 212, 216 (S.D.N.Y. 2003).

Spoliation sanctions are proper when "(1) a party has a duty to preserve evidence because it knew or should have known[] that litigation was imminent, and (2) the adverse party was prejudiced by the destruction of the evidence." *** Further, Federal Rule of Civil Procedure 37(e) provides:

> If electronically stored information that should have been preserved in the anticipation or conduct of litigation is lost because a party failed to take reasonable steps to preserve it, and it cannot be restored or replaced through additional discovery, the court: (1) upon finding prejudice to another party from loss of the information, may order measures no greater than necessary to cure the prejudice.

Fed. R. Civ. P. 37(e). An aggrieved party must demonstrate bad faith to warrant an adverse inference sanction. ***

Generally, upon reasonably anticipating litigation, a party "must suspend its routine document retention/destruction policy and put in place a 'litigation hold' to ensure the preservation of relevant documents" and other tangible evidence. *** Litigation holds are required for both tangible evidence and electronic data. ***

II. Background

On January 9, 2018, Plaintiff John Carrillo was installing striping along northbound U.S. Highway 285, outside the City of Artesia in Eddy County, New Mexico. At the same time, Defendant Shifflett was driving a tractor trailer on behalf of Defendant New Bern, and allegedly Defendant PepsiCo, northbound on the same highway. A mounted attenuator trailer was positioned behind Plaintiff John Carrillo's work truck, and he was working nearby on the passenger side of his vehicle. Defendant Shifflett collided into the rear of the mounted attenuator trailer and work truck which then struck Plaintiff John Carrillo causing serious injuries to him.

Defendant Shifflett reported that, just prior to the collision, he was distracted by the instrument gauges in his tractor, which he claims were malfunctioning. In his written statement, he explained:

> My truck was sounding weird so I reduced my speed and starting [sic] checking my gauges. I seen trucks in front of me, but didn't see any warning lights. I look down again to check my gauges, and when I look up I realized I was about to make impact with another veh[icle].

Similarly, Defendant Shifflett testified during his deposition: "I looked down at my gauges and then I looked up. I seen a truck in front of me roughly 100 yards, and I looked down at my gauges again and then when I looked up again it was impact."

It is undisputed that Defendant Shifflett denied using his personal or business cellphone at the time of the accident. Chris Gonzales, Associate Manager of Bottling Group, LLC, testified that he did not ask Defendant Shifflett to turn over his personal cell phone following the collision, explaining: "That's where I decided not to go to try and request a personal device. Asked him and hoped that he was going to be full, fair and transparent." Defendant New Bern did, however, terminate Defendant Shifflett's employment on January 19, 2018.

On March 2, 2018, Plaintiffs' counsel issued a "Notice of Representation [and] Notice of Preservation/Spoliation" to Pepsi - Cola Co.'s Risk Manager and the Ace American Insurance Company's Claims Department. The letter indicated that counsel was representing Plaintiff John Carrillo and demanded that the recipients preserve certain enumerated items for the "past 3 years." *** "Data from tele-communications system" and "Driver's personal and business cell phone record" were among the 62 items for which preservation was demanded. *** Plaintiffs later filed suit against Defendants in State Court on June 5, 2018.

Following the commencement of litigation, the parties engaged in formal discovery. In his responses to Plaintiffs' First Set of Interrogatories, Defendant Shifflett stated that he was in possession of two mobile phones on the day of the collision, his personal cell phone,

(757-358-2671), and a cell phone issued by Defendant New Bern. He asserted that his personal cell phone, however, remained "in a bag in the cab of the tractor" at the time of the collision, while the phone issued by Defendant New Bern was "in the cab of the tractor." Id. Later, in his responses to Plaintiffs' Supplemental Interrogatories, Defendant Shifflett admitted that he was no longer in possession or control of the personal cell phone that he used at the time of the collision. He explained that "to the best of [his] recollection, the phone was discarded sometime during July and/or August 2018 as a byproduct of the process of moving across the country back to Virginia and/or the packing and unpacking process." According to Defendant Shifflett, he discarded the phone because he "was not pleased with the quality of service from T-Mobile."

Additionally, Defendants did not produce Defendant Shifflett's phone records for his personal phone for the day of the collision. Instead, Plaintiffs obtained them directly from T-Mobile Wireless. In their First Supplemental Requests for Admissions, Plaintiffs asked Defendant Shifflett to admit that the records they had obtained were, in fact, his personal phone records from the relevant period. Defendant Shifflett responded that "[s]ubject to and without waiving [his] objection, ... the records appear to be T-Mobile records" for the personal cell phone he owned at the time of the collision. ***

Plaintiffs retained Ben Levitan as their cell phone expert in this case. In Mr. Levitan's Preliminary Report, which is attached to Plaintiffs' Motion, Mr. Levitan opined that Defendant Shifflett's cell phone records and other material sent to him by Plaintiffs' counsel "show, with scientific certainty, that Mr. Shifflett was highly distracted at the time of the accident and this impairment caused by his cell phone use was a substantial cause of the crash." According to Mr. Levitan, Defendant was actively on a voice call on his personal cell phone with Familia Dental when the accident took occurred. Moreover, based upon a review of Defendant Shifflett's cell phone records and driver's log, Mr. Levitan observed that Defendant "Shifflett routinely [drove] while using his personal phone."

III. Analysis

As a preliminary matter, Plaintiffs insist that Defendants' Response to their Motion for Sanctions was untimely, having been due April 1, 2019, but filed April 12, 2019. While the Court does not condone the lateness of Defendants' filing, and indeed cautions Defendants that they should more closely follow the deadlines set out in D.N.M.LR-Civ. 7.4(a), it favors a determination on the merits of Plaintiffs' Motion for Sanctions. Defendants response, albeit untimely, aids the Court in a full consideration of the issues in Plaintiffs' motion and will not be stricken.

In their Motion for Sanctions, Plaintiffs ask the Court to sanction Defendants for "intentionally destroying Defendant ... Shifflett's ... mobile phone device, and for their failure to preserve the mobile phone data of Shifflett's personal cell phone from the day of the collision in this case." Plaintiffs explain that Defendant Shifflett discarded his cell phone in July or August of 2018, even after Plaintiffs provided Defendants with a preservation letter on March 2, 2018 and initiated formal litigation in State Court on June 5, 2018. They maintain that Defendants thereby engaged in overt acts to knowingly destroy critical evidence in bad faith. Further, they contend that Defendant New Bern and Defendant PepsiCo failed to take any independent actions to preserve the mobile phone data or to adopt a policy to manage data regarding personal cell phone usage. They request, as sanctions, an adverse inference instruction, an order allowing the introduction of evidence of willful spoliation, an order allowing the introduction of Shifflett's person mobile phone records, an order precluding Defendants from questioning the veracity of T-Mobile's records, an order precluding evidence regarding faulty gauges, and an order precluding arguments by Defendants as to comparative fault. In response, Defendants insist that they properly complied with Plaintiffs' March 2, 2018 preservation letter and that the spoliation factors cannot be met, nor can prejudice be shown.

As the Court explained in *Zubulake v. UBS Warburg LLC*, "identifying the boundaries of the duty to preserve involves two related inquiries: when does the duty to preserve attach, and what evidence must be preserved?" *** Plaintiffs' motion, first, takes up the issue of when Defendants' duty to preserve arose.

Generally, the filing of a lawsuit generally triggers the duty to preserve evidence. Cache La Poudre Feeds, LLC at 621. Sometimes, however, the obligation arises earlier. Here, Plaintiffs maintain that such a duty arose the moment Defendants became aware of the collision between Plaintiff John Carrillo and Defendant Shifflett, on January 9, 2018. In support of this proposition, they refer the Court to *Browder v. City of Albuquerque*. In *Browder*, a discovery dispute arose over video footage from intersections near the site of a fatal collision. Although the footage was initially available for viewing by officials from the City of Albuquerque, it was later lost and unavailable to the plaintiffs. *** The plaintiffs moved to sanction the defendants for spoliation, and Judge Brack of this District concluded that a duty to preserve relevant evidence arose the moment the City became aware that one of its police officers was involved in a fatal traffic accident. ***

The Court agrees that a similar finding may be warranted here. That is, just as litigation was reasonably foreseeable to the City in Browder when it learned that one of its officers was involved in a fatal traffic accident, litigation was arguably foreseeable here when Defendants learned that Defendant Shifflett's tractor-trailer had rear-ended a stationary or slow-moving vehicle installing striping along the highway and seriously injured Plaintiff John Carrillo. This is especially true given Defendant Shifflett reports to his employers that he was looking away from the road immediately before impact. But, even if the accident itself did not place Defendants on notice that litigation was likely, Mr. Chavez's March 2, 2018 preservation letter certainly did. Yet, Defendant Shifflett testified that he disposed of the subject cell phone four or five months later in July or August of 2018, after the preservation letter and even after the June 2018 commencement of this action. In short, the cell phone was discarded after a duty to preserve evidence arose.

Defendants focus their arguments on the second prong of the preservation inquiry, the scope of their duty, maintaining that they were under no duty to preserve Defendant Shifflett's personal cell phone. Defendants note that although Plaintiffs itemized 62 items for preservation in their March 2, 2018 letter, Defendant Shifflett's cell phone was not among them. While Mr. Chavez's letter enumerates "Driver's personal and business cell phone records" as items to be preserved, he does not specifically request preservation of any cell phones. As such, Defendants insist that they have complied with Plaintiffs' Preservation Notice, as "Plaintiffs possess driver's personal and cell phone records and data from telecommunication system[s]."

Common sense dictates that Mr. Chavez's omission of cell phones from the preservation letter, while at the same time identifying so many other potentially relevant items for preservation, diminishes the culpability of Defendants with respect to the discarded cell phone. Indeed, absent some knowledge by Defendants that there was relevant evidence contained on the cell phone itself, neither its disposal nor the failure to advise against its disposal would seem to warrant sanctions. In other words, Defendants' duty to preserve Defendant Shifflett's personal cell phone turns, at least in part, on what the respective defendants knew about its relevance to the instant litigation. Such an inquiry overlaps with the culpability analysis that the Court must undertake in assessing the appropriateness of spoliation sanctions.

Under the spoliation analysis, the "two most important factors" are: (1) the culpability of the offending party, and (2) the actual prejudice to the other party. *** With respect to the first factor, Plaintiffs allege that Defendants are culpable because they engaged in "overt acts to knowingly destroy and dispose of critical evidence to a crucial fact at issue in this case in bad faith." The Court finds this allegation overstated, particularly when it comes to Defendants New Bern and PepsiCo. After all, Plaintiffs do not identify any actions to destroy or discard Defendant Shifflett's phone taken by Defendants New Bern or Defendant PepsiCo. Nor is the Court persuaded, under the circumstances, that the failure of these defendants to collect his personal cell phone somehow equates to a bad faith action to destroy it.

Plaintiffs have not demonstrated that Defendant New Bern or Defendant PepsiCo were aware of any specific relevance of the cell phone that was not redundant of the cell phone records that Plaintiffs had already obtained from T-Mobile. Once again, Plaintiffs did not specifically request preservation of Defendant Shifflett's personal cell phone, though they requested preservation of many other items of potential relevance. And Defendant Shifflett had reported to his employers that he was distracted by his gauges at the time of the collision, not by his personal cell phone, which he claimed was in a bag in the cab of the tractor.

Further, Defendants emphasize that Defendant Shifflett was no longer employed by Defendant New Bern after January 19, 2018. Even assuming, without deciding, that

Defendant New Bern or Defendant PepsiCo had an obligation to advise a former employee concerning the retention of his personal cell phone, the sanctions that Plaintiffs seek against these defendants are simply not appropriate under the facts of this case. That is, the Court is not inclined to penalize a party for failing to prevent a former employee from discarding a personal cell phone when that phone was omitted from the opposing party's comprehensive preservation request. This case is distinguishable from Browder, where Judge Brack determined that the City's irresponsible evidence retention practices actually caused the loss of critical evidence requested by the opposing party. ***

On the other hand, Plaintiffs have proffered some evidence bearing on Defendant Shifflett's culpability in discarding his personal cell phone. More specifically, they offer for the Court's consideration expert opinion testimony from Mr. Levitan, suggesting that Defendant Shifflett was on a voice call with a dentist office at the time of the collision. This testimony, if believed, does two things. First, it increases the likelihood that Defendant Shifflett was culpable in discarding his cell phone. For if Mr. Levitan's opinion is to be relied upon, Defendant Shifflett testified untruthfully when he testified that he was not on the phone at the time of the crash, as it is unlikely that he would have simply forgotten that he was on a personal phone call at the time of the collision.

As both parties acknowledge, spoliation "occurs along a continuum of fault ranging from innocence through the degrees of negligence to intentionality[, and] resulting penalties vary correspondingly." *** Here, Defendants maintain that Defendant Shifflett's disposal of his cell phone was at most negligent. Critically, though, Mr. Levitan's opinion at least suggests that Defendant Shifflett may have discarded his cell phone despite knowing that it contained inculpatory evidence concerning his phone usage at the time of the collision. That, in turn, would tend to show that his actions in discarding the phone were culpable if not intentional. But even if Plaintiffs cannot fully establish the requisite "bad faith" required for the imposition of an adverse inference, lesser sanctions may still be warranted. *** Pursuant to Federal Rule of Civil Procedure 37(e) when a party fails to take "reasonable steps to preserve" evidence that "should have been preserved" in the anticipation or conduct of litigation, a court must impose the sanctions necessary to cure any resulting prejudice. Fed. R. Civ. P. 37(e).

But Plaintiffs must establish prejudice. Mr. Levitan's opinion about Defendant Shifflett's voice call increases the likelihood of culpability by Defendant Shifflett in discarding his phone, but they, at the same time, minimize any prejudice to Plaintiffs in the loss of that phone. If Mr. Levitan can, as he submits, testify with "scientific certainty" that Defendant Shifflett was on the phone at or around the time of the crash, the loss of the cell phone itself cannot be described as devastating to Plaintiff's case. In other words, Mr. Levitan's opinions suggest culpability by Defendant Shifflett but they also undermine Plaintiffs' claims of prejudice. Indeed, when asked at his deposition whether access to Defendant Shifflett's personal cell phone would have allowed him to give testimony with great certainty, Mr. Levitan responded: "What I have said is 100 percent accurate. Any additional information such as additional Geotab information, forensic of the phone is only going to enhance my opinion.

Plaintiffs also complain that Defendants failed to preserve or produce Defendant Shifflett's personal mobile phone records. Notably, however, Plaintiffs' do not contend that the failure to preserve these cell phone records has prejudiced them; nor could they, as they now have those records in their possession.

Ultimately, considering the two most important spoliation factors of culpability and prejudice, the Court declines to impose the most severe sanctions requested by Plaintiffs for Defendant Shifflett's spoliation of his personal cell phone (*i.e.* preventing any argument as to comparative fault or giving an adverse inference instruction). Although the opinions of Mr. Levitan would suggest some culpability by Defendant Shifflett in discarding the phone, the Court is not convinced that Plaintiffs have suffered severe prejudice. According to Mr. Levitan, a forensic evaluation of the phone may have bolstered his opinion, but he remains able to confidently opine about Defendant Shifflett's use of his phone even without inspecting the phone itself. Balancing the spoliation considerations, the Court will allow Plaintiffs to introduce evidence of Defendant Shifflett's purported willful spoliation of his personal cell phone and will also allow Plaintiffs to introduce Defendant Shifflett's personal cell phone records from T-Mobile. The Court reserves for ruling for trial as to whether an adverse inference instruction is warranted as to Defendant Shifflett.

IT IS HEREBY ORDERED that Plaintiff's Opposed Motion for Sanctions for Defendants' Failure to Preserve Mobile Phone Data is granted in part.

***

DRIVETIME CAR SALES COMPANY, LLC V. PETTIGREW
No.: 2:17-cv-371 2019 WL 1746730 (S.D. Ohio 2019)

SMITH, Judge

I. BACKGROUND

Plaintiff DriveTime Car Sales Company, LLC ("DriveTime"), a citizen of Arizona, is a used vehicle retailer who acquires its vehicles primarily from used vehicle auctions around the country. Defendant Bryan Pettigrew, a citizen of Ohio, is a former employee of DriveTime, who was responsible for purchasing vehicles on DriveTime's behalf.

DriveTime's buyers, like Pettigrew, were provided with a buying guide that contained maximum purchase prices for different models, makes, and years. DriveTime's buyers also used industry standard pricing information from the National Automotive Dealers Association ("NADA") when evaluating used cars for purchase. There is conflicting evidence as to whether buyers were permitted to exercise discretion to purchase vehicles above the maximum prices in the buying guides.

Much of Pettigrew's buying activity for DriveTime occurred at the Columbus Fair Auto Auction (the "Auction"). Sellers bring their cars to the Auction, where buyers like Pettigrew bid on and purchase them. The parties dispute whether the purchase contract for each vehicle is entered into with the Auction, as consignee, or directly with the vehicle sellers.

During the period of January through June 2016, Pettigrew purchased at the Auction what DriveTime contends was an unusually large number of vehicles from Defendant Pauley Motor, and those vehicles were purchased at what DriveTime contends were above-market rates. DriveTime had available to it the buying guide and NADA pricing information for all vehicles purchased by Pettigrew, as well as the prices he agreed to for each vehicle, as each purchase was made. In March 2016, Pettigrew's supervisor spoke with him regarding the high volume and prices for vehicles he purchased from Pauley Motor.

In June 2016, DriveTime received a report from another of its buyers, Mitch Tyler. Tyler reported that he had been told by Shawn Stratton, another car dealer who sold vehicles at the Auction, that Stratton witnessed Bruce Pauley, of Pauley Motor, giving Pettigrew "a bunch of hundreds in the restroom ..." However, Tyler is adamant that "[t]he only stuff I knew is what I was told about. And I never witnessed anything, I never saw anything. Nothing. I was told it by another buyer/seller that he witnessed Bryan taking money from Bruce. I never witnessed anything, I never saw it. So really, it's hearsay. That's all I know." More importantly, when Stratton was deposed, he categorically denied Tyler's report:

Q: At any time, have you ever told Mitchell Tyler that you have seen, personally observed, Bryan Pettigrew take cash from anyone?

A: Okay, So, I'm going to answer the question as I don't recall that conversation. I've never seen Bryan Pettigrew take any money from Bruce Pauley or any of the Pauley associates.

Q: Have you seen him take money from anyone?

A: I have not.

However, prior to Stratton's deposition, DriveTime was prompted by Tyler's report to look more closely at Pettigrew's buying patterns. DriveTime's analysis revealed that Pettigrew paid noticeably more for Pauley Motor vehicles (on average 106.75% of NADA value) than he did for vehicles purchased from other sellers (99.53%). Additionally, Pettigrew paid noticeably more for Pauley Motor vehicles (106.75%) than did Tyler when he purchased vehicles from Pauley Motor (98.71%). Finally, during discovery, Pettigrew's bank records showed that on at least five occasions, he made cash deposits of at least $1,000 within 24 hours of making a purchase from Pauley Motor.

DriveTime also learned that Pauley Motor regularly offered a $100 Visa gift card to the successful bidder for each of its vehicles sold at the Auction. Pettigrew had never forwarded the gift cards offered for the vehicles he purchased from Pauley Motor, despite an alleged DriveTime policy requiring buyers to accept any gift cards or other valuable property offered to them and to forward the items to DriveTime's home office. Pettigrew disputes that such a policy was in place.

On the basis of Tyler's report, Pettigrew's buying patterns, and Pettigrew's failure to turn over the gift cards, DriveTime commenced this action on May 1, 2017. DriveTime's Amended Complaint alleged that Pettigrew and Pauley Motor entered into a kickback scheme whereby Pauley Motor would provide Pettigrew with cash payments in exchange for his agreement to higher purchase prices for Pauley Motor vehicles. DriveTime also sought recovery for the value of the gift cards Pettigrew failed to turn over. After certain claims were dismissed on Pauley Motor's motion for judgment on the pleadings, DriveTime asserts the following remaining claims: (1) theft of the gift cards, under Ohio Revised Code § 2703.61, against Pettigrew; (2) conversion of the gift cards, against Pettigrew; (3) fraud, against Pettigrew; (4) breach of the duty of good faith and loyalty, against Pettigrew; and (5) unjust enrichment, against Pauley Motor. Defendants now move for summary judgment on all remaining claims against them.

DriveTime has also filed a motion for spoliation sanctions against Pauley Motor. During discovery, Pauley Motor first stated in its interrogatory responses that no text messages between Pauley Motor representatives and Pettigrew exist; however, in his deposition as Pauley Motor's representative under Fed.R.Civ.P. 30(b)(6), Bruce Pauley stated that he had exchanged text messages with Pettigrew. Bruce Pauley was ultimately unable to produce the content of the text messages because he had obtained a new phone and had not preserved the contents of his previous phone, despite being put on notice to do so in November of 2016 by a litigation hold letter issued by DriveTime's counsel. DriveTime asks that, as a sanction for Pauley Motor's failure to take reasonable steps to preserve the text messages, the Court impose a mandatory adverse inference that the content of the text messages was unfavorable to Pauley Motor.

II. DRIVETIME'S MOTION FOR SPOLIATION SANCTIONS

The Court turns first to DriveTime's motion for spoliation sanctions because its requested remedy—a mandatory adverse inference that the missing text messages were unfavorable to Pauley Motor—could affect the evidence the Court will consider in deciding the Defendants' motions for summary judgment.

Prior to the Federal Rule of Civil Procedure amendments of 2015, the standard in the Sixth Circuit was that a party seeking spoliation sanctions must establish: "(1) that the party having control over the evidence had an obligation to preserve it at the time it was destroyed; (2) that the records were destroyed with a culpable state of mind; and (3) that the destroyed evidence was relevant to the party's claims or defenses such that a reasonable trier of fact could find that it would support that claim or defense." However, effective December 1, 2015, Federal Rule of Civil Procedure 37(e) was amended to include the following:

> (e) Failure to Preserve Electronically Stored Information. If electronically stored information that should have been preserved in the anticipation or conduct of litigation is lost because a party failed to take reasonable steps to preserve it, and it cannot be restored or replaced through additional discovery, the court:
> (1) upon finding prejudice to another party from loss of the information, may order measures no greater than necessary to cure the prejudice; or
> (2) only upon finding that the party acted with the intent to deprive another party of the information's use in the litigation may:
> (A) presume that the lost information was unfavorable to the party;
> (B) instruct the jury that it may or must presume the information was unfavorable to the party; or
> (C) dismiss the action or enter a default judgment.

Although the amended rule clearly supplants certain aspects of the Sixth Circuit's standard, courts within the Sixth Circuit have continued to apply *Beavin* and amended Rule 37(e) in concert where they do not conflict. In particular, *Beavin*'s requirement that there be an obligation to preserve at the time of destruction, and that the destroyed evidence must have been relevant to the claims or defenses of the party seeking sanctions, are left intact by amended Rule 37(e).

However, the *Beavin* standard's "culpable state of mind" no longer applies to less severe sanctions under Rule 37(e)(1); instead, the party seeking sanctions under Rule 37(e)(1) must only demonstrate prejudice. *Yoe v. Crescent Sock Co.*, No. 1:15-CV-3-SKL, 2017 WL 5479932, at *11 (E.D. Tenn. Nov. 14, 2017). On the other hand, to obtain the more severe sanctions available under Rule 37(e)(2), the party seeking sanctions must establish that the opposing party "acted with the intent to deprive another party of the information's use in the litigation." Fed.R.Civ.P. 37(e)(2). "A showing of negligence or even gross negligence," which would have sufficed as a culpable state of mind under *Beavin*, "will not do the trick." *Applebaum v. Target Corp.*, 831 F.3d 740, 745 (6th Cir. 2016).

Here, Pauley Motor does not dispute that it had an obligation to preserve text messages between its representatives and Pettigrew or that it failed to take reasonable steps to preserve them. DriveTime has also established that the text messages cannot be restored or replaced through additional discovery, because neither Pettigrew nor the wireless carriers for Pauley Motor's representatives have access to them either. Thus, in order to obtain the mandatory adverse inference it seeks under Rule 37(e)(2), the only additional requirement under the Rule is that Pauley Motor acted with the intent to deprive DriveTime of the text messages' use in the litigation when it failed to preserve them.

The Court finds that DriveTime has not sufficiently demonstrated that Pauley Motor acted with the requisite intent. "Rule 37(e)(2)'s intent standard is stringent and does not parallel other discovery standards." As noted by the Advisory Committee in connection with the December 2015 amendments to Rule 37, [A] party's intentional loss or destruction of evidence to prevent its use in litigation gives rise to a reasonable inference that the evidence was unfavorable to the party responsible for loss or destruction of the evidence. Negligent or even grossly negligent behavior does not logically support that inference.

Information lost through negligence may have been favorable to either party, including the party that lost it, and inferring that it was unfavorable to that party may tip the balance at trial in ways the lost information never would have.

Rule 37, Advisory Committee Notes, 2015 Amendment. Accordingly, the Advisory Committee's intent was "to limit the most severe measures [to cure prejudice caused by the loss of electronically stored information] to instances of intentional loss or destruction." These concerns apply equally to "the court's authority to presume or infer that the lost information was unfavorable to the party who lost it when ruling on a pretrial motion or presiding at a bench trial." Therefore, the Court's analysis is not altered by the case's summary judgment posture.

Although Bruce Pauley failed to take reasonable steps to preserve the text messages when he switched to a different phone, there is no evidence that he did so intentionally beyond DriveTime's speculation. This is not sufficient to impose a mandatory adverse inference under Rule 37(e)(2). See *Yoe v. Crescent Sock Co.*, No. 1:15-CV-3-SKL, 2017 WL 5479932, at *14 (E.D. Tenn. Nov. 14, 2017) (even where corporate plaintiff's data was destroyed intentionally, Rule 37(e)(2) sanctions were not warranted where the individual responsible destroyed it due to concerns that the defendant would commence a separate legal action against him personally, and not to deprive the defendant of its use in the current litigation).

However, less severe sanctions are available to DriveTime under Rule 37(e)(1) upon a finding of prejudice. The Advisory Committee notes make clear that "[t]he rule does not place a burden of proving or disproving prejudice on one party or another." Rule 37, Advisory Committee Notes, 2015 Amendment. In certain cases, such as when "the content of the lost information may be fairly evident, the information may appear to be unimportant, or the abundance of preserved information may appear sufficient to meet the needs of all parties," it may be reasonable to require the party seeking curative measures to prove prejudice. But none of these circumstances are present here.

If, as DriveTime alleges, Pauley Motor and Pettigrew entered into a kickback scheme, text messages between the two might provide highly relevant information. On the other hand, they might not, and at this point, we will never know. But the reason we will never know is that Pauley Motor failed to take reasonable measures to preserve the text messages, despite being on notice to do so via DriveTime's November 22, 2016 litigation hold letter ... expressly requesting Pauley Motor to preserve "text messages" stored on "PDAs (e.g. iPhones or Blackberries)"... It would be unjust to place the burden of proving prejudice on DriveTime under these circumstances. And while Pauley Motor rightly points out that the record is devoid of any direct evidence of a kickback scheme, this fact alone does not conclusively establish that DriveTime has not been prejudiced by the loss of the text messages.

Accordingly, the Court will order curative measures under Rule 37(e)(1). The available measures are within the Court's discretion so long as they are "no greater than necessary to cure the prejudice" and "do not have the effect of measures that are permitted under subdivision (e)(2)." Rule 37(e)(1), Advisory Committee Notes, 2015 Amendment. In this case, the Court finds it appropriate to order that DriveTime will be permitted to introduce evidence at trial, if it wishes, of the litigation hold letter and Pauley Motor's subsequent failure to preserve the text messages. DriveTime may argue for whatever inference it hopes the jury will draw. Pauley Motor may present its own admissible evidence and argue to the jury that they should not draw any inference from Pauley Motor's conduct.

Additionally, "the Court recognizes that its ruling places [Pettigrew] in a precarious position." In *HLV*, one defendant negligently disposed of his phone after receipt of a litigation hold letter, and the Court permitted introduction of similar evidence as outlined above as a discovery sanction. Recognizing that an inference adverse to the negligent defendant would also affect an alleged co-conspirator who was not implicated in the disposal of the phone, the *HLV* court also permitted the alleged co-conspirator "to move for a jury instruction, if necessary, that he be held harmless for [the negligent defendant's] disposal of the phone-assuming the trial proofs are consistent with the conclusion that he did not take part in [the] disposal of the phone." The Court finds a similar allowance for Pettigrew to be appropriate here: he may move for a jury instruction, if necessary, that he be held harmless for Pauley Motor's failure to preserve the text messages, assuming the trial proofs are consistent with the conclusion that he did not take part in Pauley Motor's loss of the text messages.

Finally, in ruling on the defendants' motions for summary judgment, any inferences to be drawn from Pauley Motor's negligent failure to preserve the text messages must be left to the finder of fact. Thus, the Court will not bind itself to any adverse inference at this stage.

***

NUNES V. RUSHTON
No. 2:14-cv-00627-JNP-DBP (D. Ut. 2018)

PARRISH, District Judge.

Before the court is Rachel Nunes's motion to sanction Tiffanie Rushton for spoliation of evidence. The court grants the motion in part.

BACKGROUND

Rushton infringed Nunes's copyright in her novel, *A Bid for Love*, by copying protected elements of the book and distributing copies of the infringing work to reviewers and bloggers for promotional purposes. Around this time, Rushton created a number of "sock puppet" accounts on Google and Yahoo by registering these accounts under usernames that did not identify her as the individual controlling the accounts. Rushton used these Google and Yahoo accounts to create several sock puppet accounts on Facebook, Goodreads, and Amazon. Rushton then used the Goodreads and Amazon sock puppet accounts to post positive reviews of her own books and negative reviews of Nunes's books. Rushton also created a Twitter account and a Blogspot account under her pen name, Sam Taylor Mullens, to promote her books.

On August 1, 2014, one of the reviewers of Rushton's infringing novel contacted Nunes and reported that it was very similar to *A Bid for Love*. Nunes attempted to obtain an advance copy of the infringing novel and discover the true identity of Sam Taylor Mullens. Rushton used her sock puppet social media accounts to anonymously criticize Nunes's efforts to investigate the infringing novel. Sometime in August or September of 2014, after Nunes had discovered Rushton's identity, Rushton deleted most of her sock puppet accounts on Facebook, Goodreads, and Amazon. Rushton also deleted her Sam Taylor Mullens Twitter and Blogspot accounts. It is unclear whether these deletions occurred before or after the date when Nunes filed this lawsuit, August 28, 2014.

During the ensuing litigation, Nunes made a discovery request for documents stored on Rushton's various Google and Yahoo accounts. On August 12, 2015, while this discovery request was pending, Rushton deleted one of her Google sock puppet accounts. On February 18, 2016, Judge Pead granted a motion to compel Rushton to produce documents from her Google and Yahoo accounts. Counsel for Rushton represented that she had lost the passwords to the accounts. So on February 24, 2016, Rushton stipulated that Nunes could subpoena Google and Yahoo for all documents found on her accounts. Rushton represents that after the subpoenas were served she found a notebook containing all of the passwords to her Google and Yahoo sock puppet accounts. She deleted all of the remaining accounts on March 21, 2016. Rushton asserts that she did so because she believed that all of the documents associated with the accounts had been or would be produced by Google and Yahoo pursuant to the subpoenas.

On March 28, 2016, Google responded to the subpoena by notifying the parties that the accounts had been deleted. Google stated that the account deleted on August 12, 2015 could not be recovered because too much time had passed. But Google preserved the accounts that had been deleted on March 21, 2016.

Google stated that it was up to Rushton to recover the accounts through its online recovery tool. On March 31, 2016, counsel for Rushton represented that she would recover the accounts and stipulated to additional subpoenas to Google and Yahoo.

ANALYSIS

Nunes asks this court to sanction Rushton for deleting the various sock puppet accounts by instructing the jury that it should presume that that the destroyed evidence would have been unfavorable. "Spoliation sanctions are proper when '(1) a party has a duty to preserve evidence because it knew, or should have known, that litigation was imminent, and (2) the adverse party was prejudiced by the destruction of the evidence.'" *** "[I]f the aggrieved party seeks an adverse inference to remedy the spoliation, it must also prove bad faith. 'Mere negligence in losing or destroying records is not enough because it does not support an inference of consciousness of a weak case.'" ***

Spoliation sanctions are not appropriate for Rushton's deletion of the Goodreads, Amazon, and Facebook accounts because Nunes has not shown that she suffered any prejudice. Rushton used the Goodreads and Amazon accounts to post positive reviews of her books and negative reviews of Nunes's books. Rushton used the Facebook accounts to post public comments on Nunes's Facebook page that criticized her efforts to investigate the infringement. The deletion of these accounts did not erase these public reviews and comments. Indeed, Nunes produced numerous reviews and comments posted through these accounts in support of her motions for summary judgment. Because Nunes failed to identify any information that was lost when these accounts were deleted, she has not shown any prejudice from the deletion of these accounts.

The court, likewise, may not sanction Rushton for deleting her Sam Taylor Mullens Blogspot account and Twitter account. She used these social media accounts to post messages about her novels in particular and romance novels in general in order to promote her books. Although these blog entries and tweets were public, they presumably were no longer accessible after Rushton deleted these accounts. But it appears that Nunes was able to save the content of these two accounts before Rushton deleted them. Nunes produced several screen captures of both the Blogspot account and the Twitter account in support of her motions for summary judgment. Nunes, moreover, makes no attempt to show that the posts and comments on these accounts were irretrievably lost.

Furthermore, Nunes has not proven that she was prejudiced by the March 21, 2016 deletion of the Google and Yahoo accounts. Google indicated that the accounts deleted on this date had been preserved and were retrievable. Counsel for Rushton subsequently stated that she would recover the Google and Yahoo accounts, and the docket suggests that the accounts were, in fact restored. On April 6, 2016, Nunes stipulated to an extension of time for Yahoo to produce documents from the previously deleted accounts, representing that she and Yahoo had come to an agreement regarding the production of documents from these accounts. And on April 18, 2016, Rushton stipulated that she would use each of the previously deleted Google accounts to send a message to Google authorizing it to provide additional information about the accounts. Thus, although the motion for sanctions and the response were curiously silent on efforts to retrieve the contents of these deleted accounts, it appears that Nunes was not prejudiced because she obtained the requested documents and emails from these accounts.

Finally, the court addresses Rushton's August 12, 2015 deletion of one of the Google accounts. At the time of the deletion, Rushton had a duty to preserve this account because litigation was pending. The court also finds that Nunes was prejudiced by the deletion because any documents or emails stored on this account were irretrievably lost. The only question that remains, therefore, is whether Rushton deleted the account in bad faith. Notably, Rushton attempts to explain the deletion of the social media and Amazon accounts around the time that Nunes sued her. She represents that she was not represented by counsel at the time and that she deleted the accounts in an attempt to placate Nunes, not to destroy evidence. She also represents that she deleted the Google and Yahoo accounts on March 21, 2018 because she thought that any documents associated with the accounts would be produced pursuant to the stipulated subpoenas that had issued about a month earlier. But Rushton has not proffered an explanation for the August 12, 2015 deletion of the Google account. Given that litigation had been pending for almost a year, that Rushton was represented by counsel, and that Nunes had requested the production of documents associated with this Google account, the court infers that Rushton's August 12, 2015 deletion of one of her Google accounts was done in bad faith.

The court, therefore, shall sanction Rushton for the August 12, 2015 deletion by instructing the jury that Rushton deleted one of her Google accounts while litigation was pending and that the jury may presume that the documents and emails stored on this account would have been unfavorable to her. ***

CONCLUSION

As described above, the court GRANTS IN PART Nunes's motion for an adverse instruction regarding destroyed evidence.

***

BROWN V. SSA ATLANTIC, LLC
No. CV419-303 (S.D. Ga. 2021)

RAY, Magistrate Judge

***

I. BACKGROUND

This case arises out of a vehicle collision. Plaintiffs' Amended Complaint alleges:

On August 13, 2019, Plaintiff John Brown, Jr. was assigned to drive a jockey truck by his employer .... The assigned jockey truck was parked in a parking space ..., and as Plaintiff ... was entering the cab through its back doors ... , an employee of Defendant ... attempted to pass the vehicle. [That employee], misjudging his clearance and traveling at an excessive speed, struck the flatbed trailer which was attached to Plaintiff['s] jockey truck. As a result of the tremendous impact, Plaintiff ... , was ejected through the back doors of the jockey truck cab, ultimately landing on the flatbed trailer.

As a result of the collision, John Brown allegedly sustained injuries. Plaintiffs have asserted various tort claims, based on a theory of *respondeat superior*, against SSA, including negligence, negligence per se, and loss of consortium on behalf of plaintiff Javonna Brown.

The parties conducted discovery; as relevant to this motion plaintiff John Brown responded to defendant's requests for production of documents, and defendant deposed plaintiff John Brown. In both the deposition and written discovery responses, Brown disclosed one Facebook account. In his written response plaintiff claimed he had deactivated the account before the collision occurred, but in his deposition, he conceded it was deactivated after the collision. *** Defendant also alleges that it has discovered Plaintiff has at least two other Facebook accounts, and possibly four, that were undisclosed.

Plaintiff's response effectively concedes that he had no fewer than three "burner" accounts. Defendant requests that Plaintiff's complaint be stricken as a sanction for the alleged spoliation, or, alternatively the jury should be instructed to draw an adverse inference. *** Failing either of those sanctions, SSA requests that plaintiff be ordered to produce the requested account information. ***

Plaintiff objects that defendant failed to seek an informal resolution of this issue before filing its motion. He also responds with the suggestion that the Facebook information may yet be retrievable, if he "reactivated" his account. SSA replies that motions for spoliation sanctions are not governed by the provisions of the Federal Rules related to discovery, and so they are subject to neither the Rules' requirement of attempts at informal resolution nor the requirements of the undersigned's standing order.

As discussed more fully below, the Court ultimately agrees with both parties. SSA is correct that plaintiff's discharge of his discovery obligations has been woefully deficient. Plaintiff is correct that the discovery-dispute procedures would have provided a more appropriate avenue to raise the issue. What plaintiff, unfortunately, fails to appreciate is that SSA's failure is, at most, a procedural gaffe. His own conduct, as SSA points out perhaps too emphatically, is much more troubling.

As this Court has previously been compelled to explain, "litigation is not an exercise in catching one's opponent in some technical misstep to secure advantage. It is a search for truth and justice. The procedural rules should facilitate that search, not impede it." *** Then, as now, "[t]his Court will not abide any party or counsel's attempt to reduce its procedures to a game of 'Gotcha!'" Plaintiff's response appears to be little more than an attempt to hide a substantive mountain behind a procedural molehill. If that was his intent, it has failed. Given the Court's broad discretion to manage discovery, *** and the Federal Rules' injunction that procedure should be administered "to secure the just, speedy, and inexpensive determination of every action and proceeding," Fed. R. Civ. P. 1, the Court will endeavor to resolve the discovery dispute without further delay.

II. ANALYSIS

"Spoliation is the destruction or significant alteration of evidence, or the failure to preserve property for another's use as evidence in pending or reasonably foreseeable litigation." *** The Court has "broad discretion" to impose sanctions as part of its "inherent power to manage its own affairs and to achieve the orderly and expeditious disposition of cases." *** Spoliation sanctions may include dismissal, exclusion of testimony, or an instruction to the jury to presume that the evidence would have been unfavorable to the spoliator.

Plaintiff makes much of SSA's failure to engage in informal discovery dispute processes. *** However, SSA plausibly argues that motions for spoliation sanctions are treated differently than other discovery disputes. *** As SSA's brief points out, courts have not treated motions alleging spoliation of evidence exclusively under the Federal Rules of Civil Procedure. To the extent that such a motion invokes the Court's inherent power, and not the Federal Rules, it is, at best, unclear whether the Rules-derived requirement of a conference applies; regardless of whether that requirement is imposed by the Rules themselves or from the Court's orders invoking them. ***

The Court does, however, agree that SSA's presentation of this issue as a motion for spoliation sanctions, pursuant to the Court's inherent power, is perhaps not the most natural. In the first place, despite the defendant's characterization, it is not clear that any evidence has been spoliated, as opposed to withheld. Defendant's brief explains the distinction between "deactivating" and "deleting" a Facebook account. *** As the Court in Bruner v. City of Phoenix explains, "deactivation" primarily prevents third-party access to the Facebook account, and "reactivation" remains possible. *** "Deletion," in contrast, "is a much more permanent step, and it means that the account information will be erased from the site completely." SSA does not dispute that, based on the information currently available, Brown has only "deactivated" and not "deleted" his Facebook account(s).

Despite recognizing the distinction between deactivation and deletion, SSA contends "[d]eactivation of Facebook accounts during discovery constitutes spoliation." The cases it cites do not, however, suggest that deactivation amounts to spoliation, as opposed to a more generalized discovery violation. In *Bruner*, the principal case cited, the court cites to discovery rules—Rules 37 and 26—but never once mentions "spoliation." Moreover, the motions at issue were brought pursuant to Rule 37. *** Finally, *Bruner* involved allegations of deletion of data, not merely deactivation of the account. *** The other cases cited recite similar information. *** None of those cases, then, stand for the proposition that "deactivating" a Facebook account, without concomitant destruction or irremediable alteration, amounts to spoliation.

To the extent that court-ordered production of the material remains as a potential form of relief, Rule 37 appears to be a more natural procedure. *See* Fed. R. Civ. P. 37(a)(3)(B)(iv) (motion to compel production of documents). Indeed, even if plaintiff's conduct were sufficiently willful to warrant sanctions, Rule 37 includes applicable provisions. *See* Fed. R. Civ. P. 37(a)(4) (evasive or incomplete responses are to be treated as failures to respond); (d) (motion for sanctions for failure to respond to request for production of documents). Finally, Rule 37(e) includes specific procedures applicable "[i]f electronically stored information that should have been preserved in the anticipation or conduct of litigation is lost because a party failed to take reasonable steps to preserve it, and it cannot be restored or replaced through additional discovery." Fed. R. Civ. P. 37(e). Given the facts as they currently appear, SSA might have used those procedures to secure the relief it seeks.

However, the Court, and possibly the parties, simply can't tell from the pleadings whether information has, even allegedly, been irretrievably lost. *** If the information has not been destroyed, but "only" withheld, Rule 37, with its attendant prerequisites, provides a more appropriate procedure. In the absence of a clear showing that information has been destroyed or significantly altered, the Motion for Spoliation Sanctions is DENIED, in part.

Although the Court disagrees with SSA's procedural choice, the substance of its motion is spot on. Brown's alleged conduct related to the social media discovery, which he never really disputes, is troubling. The defense of his objection to the written request is dubious, at best. Although he tries to brush off the issue as harmless, plaintiff concedes that his response was inaccurate when it was provided. The concluding contention that "there are appropriate procedures" SSA could have used to gain access to the deactivated Facebook account is particularly brazen, given that the original discovery request seems like exactly the "appropriate procedure," which Brown's inadequate response obstructed. Even if a conference was technically required, plaintiff might have mooted the issue by producing the requested material when the motion was filed or initiating the meet-and-confer process himself. Despite his response effectively conceding that his original discovery response was defective, plaintiff still does not propose to make good his failure. *** In the absence of any indication that he—or perhaps more accurately his attorneys—took any of those good-faith steps, the brief's indignation rings particularly hollow.

Although the Court cannot find that any evidence has been spoliated, under the circumstances it need not wait to rectify the situation. Since plaintiff's brief effectively concedes that his response to the written discovery request was "evasive or incomplete," his objection is deemed waived. *** The Court, therefore, GRANTS SSA's alternative request to compel production of the Facebook data.

Brown is DIRECTED to produce account data for the period of January 2018 through the present for each Facebook account he maintains or maintained, whether the account is "deactivated" or not, to SSA by no later than seven (7) days after the entry of this Order. SSA's request for attorneys' fees, however, is DENIED. *See* Fed. R. Civ. P. 37(a)(5)(A)(i). If, upon review of the material produced, SSA concludes that additional, limited-purpose, discovery is necessary, the Court will consider modification of the Scheduling Order. If SSA concludes that substantive information was, in fact, lost or destroyed because of the "deactivation," it is free to renew its motion for spoliation sanctions.

III. Potentially Improper Certification of Discovery Responses

Although the Court cannot find that spoliation sanctions are appropriate, plaintiff's own argument exposes a deeper problem that the Court cannot ignore. The Federal Rules of Civil Procedure impose a duty on attorneys to sign discovery responses, certifying them. *See* Fed. R. Civ. P. 26(g). Certification implicitly imposes a duty upon the signing attorney to make "a reasonable inquiry into the factual basis of his response, request, or objection." ***

Plaintiff's brief argues that his undisclosed, so-called "burner," Facebook accounts did not need to be disclosed because they were available "in a publicly viewable location on the internet for anyone to see; identified using John Brown's own name (and for two of [the additional accounts], a picture of his face)." If those profiles were so obvious and easy to discover, the Court must inquire why they were not revealed by plaintiff's counsel's required inquiry and identified notwithstanding the objection. *See* Fed. R. Civ. P. 34(b)(2)(C) ("An objection must state whether any responsive materials are being withheld on the basis of that objection") ***.

"'The decision whether to impose sanctions under Rule 26(g)(3) is not discretionary,' and '[o]nce the court makes the factual determination that a discovery filing was signed in violation of the rule it must impose æan appropriate sanction.'" *** However, the Rule only mandates sanctions when the violating certification lacks "substantial justification." Fed. R. Civ. P. 26(g)(3). It may well be that such justification exists in this case. In order to determine whether the omitted disclosure of the existence of the "publicly viewable" Facebook accounts was substantially justified, notwithstanding the reasonable-inquiry requirement, plaintiff and the attorney who signed the responses, R. Brian Tanner, are DIRECTED to respond within thirty days of the date of this Order and SHOW CAUSE why sanctions, pursuant to Rule 26(g)(3), should not be imposed.

IV. CONCLUSION

In order to get this case back on track, defendant's motion is GRANTED, in part, and DENIED, in part, without prejudice to refiling. Plaintiff is DIRECTED to produce data from his Facebook account(s) for the period of January, 2018 through the present, as requested in Request No. 16 of Defendant's First Request for Production of Documents, no later than seven (7) days from the date of this Order. Further, plaintiff and attorney R. Brian Tanner are DIRECTED to respond to this Order within thirty days and SHOW CAUSE why sanctions should not be imposed, pursuant to Federal Rule of Civil Procedure 26(g).

***

HERZIG V. ARK. FOUNDATION FOR MED. CARE
No. 2:18-CV-02101 2019 WL 2870106 (W.D. Ark. 2019)

HOLMES, District Judge

***

II. Facts

Herzig and Martin's responsive statement of facts does not cite to evidence in the record to support the disputes it identifies with AFMC's statement of facts. Herzig and Martin fail to show their disputes are genuine. Furthermore, most of the identified disputes concern facts immaterial to the resolution of Herzig and Martin's age discrimination claims. The material facts in AFMC's statement of facts are deemed admitted, though the Court will continue to draw factual inferences in Herzig and Martin's favor and will consider their legal disputes with AFMC's interpretation of the material facts.

AFMC provides medical necessity review services related to Medicaid under contract with the State of Arkansas. AFMC receives, uses, and transfers protected health information and must observe privacy and security requirements imposed by the Health Insurance Portability and Accountability Act ("HIPAA"). Among those requirements are that AFMC must limit access to protected health information to the minimum personnel necessary to perform AFMC's contractual obligations, AFMC must log electronic access to protected health information for audit purposes, and AFMC must implement appropriate disciplinary actions against individuals who violate HIPAA.

Plaintiff Brian Herzig began working at AMFC in 2005 as a Software Applications Developer and eventually was promoted to Director of Information Technology in 2009. In that position, he was responsible for development, production, and maintenance of AFMC's IT systems and for ensuring employee compliance with data confidentiality and security policies. Herzig reported directly to Nathan Ray, AFMC's Chief Technology Officer.

Plaintiff Neal Martin began working at AFMC in 2010 as Manager of Programming and eventually was promoted to Assistant Director of Information Technology in October, 2016. In that position, he was responsible for application development projects and implementation of programs and applications. Martin's position as Assistant Director was newly-established when he was promoted, and Martin reported directly to Herzig.

In 2016, AFMC designed and developed in-house medical necessity review software called "ReviewPoint." ReviewPoint was intended to integrate servers hosting protected health information through a software platform called "Laserfiche" with customized and default features of a software platform called "Salesforce." AFMC's Business Intelligence Department in Little Rock was in charge of AFMC's implementation and use of Salesforce. AFMC's IT Department in Fort Smith was in charge of the ReviewPoint project. Because AFMC's IT Department had the only employees with computer program development knowledge and responsibilities, the IT Department was responsible for the Laserfiche Integration Program, which would allow Salesforce to access the Laserfiche-based protected health information in a way that complied with AFMC's HIPAA obligations to limit and log personnel access to that information. Mark Gossman was the lead programmer responsible for writing the computer code for the Laserfiche Integration Program and was directly supervised by Martin.

At meetings attended by Herzig, Martin, Chief Technology Officer Ray, AFMC Manager of Security D.J. Blaylock, and AFMC General Counsel and HIPAA Privacy Officer Breck Hopkins, the need to meet HIPAA security and logging requirements was emphasized, and Herzig, Martin, and Blaylock agreed that necessary security and logging protections either could be developed or were already in place. Prior to AFMC's deployment of ReviewPoint on January 13, 2017, Blaylock submitted a security report and Martin assured AFMC leadership that the Laserfiche Integration Program was effective at secure, HIPAA-compliant retrieval of Laserfiche-based protected health information.

On March 7, 2017, employees in the Business Intelligence Department learned of an exploit that they believed would allow a ReviewPoint user to bypass ReviewPoint security and gain unauthorized access to protected health information by changing the document number displayed in the URL on ReviewPoint. The employees contacted HIPAA Privacy Officer Hopkins and demonstrated the exploit. Hopkins reported the exploit to Chief Technology Officer Ray and to AFMC Chief Operating Officer Marilyn Little. Thereafter, AFMC disabled the Laserfiche Integration Program, preventing ReviewPoint users from uploading medical records. This in turn prevented AFMC personnel from using ReviewPoint to conduct medical necessity reviews pursuant to AFMC's Arkansas Medicaid contract. Hopkins then reviewed the logs for Laserfiche to determine if anyone had actually used the exploit to unnecessarily access protected health information in violation of HIPAA. During that review, Hopkins learned of a second potential problemùLaserfiche was not logging access by users who actually accessed protected health information. Instead, after a user entered his or her credentials into ReviewPoint and then accessed a Laserfiche document containing protected health information, ReviewPoint's security features were bypassed and Laserfiche logged access by Mark Gossman because Gossman had hardcoded his administrative credentials into the Laserfiche Integration Program's code.

On March 7, following the discovery of these issues, Chief Operating Officer Little asked Herzig who, if anyone, had conducted a secondary code review of Gossman's work on the Laserfiche Integration Program. Neither Herzig nor Martin had reviewed the code, and Herzig was initially unable to provide an answer. Little directed Chief Technology Officer Ray to investigate the root cause of the vulnerability. On March 13, Ray asked Herzig about the IT Department's quality control methods, and on March 16, Little again asked Herzig about secondary code review. Herzig remained unable to provide an answer. Herzig then directed Martin by text message to communicate with IT Department staff and find out the answer. After communicating with Gossman and Vieng Siripoun, another programmer in the IT Department, Martin determined that no one fully reviewed the code prior to AFMC's deployment of the Laserfiche Integration Program and on March 17, 2017 sent an email to Herzig communicating that. Shortly thereafter, Herzig informed Little and Ray that development team members Jarrod Thrift and Vieng Siripoun performed the secondary code review.

Herzig and Martin then had Gossman, Siripoun, and another IT Department employee draft a summary of the quality control and testing methods used in the Laserfiche Integration Program's development. Siripoun noted that the summary ultimately did not make a good case for the IT Department, and accepted complete blame for the Laserfiche Integration Program failures. In addition to providing the summary to their superiors, Herzing and Martin suggested that a change made by the Business Intelligence Department may have contributed to the vulnerability. Ray contacted Jason Scheel, Director of the Business Intelligence Department, regarding this matter. Business Intelligence Department personnel did not have access to or responsibility for developing Laserfiche Integration Program code. Scheel communicated that the Business Intelligence Department made a change to the ReviewPoint page layout, and that the IT Department had been involved in that change. Ray reported to AFMC during his preliminary investigation that the Business Intelligence Department did not contribute to the root cause of the Laserfiche Integration Program issues.

On March 28, 2017, Chief Operating Officer Little put Herzig, Martin, Gossman, and Blaylock on administrative leave with pay pending final completion of AFMC's investigation. Each of them was given a final opportunity to provide information for AFMC's consideration. Gossman took responsibility for the contribution of his coding error to any issues with the Laserfiche Integration Program. Herzig expressed disappointment in his development staff and in Martin, and communicated that he held them accountable for these issues. Martin noted that Chief Technology Officer Ray's preliminary investigation did not include a review of information Martin had provided, which he believed indicated that whatever code errors might exist, any vulnerability was created only when the Business Intelligence Department incorrectly set ReviewPoint user permissions.

Chief Technology Officer Ray finalized his investigation and submitted a final report recommending that Herzig, Martin, Gossman, and Blaylock be terminated for their contributions to the Laserfiche Integration Program's vulnerabilities and, in Herzig and Martin's case, for repeated misrepresentations to AFMC that the Laserfiche Integration Program was secure and HIPAA-compliant. HIPAA Privacy Officer Hopkins supported and independently made these recommendations. Chief Operating Officer Little agreed and directed Ray to terminate Herzig, Martin, Gossman, and Blaylock's employment. All four were fired on April 4, 2017. At that time, Herzig was 44 years old and Martin was 41 years old. Additionally, Blaylock was 37, Little was 63, Hopkins was 63, and Scheel was 42.

In September 2017, AFMC hired Michael Troop to replace Herzig as Director of Information Technology. At the time of his hire, Troop was 55 years old. AFMC did not hire anyone to fill the position of Assistant Director of Information Technology. That same month, Herzig and Martin filed discrimination charges with the Equal Employment Opportunity Commission, alleging age discrimination. Following receipt of their right-to-sue letters, Herzig and Martin filed the complaint in this action alleging their employment was terminated in violation of the Age Discrimination in Employment Act ("ADEA"), 29 U.S.C. § 621, *et seq.*

When the parties conferred pursuant to Federal Rule of Civil Procedure 26(f), they agreed that AFMC might request data from Herzig and Martin's mobile phones and that the parties had taken reasonable measures to preserve potentially discoverable data from alteration or destruction. On July 18, 2018 AFMC served requests for production on Herzig and Martin, including a request for production of documents related to communications with current or former AFMC employees relevant to Herzig and Martin's lawsuit. On August 22, 2018, Herzig and Martin served their responses. Herzig agreed to produce responsive documents. Martin claimed to have no responsive documents. Responsive documents were not produced at that time, however. Rather, on September 4, 2018, Herzig and Martin produced screenshots of parts of text message conversations from Martin's mobile phone, including communications between Herzig and Martin. All produced text message portions ended on August 20, 2018, and Herzig and Martin produced no additional messages. Following a motion to compel, Herzig and Martin produced additional text messages from those text message conversations, but nothing more recent than August 20, 2018. After the August production, Martin installed the application Signal on his phone (Herzig had done so while working at AFMC), and Herzig and Martin used that application for communicating, not only with each other but with Blaylock. Signal allows users to send and receive encrypted text messages accessible only to sender and recipient, and to change settings to automatically delete these messages after a short period of time. Herzig and Martin set the application to delete their communications. Herzig and Martin disclosed no additional text messages to AFMC, and AFMC was unaware of their continued communication using Signal until Herzig disclosed it in his deposition near the end of the discovery period. Herzig and Martin allege that they used the application only to arrange meetings with one another or their attorney, and no longer had any text message communications responsive to AFMC's request for production.

III. Analysis

A. Spoliation Motion

In its motion for dismissal or adverse inference on the basis of spoliation, AFMC argues that despite Herzig and Martin's duty to impose litigation holds and to update responses to requests for production following their initial and reluctant production of text messages, Herzig and Martin instead intentionally acted to withhold and destroy discoverable evidence by installing and using the Signal application on their mobile devices. Herzig and Martin respond that they had no duty to allow AFMC to see all their communications, only communications responsive to the requests for production, and AFMC has no evidence that Herzig and Martin had responsive communications using Signal or that the destruction of those communications was in bad faith.

Herzig and Martin had numerous responsive communications with one another and with other AFMC employees prior to responding to the requests for production on August 22, 2018 and producing only some of those responsive communications on September 4, 2018. They remained reluctant to produce additional communications, doing so only after AFMC's motion to compel. Thereafter, Herzig and Martin did not disclose that they had switched to using a communication application designed to disguise and destroy communications until discovery was nearly complete. Based on the content of Herzig and Martin's earlier communications, which was responsive to the requests for production, and their reluctance to produce those communications, the Court infers that the content of their later communications using Signal were responsive to AFMC's requests for production. Based on Herzig and Martin's familiarity with information technology, their reluctance to produce responsive communications, the initial misleading response from Martin that he had no responsive communications, their knowledge that they must retain and produce discoverable evidence, and the necessity of manually configuring Signal to delete text communications, the Court believes that the decision to withhold and destroy those likely-responsive communications was intentional and done in bad faith.

This intentional, bad-faith spoliation of evidence was an abuse of the judicial process and warrants a sanction. The Court need not consider whether dismissal, an adverse inference, or some lesser sanction is the appropriate one, however, because in light of the motion for summary judgment, Herzig and Martin's case can and will be dismissed on the merits.

***

B. Types of Sanctions

Adverse inference instruction

NUTRITION DISTRIBUTION LLC V. PEP RESEARCH, LLC
No.: 16-cv-2328-WQH-BLM, 2018 WL 3789162 (S.D. Cal. 2018)

HAYES, Judge

I. BACKGROUND

On September 15, 2016, Plaintiff initiated this action by filing a Complaint, alleging violation of the Lanham Act by Defendants PEP Research LLC (PEP), Brian Reynders, and Fred Reynders. On December 30, 2016, Plaintiff filed an amended complaint, the operative complaint in this action, alleging the same claims. Plaintiff alleges that Defendants' supplement company, a competitor of Plaintiff, engaged in false and misleading advertising of certain prescription-only drugs and synthetic peptides. The docket reflects that the parties have engaged in discovery proceedings.

On August 9, 2018, the Magistrate Judge ordered that Plaintiff's motion for monetary sanctions pursuant to Fed. R. Civ. P. 37(d) be granted on the grounds "that Defendants failed to comply with several parts of the Court's March 9, 2018 discovery order and failed to adequately prepare and present a deponent pursuant to Fed. R. Civ. P. 30(b)(6)." The Magistrate Judge concluded Defendants had inadequately responded to Plaintiff's requests for production of documents. The Magistrate Judge concluded that Brent Reynders, Defendants' Fed. R. Civ. P. 30(b)(6) witness, admitted he "was not adequately prepared or sufficiently knowledgeable to testify as a corporate witness" regarding the identified financial topics, and was "unable or unwilling to adequately respond to Plaintiff's counsel's questions which were squarely in line with the noticed deposition topic." The Magistrate Judge imposed sanctions against both Defendants and Defendants' counsel because "the evidence presented to the Court indicates that counsel did contribute to the discovery violations and failures to comply."

The Magistrate Judge also issued a report and recommendation. The Magistrate Judge found evidence supporting all elements of spoliation as to certain deleted social media posts. The Magistrate Judge concluded, and Defendants did not dispute, the obligation to preserve relevant evidence arose "no later than June 1, 2016." The Magistrate Judge concluded the evidence established a culpable state of mind, based on Brent Reynder's deposition testimony that he deleted Facebook posts after September 2016, that "[i]t's possible" the deleted posts had to do with the lawsuit, and that "I have the right to do whatever I want to do with my Facebook account, regardless of a lawsuit or not. If I wanted to -- if I want to delete every single post on my Facebook page, I have the right to do so." The Magistrate

Judge found this deposition testimony contradicted Defendants' declaration that posts were deleted before the litigation and were not intentionally deleted for litigation purposes. The Magistrate Judge concluded that "the evidence establishes that Defendant deleted relevant social media posts after this case was filed and the law does not require that Defendants destroyed or deleted the posts 'intentionally for this litigation;' it merely requires destruction after notice to preserve or negligence."

The Magistrate Judge concluded, and Defendants did not dispute, the deleted evidence was relevant to Plaintiff's claims. The Magistrate Judge stated "Initially, Defendants' deposition testimony and the lack of any legitimate explanation for the destruction of evidence establishes bad faith," which suffices to demonstrates relevance. The Magistrate Judge concluded Plaintiff had established prejudice, as "Plaintiff only has some Facebook and Twitter posts regarding the challenged products which it obtained during its pre-lawsuit investigation."

The Magistrate Judge concluded that Plaintiff's evidence did not support a finding of spoliation as to financial data and emails lost in a June 2017 computer upgrade. The Magistrate Judge recommended that this Court issue an order:

(1) approving and adopting this Report and Recommendation;

(2) FINDING that Defendants spoiled social media evidence,

(3) GRANTING Plaintiff's motion for an adverse inference instruction "that the social media posts deleted were false advertising of products that compete with Plaintiff,"

(4) DENYING Plaintiff's request for an adverse inference instruction that "the spoliated financial information would demonstrate proximate cause and commercial injury to Plaintiff," and

(5) DENYING Plaintiff's request for monetary sanctions related to spoliation.

The Magistrate Judge ordered objections to be filed by August 24, 2018. On August 24, 2018, Defendants filed objections, supported by the Declaration of Brent Reynders. On September 7, 2018, Plaintiff filed a reply to Defendants' objections, supported in part by the Declaration of Valerie Saryan.

II. DISCUSSION

A. Sanctions Against Defendants' Counsel

Defendants dispute the monetary sanctions imposed by the Magistrate Judge on the grounds that counsel was not on notice of the requirement to show counsel was not responsible for any discovery noncompliance. Defendants contend that sanctions were unfairly imposed on counsel, in part because counsel represents Defendants pro bono. Defendants contend that counsel properly advised appropriate production of documents. Defendants contend that the statements of an unsophisticated and defensive deponent do not show counsel's failings. Defendants contend sufficient documents have been produced.

Plaintiff contends sanctions against Defendants' counsel are proper. Plaintiff asserts that Defendants' counsel was notified of the potential sanctions order because Plaintiff expressly requested the order in the motion for sanctions, and Defendants and Defendants' counsel had already received discovery sanctions in this action. Plaintiff asserts that Defendants' counsel was paid, and deserves no leniency based on pro bono service.

A district court judge "may designate a magistrate judge to hear and determine any pretrial matter pending before the court" with a limited number of exceptions. 28 U.S.C. § 636(b)(1)(A). "A judge may reconsider any pretrial matter ... where it has been shown that the magistrate judge's order is clearly erroneous or contrary to law." Rule 72(a) of the Federal Rules of Civil Procedure states,

> When a pretrial matter not dispositive of a party's claim or defense is referred to a magistrate judge to hear and decide, the magistrate judge must promptly conduct the required proceedings and, when appropriate, issue a written order stating the decision. A party may serve and file objections to the order within 14 days after being served with a copy. A party may not assign as error a defect in the order not timely objected to. The district judge in the case must consider timely objections and modify or set aside any part of the order that is clearly erroneous or is contrary to law.

Fed. R. Civ. P. 72(a). A magistrate judge's nondispositive order may be set aside or modified by a district court only if it is found to be clearly erroneous or contrary to law. *Bhan v. Hosps., Inc.* 929 F.2d 1404, 1414 (9th Cir. 1991).

Matters concerning discovery generally are considered nondispositive of the litigation and reviewed under the clearly erroneous standard.

Defendants object only to the portion of the Magistrate Judge's order imposing monetary sanctions against Defendants' counsel. Defendants do not object to, and the Court does not review, the appropriateness of discovery sanctions under Fed. R. Civ. P. 37(b)(2) in this case. The Court has reviewed the order, the parties' briefings, and the record in full.

The imposition of 37(b)(2) sanctions is nondispositive in this case. The Magistrate Judge referenced deposition testimony of Brent Reynders and Fred Reynders, who stated they would produce certain documents only upon instruction from the judge or counsel. The Magistrate Judge stated those documents were within the scope of the court's previous discovery orders, and that Defendants had produced no evidence showing counsel had explained the previous orders or instructed that the documents be produced. Id. Defendants provide a declaration by Brent Reynders, stating that "certainly our counsel advised us to preserve our relevant documents, and produce everything we have that could possibly be relevant, not just documents sufficient to respond to Plaintiff's specific requests."

The evidence in the record tends to establish that Defendants' counsel was responsible for the discovery noncompliance. Defendants do not provide cases or other law to support the assertion that sanctions against pro bono counsel are inappropriate under the circumstances. The Magistrate Judge's imposition of sanctions against Defendants' counsel was not clearly erroneous or contrary to law. Counsel's failure to oversee Defendants' discovery efforts can give rise to sanctions. *See Knickerbocker v. Corinthian Colls.*, 298 F.R.D. 670, 678 (W.D. Wash. 2014) (collecting Southern District of California cases imposing sanctions on attorneys for discovery failures). Defendants' objections to the sanctions Order are overruled.

B. Report & Recommendation

Defendants object to the Magistrate Judge's finding of a culpable state of mind as to the deleted social media posts. Defendants contend the Magistrate Judge's findings are insufficiently supported by the "bluster and sass" of an "unsophisticated," "defensive and testy," "annoyed and exasperated" deponent, who denies spoliation in a sworn Declaration. Defendants assert that PEP "would stipulate to the content of the alleged 'false advertising' at issue; as such, finding duplicative Facebook posts making the same statements would not be a 'proportional' use of the discovery process." Defendants assert that the Magistrate Judge inappropriately placed the burden on PEP to disprove spoliation.

Defendants assert that the recommended adverse instruction goes too far, because Plaintiff has done no business recently, specifically no business competing with PEP. Defendants contend the instruction should at most state, "that the 'social media posts' support Plaintiff's claim that PEP makes the alleged statements in its advertising of 'not for human consumption' and 'intended for laboratory research only.'"

Plaintiff asserts that the evidence supports the recommended adverse inference instruction, and that Defendants' objections and supporting declaration are unsubstantiated and misleading.

Federal Rule of Civil Procedure 72(b) and 28 U.S.C. § 636(b) set forth the duties of the district court as to a report and recommendation issued by a magistrate judge. The district judge must "make a *de novo* determination of those portions of the report ... to which objection is made," and "may accept, reject, or modify, in whole or in part, the findings or recommendations made by the magistrate." 28 U.S.C. § 636(b). The district court need not review *de novo* those portions of a report and recommendation to which neither party objects.

There is no objection filed to the Magistrate Judge's recommendation to deny an adverse inference instruction as to spoliated financial information, or the recommendation to deny the request for monetary sanctions related to spoliation. Defendants object to, and the Court reviews de novo, the Magistrate Judge's recommended finding of spoliation of social media evidence, and recommended adverse inference instruction.

Courts in the Ninth Circuit apply a three-element test when a party seeks an adverse inference instruction on grounds of spoliation: (1) the person in control of the evidence had the obligation to preserve relevant evidence at the time of destruction, (2) the evidence was destroyed with a culpable state of mind, and (3) the evidence was relevant. *See Compass Bank v. Morris Cerullo World Evangelism*, 104 F. Supp. 3d. 1040, 1054 & n.2 (S. D. Cal. 2015) (collecting cases). For the second element, a "culpable state of mind" requires a showing of at least negligence. *See Sherwin-Williams Co. v. JB Collision Servs., Inc.*, No. 13cv1946-LAB(WVG), 2015 WL 4077732, at *4 (S.D. Cal. July 3, 2015); *Cottle-Banks v. Cox Commc'ns, Inc.*, No. 10cv2133-GPC(WVG), 2013 WL 2244333, at *14 (S.D. Cal. May 21, 2013). For the third element, "relevance" requires a showing that the evidence was destroyed in bad faith, or that the evidence would have helped the innocent party prove its claim or defense. See *Sherwin Williams*, 2015 WL 4077732, at *4 ***.

The Magistrate Judge found that the duty to preserve relevant evidence arose no later than June 1, 2016. The Magistrate Judge found that the social media posts at issue were deleted after June 1, 2016. The Magistrate Judge found that Defendants had control over the social media accounts at issue. Defendants do not object to these findings and the Court concludes the Defendants were in control of the evidence and had an obligation to preserve the evidence at the time of destruction. The first element is satisfied.

The second element, a culpable state of mind, requires only a negligent failure to preserve the evidence. The Magistrate Judge found that the social media posts were deleted while Defendants were under a duty to preserve relevant evidence. Defendants do not object to this finding and the Court concludes that the second element is satisfied.

Regarding the third element, relevance, Defendants assert that Plaintiff does not need the deleted postings to prove the Lanham Act claim because Plaintiff already possesses some postings. Plaintiff's claim requires proof that Defendants made false statements of fact in advertising the product at issue in this case. *See Southland Sod Farms v. Stover Seed Co.*, 108 F.3d 1134, 1139 (9th Cir. 1997). Plaintiff cannot use the deleted posts and that impairs Plaintiff's ability to establish the false advertising claim. The Court concludes that the evidence would have helped Plaintiff prove the Lanham Act claim. The third element is satisfied. The Court finds Defendants spoliated social media evidence. An adverse inference instruction is justified.

An adverse inference instruction is a harsh sanction. *See Apple*, 888 F. Supp. 2d at 994 (collecting cases observing harshness or severity of adverse inference instructions). Courts vary the language of an adverse inference instruction according to the degree of fault of the spoliating party. *See Compass Bank*, 104 F. Supp. 3d at 1054; *Victorino v. FCA US LLC*, No. 16cv1617-GPC(JLB), 2017 WL 4541653, at *9 (S.D. Cal. Oct. 11, 2017). The harshest adverse inference instruction deems certain facts admitted, which the jury must accept as true. The harshest instruction is appropriate when the spoliating party acted willfully or in bad faith. The next harshest instruction is a mandatory, rebuttable presumption, appropriate when the spoliating party was willfull or reckless. The least harsh instruction gives the jury the option to presume the lost evidence is relevant and favorable to the innocent party, in which case the jury considers rebuttal evidence and determines whether to draw an adverse inference. A court must consider the degree of prejudice to the nonspoliating party and impose the least harsh sanction that adequately deters spoliation and places the risk of an incorrect judgment on the party who created that risk. *See Reisendorf v. Sketchers U.S.A., Inc.*, 296 F.R.D. 604, 626 (C.D. Cal. 2013).

Plaintiff asserts, and the Magistrate Judge concluded, that Defendants acted with a culpable state of mind. The deposition testimony regarding the deleted posts, in addition to Defendants' reluctance to comply with other discovery orders, support a finding of a culpable state of mind. Given the nature of the claim in this case, however, the instruction that the deleted social media posts were false advertising of products that compete with Plaintiff's products is tantamount to entry of judgment. *See In re Black Diamond Min. Co., LLC*, 514 B.R. 230, 243 (E.D. Ky. 2014) (finding mandatory instructions of "parties' negligent failure to purchase coal or failure to exercise sound business judgment" tantamount to entry of judgment against those parties) (*citing Flagg v. City of Detroit*, 715 F.3d 165, 177 (6th Cir. 2013)). The record shows that Plaintiff has preserved some social media postings. Defendants offer to stipulate to the contents of the posts.

The Court will give an adverse inference instruction. ***

III. CONCLUSION

***

Defendants have failed to preserve social media posts for Plaintiff's use in this litigation after Defendants' duty to preserve arose. You may, but are not obligated to, infer that the deleted social media posts were favorable to Plaintiff and unfavorable to Defendants.

***

Monetary Sanctions

PAISLEY PARK ENTERPRISES, INC. v. BOXILL
No. 17-cv-1212 (WMW/TNL) (D. Minn. 2019)

LEUNG, Magistrate Judge

This matter is before the Court on Plaintiffs' Motion for Sanctions Due to Spoliation of Evidence and Plaintiffs' Motion to Compel Discovery from Defendant Brown & Rosen, LLC. ***

I. BACKGROUND

Plaintiff Comerica Bank & Trust, N.A. is the personal representative for the estate of the late internationally known musician Prince Rogers Nelson ("Prince" and "Prince Estate"). The Prince Estate owns Plaintiff Paisley Park Enterprises, Inc. The Prince Estate has an interest in various songs created by Prince, including those not released to the public. Plaintiffs allege that Defendants have taken steps to release songs that Prince created but did not previously release to the public without the permission of the Prince Estate. In particular, Plaintiffs allege that Defendant George Ian Boxill, a sound engineer who worked with Prince previously, took tracks of certain songs that he worked on with Prince, edited, and released those songs with the assistance of Defendant Rogue Music Alliance ("RMA"), an LLC whose principals are David Staley and Gabriel Solomon Wilson. Plaintiffs also allege that Boxill, Staley, and Wilson formed Deliverance, LLC to release the music and that the law firms Sidebar Legal, PC and Brown & Rosen, LLC ("Brown") assisted in the infringement.

On February 11, 2017, before releasing the music at issue in this lawsuit, Staley sent an e-mail to Nate Yetton of Sensibility Music wherein Staley indicated that Boxill had indemnified RMA in case the Prince Estate chose to challenge the release of the music. On March 16, 2017 after learning that Defendants intended to release the music, the Prince Estate sent a cease and desist letter. Plaintiffs followed up with a second letter demanding that the music be returned. They then filed suit against Boxill in state court on April 14, 2017. Boxill removed the lawsuit to federal court on April 18, 2017. ***

In December 2017, after Plaintiffs filed their first amended complaint, they, RMA, Deliverance, and Boxill, stipulated to certain protocols regarding the discovery of electronically stored information ("ESI"). In that stipulation, the parties indicated that they had taken "reasonable steps to preserve reasonably accessible sources of ESI." The Court indicated that it would enforce the parties' agreement but did not enter an order concerning the stipulation.

The Court then issued its pretrial scheduling order on January 10, 2018. In that order, the Court directed the parties to preserve "all electronic documents that bear on any claims, defenses, or the subject matter of this lawsuit." The Court warned failure to comply with any provision of this order would subject the non-complying party to "any and all appropriate remedies," including sanctions, assessment of costs, fines and attorneys' fees and disbursements, and any other relief the Court might deem appropriate. The Court issued amended pretrial scheduling orders on June 27, 2018 and October 4, 2018. Each order contained language regarding ESI discovery and the potential consequences of a violation of the Court's order.

Plaintiffs served written discovery on RMA and Deliverance on December 1, 2017. Included in their discovery were requests for the production of all documents related to the timing, circumstances, format, and content of the music at issue in this lawsuit, communications with any third-party regarding Boxill, Prince, and items at issue in this lawsuit, and all documents related to Boxill, Prince, the music at issue here, Paisley Park Enterprises, and this lawsuit. Plaintiffs indicated in their requests that the term document had the broadest possible meaning ascribed to it under Rule 34. Plaintiffs sent a letter outlining certain deficiencies with RMA and Deliverance's responses on March 2, 2018, including the failure to produce text messages responsive to their requests.

Shortly thereafter, Plaintiffs received a third-party production of documents from a public relations firm that Defendants had hired. Included in that production were text messages that Wilson sent to an employee of the public relations firm. Plaintiffs then filed a motion to compel discovery from RMA, seeking production of text messages that Staley and Wilson sent to each other and third parties. The Court ordered that Defendants produce all responsive text messages on July 19, 2018.

Counsel for Plaintiffs, Wilson, Staley, RMA and Deliverance then held a meet-and-confer on September 21, 2018. There, counsel for Wilson, Staley, RMA and Deliverance indicated that they could not produce responsive text messages because they had not preserved their text messages. They indicated that text messages had not been preserved because Staley and Wilson did not disengage the auto-delete function on their phones and because Staley had wiped and discarded his phone in October 2017 and Wilson had wiped and discarded his phone in January 2018 and then wiped and discard his new phone in May 2018. They also indicated that no back-up data existed for either phone, though they were later able to produce a screenshot captured from Staley's phone, which he had uploaded to his cloud storage space. An e-discovery lawyer for Plaintiffs' law firm indicates that had Staley and Wilson not wiped and discarded their phones, it might have been possible to recover the deleted messages.

Plaintiffs also served written discovery on Brown, the law firm that issued an opinion letter regarding Boxill's right to release the music. In those requests, Plaintiffs sought discovery regarding information and documents that Brown considered prior to writing the opinion letter, identification of evidence regarding Prince's intent, research and analysis that Brown conducted regarding the music at issue here, and issues related to Brown's competency to author the opinion. Plaintiffs also sought the production of documents related to Brown's experience in teaching intellectual property law. Brown objected to each of those requests on grounds of irrelevancy, privilege, or the fact that the opinion letter spoke for itself.

Plaintiffs have filed a motion for sanctions against RMA, Deliverance, Staley, and Wilson and a motion to compel against Brown. RMA, Deliverance, Staley, and Wilson filed a memorandum in response on November 6, 2018 and Brown filed a response on January 4, 2019. The Court heard argument on both matters on January 15, 2019 and took both under advisement.

II. ANALYSIS

A. Motion for Sanctions

Plaintiffs first move to sanction RMA, Deliverance, Staley, and Wilson ("RMA Defendants") for the destruction of text messages. They seek sanctions under Rule 37(e)(1), 37(e)(2) and 37(b)(2)(A). The RMA Defendants argue that they took reasonable steps to preserve relevant evidence, that Plaintiffs failed to show prejudice, and that the record shows that they did not act with intent to deprive Plaintiffs of relevant evidence. The RMA Defendants do not dispute, however, that some evidence has been lost and likely cannot be replaced in its original form.

The Federal Rules of Civil Procedure require that parties take reasonable steps to preserve ESI that is relevant to litigation. Fed. R. Civ. P. 37(e). The Court may sanction a party for failure for failure to do so, provided that the lost ESI cannot be restored or replaced through additional discovery. Rule 37(e) makes two types of sanctions available to the Court. Under Rule 37(e)(1), if the adverse party has suffered prejudice from the spoliation of evidence, the Court may order whatever sanctions are necessary to cure the prejudice. But under Rule 37(e)(2), if the Court finds that the party "acted with the intent to deprive another party of the information's use in the litigation," the Court may order more severe sanctions, including a presumption that the lost information was unfavorable to the party or an instruction to the jury that it "may or must presume the information was unfavorable to the party." The Court may also sanction a party for failing to obey a discovery order. Fed. R. Civ. P. 37(b). Sanctions available under Rule 37(b) include an order directing that certain designated facts be taken as established for purposes of the action, payment of reasonable expenses, and civil contempt of court.

A party is obligated to preserve evidence once the party knows or should know that the evidence is relevant to future or current litigation. *E*Trade Sec. LLC v. Deutsche Bank AG*, 230 F.R.D. 582, 588 (D. Minn. 2005); see also Fed. R. Civ. P. 37(e), advisory committee's note to 2015 amendment (stating that rule requires preservation of evidence when litigation is reasonably foreseeable). "A variety of events may alert a party to the prospect of litigation." Fed. R. Civ. P. 37(e), advisory committee's note to 2015 amendment. "The duty to preserve relevant evidence must be viewed from the perspective of the party with control of the evidence."

In this case, the Court finds the duty to preserve evidence arose no later than February 11, 2017 when Staley sent an e-mail regarding his plans to release the music at issue here. In that e-mail, Staley acknowledged the riskiness of his and RMA's position and indicated that the Prince Estate could challenge their actions. Staley referred specifically to the possibility of litigation in that e-mail, noting that RMA was not concerned by a lawsuit because it had been indemnified by Boxill. It is apparent, based on this letter, that the RMA Defendants anticipated litigation following their release of the Prince music. The duty to preserve therefore attached on February 11, 2017.

The next question the Court must consider is whether the RMA Defendants took reasonable steps to preserve relevant ESI. Even when litigation is reasonably foreseeable, a party is under no obligation "to keep every shred of paper, every e-mail or electronic document and every backup tape." *In re Ethicon, Inc. Pelvic Repair Sys. Prod. Liability Lit.*, 299 F.R.D. 502, 517-518 (S.D. W. Va. 2014) (citation and internal quotation marks omitted); see also Fed. R. Civ. P. 37(e), advisory committee's note to 2015 amendment (stating the scope of information that should be preserved often is uncertain). The "duty to preserve evidence extends to those [persons] likely to have relevant information—the key players in the case, and applies to unique, relevant evidence that might be useful to the adversary."

There is no doubt that Staley and Wilson are the types of persons likely to have relevant information, given their status as principals of RMA and owners of Deliverance. Nor can there be any reasonable dispute as to the fact that their text messages were likely to contain information relevant to this litigation. In fact, Boxill and other third parties produced text messages that they sent to or received from Staley and Wilson. Neither party disputes that those text messages were relevant to this litigation. Thus, the RMA Defendants were required to take reasonable steps to preserve Staley and Wilson's text messages.

The RMA Defendants did not do so. First, Staley and Wilson did not suspend the auto-erase function on their phones. Nor did they put in place a litigation hold to ensure that they preserved text messages. The principles of the "standard reasonableness framework" require a party to "suspend its routine document retention/destruction policy and put in place a `litigation hold' to ensure the preservation of relevant documents." It takes, at most, only a few minutes to disengage the auto-delete function on a cell phone. It is apparent, based on Staley's affidavit, that he and Wilson could have taken advantage of relatively simple options to ensure that their text messages were backed up to cloud storage. These processes would have cost the RMA Defendants little, particularly in comparison to the importance of the issues at stake and the amount in controversy here. Failure to follow the simple steps detailed above alone is sufficient to show that Defendants acted unreasonably.

But that is not all the RMA Defendants did and did not do. Most troubling of all, they wiped and destroyed their phones after Deliverance and RMA had been sued, and, in the second instance for Wilson, after the Court ordered the parties to preserve all relevant electronic information, after the parties had entered into an agreement regarding the preservation and production of ESI, and after Plaintiffs had sent Defendants a letter alerting them to the fact they needed to produce their text messages. As Plaintiffs note, had Staley and Wilson not destroyed their phones, it is possible that Plaintiffs might have been able to recover the missing text messages by use of the "cloud" function or through consultation with a software expert. But the content will never be known because of Staley and Wilson's intentional acts. The RMA Defendants' failure to even consider whether Staley and Wilson's phones might have discoverable information before destroying them was completely unreasonable. This is even more egregious because litigation had already commenced.

The RMA Defendants make a number of arguments as to why their decision not to preserve text messages was reasonable. None of these arguments is persuasive. First, they argue that Plaintiffs did not issue a litigation hold letter to Defendants informing them that Plaintiffs were likely to seek discovery on text messages. Rule 37 requires the party from whom the information is sought to ensure they are taking reasonable steps to preserve evidence. See Fed. R. Civ. P. 37(e) The rule does not require that the requesting party issue a document preservation letter identifying all types of ESI that it might seek in the future. That burden rests with the preserving party. *See id.* The fact that Plaintiffs did not sua sponte issue a litigation hold letter to RMA Defendants is of little or no relevance here.

Second, the RMA Defendants surprisingly argue they could not possibly be expected to know that they should preserve text messages. They further note that their previous counsel never told them to preserve text messages and that the document requests that Plaintiffs served did not identify text messages as a form of document sought. But parties are responsible for the conduct of their attorneys; an adverse party is not required to bear the burden of misconduct committed by the opposing side's counsel. *Siems v. City of Minneapolis*, 560 F.3d 824, 827 (8th Cir. 2009) (affirming sanctions where the "record does not contain any evidence that [the party] contributed in any way to the dilatory actions of his counsel"); *Comiskey v. JFTJ Corp.*, 989 F.2d 1007, 1010 (8th Cir. 1993) (affirming default judgment sanction for discovery violations that were the sole fault of party's prior counsel); *Boogaerts v. Bank of Bradley*, 961 F.2d 765, 768 (8th Cir. 1992) ("Although the sanction was imposed against the plaintiff, it is of no consequence that the discovery abuse perpetrated was by counsel rather than the plaintiff-client."). And Rule 34 requires the production of any document, including, "data or data compilations-stored in any medium from which information can be obtained ... directly." Fed. R. Civ. P. 34(a)(1)(A). It is well established that text messages "fit comfortably within the scope of materials that a party may request under Rule 34." *Flagg v. City of Detroit*, 252 F.R.D. 346, 352-53 (E.D. Mich.

2008); *see Lalumiere v. Willow Springs Care, Inc.*, No. 16-cv-3133, 2017 WL 6943148 *2 (E.D. Wa. Sept. 18, 2017) (concluding text messages may be requested under Rule 34); *see also* Fed. R. Civ. P. 34, advisory committee's note to 2006 amendments (explaining that Rule 34 plainly encompasses electronic communications and copies of such communications preserved in electronic form). In the contemporary world of communications, even leaving out the potential and reality of finding the modern-day litigation equivalent of a "smoking gun" in text messages, e-mails, and possibly other social media, the Court is baffled as to how Defendants can reasonably claim to believe that their text messages would be immune from discovery.

Third, the RMA Defendants also argue that given the personal nature of their phones, it is unreasonable for the Court to expect them to know they should preserve information contained on those devices. In support of this claim, they note that they provided discovery from other sources of ESI, including their work computers. They also note that they cooperated with a forensic data firm to ensure Plaintiffs obtained everything they sought. They further claim that Plaintiffs never asked to inspect their cell phones during this process.

This argument too is without merit. It is obvious, based on text messages that other parties produced in this litigation, that Staley and Wilson used their personal cell phones to conduct the business of RMA and Deliverance. It is not Plaintiffs' responsibility to question why RMA Defendants did not produce any text messages; in fact, it would be reasonable for Plaintiffs to assume that Defendants' failure to do so was on account of the fact that no such text messages existed. This is because the RMA Defendants are the only ones who would know the extent that they used their personal cell phones for RMA and Deliverance business at the time they knew or should have reasonably known that litigation was not just possible, but likely, or after Plaintiffs filed suit or served their discovery requests.

Furthermore, the RMA Defendants do not get to select what evidence they want to produce, or from what sources. They must produce all responsive documents or seek relief from the court. *See* Fed. R. Civ. P. 26(c) (outlining process for obtaining protective order). In fact, in cases that predate Rule 37(e) in its current form, courts had concluded that the failure to preserve some types of ESI while destroying others is a reasonable basis to infer that the destroying party acted with bad faith. The Court will not permit the RMA Defendants to claim that it was reasonable to assume data on their personal cell phones would not be subject to discovery when the record clearly shows that they used their phones for work purposes. As will be discussed more fully later, the record here establishes that the RMA Defendants acted willfully and with intent to destroy discoverable information.

Finally, Wilson and Staley argue that sanctions should not be imposed against them in their personal capacities because they were not named as defendants in this lawsuit until June 2018. But the duty to preserve still attached upon both individuals in February 2017, when they recognized litigation to be a possibility upon release of the music at issue here.

Nothing in the intervening months relieved either individual of this duty. Both Staley and Wilson participated in the destruction of the text messages. They cite to no authority to support the proposition that a spoliation motion cannot be brought against an individual simply because the conduct occurred long before they were named as individual defendants.

Having concluded that the RMA Defendants did not take reasonable steps to preserve and in fact intended to destroy relevant ESI, the Court must next consider whether the lost ESI can be restored or replaced from any other source. Because ESI "often exists in multiple locations, loss from one source may often be harmless when substitute information can be found elsewhere." Fed. R. Civ. P. 37, advisory committee's note to 2015 amendments. For example, Rule 37 sanctions are not available when "e-mails are lost because one custodian deletes them, but they remain available in the records of another custodian." Logically, the same principle holds true for text messages.

While it is true that Plaintiffs have obtained text messages that Boxill and other parties sent to or received from Staley and Wilson, that does not mean that all responsive text messages have been recovered or that a complete record of those conversations is available. In particular, because Wilson and Staley wiped and destroyed their phones, Plaintiffs are unable to recover text messages that the two individuals sent only to each other. Nor can they recover text messages that Staley and Wilson sent to third parties to whom Plaintiff did not send Rule 45 subpoenas (likely because they were not aware that Wilson or Staley communicated with those persons). The RMA Defendants do not dispute that text messages sent between Staley and Wilson are no longer recoverable.

The fact that the information contained in the missing text messages might also be cumulative to e-mails that the RMA Defendants already produced is insufficient to restore or replace the text messages. First, it will never be known whether such information would or would not have been cumulative because it is impossible to know what it was or to whom it may have been communicated. Second, even when the information lost is "cumulative to some extent," the loss of the information still has an impact because Plaintiffs "cannot present the overwhelming quantity of evidence [they] otherwise would have to support [their] case." *Victor Stanley, Inc. v. Creative Pipe, Inc.*, 269 F.R.D. 497, 533 (D. Md. 2010) (considering spoliation motion before Rule 37(e) amendment). At most, Plaintiffs now can obtain only "scattershot texts and [e-mails]," rather than "a complete record of defendants' written communications from defendants themselves." The Court therefore finds that the missing text messages cannot be replaced or restored by other sources.

The Court now turns to what, if any, sanctions are appropriate for the RMA Defendants' failure to preserve relevant text messages. As set forth above, Rule 37(e) allows the Court two options. If the Court finds that Plaintiffs have suffered prejudice from the RMA Defendants' failure to preserve relevant evidence, the Court may order only those sanctions necessary to cure the prejudice. Fed. R. Civ. P. 37(e)(1). But if the Court finds that the RMA Defendants acted with "intent to deprive" Plaintiffs of the information's use, then the Court may order more severe sanctions, including a presumption the lost information was unfavorable or an instruction to the jury that it may or must presume the missing information was unfavorable. Fed. R. Civ. P. 37(e)(2). As for the violation of the Court's pretrial scheduling order, the Court may issue any "just order[]," including the striking of pleadings, prohibiting the disobedient party from supporting or opposing certain claims, or ordering the payment of costs and fees. Fed. R. Civ. P. 37(b)(2)(A); 37(b)(2)(C). The Court's pretrial scheduling order also puts parties on notice that failure to comply with any provision could result in the assessment of costs and fees or a monetary fine. In this case, the Court finds it appropriate to issue sanctions under both Rules 37(b) and 37(e) and the Court's pretrial scheduling order.

There is no doubt that Plaintiffs are prejudiced by the loss of the text messages. Prejudice exists when spoliation prohibits a party from presenting evidence that is relevant to its underlying case. As set forth above, in the Court's discussion regarding their ability to replace or restore the missing information, Plaintiffs are left with an incomplete record of the communications that Defendants had with both each other and third parties. Neither the Court nor Plaintiffs can know what ESI has been lost or how significant that ESI was to this litigation. The RMA Defendants' claim that no prejudice has occurred is "wholly unconvincing," given that "it is impossible to determine precisely what the destroyed documents contained or how severely the unavailability of these documents might have prejudiced [Plaintiffs'] ability to prove the claims set forth in [their] Complaint." *Telectron, Inc. v. Overhead Door Corp.*, 116 F.R.D. 107, 110 (S.D. Fl. 1987); *see also Multifeeder Tech., Inc. v. British Confectionary Co. Ltd*, No. 09-cv-1090, 2012 WL 4128385 *23 (D. Minn. Apr. 26, 2012) (finding prejudice because Court will never know what ESI was destroyed and because it was undisputed that destroying parties had access to relevant information). Plaintiffs are now forced to go to already existing discovery and attempt to piece together what information might have been contained in those messages, thereby increasing their costs and expenses. Sanctions are therefore appropriate under Rule 37(e)(1).

Sanctions are also appropriate under Rule 37(e)(2) because the Court finds that the RMA Defendants acted with the intent to deprive Plaintiffs of the evidence. "Intent rarely is proved by direct evidence, and a district court has substantial leeway to determine intent through consideration of circumstantial evidence, witness credibility, motives of the witnesses in a particular case, and other factors." There need not be a "smoking gun" to prove intent. But there must be evidence of "a serious and specific sort of culpability" regarding the loss of the relevant ESI.

Were the missing ESI only the result of Wilson and Staley's failure to disengage the auto-delete function on their phones, then the Court might consider the loss of evidence to be the result of mere negligence. But that is not the case here. As noted previously, Wilson and Staley failed not only to turn off the auto-delete function when they anticipated litigation in February 2017, they also wiped and discarded their phones (twice, in Wilson's case) after Plaintiffs filed suit against RMA and Deliverance. This despite the fact that, as evidenced by the fact that Staley backed up photographs from his phone to his cloud storage space and Dropbox, they knew how to preserve information on their phones and knew that information on their phone might be discoverable. The Court finds from these circumstances alone that the RMA Defendants intentionally destroyed evidence.

The wiping and destruction of Wilson's phone for a second time are perhaps the most egregious or unkindest acts of all. Wilson got rid of his phone in May 2018, after: (1) litigation had commenced; (2) Plaintiffs served discovery; (3) Plaintiffs expressly informed the RMA Defendants that they intended to seek discovery regarding Wilson and Staley's text messages; and (4) the Court ordered the parties to preserve all relevant electronically stored information in its pretrial scheduling order. Any one of these events should have been sufficient to put the RMA Defendants on notice that they needed to preserve their text messages and phones. The Court can draw only one conclusion from this set of circumstances: that they acted with the intent to deprive Plaintiffs from using this information. Rule 37(e)(2) sanctions are particularly appropriate as to Wilson, RMA, and Deliverance for this reason as well.

Finally, sanctions under Rule 37(b) as to Wilson, RMA, and Deliverance are also appropriate because those Defendants violated the Court's pretrial scheduling orders, all of which directed them to preserve electronically stored information. The pretrial scheduling orders also put those Defendants on notice that failure to comply with any provision in those orders might result in a number of sanctions, including an assessment of attorney's fees and costs or a fine. The Court will consider sanctions authorized under these authorities as well.

As to Rule 37(e)(2), Plaintiffs seek the following sanctions: a presumption that the evidence destroyed was unfavorable to the party that destroyed it or, alternatively, an adverse inference instruction. As to Rule 37(e)(1), Plaintiffs seek monetary sanctions and an instruction to the jury that the RMA Defendants had an obligation to preserve the text messages, but failed to do so, making that evidence no longer available. Plaintiffs seek similar sanctions for Rule 37(b), including an instruction to the jury that the RMA Defendants had an obligation to preserve text messages, that they took active steps to destroy those messages, and that as a result, the evidence is no longer available. Plaintiffs also seek their costs and attorney's fees.

The Court believes that Plaintiffs' request for an order presuming the evidence destroyed was unfavorable to the RMA Defendants and/or for an adverse inference instruction may well be justified. But given the fact that discovery is still on-going, the record is not yet closed, and the case is still some time from trial, the Court believes it more appropriate to defer consideration of those sanctions to a later date, closer to trial. *See Monarch Fire Protection Dist. v. Freedom Consulting & Auditing Servs., Inc.*, 644 F.3d 633, 639 (8th Cir. 2011) (holding that it is not an abuse of discretion to defer sanction considerations until trial). At that point, the trial judge will have the benefit of the entire record and supplemental briefing from the parties regarding the parameters of any such instruction or presumption.

The Court will, however, order the RMA Defendants to pay monetary sanctions pursuant to Rules 37(b), and 37(e) and the Court's pretrial scheduling orders. In reaching this decision, the Court notes that neither Rule 37(e)(1) nor 37(e)(2) expressly authorizes the imposition of monetary sanctions. But Rule 37(e)(1) allows the Court to impose any measures necessary to cure the prejudice resulting from spoliation. The range of sanctions available to the Court is "quite broad" and "[m]uch is left to the court's discretion. Fed. R. Civ. P. 37(e), advisory committee's note to 2015 amendment. Many courts have imposed monetary sanctions under Rule 37(e)(1). On this basis alone, there is a good argument that the Court could do the same here.

But, given the facts of this case, the conduct of the RMA Defendants is egregious--they willfully and intentionally destroyed discoverable information. Thus, monetary sanctions are available under Rule 37(e)(2). Though that provision contains a list of three different sanctions that may be imposed upon a finding that a party acted with the intent to deprive another of the use of information in litigation, those sanctions do not constitute an exhaustive list of those available to the Court. Instead, the Court may order any remedy that "fit[s] the wrong." Fed. R. Civ. P. 37(e), advisory committee's note to 2015 amendment. Thus, the Court concludes that monetary sanctions are available under this provision of Rule 37.

The Court will therefore order, pursuant to Rules 37(b)(2)(C), 37(e)(1), and 37(e)(2) and the Court's pretrial scheduling orders, the RMA Defendants to pay reasonable expenses, including attorney's fees and costs, that Plaintiffs incurred as a result of the RMA Defendants' misconduct. The Court will order Plaintiffs to file a submission with the Court detailing such expenses and allow the RMA Defendants the opportunity to respond to that submission. In addition, pursuant to Rule 37(e)(2) and the Court's pretrial scheduling order, the Court will also order the RMA Defendants to pay into the Court a fine of $10,000. This amount is due within 90 days of the date of this Order.

***

DAVIS V. ELECTRONIC ARTS INC.
No. 10-cv-03328-RS (DMR) 2018 WL 1609289 (N.D. Cal. 2018)

RYU, Magistrate Judge

***

I. BACKGROUND
A. Background

Plaintiffs are retired NFL football players. EA develops and publishes video games. In July 2010, Plaintiffs filed a complaint on behalf of themselves and a proposed class of approximately 6,000 retired NFL players alleging that EA violated Plaintiffs' statutory and common law rights of publicity through unauthorized use of their likenesses in EA's Madden NFL video game franchise. Specifically, Plaintiffs allege that EA releases new Madden NFL video games every year, producing different editions for different video game platforms, and that many editions of the games include "historic teams." According to Plaintiffs, EA misappropriated the likenesses of retired NFL players on these historic teams by describing in each player's profile details such as the player's position, years in the NFL, height, weight, skin tone, and skill level in different aspects of the game. Plaintiffs assert that these characteristics are "consistently identical or so close to the actual player's characteristics that the consumers of the game can readily discern which player is being represented." The only player characteristic that EA changes from the real-life retired NFL players is the jersey number. Plaintiffs allege that EA did not obtain required licenses or authorizations for the use of the putative class members' likenesses.

***

B. EA's Sanctions Motion

In July 2017, EA filed unilateral discovery letter briefs in which it moved to compel Plaintiffs to provide further responses to discovery. The court ordered the parties to meet and confer regarding the disputes set forth in the letters and to file joint letters regarding any remaining disputes. The court held a hearing on September 14, 2017 regarding the issues raised in the parties' subsequent joint letters and granted in part EA's motions to compel further responses to requests for the production of documents ("RFPs"), interrogatories, and requests for admission ("RFA").

The court ordered Plaintiffs to serve amended responses by dates certain. It also ordered Plaintiffs to lodge and serve a privilege log listing documents responsive to RFPs 56-58, and to lodge for in camera review documents responsive to RFP 58 by September 28, 2017.

On September 29, 2017, one day after the court-ordered deadline, Plaintiffs lodged a document entitled, "Plaintiffs' Privilege Log and Statement of No Responsive Documents to EA's RFP No. 58." In the document, Plaintiffs state that they "engaged in a reasonable and diligent search for documents responsive to Request No. 58" and "did not locate any responsive documents." In a footnote, Plaintiffs note the delay in submitting the privilege log, describing a computer problem that "rendered it unusable." EA asserts that Plaintiffs did not send EA a copy of the privilege log until September 30, 2017. Mot. 3. Moreover, EA contends that Plaintiffs' representation that they have no documents responsive to RFP 58 is inconsistent with Plaintiffs' own deposition testimony about communications between the named plaintiffs.

In addition to Plaintiffs' late submission of a privilege log, EA asserts that Plaintiffs failed to comply with other aspects of the court's order. Specifically, on the September 28, 2017 deadline for Plaintiffs to serve responsive documents and amended responses to RFPs, RFAs, and interrogatories, Plaintiffs produced 363 files and emailed to EA their purported responses to EA's interrogatories. However, the document purporting to be Plaintiffs' interrogatory responses was incomplete and unsigned, and appeared to be a two-page excerpt from a longer response. Plaintiffs did not send EA full responses to the interrogatories until October 2, 2017. Plaintiffs also did not serve amended responses to the RFAs by the September 28, 2017 deadline, instead emailing EA with the RFA responses on October 2, 2017.

Notably, Plaintiffs provided their court-ordered discovery responses to EA by email alone, even though EA has not consented to service by email. *** EA also contends that Plaintiffs have never produced documents responsive to RFP 46 or confirmed in writing that they have no such documents.

Most importantly, EA further asserts that Plaintiffs' late responses to the interrogatories and RFAs remain deficient and do not comply with the court's guidance at the September 14, 2017 hearing.

EA now moves for sanctions pursuant to Rule 37, the court's inherent powers, and the Civil Local Rules. They ask for evidentiary sanctions specifically tied to the discovery responses that it contends remain deficient, an order directing Plaintiffs to appear in San Francisco for one-hour depositions at Plaintiffs' expense, and monetary sanctions. Plaintiffs oppose the motion.

II. LEGAL STANDARD

Rule 37 authorizes the imposition of various sanctions for discovery violations, including a party's failure to obey a court order to provide or permit discovery and failure to timely supplement initial disclosures and/or discovery responses pursuant to Rule 26(e). Fed. R. Civ. P. 37(b)(2)(A), (c)(1). Such sanctions may include ordering a party to pay the reasonable expenses, including attorneys' fees, caused by its failure to comply with the order or rule. Fed. R. Civ. P. 37(b)(2)(C), (c)(1)(A). Where a party has violated a discovery order or Rule 26's disclosure requirements, a court may direct that certain facts be taken as established for purposes of the action and/or prohibit the party "from introducing designated matters in evidence." Fed. R. Civ. P. 37(b) (2)(A)(i), (ii), (c)(1)(C). In addition, a party in violation of Rule 26 may also be prohibited from using "information or [a] witness to supply evidence on a motion, at a hearing, or at trial," unless the failure to disclose the information or witness "was substantially justified or is harmless." Fed. R. Civ. P. 37(c)(1).

Additionally, courts are vested with inherent powers arising out of "`the control necessarily vested in courts to manage their own affairs so as to achieve the orderly and expeditious disposition of cases.'" \*\*\* A court's inherent powers include "the `broad discretion to make discovery and evidentiary rulings conducive to the conduct of a fair and orderly trial.'" ***

Finally, Civil Local Rule 1-4 provides that "[f]ailure by counsel or a party to comply with any duly promulgated local rule or any Federal Rule may be a ground for imposition of any authorized sanction."

III. DISCUSSION
A. EA's Entitlement to Sanctions

The court's September 15, 2017 order directed Plaintiffs to serve further responses to certain interrogatories, RFAs, and RFPs, and to lodge and serve a privilege log by September 28, 2017. Plaintiffs do not dispute that they served their responses to the interrogatories and RFAs and their privilege log after the court-ordered deadline. However, they assert that they timely produced approximately 13,000 pages of "reference materials" and 30 gigabytes of data in response to the RFPs, in accordance with the court's order that they produce certain documents by September 28, 2017. Counsel states that "due to technical difficulties caused by a computer failure ... there were issues in the transmission of Plaintiffs' amended responses to the written discovery requests."

Plaintiffs' counsel states that he "made numerous attempts to repairs [sic] the issues while [he] was out of town on September 28 and 29, but was unable to do so." According to Plaintiffs, EA has suffered no prejudice as a result of their failure to timely serve discovery responses, as Plaintiffs provided responses within two business days of the due date. Counsel also states that Plaintiffs believe that their substantive responses are "full and complete and in compliance" with the September 15, 2017 order, and that he has offered to meet and confer with EA regarding the responses if it contends otherwise.

It is undisputed that Plaintiffs violated the September 15, 2017 order by sending untimely amended responses. Generally, in the absence of demonstrable prejudice, a two business-day delay in serving discovery responses without more would not be sanctionable. However, EA's sanctions motion is not based solely on the issue of untimeliness. EA also disputes the sufficiency of the late responses. EA argues that the discovery at issue goes to the heart of many of Plaintiffs' claims, and that Plaintiffs' failure to timely serve full and complete responses have precluded its ability to move for summary judgment.

After reviewing the amended responses, the court agrees that they are deficient and do not comply with its orders at the September 14, 2017 hearing, as detailed below.

1. Interrogatories

***

2. RFAs

***

3. RFPs

a. Plaintiffs' September 28, 2017 Document Production

EA contends that Plaintiffs' September 28, 2017 document production skirts the court's September 15, 2017 order in two ways. First, RFP No. 46 requested all documents related to the Parrish litigation, which involved the licensing of retired football players' images. The court ordered Plaintiffs to produce documents responsive to RFP No. 46, or confirm in writing that Plaintiffs had no such documents. According to EA, Plaintiffs have never produced the requested documents or provided confirmation that no documents are in their possession, custody, or control. Plaintiffs do not contest this assertion.

Second, EA contends that Plaintiffs' discovery responses attempt to circumvent the September 28, 2017 deadline to produce documents. In their amended responses to Interrogatory Nos. 9 and 9.2, Plaintiffs state, "Plaintiffs do not possess a complete set of such documents and reserve the right to supplement their responses to [the interrogatories] with additional information and facts." EA argues that Plaintiffs' "efforts to keep the production door open" after the close of discovery is improper. The court agrees. Plaintiffs' amended responses do not comply with the court's September 15, 2017 order that they produce "all responsive documents which support their claims by [September 28, 2017]." Accordingly, Plaintiffs are prohibited from introducing or relying upon, in a motion, at a hearing, or at trial, any documents that they have not previously produced in discovery, absent substantial justification. See Fed. R. Civ. P. 37(c)(1).

b. RFP No. 58

Finally, EA challenges Plaintiffs' privilege log and representation that they did not locate any documents responsive to RFP No. 58. RFP No. 58 asks for "[a]ll documents related to this litigation or Madden NFL that you have received from or sent to other retired football players, including but not limited to those retired football players who objected at any point to this litigation, to you as a class representative, or to your counsel as class counsel." Plaintiffs' counsel previously represented that there are no responsive communications between Plaintiffs and the putative class members. See id. However, at the September 2017 hearing, Plaintiffs' counsel stated, "I believe there's regular communications between [the named Plaintiffs] ... regarding the case." Similarly, Plaintiff Davis testified at deposition that he typically communicates by email and phone with the other retired players about the lawsuit.

Therefore, EA argues, Plaintiffs' statement that there are no responsive documents appears inconsistent with counsel and Davis's previous representations.

At the January 2018 hearing, given the inconsistencies between counsel and Plaintiffs' statements about communications between Plaintiffs about this litigation or Madden NFL, the court expressed its concern about the adequacy of Plaintiffs' search for responsive documents. The court ordered Plaintiffs' counsel to immediately contact his clients in writing and by telephone to communicate the court's order that they each "search thoroughly all ... email, going all the way back, for communications between [Plaintiffs] and other people who are not lawyers about this case," and ordered counsel to confirm the completeness of the search. The court also ordered a further one-hour deposition of Davis on the subject of his search for responsive documents and communications he had with other retired football players about the case, with the costs of the deposition to be borne by Plaintiffs (not including attorneys' fees).

4. Monetary Sanctions

EA also requests $45,000 in monetary sanctions. The court finds that monetary sanctions are appropriate in this case, in addition to the evidentiary sanctions described above. After the court gave detailed instructions and ordered Plaintiffs to provide amended responses to the discovery at issue, Plaintiffs served untimely, deficient responses, and continued to take indefensible positions that were not substantially justified. This conduct forced EA and the court to continue to expend significant resources to address Plaintiffs' failure to meet its discovery obligations and provide basic discovery. Monetary sanctions are therefore warranted.

The court determines reasonable attorneys' fees according to the lodestar analysis, which multiplies the number of hours reasonably expended on the matter by a reasonable hourly rate. *** The reasonable hourly rate depends on "the prevailing market rates in the relevant community." *** Although the court presumes that the lodestar represents a reasonable fee ***, the court may adjust the award if other factors make it unreasonable. *** The court "should ... exclude from the lodestar fee calculation any hours that were not 'reasonably expended,' such as hours that are excessive, redundant, or otherwise unnecessary." ***

EA submitted supporting evidence in the form of a spreadsheet with itemized billing records covering the period July 5, 2017 through January 11, 2018, the date of the hearing on the motion for sanctions. EA's billing records reflect attorneys' fees totaling $114,866.10, and include work performed by four timekeepers: attorneys R. James Slaughter, R. Adam Lauridsen, Nic Marais, and Chessie Thatcher. Slaughter explains that EA does not seek the full amount of fees, and instead is limiting its request for monetary sanctions to the sum requested in the motion, which is $45,000. EA has excluded time spent by Slaughter as well as time spent after the September 14, 2017 hearing, including time spent on the motion for sanctions. Slaughter explains that the fees requested are also limited to those incurred for work performed by Lauridsen, Marais, and Thatcher "on relevant issues from July 5, 2017 through September 14, 2017," and that EA has further reduced the fees incurred by one quarter, resulting in the total request of $45,000. EA seeks hourly rates of $652.50, $495, and $495 for Lauridsen, Marais, and Thatcher, respectively, for work necessitated by Plaintiffs' discovery misconduct. Lauridsen is a 2005 law school graduate and partner. Marais and Thatcher, who are associates, are each 2011 law school graduates.

The court has carefully reviewed EA's billing records, which are organized chronologically and reflect fees incurred in connection with: 1) preparing the July 2017 unilateral discovery briefs including meeting and conferring; 2) preparing the joint discovery letter briefs heard on September 14, 2017, including preparing for the hearing; and 3) preparing the motion for sanctions, including preparing for the hearing. The billing records do not segregate the fees by task or category, which makes it difficult to evaluate the reasonableness of the time expended, or to calculate precise sums that should be allowed or disallowed. For example, if the time were broken out by category, the court would disallow time spent meeting and conferring prior to the filing of EA's July 2017 unilateral discovery briefs in which they moved to compel, because EA was required to meet and confer with Plaintiffs prior to moving to compel pursuant to Federal Rule of Civil Procedure 37(a)(1) and Local Rule 37-1(a). The court would also disallow time spent drafting the unilateral discovery briefs, because the court declined to rule on those motions before the parties had submitted joint letters on the same disputes. Notwithstanding the problems with EA's billing records, it is clear that EA incurred substantial attorneys' fees in attempting to obtain Plaintiffs' compliance and seeking court intervention. For example, by the court's calculation, attorneys Lauridsen and Marais together billed nearly $20,000 for work on the sanctions motion alone. The court finds that a sanction of $25,000 is justified in these circumstances, and acknowledges that this amount represents a significant discount from the actual attorneys' fees incurred by EA as a result of Plaintiffs' counsel's actions. The court finds that $25,000, coupled with the evidentiary consequences set forth above, are an appropriate sanction here. The entire $25,000 shall be paid by Plaintiffs' counsel to EA within 30 days of the date of this order.

IV. CONCLUSION

For the foregoing reasons, EA's motion for sanctions is granted in part. The court awards attorneys' fees in the amount of $25,000, which must be paid by Plaintiffs' counsel within 30 days of the date of this order.

***

DOCTOR JOHN'S INC. v. CITY OF SIOUX CITY, IOWA
486 F. Supp. 2d 953 (N.D. Iowa 2007)

BENNETT, District Judge

***

A first year law student should have—and most would have—known that a party must retain documents or records that are likely to be relevant in pending litigation. The City's claim that it was simply following state law in destroying key evidence is laughable and frivolous. No state or federal statute, rule, or common law allows a party to destroy critical evidence during the pendency of litigation, and the City policy that permitted destruction of certain documents after a specified period of time certainly did not require destruction of such documents.

Indeed, both state and federal law require just the opposite, retention of evidence potentially relevant to pending or reasonably anticipated litigation. *See, e.g., Dillon v. Nissan Motor Co., Ltd.*, 986 F.2d 263, 268 (8th Cir. 1993) ("[T]he destruction of evidence that a party knew or should have known was relevant to imminent litigation certainly justifies a sanction under the court's inherent power comparable to the Rule 37 sanctions."); *see also Silvestri v. Gen. Motors Corp.*, 271 F.3d 583, 591 (4th Cir. 2001) ("The duty to preserve material evidence arises not only during litigation but also extends to that period before litigation when a party reasonably should know that the evidence may be relevant to anticipated litigation."); *Fujitsu Ltd. v. Federal Express Corp.*, 247 F.3d 423, 436 (2d Cir.2001) ("The obligation to preserve evidence arises that when the party has notice that the evidence is relevant to litigation or when a party should have known that the evidence may be relevant to future litigation."); *Kronisch v. United States*, 150 F.3d 112, 126 (2d Cir. 1998) (the obligation to preserve evidence arises when a party "should have known that the evidence may be relevant to future litigation"); *Zubulake v. UBS Warburg LLC*, 220 F.R.D. 212, 216 (S.D.N.Y. 2003) ("The duty to preserve attached at the time that litigation was reasonably anticipated.").

Thus, the City's failure to preserve the tape recordings of the City Council's closed-session meetings, and the consequential destruction of critical evidence in this case, was clearly and unquestionably improper conduct.

Moreover, the court has the inherent power to sanction such improper conduct subject to review for abuse of discretion. *** A court's inherent power includes the discretionary ability to fashion an appropriate sanction for conduct which abuses the judicial process. *** Thus, the court must determine whether and what sanctions are appropriate for the City's improper destruction of records in this case.

The Eighth Circuit Court of Appeals has recognized that, under a court's inherent power to sanction parties, "a finding of bad faith is not always necessary to the court's exercise of its inherent power to impose sanctions." *** [H]owever, the court concluded that a finding of "bad faith" is required to impose sanctions in the form of an adverse inference instruction or award of attorney fees to the opposing party. *** Consequently, this court will assume that a finding of "bad faith" is required to impose other monetary sanctions.

Here, a substantial monetary sanction against the City is easily justified by the City's outrageous conduct in failing to preserve the key evidence of recordings of closed-session meetings. That conduct was of a kind that "abuses the judicial process" and "defile[s] the temple of justice" because it went to the very heart of the plaintiff's ability to prove the City's motivation in passing the challenged ordinances. Moreover, the circumstances give rise to a powerful inference of intentional destruction indicating a desire to suppress the truth, notwithstanding the City's contention that the records were destroyed pursuant to a document retention policy.

More specifically, as noted above, the contention that the document retention policy mandated by state law excused destruction of the records in question is laughable and frivolous, because that policy plainly did not require the destruction of any documents, and certainly did not authorize the destruction of records pertinent to pending litigation. Moreover, purported adherence to the policy by destroying records that the policy did not mandate for destruction was unreasonable and amounted to bad faith conduct where litigation was pending. Indeed, this case seems to this court to fall well within, not to test the limits of, conduct that constitutes bad faith destruction of documents, where the City had not simply been made aware of the circumstances giving rise to a potential lawsuit, but was in the throes of litigating a lawsuit over the constitutionality of its sex shop ordinances at the time that it destroyed records of closed sessions in which the City Council considered those ordinances. Moreover, while the City destroyed these records, the City went out of its way to provide evidence and even to generate new evidence to try to justify the ordinances long after they were passed, enjoined, and partially struck down. Finally, the recordings of the closed sessions in question here were the only contemporaneous evidence of the motives of the decision makers at the time certain decisions were made, and as such—where the motives of the decision makers were plainly at issue—the evidence was highly relevant to pending litigation.

To the same extent and for essentially the same reasons that the court finds that the City's conduct in destroying the records in question was in "bad faith," the court also finds that such conduct was prejudicial to the plaintiff. Again, the City's motive in passing the challenged ordinances was a critical element of the plaintiffs' proof, and the City's destruction of contemporaneous recordings of closed sessions of City Council meetings in which the ordinances were discussed patently prejudiced the plaintiffs' ability to prove that critical element.

In this case, the court finds that a monetary sanction in the amount of $50,000 is warranted for the City's destruction of plainly relevant records. ***

On the other hand, because of the City's ill-conceived, illegal, and unconstitutional actions in targeting and attempting to trample the plaintiffs First Amendment rights, the taxpayers have already paid dearly, to the tune of over $600,000. No matter how you fry it, that's a ton of Sneaky's chicken. Also, notwithstanding various City Council Members' attempts to save face by claiming that the City would have ultimately prevailed in this litigation—just how those City Council Members became such enlightened, sophisticated, and prophetic federal constitutional scholars remains a prodigious mystery—the City and Doctor John's have worked diligently to reach a settlement. In so doing, both sides engaged in substantial compromise from their equally unreasonable legal positions. Moreover, the City Council has voluntarily and wisely changed its record retention policy to prevent the destruction of such evidence in the future during pending litigation. Thus, having recognized the error of its ways, the City moved swiftly to correct its mistake.

Balancing all of these factors, the court finds that the scales of justice tip ever so slightly in favor of declining to impose sanctions against the City for destruction of relevant records. Any similar litigation misconduct in the future, however, will be dealt with severely, in light of the City's "get out of jail free" card here.

***

Sanctioning Counsels

QUALCOMM INC. V. BROADCOM CORP.
No. 05 Civ. 1958-13, 2008 WL 66932 (S.D. Ca. 2008)

MAJOR, Magistrate Judge

At the conclusion of trial, counsel for Broadcom Corporation ("Broadcom") made an oral motion for sanctions after Qualcomm Incorporated ("Qualcomm") witness Viji Raveendran testified about emails that were not produced to Broadcom during discovery. The trial judge, United States District Court Judge Rudi M. Brewster, referred the motion to this Court ***. On May 29, 2007, Broadcom filed a written motion requesting that the Court sanction Qualcomm for its failure to produce tens of thousands of documents that Broadcom had requested in discovery. ***

After hearing oral argument and reviewing Judge Brewster's Order on Remedy for Finding of Waiver ("Waiver Order") and Order Granting Broadcom Corporation's Motion for Exceptional Case Finding and for an Award of Attorney's Fees (35 U.S.C. § 285) ("Exceptional Case Order"), this Court issued an Order to Show Cause Why Sanctions Should Not be Imposed against Qualcomm's retained attorneys ("OSC"). Specifically, this Court ordered James R. Batchelder, Adam A. Bier, Craig H. Casebeer, David E. Kleinfeld, Kevin K. Leung, Christian E. Mammen, Lee Patch, Kyle Robertson, Victoria Q. Smith, Barry J. Tucker, Jaideep Venkatesan, Bradley A. Waugh, Stanley Young, Roy V. Zemlicka, and any and all other attorneys who signed discovery responses, signed pleadings and pretrial motions, and/or appeared at trial on behalf of Qualcomm to appear and show cause why sanctions should not be imposed for their failure to comply with this Court's orders.

On October 3, 2007, nineteen attorneys filed declarations and briefs responsive to the OSC. Qualcomm filed a brief and four declarations. ***

Having considered all of the written and oral arguments presented and supporting documents submitted, and for the reasons set forth more fully below, the Court GRANTS IN PART and DENIES IN PART Broadcom's motion for sanctions against Qualcomm, REFERS TO THE STATE BAR OF CALIFORNIA six attorneys, and SANCTIONS Qualcomm and six of its retained lawyers.

BACKGROUND

A. The Patent Infringement Case

Qualcomm initiated this patent infringement action on October 14, 2005, alleging Broadcom's infringement of Qualcomm patent numbers 5,452,104 (the "'104 patent'") and 5,576,767 (the "'767 patent'") based on its manufacture, sale, and offers to sell H.264—

compliant products. Qualcomm sought injunctive relief, compensatory damages, attorneys' fees and costs. On December 8, 2006, Broadcom filed a First Amended Answer and Counterclaims in which it alleged (1) a counterclaim that the '104 patent is unenforceable due to inequitable conduct, and (2) an affirmative defense that both patents are unenforceable due to waiver. Broadcom's waiver defense was predicated on Qualcomm's participation in the Joint Video Team ("JVT") in 2002 and early 2003. The JVT is the standards-setting body that created the H.264 standard, which was released in May 2003 and governs video coding.

B. Evidence of Qualcomm's Participation in the JVT

Over the course of discovery, Broadcom sought information concerning Qualcomm's participation in and communications with the JVT through a variety of discovery devices.

***

In response to Broadcom's request for JVT documents, Qualcomm, in a discovery response signed by attorney Kevin Leung, stated "Qualcomm will produce non-privileged relevant and responsive documents describing QUALCOMM's participation in the JVT, if any, which can be located after a reasonable search." Similarly, Qualcomm committed to producing "responsive non-privileged documents that were given to or received from standards-setting body responsible for the ISO/IEC MPEG-4 Part 10 standard, and which concern any Qualcomm participation in setting the ISO/IEC MPEG-4 Part 10 standard." When asked for "the facts and circumstances of any and all communications between Qualcomm and any standards setting body relating to video technology, including ... the JVT ...," Qualcomm responded that it first attended a JVT meeting in December 2003 and that it first submitted a JVT proposal in January 2006. In response to Interrogatory No. 13, Qualcomm stated that it submitted four proposals to the JVT in 2006 but had no earlier involvement. This response included the statement that "Qualcomm's investigation concerning this interrogatory is ongoing and Qualcomm reserves the right to supplement its response to this interrogatory as warranted by its investigation." Kevin Leung signed both of these interrogatory responses.

Qualcomm's responses to Broadcom's Rule 30(b)(6) deposition notices were more troubling. Initially, Qualcomm designated Christine Irvine as the corporation's most knowledgeable person on the issue of Qualcomm's involvement in the JVT. Although attorney Leung prepared Irvine for her deposition, Qualcomm did not search her computer for any relevant documents or emails or provide her with any information to review. Irvine testified falsely that Qualcomm had never been involved in the JVT. Broadcom impeached Irvine with documents showing that Qualcomm had participated in the JVT in late 2003. Qualcomm ultimately agreed to provide another Rule 30(b)(6) witness.

Qualcomm designated Scott Ludwin as the new representative to testify about Qualcomm's knowledge of and involvement in the JVT. Leung prepared and defended Ludwin at his deposition. Qualcomm did not search Ludwin's computer for any relevant documents nor take any other action to prepare him. Ludwin testified falsely that Qualcomm only began participating in the JVT in late 2003, after the H.264 standard had been published. Id. In an effort to impeach him (and extract the truth), Broadcom showed Ludwin a December 2002 email reflector list from the Advanced Video Coding ("AVC") Ad Hoc Group that listed the email address viji@qualcomm.com. Although Ludwin did not recognize the document, Broadcom utilized the document throughout the litigation to argue that Qualcomm had participated in the JVT during the development of the H.264 standard.

As the case progressed, Qualcomm became increasingly aggressive in its argument that it did not participate in the JVT during the time the JVT was creating the H.264 standard. This argument was vital to Qualcomm's success in this litigation because if Qualcomm had participated in the creation of the H.264 standard, it would have been required to identify its patents that reasonably may be essential to the practice of the H.264 standard, including the '104 and '767 patents, and to license them royalty-free or under non-discriminatory, reasonable terms. Thus, participation in the JVT in 2002 or early 2003 during the creation of the H.264 standard would have prohibited Qualcomm from suing companies, including Broadcom, that utilized the H.264 standard. In a nutshell, the issue of whether Qualcomm participated in the JVT in 2002 and early 2003 became crucial to the instant litigation.

C. Trial and Decision Not to Produce avc_ce Emails

Trial commenced on January 9, 2007, and throughout trial, Qualcomm argued that it had not participated in the JVT in 2002 and early 2003 when the H.264 standard was being created. In his opening statement, Qualcomm's lead attorney, James Batchelder, stated:

> Later, in May of '03, the standard is approved and published. And then Qualcomm, in the fall of 2003, it begins to participate not in JVT because it's done. H.264 is approved and published. Qualcomm begins to participate in what are called professional extensions, things that sit on top of the standard, additional improvements.

While preparing Qualcomm witness Viji Raveendran to testify at trial, attorney Adam Bier discovered an August 6, 2002 email to viji@qualcomm.com welcoming her to the avc_ce mailing list. Several days later, on January 14, 2007, Bier and Raveendran searched her laptop computer using the search term "avc_ce" and discovered 21 separate emails, none of which Qualcomm had produced in discovery. The email chains bore several dates in November 2002 and the authors discussed various issues relating to the H.264 standard. While Raveendran was not a named author or recipient, the emails were sent to all members of two JVT email groups (jvt-experts and avc_ce) and Raveendran maintained them on her computer for more than four years. The Qualcomm trial team decided not to produce these newly discovered emails to Broadcom, claiming they were not responsive to Broadcom's discovery requests. The attorneys ignored the fact that the presence of the emails on Raveendran's computer undercut Qualcomm's premier argument that it had not participated in the JVT in 2002. The Qualcomm trial team failed to conduct any investigation to determine whether there were more emails that also had not been produced.

Four days later, during a sidebar discussion, Stanley Young argued against the admission of the December 2002 avc_ce email reflector list, declaring: "Actually, there are no emails—there are no emails—there's no evidence that any email was actually sent to this list. This is just a list of email addresses. There's no evidence of anything being sent." None of the Qualcomm attorneys who were present during the sidebar mentioned the 21 avc_ce emails found on Raveendran's computer a few days earlier.

During Raveendran's direct testimony on January 24th, attorney Lee Patch pointedly did not ask her any questions that would reveal the fact that she had received the 21 emails from the avc_ce mailing list; instead, he asked whether she had "any knowledge of having read" any emails from the avc_ce mailing list. But on cross-examination, Broadcom asked the right question and Raveendran was forced to admit that she had received emails from the avc_ce mailing list. Immediately following this admission, in response to Broadcom's request for the emails, and despite the fact that he had participated in the decision three days earlier not to produce them, Patch told the Court at sidebar:

> [I]t's not clear to me [the emails are] responsive to anything. So that's something that needs to be determined before they would be produced ... I'm talking about whether they were actually requested in discovery ... I'm simply representing that I haven't seen [the emails], and [whether Broadcom requested them] hasn't been determined.

Over the lunch recess that same day, Qualcomm's counsel produced the 21 emails they previously had retrieved from Raveendran's email archive.

On January 26, 2007, the jury returned unanimous verdicts in favor of Broadcom regarding the non-infringement of the '104 and '767 patents, and in favor of Qualcomm regarding the validity and non-obviousness of the same. The jury also returned a unanimous advisory verdict in favor of Broadcom that the '104 patent is unenforceable due to inequitable conduct and the '104 and '767 patents are unenforceable due to waiver.

On March 21, 2007, Judge Brewster found (1) in favor of Qualcomm on Broadcom's inequitable conduct counterclaim regarding the '104 patent, and (2) in favor of Broadcom on Broadcom's waiver defense regarding the '104 and '767 patents. On August 6, 2007, Judge Brewster issued a comprehensive order detailing the appropriate remedy for Qualcomm's waiver. After a thorough overview of the JVT, the JVT's policies and guidelines, and Qualcomm's knowledge of the JVT and evidence of Qualcomm's involvement therein, Judge Brewster found:

by clear and convincing evidence that Qualcomm, its employees, and its witnesses actively organized and/or participated in a plan to profit heavily by (1) wrongfully concealing the patents-in-suit while participating in the JVT and then (2) actively hiding this concealment from the Court, the jury, and opposing counsel during the present litigation.

Judge Brewster further found that Qualcomm's "counsel participated in an organized program of litigation misconduct and concealment throughout discovery, trial, and post-trial before new counsel took over lead role in the case on April 27, 2007." Based on "the totality of the evidence produced both before and after the jury verdict," and in light of these findings, Judge Brewster concluded that "Qualcomm has waived its rights to enforce the '104 and '767 patents and their continuations, continuations-in-part, divisions, reissues, or any other derivatives of either patent." Also on August 6, 2007, Judge Brewster granted Broadcom's Motion for an Award of Attorneys' Fees pursuant to 35 U.S.C. § 285. Judge Brewster found clear and convincing evidence that Qualcomm's litigation misconduct, as set forth in his Waiver Order, justified Qualcomm's payment of all "attorneys' fees, court costs, expert witness fees, travel expenses, and any other litigation costs reasonably incurred by Broadcom" in the defense of this case. On December 11, 2007, Judge Brewster adopted this court's recommendation and ordered Qualcomm to pay Broadcom $ 9,259,985.09 in attorneys' fees and related costs, as well as post-judgment interest on the final fee award of $ 8,568,633.24 at 4.91 percent accruing from August 6, 2007.

D. Qualcomm's Post-Trial Misconduct

Following trial, Qualcomm continued to dispute the relevancy and responsiveness of the 21 Raveendran emails. Qualcomm also resisted Broadcom's efforts to determine the scope of Qualcomm's discovery violation. By letter dated February 16, 2007, Bier told Broadcom "[w]e continue to believe that Qualcomm performed a reasonable search of Qualcomm's documents in response to Broadcom's Requests for Production and that the twenty-one unsolicited emails received by Ms. Raveendran from individuals on the avc_ce reflector are not responsive to any valid discovery obligation or commitment." In response to Broadcom's request that Qualcomm conduct additional searches to determine the scope of Qualcomm's discovery violation, Bier stated in a March 7, 2007 letter, we "believe your negative characterization of Qualcomm's compliance with its discovery obligation to be wholly without merit" but he advised that Qualcomm agreed to search the current and archived emails of five trial witnesses using the requested JVT, avc_ce and H.264 terms. Bier explained that Qualcomm has "not yet commenced these searches, and [does] not yet know the volume of results we will obtain." Throughout the remainder of March 2007, Bier repeatedly declined to update Broadcom on Qualcomm's document search.

But, on April 9, 2007, James Batchelder and Louis Lupin, Qualcomm's General Counsel, submitted correspondence to Judge Brewster in which they admitted Qualcomm had thousands of relevant unproduced documents and that their review of these documents "revealed facts that appear to be inconsistent with certain arguments that [counsel] made on Qualcomm's behalf at trial and in the equitable hearing following trial." Batchelder further apologized "for not having discovered these documents sooner and for asserting positions that [they] would not have taken had [they] known of the existence of these documents."

As of June 29, 2007, Qualcomm had searched the email archives of twenty-one employees and located more than forty-six thousand documents (totaling more than three hundred thousand pages), which had been requested but not produced in discovery. Qualcomm continued to produce additional responsive documents throughout the summer.

DISCUSSION

As summarized above, and as found by Judge Brewster, there is clear and convincing evidence that Qualcomm intentionally engaged in conduct designed to prevent Broadcom from learning that Qualcomm had participated in the JVT during the time period when the H.264 standard was being developed. To this end, Qualcomm withheld tens of thousands of emails showing that it actively participated in the JVT in 2002 and 2003 and then utilized Broadcom's lack of access to the suppressed evidence to repeatedly and falsely aver that there was "no evidence" that it had participated in the JVT prior to September 2003. Qualcomm's misconduct in hiding the emails and electronic documents prevented Broadcom from correcting the false statements and countering the misleading arguments.

A. Legal Standard

The Federal Civil Rules authorize federal courts to impose sanctions on parties and their attorneys who fail to comply with discovery obligations and court orders. Rule 37 authorizes a party to file a motion to compel an opponent to comply with a discovery request or obligation when the opponent fails to do so initially. Fed. R. Civ. P. 37(a). If such a motion is filed, the rule requires the court to award reasonable attorney's fees to the prevailing party unless the court finds the losing party's position was "substantially justified" or other circumstances make such an award unjust. *Id.* Depending upon the circumstances, the court may require the attorney, the client, or both to pay the awarded fees. *Id.* If the court grants a discovery motion and the losing party fails to comply with the order, the court may impose additional sanctions against the party. Fed. R. Civ. P. 37 (b). There is no requirement under this rule that the failure be willful or reckless; "sanctions may be imposed even for negligent failures to provide discovery."

The Federal Rules also provide for sanctions against individual attorneys who are remiss in complying with their discovery obligations:

> Every discovery request, response or objection made by a party ... shall be signed by at least one attorney [and] [t]he signature of the attorney ... constitutes a certification that to the best of the signer's knowledge, information, and belief,

formed after a reasonable inquiry, the request, response, or objection is: consistent with the rules and law, not interposed for an improper purpose, and not unreasonable or unduly burdensome or expensive.

Fed. R. Civ. P. 26 (g)(2) (emphasis added). "[W]hat is reasonable is a matter for the court to decide on the totality of the circumstances." ***

If an attorney makes an incorrect certification without substantial justification, the court must sanction the attorney, party, or both and the sanction may include an award of reasonable attorney's fees. Fed. R. Civ. P. 26 (g) (3). If a party, without substantial justification, fails "to amend a prior response to discovery as required by Rule 26(e)(2)," the court may prevent that party from using that evidence at trial or at a hearing and impose other appropriate sanctions, including the payment of attorney's fees. Fed. R. Civ. P. 37(c)(1). As the Supreme Court confirmed, Rule 26(g), like Rule 11, requires that the court impose "an appropriate sanction" on the attorney; in other words, one which is commensurate with the discovery harm. ***

In addition to this rule-based authority, federal courts have the inherent power to sanction litigants to prevent abuse of the judicial process. All "federal courts are vested with inherent powers enabling them to manage their cases and courtrooms effectively and to ensure obedience to their orders." As a function of this power, courts can dismiss cases in their entirety, bar witnesses, award attorney's fees and assess fines. Sanctions are appropriate in response to "willful disobedience of a court order--or when the losing party has acted in bad faith, vexatiously, wantonly, or for oppressive reasons." When a court order is violated, a district court considering the imposition of sanctions must also examine the risk of prejudice to the complying party and the availability of less drastic sanctions.
***

C. Sanctions

The Court's review of Qualcomm's declarations, the attorneys' declarations, and Judge Brewster's orders leads this Court to the inevitable conclusion that Qualcomm intentionally withheld tens of thousands of decisive documents from its opponent in an effort to win this case and gain a strategic business advantage over Broadcom. Qualcomm could not have achieved this goal without some type of assistance or deliberate ignorance from its retained attorneys. Accordingly, the Court concludes it must sanction both Qualcomm and some of its retained attorneys.
***

2. Attorneys' Misconduct

The next question is what, if any, role did Qualcomm's retained lawyers play in withholding the documents? The Court envisions four scenarios. First, Qualcomm intentionally hid the documents from its retained lawyers and did so so effectively that the lawyers did not know or suspect that the suppressed documents existed. Second, the retained lawyers failed to discover the intentionally hidden documents or suspect their existence due to their complete ineptitude and disorganization. Third, Qualcomm shared the damaging documents with its retained lawyers (or at least some of them) and the knowledgeable lawyers worked with Qualcomm to hide the documents and all evidence of Qualcomm's early involvement in the JVT. Or, fourth, while Qualcomm did not tell the retained lawyers about the damaging documents and evidence, the lawyers suspected there was additional evidence or information but chose to ignore the evidence and warning signs and accept Qualcomm's incredible assertions regarding the adequacy of the document search and witness investigation.

Given the impressive education and extensive experience of Qualcomm's retained lawyers (see exhibit A), the Court rejects the first and second possibilities. It is inconceivable that these talented, well-educated, and experienced lawyers failed to discover through their interactions with Qualcomm any facts or issues that caused (or should have caused) them to question the sufficiency of Qualcomm's document search and production. Qualcomm did not fail to produce a document or two; it withheld over 46,000 critical documents that extinguished Qualcomm's primary argument of non-participation in the JVT. In addition, the suppressed documents did not belong to one employee, or a couple of employees who had since left the company; they belonged to (or were shared with) numerous, current Qualcomm employees, several of whom testified (falsely) at trial and in depositions. Given the volume and importance of the withheld documents, the number of involved Qualcomm employees, and the numerous warning flags, the Court finds it unbelievable that the retained attorneys did not know or suspect that Qualcomm had not conducted an adequate search for documents.

The Court finds no direct evidence establishing option three. Neither party nor the attorneys have presented evidence that Qualcomm told one or more of its retained attorneys about the damaging emails or that an attorney learned about the emails and that the knowledgeable attorney(s) then helped Qualcomm hide the emails. While knowledge may be inferred from the attorneys' conduct, evidence on this issue is limited due to Qualcomm's assertion of the attorney-client privilege.

Thus, the Court finds it likely that some variation of option four occurred; that is, one or more of the retained lawyers chose not to look in the correct locations for the correct documents, to accept the unsubstantiated assurances of an important client that its search was sufficient, to ignore the warning signs that the document search and production were inadequate, not to press Qualcomm employees for the truth, and/or to encourage employees to provide the information (or lack of information) that Qualcomm needed to assert its non-participation argument and to succeed in this lawsuit. These choices enabled Qualcomm to withhold hundreds of thousands of pages of relevant discovery and to assert numerous false and misleading arguments to the court and jury. This conduct warrants the imposition of sanctions.

a. Identity of Sanctioned Attorneys

The Court finds that each of the following attorneys contributed to Qualcomm's monumental discovery violation and is personally responsible: James Batchelder, Adam Bier, Kevin Leung, Christopher Mammen, Lee Patch, and Stanley Young ("Sanctioned Attorneys").

Attorneys Leung, Mammen and Batchelder are responsible for the initial discovery failure because they handled or supervised Qualcomm's discovery responses and production of documents. The Federal Rules impose an affirmative duty upon lawyers to engage in discovery in a responsible manner and to conduct a "reasonable inquiry" to determine whether discovery responses are sufficient and proper. Fed. R. Civ. P. 26(g); Fed. R. Civ. P. 26 Advisory Committee Notes (1983 Amendment). In the instant case, a reasonable inquiry should have included searches using fundamental terms such as JVT, avc_ce or H.264, on the computers belonging to knowledgeable people such as Raveendran, Irvine and Ludwin. As the post-trial investigation confirmed, such a reasonable search would have revealed the suppressed documents. Had Leung, Mammen, Batchelder, or any of the other attorneys insisted on reviewing Qualcomm's records regarding the locations searched and terms utilized, they would have discovered the inadequacy of the search and the suppressed documents. 10Link to the text of the note Similarly, Leung's difficulties with the Rule 30(b)(6) witnesses, Irvine and Ludwin, should have alerted him (and the supervising or senior attorneys) to the inadequacy of Qualcomm's document production and to the fact that they needed to review whose computers and databases had been searched and for what. Accordingly, the Court finds that the totality of the circumstances establishes that Leung, Mammen and Batchelder did not make a reasonable inquiry into Qualcomm's discovery search and production and their conduct contributed to the discovery violation.

Attorneys Bier, Mammen and Patch are responsible for the discovery violation because they also did not perform a reasonable inquiry to determine whether Qualcomm had complied with its discovery obligations. When Bier reviewed the August 6, 2002 email welcoming Raveendran to the avc_ce email group, he knew or should have known that it contradicted Qualcomm's trial arguments and he had an obligation to verify that it had been produced in discovery or to immediately produce it. If Bier, as a junior lawyer, lacked the experience to recognize the significance of the document, then a more senior or knowledgeable attorney should have assisted him. To the extent that Patch was supervising Bier in this endeavor, Patch certainly knew or should have recognized the importance of the document from his involvement in Qualcomm's motion practice and trial strategy sessions.

Similarly, when Bier found the 21 emails on Raveendran's computer that had not been produced in discovery, he took the appropriate action and informed his supervisors, Mammen and Patch. Patch discussed the discovery and production issue with Young and Batchelder. While all of these attorneys' assert that there was a plausible argument that Broadcom did not request these documents, only Bier and Mammen actually read the emails. Moreover, all of the attorneys missed the critical inquiry: was Qualcomm's document search adequate? If these 21 emails were not discovered during Qualcomm's document search, how many more might exist? The answer, obviously, was tens of thousands. If Bier, Mammen, Patch, Young or Batchelder had conducted a reasonable inquiry after the discovery of the 21 Raveendran emails, they would have discovered the inadequacy of Qualcomm's search and the suppressed documents. And, these experienced attorneys should have realized that the presence on Raveendran's computer of 21 JVT/avc_ce emails from 2002 contradicted Qualcomm's numerous arguments that it had not participated in the JVT during that same time period. This fact, alone, should have prompted the attorneys to immediately produce the emails and to conduct a comprehensive document search.

Finally, attorneys Young, Patch, and Batchelder bear responsibility for the discovery failure because they did not conduct a reasonable inquiry into Qualcomm's discovery production before making specific factual and legal arguments to the court. Young decided that Qualcomm should file a motion for summary adjudication premised on the fact that Qualcomm had not participated in the JVT until after the H.264 standard was adopted in May 2003. Given that non-participation was vital to the motion, Young had a duty to conduct a reasonable inquiry into whether that fact was true. And, again, had Young conducted such a search, he would have discovered the inadequacy of Qualcomm's document search and production and learned that his argument was false. Similarly, Young had a duty to conduct a reasonable inquiry into the accuracy of his statement before affirmatively telling the court that no emails were sent to Raveendran from the avc_ce email group. Young also did not conduct a reasonable (or any) inquiry during the following days before he approved the factually incorrect JMOL. A reasonable investigation would have prevented the false filing.

Patch was an integral part of the trial team-familiar with Qualcomm's arguments, theories and strategies. He knew on January 14th that 21 avc_ce emails had been discovered on Raveendran's computer. Without reading or reviewing the emails, Patch participated in the decision not to produce them. Several days later, Patch carefully tailored his questions to ensure that Raveendran did not testify about the unproduced emails. And, after Broadcom stumbled into the email testimony, Patch affirmatively misled the Court by claiming that he did not know whether the emails were responsive to Broadcom's discovery requests. This conduct is unacceptable and, considering the totality of the circumstances, it is unrealistic to think that Patch did not know or believe that Qualcomm's document search was inadequate and that Qualcomm possessed numerous, similar and unproduced documents.

Batchelder also is responsible because he was the lead trial attorney and, as such, he was most familiar with Qualcomm's important arguments and witnesses. Batchelder stated in his opening statement that Qualcomm had not participated in the JVT before late 2003. Despite this statement and his complete knowledge of Qualcomm's legal theories, Batchelder did not take any action when he was informed that JVT documents that Qualcomm had not produced in discovery were found on Raveendran's computer. He did not read the emails, ask about their substance, nor inquire as to why they were not located during discovery. And, he stood mute when four days later, Young falsely stated that no emails had been sent to Raveendran from the avc_ce email group. Finally, all of the pleadings containing the lie that Qualcomm had not participated in the JVT in 2002 or early 2003 were sent to Batchelder for review and he approved or ignored all of them. [3Link to the text of the note] The totality of the circumstances, including all of the previously-discussed warning signs, demanded that Batchelder conduct an investigation to verify the adequacy of Qualcomm's document search and production. His failure to do so enabled Qualcomm to withhold the documents.

For all of these reasons, the Court finds that these attorneys did not conduct a reasonable inquiry into the adequacy of Qualcomm's document search and production and, accordingly, they are responsible, along with Qualcomm, for the monumental discovery violation.

b. Identity of Non-Sanctioned Attorneys

Based upon the Court's review of the submitted declarations, the Court finds that the following attorneys do not bear any individual responsibility for the discovery violation and, on that basis, declines to sanction them: Ruchika Agrawal, Howard Loo, William Nelson, Ryan Scher, Bradley Waugh, David Kleinfeld, Barry Tucker, Heidi Gutierrez, Victoria Smith, Roy Zemlicka, Craig Casebeer, Jaideep Venkatesan, and Kyle Robertson.

The Court declines to sanction attorneys Agrawal, Loo, Nelson, Scher, Waugh and Guiterrez because they did not significantly participate in the preparation or prosecution of the instant case or primarily participated in aspects of the case unrelated to those at issue in this Order and Judge Brewster's Waiver Order and Exceptional Case Order.

The Court also declines to sanction Heller Ehrman attorneys Kleinfeld and Tucker. These attorneys primarily monitored the instant case for its impact on separate Qualcomm/Broadcom litigation. However, for logistical reasons, both attorneys signed as local counsel pleadings that contained false statements relating to Qulacomm's non-participation in the JVT. Given the facts of this case as set forth above and in the declarations, the limitations provided by the referral, and the totality of the circumstances, the Court finds that it was reasonable for these attorneys to sign the pleadings, relying on the work of other attorneys more actively involved in the litigation.

***

Case dismissal

LAWRENCE V. CITY OF NEW YORK
No. 15cv8947 WL 3611963 (S.D.N.Y. 2018)

PAULEY, Senior District Judge

***

BACKGROUND

This Opinion & Order showcases the importance of verifying a client's representations. In November 2015, Leventhal filed this civil rights action on behalf of Lawrence. The complaint alleged that in August 2014, NYPD officers entered Lawrence's home without a warrant, pushed her to the floor, damaged her property, and stole more than $1,000 in cash.

In September 2016, Lawrence provided photographs that she claimed depicted the condition of her apartment several days after the incident. Leventhal accepted his client's representations and after reviewing the photographs, saved them to a PDF, Bates-stamped them, and produced them to Defendants. At that time, Leventhal was unfamiliar with electronically stored metadata and "did not doubt [that] the photographs were taken contemporaneously with the occurrence of the damage."

During a December 2016 deposition, Lawrence testified that her son or a friend took the photographs two days after the incident. In a subsequent deposition in April 2017, Lawrence asserted that she had taken most of the pictures, that her son had taken a few, and that none of them were taken by the previously described friend. At that juncture, Leventhal believed his client had memory problems but did not believe she was testifying falsely. In view of Lawrence's conflicting testimony, Defendants requested the smartphones which Lawrence claimed were used to take the photos. In August 2017, Leventhal objected, but agreed to produce the photographs' native files, which included metadata.

When Defendants checked the photographs' metadata, they learned that 67 of the 70 photographs had been taken in September 2016--two years after the incident and immediately before Lawrence provided them to Leventhal. In September 2017, Defendants sent a Rule 11 safe-harbor letter to Leventhal.

In October 2017, Leventhal moved to withdraw as counsel, asserting that "based upon facts of which [he] was not aware ... [he] hereby disavow[ed] all prior statements made [regarding] the photographs." At an October 2017 conference, Leventhal's ethics counsel represented that at the time of production, Leventhal "did not believe or have reason to believe that there was any question about the date or provenance of the photographs." Ethics counsel also stated that other events now compelled Leventhal to withdraw. While Leventhal's motion was pending, Lawrence terminated Leventhal's representation.

In December 2017, this Court granted Leventhal's motion to withdraw and afforded Lawrence two months to secure new counsel. Lawrence was unable to engage a new lawyer and appeared pro se. By letter dated February 20, 2018, Lawrence claimed she provided the photographs to her attorney by accident because she had an eye infection. At a status conference, this Court advised Lawrence that "[t]he issue here is whether the photographs that you submitted actually depicted the damages at the time or whether it was all staged by you and then given to your attorney." Further, this Court informed Lawrence that "if evidence comes out on [Defendants'] motion that in fact this is all fabricated, at a minimum, [the Court] may be duty bound to refer it to the United States attorney," that her case could be dismissed, and that she "may be subject to substantial monetary penalties." Lawrence elected to proceed.

In the wake of Defendants' motion for sanctions, Lawrence forwarded numerous documents to this Court and attributed her production of the photographs to mental illness. She also claims that her medications prevented her from testifying truthfully during depositions. Lawrence's medical records evince a history of mental illness. Most recently, Lawrence amended her deposition testimony and now contends that the photographs were taken by her grandchild for a book report.

LEGAL STANDARD

The Federal Rules of Civil Procedure provide for sanctions based on litigation misconduct. Courts also "possess certain inherent powers, not conferred by rule or statute ... to fashion an appropriate sanction for conduct which abuses the judicial process." *** Courts have the inherent power to correct a fraud upon the court. Fraud upon the court exists where a litigant attempts to "improperly influence[] the trier" of fact, "lies to the court and h[er] adversary intentionally, repeatedly, and about issues that are central to the truth finding process," or "knowingly submit[s] fraudulent documents to the Court." *** A district court has broad discretion in fashioning sanctions under its "inherent power to manage its own affairs." ***

Discovery sanctions serve broad purposes, including: (1) to ensure "that a party will not benefit from its own failure to comply"; (2) "as specific deterrents [to] seek compliance with the particular order issued"; and (3) "as a general deterrent effect on the case at hand and on other litigation." *** In determining sanctions based on discovery misconduct, courts consider willfulness, duration of non-compliance, whether the non-compliant party had been warned of the consequences of non-compliance, and the efficacy of lesser sanctions. ***

"[D]ismissal is a harsh remedy, not to be utilized without a careful weighing of its appropriateness," and should only be employed when a court is "sure of the impotence of lesser sanctions." *** Nonetheless, "when a party lies to the court and h[er] adversary intentionally, repeatedly, and about issues that are central to the truth-finding process, it can

fairly be said that [s]he has forfeited h[er] right to have h[er] claim decided on the merits."
***

DISCUSSION

I. Rule 11

Rule 11 states that by signing a pleading, motion, or other paper, an attorney certifies that "to the best of the person's knowledge, information, and belief, formed after an inquiry reasonable under the circumstances," the document is submitted for a proper purpose, the legal claims are nonfrivolous, and "the factual contentions have evidentiary support." Fed. R. Civ. P. 11(b). "Rule 11 imposes a duty on every attorney to conduct a reasonable pre-filing inquiry into the evidentiary and factual support for [a] claim ...." *** It serves "to deter baseless filings." ***

A pleading violates Rule 11 where "a competent attorney could not form a reasonable belief that the pleading is well grounded in fact and is warranted by existing law." *** An attorney also has an obligation not to "reaffirm[] to the court and advocat[e] positions contained in [prior] pleadings and motions after learning that they cease to have merit." Fed. R. Civ. P. 11 advisory committee's note. Rule 11 "does not apply to disclosures and discovery requests, responses, objections, and motions ...." Fed R. Civ. P. 11(d).

In enforcing Rule 11, a court may "impose an appropriate sanction on any attorney, law firm, or party that violated the rule." Fed. R. Civ. P. 11(c)(1). A represented party may be sanctioned if she "had actual knowledge that the filing of the papers constituted wrongful conduct, e.g. the papers made false statements or were filed for an improper purpose." *** A court "resolves all doubts in favor of the signer." *** "Courts impose Rule 11 sanctions with discretion and caution." ***

Defendants attempt to cast what occurred here as conduct sanctionable under Rule 11. They contend that Leventhal failed to adequately investigate Lawrence's claims before filing this action and failed to drop those claims after learning that Lawrence had provided fraudulent photographs and given false testimony. But Rule 11 does not apply to this situation. Leventhal produced documents in discovery that turned out to be fraudulent. Defendants' sanctions motion rests entirely on that production. "These incidents are not sanctionable under Rule 11 because they arose in the context of discovery and thus are not within the scope of Rule 11." ***

Further, the record does not support Defendants' contention that it was unreasonable for Leventhal to bring this action. "[U]nder Rule 11, an attorney has an affirmative duty to make reasonable inquiry into the facts and the law." *** Here, Leventhal made such an inquiry. Although Defendants allege the photographs constitute the only evidence of Lawrence's claims, Leventhal also: (1) requested Lawrence's medical records, which showed that she sought treatment for difficulty sleeping, nightmares, anxiety, depression, and weight loss from the alleged incident, (2) reviewed Civilian Complaint Review Board records regarding the incident and certain police officers' prior conduct, and (3) interviewed both Lawrence and her son. This investigation was sufficient. "[A]n attorney is entitled to rely on the objectively reasonable representations of the client." ***

Accordingly, the record does not show that Leventhal failed to perform "an inquiry reasonable under the circumstances," Fed. R. Civ. P. 11(b), nor that Lawrence's claims were "utterly lacking in support," ***

This Court recognizes that the date the photographs were created became apparent only after Leventhal filed suit and Lawrence testified. "When a district court examines the sufficiency of the investigation of facts and law, it is expected to avoid the wisdom of hindsight ...." *** Even if Lawrence contradicted herself in her deposition, "submission of inconsistent statements alone is insufficient to establish that a statement was false, or was filed for an improper purpose." *** Based on the evidence supporting Lawrence's claims, including the 911 call produced in discovery, this Court cannot conclude that Leventhal had a duty to withdraw Lawrence's claims.

For similar reasons, Rule 11 does not apply to Lawrence's conduct. "Where it is the party ... and not the attorney, that is the target of Rule 11 motion, a subjective good faith test applies." *** The evidence demonstrates that Lawrence or someone on her behalf staged photographs and that she represented them to be accurate depictions of her apartment at the time of the incident. But that does not compel the conclusion that the August 2014 incident did not in fact occur. Thus, this Court cannot conclude that Lawrence "misl[ed] [her] attorney as to ... the purpose of a lawsuit." *** While Lawrence committed egregious discovery misconduct, Rule 11 sanctions are unavailable.

II. Rule 26

Rule 26 provides a parallel to Rule 11 for productions made in discovery. Under Rule 26(g), an attorney's signature on a discovery response or objection certifies that after reasonable inquiry, the production is: (1) "complete and correct as of the time it is made"; (2) consistent with existing law; (3) "not interposed for any improper purpose"; and (4) not unduly burdensome. Fed. R. Civ. P. 26(g)(1). Violation "without substantial justification" requires a court to "impose an appropriate sanction on the signer, the party on whose behalf the signer was acting, or both." Fed. R. Civ. P. 26(g)(3). "Rule 26(g) imposes on counsel an affirmative duty to engage in pretrial discovery responsibly" and to "stop and think about the legitimacy of a discovery request, a response thereto, or an objection." ***

In determining sanctions under Rule 26, a court considers whether the attorney's inquiry before a production "was objectively reasonable under the circumstances." *** "In making her inquiry, an attorney may rely, when appropriate, on representations by her client or by other attorneys." *** "Ultimately, what is reasonable is a matter for the court to decide on the totality of the circumstances." Fed. R. Civ. P. 26 advisory committee's note.

Defendants argue that Lawrence provided the photos nearly a year after this litigation commenced without ever mentioning them previously. However, as Leventhal explained in camera, Lawrence told him about photographs depicting damage to her apartment from the very beginning, but claimed that she was not "tech-savvy" and did not know how to reproduce them. Leventhal repeatedly attempted to gain access to the devices containing the photos. Further, some of the photographs appear to show damage to Lawrence's apartment consistent with her testimony, including a mattress and couch torn open, and damage to other items. Therefore, a reasonable lawyer would not have doubted that they showed what Lawrence claimed. Finally, Leventhal explains that at the time he produced the photos he was unfamiliar with the process for checking a digital photograph's metadata, which entails right-clicking it and navigating to its properties.

Based on these facts, Leventhal's production of the photos may have been careless, but was not objectively unreasonable. *** On the other hand, it is clear that Lawrence, or someone acting on her behalf, created these photographs to bolster her claims, and then she falsely testified about them. Accordingly, sanctions under Rule 26 are appropriate. *See* Fed. R. Civ. P. 26(g)(3) (sanctions under Rule 26 apply to both the signer and "the party on whose behalf the signer was acting"). But as described below, Lawrence's conduct is more properly construed as an attempted fraud on this Court, and is therefore analyzed under that standard.

III. Rule 37

Federal Rule of Civil Procedure 37 governs a party's failure to obey a discovery order or comply with discovery requests. *See* Fed. R. Civ. P. 37. It largely functions to "ensure that a party will not be able to profit from its own failure to comply" and "to secure compliance with the particular order at hand." *** In determining sanctions under Rule 37, a court considers "willfulness or bad faith of the noncompliant party; (b) the history, if any, of noncompliance; (c) the effectiveness of lesser sanctions; (d) whether the noncompliant party has been warned about the possibility of sanctions; (e) the client's complicity; and (f) prejudice to the moving party." ***

Rule 37 does not apply to this situation. This rule "provides generally for sanctions against parties or persons unjustifiably resisting discovery." Fed. R. Civ. P. 37 advisory committee's note ***. Here, Leventhal did not fail to comply with discovery orders, to supplement an earlier response, or to preserve electronically stored information. Further, there is no showing that his actions were willful or part of a pattern of noncompliance. "Willful non-compliance is routinely found ... where a party has repeatedly failed to produce documents in violation of the district court's orders." *** Instead, Leventhal was unaware of Lawrence's actions and took corrective action after learning that the photographs were taken two years later. Defendants have not shown that Leventhal handled his discovery obligations in an unethical or willfully non-compliant manner.

Defendants also contend that Leventhal should have corrected the record before seeking leave to withdraw. But Leventhal spoke numerous times with Lawrence to understand what had happened and engaged ethics counsel to advise him. Leventhal also disavowed his prior representations concerning the photographs. It appears that Leventhal's need to withdraw precluded him from taking certain steps such as voluntarily dismissing some or all of Lawrence's claims.

IV. Inherent Power of Court

"Beyond the powers conferred expressly by rule and statute, a federal court has inherent power to sanction a party for bad faith litigation conduct." ***

"Our judicial system generally relies on litigants to tell the truth ...." *** Therefore, "[f]raud upon the court ... seriously affects the integrity of the normal process of adjudication." *** "[T]ampering with the administration of justice ... involves far more than an injury to a single litigant. It is a wrong against the institutions set up to protect and safeguard the public, institutions in which fraud cannot complacently be tolerated consistently with the good order of society." ***

A litigant must prove fraud upon the court by clear and convincing evidence. *** Defendants must establish the opposing party "has acted knowingly in an attempt to hinder the fact finder's fair adjudication of the case." *** A court also considers (1) if the misconduct was performed intentionally and in bad faith; (2) whether it prejudiced the injured party; (3) if there is a pattern of misbehavior; (4) whether and when the misconduct was corrected; and (5) whether it is likely to continue. ***

The creation of staged photos was the beginning of a sustained effort by Lawrence to mislead Defendants and this Court. A brief recapitulation is necessary. Lawrence told Leventhal early on that she had photos of her apartment on a cellphone. In September 2016, she provided photos to her attorney and represented to him that they were taken days after the incident. In her December 2016 deposition, she testified that the photos were taken by her son or a friend days after the incident. She also testified that she was not suffering from any mental condition at the time of her deposition. In April 2017, Lawrence reiterated that the photos were taken immediately after the incident, but now claimed to have taken most of them herself. It was only after Defendants discovered the metadata that Lawrence acknowledged that the photos were taken in 2016.

Lawrence's attempts to explain the photographs and her deposition testimony continue a pattern of evasion and untruths. First, she asserted the production was caused by conjunctivitis, and presented her prescription for eye drops. Lawrence's conjunctivitis does not explain the creation of 67 doctored photographs or her false statements in two depositions. Only after this Court rejected that explanation did Lawrence contend that the production was due to mental illness. However, after providing that explanation, Lawrence submitted further documents in which she amended her deposition testimony and now contends that the photos were taken by her grandson as part of a school project.

These shifting explanations are as troubling as the photographs themselves. This Court does not know how it can credit any of Lawrence's explanations. In considering the factors relevant to sanctions, most, if not all, support a harsh sanction. First, it is clear that the photos were intentionally staged. Photographs do not create themselves, and Lawrence's belated attempts to explain them are not worthy of belief. From this Court's review of the photographs, it is clear that Lawrence or someone on her behalf intentionally staged scenes of her apartment, including ripped furniture, a couch turned over, a broken air-conditioner, and disassembled stereos. Whether Lawrence personally created the photographs or not, she embraced them and willingly testified that they accurately depicted the condition of her apartment as of August 2014. Second, her actions prejudiced Defendants. Third, her pattern of misbehavior appears likely to continue. ***

Further, this Court warned Lawrence of the repercussions of her actions. In December 2017, it informed her that "this is a very serious and grave matter with respect to the production of th[e] photographs, the circumstances surrounding the creation of th[e] photographs, and related matters." Again, in February, this Court told her that if the photos were staged by her, it would be a "very, very serious charge."

Finally, Lawrence's "misconduct did not concern a peripheral or an incidental matter[.] ... Rather, [it] goes to the heart of the case by making it apparent that defendants can rely only on fraudulent or defective records ...." *** "[A]ll litigants, including pro ses, have an obligation to comply with court orders. When they flout that obligation, they, like all litigants, must suffer the consequences of their actions." ***

Lawrence's deceptive conduct and shifting excuses have completely undermined her credibility. This Court has no way of knowing what story Lawrence would offer if this case went to trial. *** Any sanction less than dismissal, "such as a jury instruction, would be ineffective." *** And "merely excluding the fabricated evidence would not only fail to address ... [P]laintiff's other misconduct ... but would also send the [P]laintiff, and future litigants like [her], the message that they have everything to gain, and nothing to lose, by continuing to submit fabricated evidence." ***

This Court has considered Lawrence's explanation that the photographs were produced because of her mental illness. Courts consider mental illness as a factor in determining sanctions. *** Some courts have chosen to lessen sanctions based on a litigant's mental illness. *** Others have dismissed a case despite a litigant's mental illness. ***

Lawrence's mental illness, while a mitigating factor, does not excuse her actions. Memory lapse does not explain manufactured exhibits and perjured testimony. This Court cautioned Lawrence that she needed to provide a credible explanation for her actions. She has failed to do so. As this Court stated in February, Lawrence may not be a lawyer, but she "know[s] the difference between giving honest testimony and providing honest exhibits as opposed to giving perjured testimony and manufacturing exhibits ... [b]ecause that's the difference between right and wrong."

Whether dismissal is appropriate as a sanction is within the trial court's discretion. *** Although "dismissal is a harsh sanction to be used only in extreme situations ... [w]hen faced with a fraud upon the court ... such a[] powerful sanction is entirely appropriate." *** Lawrence's conduct "requires that the policy favoring adjudication on the merits yield to the need to preserve the integrity of the courts." *** Accordingly, this case is dismissed.

***

ABBOTT LABS. V. ADELPHIA SUPPLY USA
No. 15 CV 5826 2019 WL 3281324 (E.D.N.Y. 2019)

BLOOM, Magistrate Judge

This motion presents a cautionary tale about how not to conduct discovery in federal court. ***

On October 5, 2015, plaintiffs filed the instant trademark diversion action against hundreds of defendants, including pharmacies, distributors, importers, and online sellers alleging defendants had violated Abbott's rights by selling the international version of Abbott's FreeStyle Diabetes test strips in the On January 13, 2017, I held the first of many conferences with the parties to address various discovery issues. On January 17, 2017, I ordered all defendants to "review all formal and informal communications regarding defendants' purchases and sales of International FreeStyle test strips in 2014, including emails, text messages, purchase orders, delivery invoices, and check/wire transfers." On January 25, 2017, counsel for H&H wrote to the Court and stated that H&H "has conducted a review of all formal and information [sic] communications regarding the purchase and sale of International FreeStyle test strips for the year of 2014 ... Individual Defendants Howard Goldman and Lori Goldman do not have any responsive documents. As to H&H, there are approximately 6,000 responsive documents[.]"

On January 27, 2017, I held a telephone conference. In light of H&H's claim that producing more than one year of responsive documents would be unduly burdensome, I directed H&H to produce only the 2014 documents due to the high number of responsive documents they had identified. Only H&H was granted this modification of the Court's order to produce. All other defendants produced responsive documents for the years 2013-2015 by February 10, 2017 as the Court directed.

H&H's production was coordinated by Andrew Sweet, H&H's General Manager, and Jason Yert, H&H's counsel from Kerr, Russell and Webber PLC ("Kerr Russell").2Link to the text of the note On February 10, 2017, defendants produced 314 emails and a separate collection of invoices. On March 23, 2017, plaintiffs raised objections to defendants' February 10, 2017 production, including that the documents defendants produced were printed "in hard copy, scanning them all together, and producing them as a single, 1941-page PDF file." On March 24, 2017, the Court ordered defendants to "produce an electronic copy of the 2014 emails (1,941 pages)" including metadata. The H&H defendants electronically produced 4,074 pages of responsive documents on April 5, 2017.

On May 25, 2017, plaintiffs commenced a counterfeiting action against the H&H defendants, alleging that defendants were selling International FreeStyle test strips repackaged into counterfeit U.S. boxes. The Court entered a seizure order in the new action on May 24, 2017 authorizing Abbott to seize, *inter alia*, a copy of H&H's email server. Once plaintiffs had seized H&H's email server, plaintiffs had the proverbial smoking gun and raised its concerns anew that defendants had failed to comply with the Court's Order to produce responsive documents in the instant action. On July 12, 2017, the Court ordered the H&H defendants to "re-run the document search outlined in the Court's January 17 and January 21 Orders," "produce the documents from the re-run search to Abbott," and to produce "an affidavit of someone with personal knowledge" regarding alleged technical errors that affected the production. Pursuant to the Court's July 12, 2017 Order to re-run the search, The H&H defendants produced 3,569 responsive documents.

DISCUSSION

I. The Court's Inherent Power

Plaintiffs move for case ending sanctions under Federal Rule of Civil Procedure 37 and invoke the Court's inherent power to hold defendants in default for perpetrating a fraud upon the Court. Plaintiffs move to strike the H&H defendants' pleadings, to enter a default judgment against them, and for an order directing defendants to pay plaintiffs' attorney's fees and costs, for investigating and litigating defendants' discovery fraud. ***

II. Fraud upon the Court

A fraud upon the court occurs where it is established by clear and convincing evidence "that a party has set in motion some unconscionable scheme calculated to interfere with the judicial system's ability impartially to adjudicate a matter by ... unfairly hampering the presentation of the opposing party's claim or defense." ***

The basic tenet of a fraud upon the court is "when a party lies to the court and his adversary intentionally, repeatedly, and about issues that are central to the truth-finding process." ***

a. Defendants' Failure to Comply with the Court's Orders to Produce

The H&H defendants originally represented to the Court that for the year of 2014 there were "approximately 6,000 responsive documents." The H&H defendants then clarified at the January 27, 2017 conference that there were "6,000 pages," not 6,000 responsive documents. Given this large number, the Court modified its order issued to all defendants and directed the H&H defendants to produce documents only for the year 2014. However, on February 10, 2017, the H&H defendants produced 314 documents amounting to 2,034 pages. According to defendants, the original Sweet search produced 1,540 emails (or 3,296 documents including attachments). After the seizure order in *Abbott II*, and after plaintiffs again raised issues regarding defendants' original production, the Court ordered the H&H defendants to re-run the original search. Thereafter, the H&H defendants produced 3,569 documents.

Cooley, counsel for H&H at the time, retained the services of an outside vendor Transperfect, to re-run the original search. The H&H defendants filed a declaration from

Joseph Pochron, Director in the Forensic Technology and Consulting Division at Transperfect, which states that H&H utilized an email archiving system called Barracuda and that there are two types of Barracuda accounts, Administrator and Auditor. Pochron's declaration states that the H&H employee who ran the original search, Andrew Sweet, H&H's general manager, used the Auditor account to run the original search ("Sweet search"). When Mr. Pochron replicated the Sweet search using the Auditor account, he obtained 1,540 responsive emails. When Mr. Pochron replicated the Sweet search using the Administrator account, he obtained 1,737 responsive emails. Id. Thus, Mr. Pochron attests that 197 messages were not viewable to Mr. Sweet when the original production was made. Plaintiffs state that they have excluded those 197 messages, deemed technical errors, from their instant motion for sanctions. However, even when those 197 messages are excluded, defendants' numbers do not add up. In fact, H&H has repeatedly given plaintiffs and the Court different numbers that do not add up.

Moreover, plaintiffs argue that the H&H defendants purposely used search terms designed to fail, such as "International" and "FreeStyle," whereas H&H's internal systems used item numbers and other abbreviations such as "INT" and "INTE" for International and "FRL" and "FSL" for FreeStyle. Plaintiff's Memorandum of Law at 10-11. Plaintiffs posit that defendants purposely designed and ran the "extremely limited search" which they knew would fail to capture responsive documents, and still reported that there were 6,000 responsive documents for year 2014 which they used to claim an undue burden to obtain a modification of the Court's Order.

The H&H defendants argue that their original number of 6,000 documents represented 6,000 pages, which the H&H defendants clarified at a Court conference. Defendants' Memorandum of Law at 20-22. The H&H defendants further explain that the 314 documents/2,034 pages that were produced can be explained by "the elimination of emails from email user accounts of persons who worked for other H&H divisions that do not sell test strips ... elimination of duplicates; and consolidation of multiple email exchanges into a single email containing the entire chain." Regarding plaintiffs' assertion that defendants designed and used search terms to fail, defendants proffer that their former counsel, Mr. Yert, formulated and directed the use of the search terms. The H&H defendants state that "any problems with the search terms was the result of H&H's good faith reliance on counsel who ... decided to use parameters that were less robust than those later used[.]" The H&H defendants further state that the Sweet search results were limited because of Mr. Yert's incompetence.

From the very start of discovery in this case, the H&H defendants have proffered serial representations to the Court, many of which have been proven to be false. Defendants first represented to the Court that there were 6,000 responsive documents to the Court's discovery orders. Then defendants subsequently represented that the 6,000 documents were actually 6,000 pages. However, neither number the H&H defendants proffered makes sense. The original Sweet search produced 1,540 responsive emails which amounted to 3,296 documents. Conspicuously absent is H&H's total page count for the 3,296 documents. However, the H&H defendants state, "the initial number [6,000 pages] Mr. Yert conveyed to the Court was predicated on the search results before certain documents were removed." Thus, if the H&H defendants' position were correct, the 1,540 responsive emails (3,296 documents) represented approximately 6,000 pages, but the H&H defendants have offered no plausible explanation for this number. Accordingly, given defendants wholly unsubstantiated serial explanations, the Court finds that the H&H defendants materially misrepresented the number of responsive documents/pages to the Court, which facilitated their objective: the Court's modification of its Order to limit their search for responsive documents. ***

Similarly, the H&H defendants' attempt to lay blame on former counsel regarding the design and use of search terms is equally unavailing. It is undisputed that numerous responsive documents were not produced by the H&H defendants that should have been produced. Defendants' prior counsel conceded as much. ***

Mr. Yert was asked at his deposition about the terms that H&H used to identify their products and he testified as follows:

> Q. Tell me about the general discussions you had with the client in terms of what informed you what search terms you should be using.
>
> A. Those were the terms consistently used by H&H to identify the particular product.
>
> Q. So the client told you that FreeStyle and International are the terms they consistently used to refer to International FreeStyle test strips; is that correct?
>
> A. That's what I recall.
>
> Q. Did the client tell you that they used the abbreviation FSL to refer to FreeStyle?
>
> A. I don't recall.
>
> Q. If they had told you that, you would have included that as a search term, correct?
>
> A. I don't recall if it was or was not included as a search term, sir.

At Mr. Sweet's deposition, he testified as follows:

> Q. Okay. Sitting here today, you would agree with me, would you not, that there were many H&H documents that refer to International FreeStyle by the abbreviation I-N-T without spelling out the word "International"?

A. Only because I've seen how the different searches have been done with -- with an outside company.

Q. Yeah, but in your day-to-day business with H&H, you've certainly seen many emails where the abbreviation I-N-T is used in lieu of the full word "International"; correct?

A. This is kind of misleading, of course I've seen different abbreviations used, but in creating a filter, I was doing what I was directed to do.

Q. Okay. So putting aside what you did with the filter. I'm just asking, in your day-to-day business with H&H, you are aware that H&H routinely uses the abbreviation I-N-T in lieu of the full word "International"; correct?

A. I am aware of that, yes.

Mr. Sweet's declaration in opposition to plaintiffs' instant motion ("Sweet Decl."), states that the original search parameters were determined by Mr. Yert and that he "relied on Mr. Yert's expertise as counsel to direct the parameters and methods for a proper search that would fulfill the Court's Order."

As will be discussed below, the crux of defendants' arguments throughout their opposition to the instant motion seeks to lay blame on Mr. Yert for their actions; however, defendants cannot absolve themselves of liability here by shifting blame to their former counsel. In *Chevron Corp. v. Donziger*, 833 F.3d 74, 149-50 (2d Cir. 2016), defendants argued that they were improperly "punished ... for their Ecuadorian lawyers' failure to respond to [plaintiff's] discovery demands[.]" It has long been held that a client-principal is "bound by the acts of his lawyer agent." *** As the Second Circuit stated, "even innocent clients may not benefit from the fraud of their attorney."

Both parties cite Mr. Yert and Mr. Sweet's conflicting testimony. Despite this conflicting testimony, both sides agree that H&H's search terms were inadequate and failed to capture the documents responsive to the Court's Orders. However, notwithstanding defendants' assertion that the search terms "FreeStyle" and "International" were used in lieu of more comprehensive search terms at the behest of Mr. Yert, it is undisputed that Mr. Sweet, H&H's general manager, knew that H&H used abbreviations for these terms. Mr. Sweet admitted this at his deposition. Plaintiff's counsel asked, "[s]o putting aside what you did with the filter. I'm just asking, in your day-to-day business with H&H, you are aware that H&H routinely uses the abbreviation I-N-T in lieu of the full word "International"; correct?" Mr. Sweet answered, "I am aware of that, yes." The Court need not speculate as to why defendants did not use these search terms to comply with defendants' obligation to produce pursuant to the Court's Order. Mr. Sweet, by his own admission, states that "on several occasions he contacted Mr. Yert with specific questions about whether to include certain emails in production." It is inconceivable that H&H's General Manager, who worked closely with Mr. Yert to respond to the Court's Order, never mentioned that spelling out the terms used, "International" and "FreeStyle", would not capture the documents in H&H's email system. Mr. Sweet knew that H&H was required to produce documents regarding International FreeStyle test strips, regardless of whether H&H's documents spelled out or abbreviated the terms. Had plaintiffs not seized H&H's email server in the counterfeiting action, plaintiffs would have never known that defendants failed to produce a trove of responsive documents. H&H would have gotten away with it.

Accordingly, the Court finds that H&H's original misrepresentations to the Court and use of search terms that were designed to fail are just the first evidence of defendants' bad faith. H&H's failure to produce responsive documents in accordance with the January 2017 Court Orders is in and of itself sanctionable conduct. Standing alone, misrepresentations to the Court and the designed to fail search terms would not warrant case ending sanctions; however, as enumerated below, this conduct is but one brush stroke in the composition of discovery abuses that has colored this litigation. Moreover, plaintiffs would have never discovered the extent of defendants' withheld documents and defendants' fraud upon the court but for the seizure order entered in the subsequent counterfeiting case.

b. Documents H&H Withheld from the February 10, 2017 Production
Holland Trading, Howard Goldman, and Lori Goldman Documents
Plaintiffs allege that defendants withheld all documents regarding Holland Trading, a Dutch company, revealing that "at the time the H&H defendants were collecting and reviewing documents, they were buying and selling tens of thousands of boxes of International FreeStyle test strips that had been repackaged into counterfeit U.S. retail packaging." H&H purchased test strips from Holland Trading beginning in November 2016 and stopped when plaintiffs filed their counterfeit action in May 2017. Moreover, plaintiffs state that the H&H defendants negotiated purchases of International FreeStyle test strips from Holland Trading in 2013 and 2014 and emails were exchanged with Holland Trading concerning International FreeStyle test strips in 2014. The 2014 Holland Trading documents should have been produced in response to the January 27, 2017 Order. Plaintiffs posit that the H&H defendants intentionally withheld all documents concerning Holland Trading from the February production. Plaintiffs cite to Exhibit Z and AA as examples of withheld Holland Trading documents.

Perhaps even more troubling than the removal of all the Holland Trading documents was defendants' failure to produce a single document that referenced Howard Goldman, owner and president of H&H. Plaintiffs allege that defendants intentionally withheld "[e]very document referring to Howard Goldman." Mr. Sweet testified that he wouldn't have removed Howard Goldman documents as nonresponsive. Mr. Yert testified that all of the documents Mr. Sweet provided were produced. Plaintiffs argue that the only explanation for defendants' failure to produce any Howard Goldman documents is that the H&H defendants "intentionally removed, by hand, every single document referencing Howard Goldman."

Like the Holland Trading and Howard Goldman documents, plaintiffs allege that the H&H defendants removed all responsive documents concerning Lori Goldman. No documents concerning or referencing Lori Goldman were produced in the February 10, 2017 production. Both Lori Goldman and Howard Goldman's declarations deny Lori Goldman's involvement with H&H's business regarding diabetic test strips and stated that Lori Goldman "is not involved in and does not direct or control any of the business activities of H&H." Nonetheless, when defendants reran the search pursuant to the Court's July 12, 2017 Order, there were 16 responsive documents referencing Lori Goldman, such as emails with suppliers and an offer forwarded to Mr. Sweet concerning International FreeStyle test strips that Howard Goldman had received. The documents in the reproduction prompted plaintiffs to move for the production of additional emails from Ms. Goldman's H&H account in the counterfeiting action. The H&H defendants were ordered to produce emails from Ms. Goldman's account from "2014 through 2015[.]" According to plaintiffs, in response to the Court's Order, the H&H defendants produced 6,291 documents from Ms. Goldman's account.

The H&H defendants contend that the missing Holland Trading, Howard Goldman, and Lori Goldman documents were either removed from the production by Mr. Sweet at the direction of Mr. Yert, were not in Mr. Sweet's original search results, or were not within the scope of the Court's discovery Order. The H&H defendants maintain that Ms. Goldman's involvement in H&H's business activities was limited and that Ms. Goldman's emails do not evidence fraud by H&H.

The H&H defendants intentionally withheld all documents concerning Holland Trading, Howard Goldman, and Lori Goldman from their original production. Decisions in several cases by Courts within this circuit, namely Penthouse, McMunn, and Cerruti, are instructive here. In Penthouse, the Second Circuit affirmed dismissal of a libel suit where plaintiff failed to produce financial records relevant to the case. Although the district court held those records were relevant and thus should have been produced, plaintiff produced only part of the records and refused to turn over the balance of its financial statements. Defendant moved for Rule 37(b) sanctions, including dismissal of the action, based on plaintiff's failure to comply with the Court's production order. The Second Circuit observed that the district court "exercised enormous patience and conscientiousness" before imposing the sanction of dismissal. The Second Circuit stated:

> The financial records which Penthouse refused to furnish were relevant. Its defiance of the order climaxed a sordid pattern of prolonged and vexatious obstruction of legitimate discovery sought by Playboy, in which false testimony, material misrepresentations by [counsel] and foot-dragging were used in an effort to prevent Playboy from getting at Penthouse records that were relevant to the central issue in this case, which was whether Penthouse suffered any [pecuniary] damages...

"Where justified ... the imposition of sanctions for discovery abuse is essential to the sound administration of justice." Thus, the Second Circuit affirmed the entry of default in Penthouse where there was an abundance of evidence that plaintiff disobeyed an "order to produce in full all of [their] financial statements," engaged in "prolonged and vexatious obstruction of discovery with respect to closely related and highly relevant records," gave "false testimony and representations that [financial records] did not exist," and provided the data only when "the scent had become too fresh and the trail too hot to risk further non-compliance."

***

In the instant action, defendants attempt to minimize their part in failing to produce the Holland Trading, Howard Goldman, and Lori Goldman documents. According to defendants, the cited Holland Trading documents were not within the Sweet search directed by Mr. Yert or were removed by Mr. Sweet per Mr. Yert's instructions.

Plaintiffs proffer seven Howard Goldman emails that were withheld. Defendants, again, seek to minimize their failure to produce the emails through Mr. Sweet's declaration. The H&H Defendants allege that plaintiffs' exhibits O, P, Q, V reflect "emails from David Gulas to Howard Goldman discussing business goals for coming months" which Mr. Sweet removed from the production; exhibit N reflects an offer that H&H never followed up on and thus Mr. Sweet removed the document from the production per Mr. Yert's instructions; and exhibits W and X were not within the search results and thus were not produced.

Likewise, no Lori Goldman documents were produced pursuant to the Court's Order despite 16 documents in the reproduction, and 6,291 total emails from Ms. Goldman's H&H email account from 2014-2015. The H&H defendants try to paint Ms. Goldman as a housewife who dropped in and out of the office with little to no responsibilities within the company. However, the record suggests otherwise. While many of the Lori Goldman emails do not specifically involve the buying and selling of diabetic test strips, other emails do and should have been produced in defendants' original production. The H&H defendants, however, through Mr. Sweet's declaration assert that Exhibit AK (an email to Lori Goldman about open unpaid invoices of FreeStyle strips) was not captured in the original Sweet search results, and Exhibit AL (an email to Ms. Goldman from a representative of Veenak International regarding an offer for test strips that the representative wanted to make sure Mr. Goldman saw) represents an offer from a company that H&H never did business with and was removed by Mr. Sweet.

The Court first notes that defendants were ordered to produce "all formal and informal communications regarding defendants' purchases and sales of International FreeStyle test strips in 2014, including emails, text messages, purchase orders, delivery invoices, and check/wire transfers." The Court's Order did not specify that the purchases or sales must have been consummated as defendants suggest. Even if the Court credits defendants' position that it understood the Court's Order to be limited to completed sales, defendants contradict their own position by producing incomplete purchases and sales. In so far as defendants argue that they believed the Court's Order limited what needed to be produced to actual purchases or sales, their argument is belied by their own production.

Moreover, the H&H defendants' account of the withheld Holland Trading, Howard Goldman, and Lori Goldman documents, again, attempts to shift the blame to Mr. Yert for their failure to produce Court ordered discovery. As discussed supra, defendants cannot absolve themselves of their failure to produce by blaming their former counsel. *** While defendants' effort to shift blame to Mr. Yert is unconvincing at best, even if defendants' effort could be credited, counsel's actions, even if they were found to be negligent, would not shield the H&H defendants from responsibility for their bad faith conduct. In Penthouse, while recognizing that counsel's actions may have been grossly negligent, the Court upheld the District Court's dismissal of the action and stated:

> [I]t is questionable whether [counsel for plaintiffs] intentionally ... misrepresented to the court material facts with respect to the existence of the relevant ... records. It is conceivable that [counsel] was misled by his client. However, the record does support ... [the] finding that [counsel] ... was grossly negligent in not pursuing the matter more diligently to ascertain the facts from his client.

Furthermore, the H&H defendants never objected to production of these documents on the basis of any privilege. The H&H defendants' entirely new attorney-client privilege argument falls flat based on the record. The H&H defendants consistently proffered that no documents were intentionally withheld. At the July 11, 2017 conference, defendants' former counsel stated:

> We [Cooley LLP] have in the days that we've been looking into this not seen evidence of deliberate withholding. What we have seen is a variety of ways in which the collection process left gaps and I can't tell the Court definitively one way or the other exactly what all those gaps are because we're still doing it and I don't want to represent something that's wrong but there were domain names that were not properly searched because they were stored as old domain names. Whether that explains the large gaps completely, I can't tell you but I have not seen any evidence of somebody excluding something.

Moreover, C&G, the H&H defendants' next counsel, conducted their own internal investigation and found that outside of documents not provided due to technical errors (197 documents), no documents were intentionally withheld. Even more damning is Mr. Yert's deposition testimony, which is consistent with the positions proffered by Cooley and C&G. Mr. Yert testified as follows:

> Q. At any time prior ù do you recall any conversations with Mr. Sweet regarding Holland Trading documents and whether they should be included or not in the document production?

> A. I don't recall any conversations with Mr. Sweet regarding Holland Trading.

However, Mr. Sweet testified as follows:

> Q. Did you remove, at any point, any documents that had the name Holland Trading in them?
>
> A. We never purchased International FreeStyle from Holland Trading.
>
> Q. Did you remove any documents that were to or from Holland Trading?
>
> A. If those were in there, those would have been removed because I know that we never bought International FreeStyle from them.

Mr. Sweet's deposition continued:

> Q. And one of the reasons that a document would be pulled from that production is that it discussed a potential sale or purchase of International FreeStyle from someone who you knew, in fact, never purchased or sold International FreeStyle with H&H; right?
>
> A. All right .... I don't remember the specifics of it, but I do remember [Mr. Yert] saying early on, that if we didn't do business with them, buy or sell, that that's not the documents we were looking to produce. So in the course of going through the filter, I realized that there was some people in there, only because I recognized the names, so those ones, I would flag and then I would ask him, you know, you sure these don't need to be in there, and he would say, remove them.
>
> Q. So what - what names did you recognize as you were going through?
>
> A. Well, one of the bigger ones that sticks out now, because of the course of the case, would have been Holland Trading.

Mr. Sweet's declaration in opposition to the instant motion is at odds with his deposition testimony where he testified as follows:

> Q. Was Howard Goldman one of the custodians that you left in Outlook as someone who potentially had something to do with the purchase and sale of FreeStyle test strips.
>
> A. That's not how we did it. We said that we removed custodians that ù as you call them, custodians that didn't have anything to do with the test strips.

> Q. Was Howard Goldman one of the people you removed.
>
> A. No.

Mr. Sweet testified as follows regarding an email between David Gulas and Howard Goldman:

> Q. Okay. I take it from your testimony that this is not the type of document that you would have removed from production if you reviewed it; is that correct?
>
> A. I don't believe so, no.
>
> Q. Because it discusses H&H's sale of International FreeStyle, it says it right there; correct?
>
> A. Well, because I'm seeing the two words together there, "International FreeStyle."
>
> Q. So this would have hit your search terms, you would have expected that correct?
>
> A. That's what I would have expected, yes.
>
> Q. And you would have not removed this email because it's an email discussing H&H's sale or purchase of International FreeStyle from 2014; correct?
>
> A. I don't believe this email would have been removed.

Contradicting counsel's assertions that documents were not intentionally removed, Mr. Sweet now admits that he intentionally removed documents relating to Holland Trading, Howard Goldman, and Lori Goldman. Moreover, despite Mr. Sweet's testimony that he wouldn't have removed the Howard Goldman document discussed above, it was removed from the original production, as was every other document referencing Howard Goldman, which could have only been removed by Mr. Sweet. The document discussed in Mr. Sweet's deposition was not one of the 197 documents identified by Mr. Pochron that Mr. Sweet using his auditor account didn't have access to, and it is undisputed that this document would have been identified by H&H's search terms "International" and "FreeStyle", yet defendants still did not produce it.

Thus, the H&H defendants' explanations regarding the Holland Trading, Howard Goldman, and Lori Goldman documents continue to change as the scent "becomes too fresh and the trail too hot to risk further non-compliance." Penthouse, 663 F.2d at 389. After three different law firms asserted that the H&H defendants did not remove documents, the H&H defendants now contend that the Holland Trading, Howard Goldman, and Lori Goldman documents were either not within the Sweet search results, or when faced with a document that was clearly in the search results that went unproduced, they now say the documents were removed at the direction of Mr. Yert. The H&H defendants' position contradicts the arguments made to the Court by three of their former counsel. Mr. Sweet's testimony contradicts H&H's position throughout this litigation. Moreover, Mr. Sweet's declaration, which the H&H defendants argue accounts for many of the withheld documents, is incredible at best. Mr. Sweet states, "I am aware that during the deposition, I testified that I 'believed' [I] would not have removed such documents. But during that deposition, I was attempting to recall what was a complicated event ... that had taken place over a year before, and in which I had no previous experience."

There is no credible explanation for why the Holland Trading, Howard Goldman, and Lori Goldman documents were not produced except that the documents were willfully withheld. Defendants' explanation that there were no documents withheld, then that any documents that weren't produced were due to technical glitches, then that the documents didn't appear in Mr. Sweet's original search, then that if documents were intentionally removed, they were removed per Mr. Yert's instructions cannot all be true. The H&H defendants have always had one more excuse up their sleeve in this "series of episodes of nonfeasance," which amounts to "deliberate tactical intransigence." *** In light of the H&H defendants' ever-changing explanations as to the withheld documents, Mr. Sweet's inconsistent testimony, and assertions of former counsel, the Court finds that the H&H defendants have calculatedly attempted to manipulate the judicial process. ***

c. The H&H Defendants' Perjured and Inconsistent Testimony

David Gulas' Deposition Testimony
Plaintiffs allege that the withheld documents freed David Gulas to commit perjury at his deposition. The Court agrees. David Gulas was the only person who bought FreeStyle test strips at H&H and was employed "for a long time, a decade plus." Mr. Gulas' deposition is riddled with conflicting testimony. The Court need not point out every lie to find that Gulas' testimony at his deposition is sanctionable conduct. As a clear example of his bad faith, Mr. Gulas testified that he could not recall whether he ever worked with Mr. Goldman directly. Mr. Gulas' testimony is belied by monthly emails with Mr. Goldman regarding sales goals; an email where Mr. Gulas obtained Mr. Goldman's approval to purchase International FreeStyle test strips; and less than two weeks before Mr. Gulas' deposition on April 18 and 19, 2017, Mr. Gulas and Mr. Goldman met with two representatives from Holland Trading.

Mr. Gulas further testified under oath that he could not recall who H&H had bought retail FreeStyle test strips from in the past year. Plaintiffs point out that Holland Trading was H&H's biggest supplier of FreeStyle test strips, and approximately two weeks prior to Mr. Gulas' deposition, H&H received a shipment of over 10,000 boxes of International FreeStyle test strips from Holland Trading. Plaintiffs' Memorandum of Law. Moreover, seven days before Mr. Gulas' deposition, he exchanged several emails with Holland Trading.

The H&H defendants argue that H&H has done business with over 200 vendors and if Mr. Gulas wanted to hide the business that they had with Holland Trading, it would have made more sense for Mr. Gulas to name some other vendor rather than to say he couldn't recall any vendor. The H&H defendants also argue that "Mr. Gulas was nervous and could not recall something when put on the spot." Id. The H&H defendants state that the monthly goals emails between Mr. Gulas and Mr. Goldman "do not reflect oral conversations, and do not reflect [that Gulas worked] with Mr. Goldman 'directly.'" Conspicuously, the H&H defendants make no mention of Mr. Gulas and Mr. Goldman's two-day meeting with Holland Trading or Exhibit AF (discussed supra) in their memorandum of law.

Generally, "[p]erjury alone does not constitute fraud upon the court." *** Nevertheless, perjury can be considered fraud upon the court "'when a party lies to the court and his adversary intentionally, repeatedly, and about issues that are central to the truth-finding process.'"

First, it is inconceivable that Mr. Gulas, H&H's diabetes test strip buyer, could not recall any vendor from whom H&H had bought retail FreeStyle test strips from in the past year. The H&H defendants, by their own assertion, state that there are over 200 vendors. It is not plausible that Mr. Gulas could not name a single vendor. Likewise, there is no explanation why Mr. Gulas would not recall Holland Trading, one of, if not H&H's biggest vendor. Moreover, the Court cannot credit the H&H defendants' argument that Mr. Gulas never worked directly with Mr. Goldman. The record demonstrates that a little more than a week before Mr. Gulas' deposition, he and Mr. Goldman had a two day in person meeting with two representatives from Holland Trading. Also, seven days before his deposition, Mr. Gulas exchanged several emails with Holland Trading. The H&H defendants' explanation that this testimony was due to Mr. Gulas' nerves has hit a nerve. The H&H defendants did not just tell one lie, but they repeatedly lied—most likely in an effort to insulate Howard Goldman. Here, as in Cerruti, defendants repeatedly lied under oath in an effort to (i) conceal their fabrication once it became apparent, (ii) establish other facts helpful to their position, and (iii) account for defendants' repeated failure to produce or locate documents. *** Accordingly, I find that David Gulas' deposition testimony is clear and convincing evidence of a fraud upon the Court.

Howard Goldman's Deposition Testimony

Plaintiffs also argue that the H&H defendants withheld all Holland Trading and Howard Goldman documents to allow Howard Goldman to commit perjury at his deposition. Like Mr. Gulas, Howard Goldman's deposition testimony is riddled with evasion, inconsistencies, and contradictions. Even on the simplest matter, Mr. Goldman could not give a straight answer. Literally on the first question, Howard Goldman was asked, "Are you president of H&H." He replied, "I'm not certain of my corporate title." Plaintiffs' counsel then asked, "If you are not the president of H&H, who might be the president of H&H?" Howard Goldman replied, "Well, if--I'm not aware of anybody that would be, so I may hold that title." Then when asked, "Who own's H&H?" Mr. Goldman replied, "I do." In fact, the record makes clear that Mr. Goldman owns one hundred percent of H&H. ***

Plaintiffs allege Mr. Goldman testified that he didn't have an office at H&H. Goldman Dep. 114:24-115:12, June 28, 2017. However, Mr. Gulas and Lori Goldman testified that he did. When Mr. Gulas was asked, "and how far is [Mr. Goldman's] office from your office?", he answered, "maybe 30 feet." "Ms. Goldman does your husband have an office at H&H?" Ms. Goldman answered, "Yes, he does." What Mr. Goldman actually testified was, "My office is wherever they have room for me," and "I'm the only guy that if somebody else needs an office, I will get kicked to the curb and I will find someplace else." Goldman Dep. 115:13-115:15, June 28, 2017. Plaintiffs also point out other instances where Mr. Goldman feigned ignorance: he claimed he did not know about prior law suits filed against H&H or claimed not to know his job responsibilities at H&H. While plaintiffs allege that Mr. Goldman's testimony amounts to "serial perjury", that may be a bit overstated. Mr. Goldman's testimony was certainly less than forthcoming and at times inconsistent, but his testimony alone would not warrant case ending sanctions. However, Howard Goldman's testimony cannot be considered in isolation. "[S]anctions must be weighed in light of the full record of the case." ***

III. Appropriate Sanction

Based on the full record of the case, there is clear and convincing evidence that defendants have perpetrated a fraud upon the court. Defendants' initial conduct of formulating search terms designed to fail in deliberate disregard of the lawful orders of the Court allowed H&H to purposely withhold responsive documents, including the Holland Trading, Howard Goldman, and Lori Goldman documents. Defendants proffered inconsistent positions with three successive counsel as to why the documents were withheld. Mr. Sweet's testimony is clearly inconsistent if not perjured from his deposition to his declaration in opposition to the instant motion. Mr. Goldman's deposition testimony is evasive and self-serving at best. Finally, Mr. Gulas' deposition testimony is clearly perjured. Had plaintiffs never seized H&H's server pursuant to the Court's Order in the counterfeiting case, H&H would have gotten away with their fraud upon this Court. H&H only complied with the Court's orders and their discovery obligations when their backs were against the wall. Their email server had been seized. There was no longer an escape from responsibility for their bad faith conduct. This is, again, similar to Cerruti, where the "defendants did not withdraw the [false] documents on their own. Rather, they waited until the falsity of the documents had been detected." *** But for being caught in a web of irrefutable evidence, H&H would have profited from their misconduct.

The Court must consider the five factors discussed earlier in considering what sanction should be imposed: (1) whether the misconduct was the product of intentional bad faith; (2) whether and to what extent the misconduct prejudiced the other party; (3) whether there is a pattern of misbehavior, rather than an isolated instance; (4) whether and when the misconduct was corrected; and (5) whether further misconduct is likely to continue in the future. ***

Several factors weigh in favor of imposing a case ending sanction in this action. First, the H&H defendants' bad faith can be inferred from the H&H defendants' deliberate and strategic non-compliance with discovery, their selective withholding of responsive documents, and their perjury as well as deceptive and evasive deposition testimony. Similar to *Schlaifer*, the actions taken by the H&H defendants throughout discovery in this case have been completely without merit. *** Plaintiffs have clearly been prejudiced by incurring the costs for having to conduct duplicative depositions while investigating defendants' fraud upon the court. In addition, plaintiffs have had to brief and argue this motion at the same time as they were preparing a motion for summary judgment. Even after the seizure of defendants' servers, the record in this case is still riddled with inconsistent and perjured testimony.

Plaintiffs' progress in this litigation was significantly impeded by defendants' discovery fraud. Moreover, this was not an isolated instance of perjury or one withheld document, rather it was a calculated pattern of pervasive misconduct that started early on and continued even after defendants were caught red handed. H&H's misconduct was egregious. The record herein when taken as a whole exposes defendants' fraud upon the court. H&H has had five different law firms represent them in this action and their current position directly contradicts prior counsels' arguments. As much as H&H seeks to lay blame on its counsel, the truth is H&H is responsible. But for the seizure of the server in *Abbott II*, H&H's fraud upon the court may never have come to light.

Defendants' discovery misconduct must be appropriately punished to deter such abuse of the Court's process. If the Court fails to impose an appropriate sanction, this "would encourage dilatory tactics, and compliance with discovery orders would come only when the backs of counsel and the litigants were against the wall." *** Thus, although the Court recognizes the strong preference for resolving disputes on the merits and not by default, this is an extreme case "because we are dealing here with repeated rather than with isolated or discrete abuses" and judgment against the offending party is the only appropriate sanction. ***

The Court finds that the H&H defendants have committed a fraud upon the court, and that the harshest sanction is warranted. Therefore, plaintiffs' motion for sanctions should be granted and a default judgment should be entered against H&H Wholesale Services, Inc., Howard Goldman, and Lori Goldman.

***

Chapter 7

Collection of Electronically Stored Information

Data collection is the most technically challenging portion of the entire ediscovery process. It involves the extraction of potentially relevant ESI from its native source into a separate repository. Many people consider data collection as solely an information technology (IT) activity, but an effective collection plan can be best achieved by actively involving both legal and IT professionals.

A. Locations where ESI resides

Virtually every form of ESI are fair game in e-discovery, and they are located in various places. While different data sources have different levels of accessibility, they also present different challenges from a collection standpoint. The following is a list of data types and locations where they can be collected for the purpose of e-discovery.

1. Active data

Active data are data that people interact with on a regular basis, such as word-processed documents, spreadsheets, databases, emails, and other traditional files that are stored on a local hard drive or network drive. Active data are considered relatively easy to access and collect.

2. Cloud servers

Data stored in cloud servers can range from software as a service application to social media accounts. Each cloud provider has its own policies for data access. In many case, e-discovery technology solutions can be used to integrate with many of the popular cloud services.

3. Mobile devices

Mobile devices typically include text messages, App data, call history, photographs and videos. Collecting ESI from mobile devices often requires specialize software tools. Expert consultants should be able to preserve and collect ESI from text messages, call logs, geolocation data, etc. (*See* Chapter 14 for details).

4. Archived data

Some non-active data are stored or archived. Even though archived data cannot be accessed over a shared server, collecting them usually presents minimal challenges as long as the physical location of the data is known.

5. Backup data

Backup files are usually compressed and are not easily searchable or accessible. But since backup systems are designed to store data in the event that it must be restored, they should not present significant collection hurdles.

6. Hidden data

Previously deleted or fragmented files that exist on various systems are usually not readily visible to regular users. These files are highly inaccessible, and attempting to recover them requires specialized tools such as forensic imaging.

7. Social media

Social media include Facebook posts, Tweets, Instagram messages, Snapchat messages, etc.

PESKOFF V. FABER
No. 04-526 (D. D.C. 2006)

FACCIOLA, Magistrate Judge

This case was referred to me for the resolution of discovery disputes. Currently pending before me is Plaintiff's Motion to Compel Discovery ("Mot. to Compel"). ***

I. BACKGROUND

Plaintiff Jonathan Peskoff ("Peskoff") brought this lawsuit against defendant Michael Faber ("Faber") to recover damages for financial injury resulting from Faber's operation of a venture capital fund, called NextPoint Partners, LP, and the fund's related entities. Peskoff alleges fraud in the inducement, breach of fiduciary duty, breach of contract, conversion, common law fraud and deceit, unjust enrichment, and violations of 10 U.S.C. §§ 1962(c) and 1964(c) (Civil RICO).

NextPoint GP, LLC ("NextPoint GP") is the general partner of the venture capital fund. Both Peskoff and Faber were managing members of NextPoint GP. As of February 13, 2004, Peskoff was no longer a managing member, but he claims the retention of a membership interest. ***

The NextPoint Management Company, Inc. ("NextPoint Management") was organized as a vehicle for receiving the management fees due from the venture capital fund to NextPoint GP and for fulfilling NextPoint GP's management responsibilities to the fund. Faber's responsibilities included handling routine finances, record keeping, and fund-raising activities. Peskoff's responsibilities included oversight of the portfolio companies in which the venture capital fund invested and identification and evaluation of potential new investments.

Plaza Street Holdings, Inc. ("Plaza Street") is a corporation controlled solely by Faber that was paid by NextPoint Management for "consulting services." Among other things, Peskoff alleges that Faber caused NextPoint Management to pay Plaza Street $400,000 for consulting services that were neither needed nor provided and that these payments were for the sole purpose of diverting funds from the NextPoint entities to Faber personally.

Peskoff now moves the Court for two orders: (1) an order compelling non-party Plaza Street to produce, in response to a subpoena *duces tecum*, certain documents relating to the payments from NextPoint Management to Plaza Street; and (2) an order compelling Faber to produce additional e-mails sent to and authored by Peskoff while he was employed at NextPoint Management. ***

B. E-Mails

Peskoff also seeks the production of e-mails that he received or authored while employed at NextPoint Management. Peskoff argues that these e-mails "are highly likely to contain information relating to the ownership issues in this case, the suspect transactions identified in the Complaint and other relevant matters." During the course of discovery, Faber produced computer disks containing documents, including e-mails, that were obtained from Peskoff's computer, but these disks did not include any e-mails that Peskoff received or authored between mid-2001 and mid-2003. In moving to compel, Peskoff argues that Faber has failed to adequately explain why these two-years worth of e-mails have not been produced, where the e-mails might be located within NextPoint's computer system or archives, or what specific steps were taken to locate the emails.

In opposition, Faber contends that "no electronic documents have been withheld" and that, if the sought after e-mails are not on the computer disks provided, then they no longer exist. Faber explains that NextPoint Management subleases space from Mintz, Levin, Cohn, Ferris, Glovsky and Popeo, PC ("Mintz Levin") and its electronic files are stored on Mintz Levin's server. When Peskoff's employment ended, counsel "caused the creation of an archive of all Peskoff electronic files, including documents stored on his computer hard drive, e-mail, and any other Peskoff electronic documents." This entire archive was produced to Peskoff.

As a threshold matter, there does not appear to be any dispute that the e-mails are likely to contain relevant information. Moreover, "[d]uring discovery, the producing party has an obligation to search available electronic systems for the information demanded." *McPeek v. Ashcroft*, 202 F.R.D. 31, 32 (D.D.C. 2001) (citing to Fed.R.Civ.P. 34(a)). The parties' disagreement turns instead on whether the missing e-mails still exist and can be located. The sought after e-mails could fall into three categories: e-mails to Peskoff, e-mails from Peskoff, and e-mails about Peskoff, and could be located in several possible places.

First, the e-mail account that Peskoff used while working at NextPoint Management might still contain the e-mails in his inbox, sent items, trash, or other named folders.

Second, the e-mails may be in the inbox, sent items, trash, and other folders of e-mail accounts of other employees, agents, officers, and representatives of the NextPoint entities, who may have been the author or recipient of the e-mails at issue.

Third, the e-mails may be on the hard drive of Peskoff's computer or within any depository for NextPoint e-mails. The e-mails may be accessible from those locations through simple search technology, such as by conducting a key word search (i.e., a search on "Peskoff" or his e-mail address). Thus, even if the e-mails cannot be located by searching particular files, they yet may be located on the hard drive or other depository by finding all files where a particular word appears.

Fourth, with the help of a computer forensic technologist, the e-mails, even if deleted, may be recoverable from other places within Peskoff's computer, such as its "slack space." *See United States v. Triumph Capital Group, Inc.*, 211 F.R.D. 31, 46 n. 7 (D. Conn. 2002) ("`Slack space' is the unused space at the logical end of an active file's data and the physical end of the cluster or clusters that are assigned to an active file. Deleted data, or remnants of deleted data can be found in the slack space...").

Finally, the e-mails may even be recoverable from periodic backups tapes or disks made of Mintz Levin's server. *See Zubulake v. UBS Warburg LLC*, 217 F.R.D. 309, 319 (S.D.N.Y. 2003).

However, based on the information before the Court, I cannot determine at what level Faber searched for the requested Peskoff e-mails. All I know is that an archive was created "of all Peskoff electronic files, including documents stored on his computer hard drive, e-mail, and any other Peskoff electronic documents." This statement tells me little, if anything about the scope of Faber's search.

Accordingly, within ten business days from the date of this memorandum opinion, Faber shall file a detailed affidavit specifying the nature of the search it conducted. Peskoff shall have ten business days therefrom to respond to the adequacy of the search described in that affidavit. Once I receive Faber's affidavit and Peskoff's response, if any, I will consider whether additional searches are necessary. I should indicate that I may have to hold an evidentiary hearing in which I take testimony from Faber's employees and other witnesses about the effectiveness and cost of any additional searches.

***

THOMPSON V. AUTOLIV ASP, INC.
No. 2:09 cv 01375, 2012 WL 2342928 (D. Nev. 2012)

FERENBACH, Magistrate Judge

Before the court are Defendant TRW Automotive U.S. LLC's ("TRW") *** [and] Plaintiff Nicole Thompson ("Nicole") ***.

Background

***.

*** Plaintiffs assert that on April 27, 2007, Plaintiff Nicole suffered "massive, life threatening, permanent, and irreversible injuries" resulting from a vehicular collision. Plaintiffs allege that Defendant ASP was "engaged in the business of manufacturing, developing, testing, inspecting, advertising, merchandising, selling and distributing seatbelt systems, including the one that had been installed" in Nicole's vehicle. Plaintiffs also allege that the seatbelt system installed in Nicole's vehicle was defective when it left Defendant ASP's manufacturing facility. Plaintiffs assert that because the seatbelt system in Nicole's vehicle was defective, the seatbelt spooled out during the crash, causing/contributing to Nicole's injuries and Plaintiffs' damages. Plaintiffs assert causes of action against Defendant ASP for negligence, gross negligence, negligence per se, and product defect.

***

Plaintiffs also allege that "as a direct and proximate result" of Nicole's injuries, Plaintiff Nicole has (i) lost a scholarship; (ii) lost her ability to play the violin as part of an orchestra that she had played with for a number of years; (iii) lost the quality and enjoyment of her life because she is restricted from engaging in most physical activities, and requires the assistance of others; (iv) experienced an increase in emotional distress due to feelings of helplessness and knowledge that her condition was negatively impacting those around her; and (v) become depressed, emotionally volatile, and her memory has become permanently and irreversibly affected.

***

Defendant moves to compel Plaintiff Nicole "to produce complete and un redacted copies of Plaintiff's Facebook and other social networking site accounts." Defendant requests wall posts, photographs, and messages from April 27, 2007, to the present. Defendant asserts that Plaintiff improperly objected to TRW's Requests for Production of Documents. Defendant also asserts that "without claiming any privilege," Plaintiff provided a redacted copy of her Facebook account history and a limited number of photographs. ***

***

Defendant TRW asserts that prior to seeking social networking documents through formal discovery requests, TRW obtained wall posts and photographs from Plaintiff's public Facebook profile that "provide evidence of Plaintiff's post accident social activities, mental state, relationship history, living arrangements, and rehabilitative progressùall of which are relevant to the claims and defenses in this lawsuit." Defendant alleges that it obtained wall posts and photographs depicting: (i) Plaintiff's ability to swing on a swing set, dance, and engage in water sports; (ii) Plaintiff's ability to care for children and pets; (iii) Plaintiff's social activities, including consumption of alcohol, bowling with friends, and late night partying; (iv) Plaintiff's sleeping habits; (v) Plaintiff's personal relationships; (vi) Plaintiff's post accident physical recovery; (vii) Plaintiff's employment; (viii) the effect of Plaintiff's medications on her emotional, physical and sexual habits; (ix) offers by Plaintiff to share medications with others; and (x) Plaintiff's enrollment in institutions of higher education.

Defendant asserts that shortly after February 8, 2011, Plaintiff changed her Facebook privacy settings, thus blocking the public from viewing Plaintiff's Facebook wall posts and photographs. On February 23, 2012, Defendant requested the production of documents and communications related to Plaintiff's Facebook and other social networking site accounts in TRW's Second Request for Production. Plaintiff objected to Defendant's request, responding with "[fifty one] heavily redacted pages" from her Facebook wall, and eight photographs. Defendant asserts that contrary to applicable discovery rules, Plaintiff limited production to information and materials that support her allegations.

Defendant requests that the Court require Plaintiff "to produce for *in camera* inspection i) an un redacted copy of Plaintiff's entire Facebook account from April 27, 2007 to the present, including wall posts and photographs, and ii) an un redacted copy of Plaintiff's entire MySpace account." Defendant argues that this is the only method through which the Court can determine whether Plaintiff has complied with her Rule 26(b)(1) production obligations. ***

Plaintiff asserts that Defendant's request for a complete copy of her social networking site accounts "amounts to nothing more than an overly broad fishing expedition." Plaintiff also asserts that the "limits of civil discovery mandate that [Defendant] not be provided with unfettered access to Plaintiff's [social networking site] account data." Plaintiff argues that Defendant has not made a sufficient showing that the material is reasonably calculated to lead to the discovery of admissible evidence, and that the information sought is irrelevant.

Plaintiff asserts that Plaintiff has produced "extensive" social networking site communications in a good faith response to Defendant's discovery requests. Plaintiff also asserts that much of the information requested by Defendant is duplicative of other information that Plaintiff has already produced, and is inadmissible. *Id.* Plaintiff argues that Defendant seeks shared information that is not under Plaintiff's control. *Id.* Plaintiff also argues that Plaintiff provided all material that is relevant to Plaintiff's claims.

Plaintiff argues that there is "no legitimate basis" for Defendant's request, and as such, that an *in camera* review of her social networking site accounts is not mandated. Plaintiff also argues that *in camera* reviews are generally limited to the determination of privilege, not relevance, and relevance is the basis of Plaintiff's objections. Plaintiff requests that Defendant's Motion be denied. Plaintiff submits that if the Court conducts an *in camera* review, Plaintiff will provide "an index of redacted [social networking site] communications to assist the court in the process of any such review of the materials, along with the basis for the objections and redactions made by Plaintiff."

B. Discussion

The court has broad discretion in controlling discovery. *Little v. City of Seattle*, 863 F.2d 681, 685 (9th Cir. 1988). Under Federal Rule of Civil Procedure 26(b)(1), "[f]or good cause, the court may order discovery of any matter relevant to the subject matter involved in the action." Fed. R. Civ. P. 26(b)(1). *Id.* Relevance within the meaning of Rule 26(b)(1) is considerably broader than relevance for trial purposes. *See Oppenheimer Fund v. Sanders*, 437 U.S. 340, 351 (1978) (citation omitted). For discovery purposes, relevance means only that the materials sought are reasonably calculated to lead to the discovery of admissible evidence. *Id.*

Because Plaintiff has not claimed that the requested information is privileged or protected, the Court finds an *in camera* review of Plaintiff's social networking site accounts unnecessary. Plaintiff opposes Defendant's Motion to Compel on the basis of relevance. Because the alleged consequences of Plaintiff's injuries include severe physical injuries, emotional distress, and impaired quality of life, evidence relating to Plaintiff's physical capabilities and social activities is relevant to Plaintiff's claims in this action. *See* Fed. R. Civ. P. 26(b)(1). The material obtained by Defendant's from Plaintiff's public Facebook account negates Plaintiff's allegations that material on her social networking site accounts is irrelevant to any party's claims and defenses. Under Rule 26(b)(1), this material is discoverable.

The Court recognizes that litigation does not permit a complete and open public display of Plaintiff's life. In permitting Defendant access to material from Plaintiff's social networking site accounts, the Court must balance Plaintiff's personal interests. *See* Fed. R. Civ. P. 26(c)(1) (stating that discovery must be conducted so as to protect parties from "annoyance, embarrassment, oppression, or undue burden"). The parties shall proceed as follows:

(1) Plaintiff shall upload onto an electronic storage device, all information from her Facebook and MySpace accounts, from April 27, 2007, to the present. Within ten (10) days from the entry of this order, Plaintiff shall provide Defendant's counsel with the electronic storage device, and an index of redacted social networking site communications.

(2) Defense counsel is not permitted to disclose this material to anyone, with the exception of counsel's support staff as necessary. Defense counsel may review downloaded material and identify material that defense counsel believes is discoverable, but was withheld from Plaintiff's production. Defense counsel must provide a list of material, identified as discoverable, to Plaintiff's counsel within seven (7) days from receipt of the storage device.

(3) If Plaintiff's counsel has a good faith basis for asserting that the listed material is not discoverable, the parties shall file a Joint Report, including (i) a copy of the material, and (ii) each party's position on the discoverability of the material, for the Court's review.

(4) Within ten (10) days after material has been reviewed, and the undersigned Magistrate has issued a ruling, or in the alternative, the parties have resolved the dispute without the Court's intervention, Plaintiff's counsel must provide Defendant's counsel with formal discovery responses, and the storage device must be returned to Plaintiff's counsel. Defense counsel may not make a copy of the material on the storage device.

***

B. Entities that Perform Collection

1. Collection by internal IT department

Collection by the internal IT department of an organization is the most common collection approach. It involves members of the IT department performing the actual data collection at the direction of the legal department. However, the data collection work may keep IT department members from other business-critical projects. Also, since IT department members may not have any experience with data collection for the purpose of e-discovery, they are likely to collect very broadly if there is no clear guidance from the legal department on what to go after specifically, which can lead to more data being collected than necessary.

2. Collection by outside IT professionals

For organizations with very limited or no internal IT resources, a third party expert can be called on to perform the data collection task. An outside expert is likely to have set procedures and all the necessary tools and skill to perform a collection that can withstand the highest level of judicial scrutiny. However, outside IT assistance can be very expensive.

3. Remote Collection

Remote collections employ a centralized internal collection system that is integrated with company data sources, which allows ESI to be collected remotely. Even though the data collection may still be performed by an IT professional, it does not require any direct interaction with the data sources themselves and can usually be performed much quicker and more efficiently than with other data collection methods. These remote collection systems also support more targeted data collections by applying search and analytic technologies. In general, remote collection is the most common and cost effective approach for organizations that deal with consistent data collection demands.

4. Employee Self-Collection

Employee self-collection involves letting the custodians themselves copy relevant files into a shared drive or portable storage device. For matters involving a relatively low volume of conventional data (such as documents and emails), employee self-collection may be sufficient and cost effective. One concern is that many employees are not technically savvy and are very likely to make mistakes and overlook key documents. In addition, employee self-collection may not constitute a "defensible" e-discovery response for some courts because of their high potential for bad actors.

Tips for selecting the appropriate entity or entities to collect ESI

The answers to the following questions will help determine which entity or entities should be engaged in performing data collection for e-discovery:

  i. What is the total data size?
  ii. How many data sources are there?
  iii. How accessible are the data sources?
  iv. Are there encrypted or sensitive data?
  v. Is there any time constraints (production deadlines, retention schedules, etc.)?

EEOC v. M1 5100 CORP.
No. 19-cv-81320 (S.D. Fl. 2020)

MATTHEWMAN, Magistrate Judge

***

I. BACKGROUND

Plaintiff filed its Complaint under the Age Discrimination in Employment Act of 1967, as amended, 29 U.S.C. § 623(a) (the "ADEA"). Plaintiff alleges that Defendant discriminated against Charging Party Angela Araujo Guerrero (a cook manager) when it reduced her pay and fired her because of her age in violation of Section 4(a) of the ADEA, 29 U.S.C. § 623(a).

In its Motion, Plaintiff originally sought responsive documents to several of its requests for production, supplemental responses to several of its interrogatories, the production of a privilege log, inspection of Defendant's electronically stored information ("ESI"), and sanctions against Defendant. However, Defendant eventually provided Plaintiff with supplemental discovery responses after the Motion was filed, and, as ordered by the Court, the parties also further conferred about the discovery disputes. After further conferral, the issue regarding the privilege log has been resolved as have the disputes regarding Interrogatories No. 6 and 10.

Thus, at this point, Plaintiff only seeks better responses to two discovery requests--Interrogatory No. 9 and Request for Production No. 18. Plaintiff is also seeking attorney's fees and costs incurred in filing the Motion. Finally, Plaintiff still seeks the opportunity to inspect Defendant's ESI because, by Defendant's counsel's own admission, Defendant "self-collected" responsive documents and information to the discovery requests without the oversight of its counsel.

As stated in open court and as further specified below, the Court finds that the Motion should be granted in part as to Interrogatory No. 9 and Request for Production No. 18. The Court will also address the "self-collection" issue regarding Defendant, order further conferral on the ESI issue, and reserve jurisdiction on Plaintiff's requests for costs and attorney's fees.

II. THE PERILS OF SELF-COLLECTION OF ESI BY A PARTY OR INTERESTED PERSON WITHOUT THE PROPER SUPERVISION, KNOWLEDGE, OR ASSISTANCE OF ITS COUNSEL

With regard to Plaintiff's request to inspect Defendant's ESI, the Court finds as follows. Defendant's counsel, Dallan Vecchio, Esq., signed Defendant's original discovery responses dated April 20, 2020. However, Defendant stated in its response to the Motion that, "[d]uring conferral, Plaintiff requested Defendant's specific search efforts regarding ESI. At that time, undersigned counsel was not aware of all the specific efforts made."

Defendant's counsel also represented at the June 29, 2020 hearing that he did not supervise his client's ESI collection efforts. Plaintiff's counsel stated at the hearing that the two individuals who searched for documents and information responsive to Plaintiff's discovery requests on Defendant's behalf are self-interested parties and are employees of the Defendant.

This issue of "self-collection" of discovery documents, and especially of ESI, by Defendant in this case, without adequate knowledge, supervision, or participation by counsel, greatly troubles and concerns the Court. The Court will first address the law regarding this issue.

Federal Rule of Civil Procedure 26(g)(1) states in relevant part that

> Every disclosure under Rule 26(a)(1) or (a)(3) and every discovery request, response, or objection must be signed by at least one attorney of record in the attorney's own name....By signing, an attorney or party certifies that to the best of the person's knowledge, information, and belief formed after a reasonable inquiry: (A) with respect to a disclosure, it is complete and correct as of the time it is made; and (B) with respect to a discovery request, response, or objection, it is (i) consistent with these rules and warranted by existing law or by a nonfrivolous argument for extending, modifying, or reversing existing law, or for establishing new law; (ii) not interposed for any improper purpose, such as to harass, cause unnecessary delay, or needlessly increase the cost of litigation; and (iii) neither unreasonable nor unduly burdensome or expensive, considering the needs of the case, prior discovery in the case, the amount in controversy, and the importance of the issues at stake in the action.

Fed. R. Civ. P. 26. "Rule 26(g) imposes an affirmative duty to engage in pretrial discovery in a responsible manner that is consistent with the spirit and purposes of Rules 26 through 37." *See* Advisory Committee Notes to the 1983 Amendments to Fed. R. Civ. P. 26(g). "An attorney is entitled to rely on the assertions of the client, provided that æthe investigation undertaken by the attorney and the conclusions drawn therefrom are reasonable under the circumstances.'" *** A party's discovery obligations also include the duty to use reasonable efforts to locate and produce ESI responsive to the opposing party's requests and within the scope of discovery. To enforce these responsibilities, the attorney's signature on a discovery response "certifies that the lawyer has made a reasonable effort to assure that the client has provided all the information ... responsive to the discovery demand' and has made reasonable inquiry into the factual basis of his response."

The Sedona Conference Working Group on Electronic Document Production, The Sedona Principles: Best Practices Recommendations & Principles for Addressing Electronic Document Production ("The Sedona Principles") p. 119 (3d. ed 2018) (quoting Advisory Comm. Note to Rule 26(g)).

The relevant rules and case law establish that an attorney has a duty and obligation to have knowledge of, supervise, or counsel the client's discovery search, collection, and production. It is clear to the Court that an attorney cannot abandon his professional and ethical duties imposed by the applicable rules and case law and permit an interested party or person to "self-collect" discovery without any attorney advice, supervision, or knowledge of the process utilized. There is simply no responsible way that an attorney can effectively make the representations required under Rule 26(g)(1) and yet have no involvement in, or close knowledge of, the party's search, collection and production of discovery. In this case, it appears that Defendant's counsel left it to the client and the client's employees to determine the appropriate custodians, the necessary search terms, the relevant ESI sources, and what documents should be collected and produced. When combined with Plaintiff's assertion that only 22 pages of documents have been produced by Defendant in this complicated age discrimination case, the Court seriously questions the efficacy of Defendant's search, collection and document production. The Court will not permit an inadequate discovery search, collection and production of discovery, especially ESI, by any party in this case.

Here, Defendant's counsel seemingly failed to properly supervise his client's ESI collection process, but then he signed off on the completeness and correctness of his client's discovery responses. An attorney's signature on a discovery response is not a mere formality; rather, it is a representation to the Court that the discovery is complete and correct at the time it is made. An attorney cannot properly make this representation without having some participatory or supervisory role in the search, collection, and production of discovery by a client or interested person, or at least having sufficient knowledge of the efficacy of the process utilized by the client. Abdicating completely the discovery search, collection and production to a layperson or interested client without the client's attorney having sufficient knowledge of the process, or without the attorney providing necessary advice and assistance, does not meet an attorney's obligation under our discovery rules and case law. Such conduct is improper and contrary to the Federal Rules of Civil Procedure.

Attorneys have a duty to oversee their clients' collection of information and documents, especially when ESI is involved, during the discovery process. Although clients can certainly be tasked with searching for, collecting, and producing discovery, it must be accomplished under the advice and supervision of counsel, or at least with counsel possessing sufficient knowledge of the process utilized by the client. Parties and clients, who are often lay persons, do not normally have the knowledge and expertise to understand their discovery obligations, to conduct appropriate searches, to collect responsive discovery, and then to fully produce it, especially when dealing with ESI, without counsel's guiding hand.

Applicable case law informs that "self collection by a layperson of information on an electronic device is highly problematic and raises a real risk that data could be destroyed or corrupted." *** In the case at hand, it is very clear that Defendant's employees self-collected ESI in order to respond to Plaintiff's document requests without sufficient attorney knowledge, participation, and counsel. This is improper and a practice that can lead to incomplete discovery production or even inadvertent destruction of responsive information and/or documents. The Court is especially concerned that Defendant has only produced 22 pages of documents total in this case and that two self-interested employees allegedly collected the responsive documents and information.

Defendant and Defendant's counsel clearly did not employ the proper practices in responding to Plaintiff's discovery requests. And, the Court is not impressed by the repeated delays in production that have occurred in this case by Defendant. This has caused the Court to seriously consider Plaintiff's request that it be permitted to inspect how Defendant's ESI was searched, collected and produced. However, "[i]nspection of an opposing party's computer system under Rule 34 and state equivalents is the exception and not the rule for discovery of ESI." The Sedona Principles at p. 128. "Special issues may arise with any request for direct access to ESI or to computer devices or systems on which it resides. Protective orders should be in place to guard against any release of proprietary, confidential, or personally identifiable ESI accessible to the adversary or its expert." *** The Court agrees with these propositions and normally only permits inspection of an opposing party's ESI collection and production procedures, computer system, cellular phone, or other platforms when all other reasonable solutions have been exhausted or when the Court suspects bad faith or other discovery misconduct.

Therefore, in light of the fact that the discovery cut-off date in this case is approximately five months ahead, the Court will give Defendant one last chance to comply with its discovery search, collection and production obligations. The Court will not permit Plaintiff to inspect Defendant's ESI at this time and will withhold ruling on that issue until the parties have had the opportunity to further confer. The discovery process, particularly when ESI is involved, is intended to be collaborative. *See* Chief Justice John Roberts, 2015 Yearûend Report on the Federal Judiciary, https://www.supremecourt.gov/publicinfo/year-end/2015 year-endreport.pdf. Thus, the Court will require the parties to further confer on or before July 9, 2020, to try to agree on relevant ESI sources, custodians, and search terms, as well as on a proposed ESI protocol. The parties can submit any proposed orders or agreements to the Court.

On or before July 10, 2020, the parties shall file a joint notice regarding the ESI search, collection and production issue, the inspection issue, whether they wish for the Court to enter any further order(s), and whether the Court needs to set another hearing and resolve any outstanding issues. The conferral process again ordered by the Court must be robust, completed in good faith, and must take as long as necessary to fully address all discovery search, collection, and production issues. Failure to comply shall result in sanctions on the offending attorney and party.

The Court once again warns Defendant and Defendant's counsel that counsel must take a role in assisting Defendant with the search, collection, and production of discovery and must ensure that Defendant's production is complete and correct at the time it is made. Fed. R. Civ. P. 26(g)(1). Counsel or Defendant may also consider retaining an ESI vendor to assist with the process if they deem it necessary. But, however it is accomplished, full discovery must be promptly provided by Defendant. Both Defendant and Defendant's counsel may be sanctioned for failing to fully and completely respond to all discovery requests.

The Court notes that it is not finding at this time that Defendant's counsel has acted in bad faith or has committed any discovery misconduct whatsoever; rather, the Court will give Defendant's counsel the benefit of the doubt and suspects that, during these difficult times of the COVID-19 pandemic, counsel's involvement in the discovery process with his client has been unusually difficult. However, the Court does not want to see these problems continue. The Court also directs Defendant's counsel to impress upon Defendant that it must promptly respond to discovery or it will be subject to sanctions. The Court expects to see no more discovery delays.

The Court reserves jurisdiction as to Plaintiff's request for an ESI inspection and for an award of costs and attorney's fees in favor of Plaintiff and against Defendant and/or its counsel. The Court will re-address these issues after the court-mandated further conferral occurs and the Court hears further from the parties.

Based on the forgoing, and as stated in open court, it is hereby ORDERED AND ADJUDGED as follows:

1. Plaintiff's Motion to Compel a Privilege Log, Better Discovery Responses, and Fees is GRANT IN PART AND DENIED IN PART.

2. The parties shall fully confer in good faith on or before July 9, 2020, and attempt to agree on relevant ESI sources, custodians, and search terms, as well as on a proposed ESI protocol and all other related discovery issues. The parties can submit any proposed orders or agreements or joint motions to the Court for its consideration. Assuming that the parties do reach an agreement, Defendant's attorneys shall counsel and supervise Defendant and Defendant's employees during the discovery search, collection, and production process and become knowledgeable of that process. If any disputes remain, the parties can list them in the joint notice, and the Court will promptly set a further hearing or rule on the papers.

3. On or before July 10, 2020, the parties shall file a joint notice regarding the ESI inspection issue, any search, collection and production issues of discovery by Defendant, and any other related discovery issues. The parties shall concisely describe the issues they have resolved, the issues in dispute (if any), the parties' respective positions, whether they wish for the Court to enter any further order, and whether the Court needs to set another hearing to resolve any outstanding issues. The Court advises the parties that it intends to closely supervise the discovery process in this case to ensure that both parties and their counsel comply with all discovery obligations.

4. The Motion is GRANTED IN PART as to Interrogatory No. 9. On or before July 9, 2020, Defendant shall fully and completely respond to Interrogatory No. 9 as narrowed by Plaintiff in the Joint Notice and also as limited by the Court to the two locations where the Charging Party worked. This ruling is without prejudice to Plaintiff's ability to later seek additional information about Defendant's other two locations if Plaintiff subsequently believes that it has a good faith basis to do so.

5. The Motion is GRANTED IN PART as to Request for Production No. 18. On or before July 9, 2020, Defendant shall fully and completely respond to Request for Production No. 18 as narrowed by Plaintiff in the Joint Notice, and as limited by the Court to the time period of May 1, 2016, through March 31, 2017, and also limited in scope to the two locations where the Charging Party worked. The Court is not ordering Defendant to prepare a list that is not already in its possession, custody or control, although it may do so if it chooses to do so, but the Court is ordering Defendant to produce any responsive documents to the narrowed interrogatory as required by the applicable rules or as agreed to by the parties. This ruling is without prejudice to Plaintiff's ability to later seek additional information about Defendant's other two locations and/or a broader time period if Plaintiff subsequently believes that it has a good faith basis to do so.

***

C. Collection Strategy

Collection strategy usually depends on the case. In some cases, it may be important to collect data immediately, while in other cases, immediate collections may not be necessary, especially when a strong preservation process is already in place.

It is easy to copy an entire hard drive or email folders of all custodians, but it is also important not to over collect because more collected data means more data needed to be processed and reviewed. Instead, implement a strong preservation and early case assessment process, and target data collections so that only the potentially relevant ESI is collected.

It is always best to perform data collection in tiers or phases instead of trying to do everything all at once. A tiered collection strategy involves prioritizing data so that only the highly relevant data are collected immediately, while less relevant data should be collected when necessary.

Differences between e-discovery and digital forensics

E-discovery involves ESI identification, preservation, collection, review, analyze, and production. In general, only active data are collected, which are easily available through file storage and programs utilized by a business or individual, such as desktop computers, laptops, mobile devices, etc. Attorneys typically work with IT professionals, with IT professionals collecting data, and attorneys performing review on the collected data.

On other hand, digital forensics is a scientific method for extracting data from a speciiic digital device, such as a hard drive. A forensic analysis of data is needed when a litigation requires a deeper look at the data. It is typically carried out by digital forensic experts in hardware and software.

Digital forensic experts are brought in to produce more than data for a case. They sorts through data in search of hidden files or deleted data to help provide more-reliable evidence that can be used in a case. They can be called on in legal proceedings to defend their claims about the information.

A forensic extraction seeks to recover everything, including active data, latent data and deleted artifacts. Examples of data that can be discovered using digital forensics includes:

1. Backup data automatically removed from a server.

2. Deleted data--any files that have been deleted will usually remain on a hard drive, as long as the hard drive has not been overwritten or wiped.

3. Wiping software--determine if any hard drive wiping software has been used. This can help make a case that data was destroyed purposely.

E-discovery is useful when the only information needed involves readily accessible files such as documents, spreadsheets, emails, databases, etc. Digital forensics are needed to further analyze the data if the data have been deleted or if someone has tampered with the data.

Logical copy and Forensic image

A logical copy of a computer hard drive is simply a copy of the contents of the active files listed in the directories of the hard drive. On the other hand, a forensic image is a complete copy of a hard drive, including the portions of the hard drive that are not allocated to active files (known as slack space). A forensic image is essentially an exact duplicate (or clone) of the hard drive, bit by bit, which provides both non-hidden files and hidden files. Hidden files can be system files intended for the operating system's usage or deleted files.

Almost anyone can make a logical copy of a hard drive since the process is not very technically intensive. However, it requires specific tools to extract a forensic image of a hard drive. Thus, forensic imaging is usually performed by a skilled technician.

In a great majority of civil matters, a logical copy will suffice. A forensic image is needed only when there is a suspicion of data tampering or in cases where previously deleted files are germane. Thus, when asking an IT professional to collect data from a hard drive, it is important to state whether a logical copy or a forensic image is needed.

D. Data Collection Tools

Data collection is generally not a process supported by a single collection tool. Different collection tools should be deployed depending on the specific collection needs and priorities. The following are some examples of collection tools.

1. In-Place Processing

Conventionally, processing takes place after collection as a separate e-discovery stage, and processing is typically performed by service providers that charge on a per gigabyte basis. Currently, there are collection tools that allow data processing to be performed at the point of data collection. This can eliminate the need to send collected data to a server provider that handles processing.

2. Pre-Collection Analytics

Pre-collection analytics are tools that crawl data sources to produce information such as document volumes, and perform filtering to locate relevant ESI.

3. Data Source Integrations

Instead of conducting manual collections, data source integrators can integrate collection software with enterprise data sources (such as email servers, structured databases, etc.) in order to streamline the collection process. Data source integrators can also perform data collection remotely, which minimize many technical complexities surrounding collections.

4. Spot Collectors

Sport collectors can grab data off a system that is not connected to a network, such as field computer used by an employee working remotely. For example, some spot collector tools are portable USB devices that allow IT professionals or custodians to crawl and collect off non-network systems. Important, spot collector tools can be pre-configured to collect only relevant files rather than complete copies of a hard drive.

5. Mobile Device Collection Tools

Mobile device collection tools are specific devices designed to extract data from mobile devices. These are for extracting data that never leaves the mobile phones, such as text messages.

E. Ensuring Data Integrity

Several procedures are employed to ensure the integrity of the ESI collected during the collection stage.

1. Chain of custody

Chain of custody is defined as the "documentation regarding the possession, movement, handling and location of evidence from the time it is identified to the time it is presented in court or otherwise transferred or submitted" by the Sedona Conference. The authenticity of a document can be demonstrated by a thorough chain of custody log that can disprove any claims of data tampering.

2. Hashing

A hash value (or hash tag or hash code) can be generated for a file by running the file through a *hashing* software (*see* Chapter 15 for details). This hash value, which is an alphanumeric code, can be used as a unique identifier that corresponds to the contents within the file. If the contents of file have been modified or otherwise changed, the file's hash value will be different when the file runs through the hashing software again, indicating that the contents in file is not the same as before.

In order to ensure data integrity for e-discovery, the hash values of a file before and after collection are compared to verify that the contents of the file, including its metadata, are identical before and after collection. Hashing can also help determine whether or not anyone has attempted to tamper with electronic evidence.

3. Audit Trail

Audit trails are automated records generated by systems that track user activity. In the context of data collection for e-discovery, audit trail can be helpful in showing when a collection took place, the amount of data collected, and which party/user initiated the collection if such information is ever requested by a judge and/or opposing party.

CHAPTER 8

TECHNOLOGY-ASSISTED REVIEW

Because of the overwhelmingly large amount of ESI in e-discovery, some attorneys have been using technology-assisted review (TAR) tools to help reducing the time required to review and identify relevant documents. Examples of TAR tools include predictive coding and artificial intelligence (AI) software. By employing technologies from information retrieval science in conjunction with human inputs, these tools are able to identify relevant documents more effectively and efficiently that relying on human efforts alone.

A. Predictive Coding

Method

Predictive coding is a machine-learning process in software that takes human input keyword searches and logic to identify relevant documents. Like many email servers that use spam filters to identify and segregate junk or unwanted emails, predictive coding uses filters to examine incoming ESI based on specific criteria provided by human, and then sorts the ESI into relevant or non-relevant categories. After a specific algorithm has been proven to work on a small scale, the same algorithm can be applied to a larger, if not the entire, document set such that the number of documents that need to be manually reviewed can be drastically reduced.

The details of any specific algorithm within predictive coding are generally proprietary, but at a very high level, the workflow of predictive coding should resemble the flowchart in Figure 8.1, and the steps are described as follows.

1. Build seed set

Initially, a *seed set* (or training set) is built by pulling a representative cross-section of documents from the full population of documents that need to be reviewed. Currently, there are two acceptable methods for building seed sets, namely, random selection and judgmental (or subjective) selection.

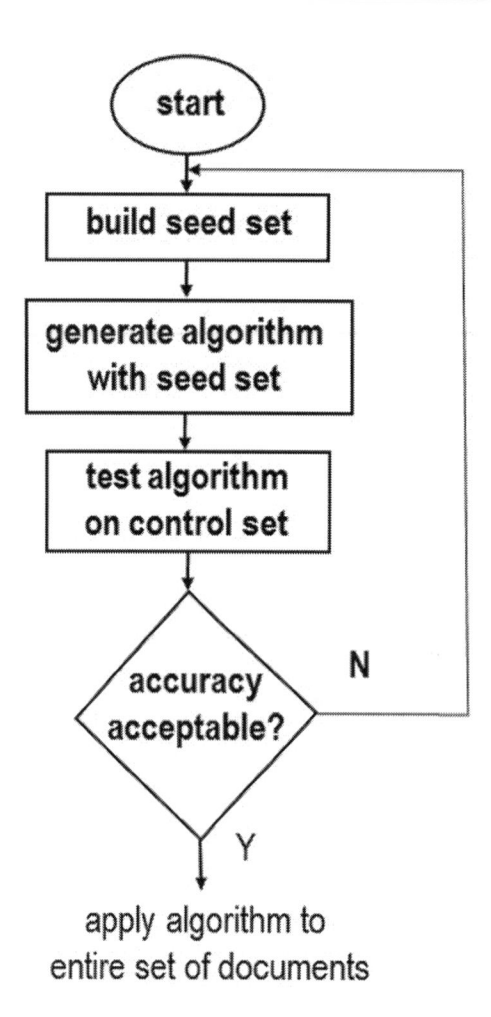

Figure 8.1

Random selection means randomly selecting a small number of documents from the entire set of documents that need to be reviewed for the inclusion in the seed set. With judgmental selection, reviewers (usually skilled attorneys) with knowledge of the case specifically select documents for the inclusion in the seed set. They represent categories of documents the reviewers feel are representative of issues in the case and are clear examples of relevant, non-relevant, or privileged documents. The reviewers label each document in the seed set as *responsive*, *nonresponsive*, privilege, or any similar variations, accordingly, and those examples are entered into the predictive coding software. Whether or not a seed set works well usually depends on the volume of material to be reviewed, the complexity of the issues involved, the reviewers' understanding of the case, and the technical skills of the predictive coding specialist.

2. Generate algorithm with seed set

The predictive coding software analyzes the seed set and generates an algorithm (predictive formula) for predicting the responsiveness of future documents. The algorithm is generated by the predictive coding software in an iterative manner. This is the machine learning portion of predictive coding.

With *passive learning*, completely random document samples are utilized to train the predictive coding software until the desired result is achieved.

With *active learning*, the seed set is repeatedly augmented by additional documents chosen specifically by the algorithm, and manually coded by the reviewers until the desired results are achieved. Specifically, the algorithm generates a model to be used to analyze other documents, and the algorithm typically assigns a numerical score to each document that reflects the probability that the document fits within the model. The reviewers take this random set of ranked documents and manually examine them to see whether or not the algorithm correctly identify the relevant and non-relevant documents. This interactive examination is repeatedly performed to ensure that the algorithm is effective in finding and categorizing documents.

3. Test algorithm on control set

The algorithm must be tested on a control set. This is typically performed by having the algorithm attempt to identify the relevant documents in the control set. The result from the control set are examined by the reviewers to see whether or not the algorithm has correctly identified relevant documents as well as correctly identifying or predicting the non-relevant and privileged documents.

Accuracy and *confidence levels*, in percentages, are typically utilized to evaluate the effectiveness of any predictive coding methodology. Suffice to say, the accuracy and confidence levels of the predictive coding algorithm are paramount. Without reliable data to indicate the predictive coding algorithm is working correctly, the user of predictive coding cannot demonstrate to the court and/or opposing party that predictive coding is accurately locating the responsive material requested.

When the accuracy and confidence levels of the predictive coding algorithm are considered acceptable, it can be applied to the entire set of documents that need to be reviewed in order to label each document as responsive or unresponsive.

Benefits of Predictive Coding

In recent years, predictive coding has secured a well-established place in the land of e-discovery because of its many benefits.

1. Augment human review

Predictive coding attempts to combine and strike a healthy balance between the speed of machine review and the accuracy of experienced human review. Unlike traditional keyword searches followed by a manual review by scores of attorneys, predictive coding only needs manual review by a small team of experienced attorneys.

Predictive coding automatically categorizes and prioritizes documents based not just on keyword frequency, but also on other qualities like document type, language, content, party, time frame, individual name, and concept meaning. These attributes allow the predictive coding algorithm to group and prioritize similar documents in a more accurate and consistent manner than human reviewers.

2. Accuracy

When performed correctly, predictive coding is more accurate than traditional manual review in locating and identifying relevant documents. This is attributed to the use of complex algorithms in a more predictable review process, which is less prone to human error or variation.

Drawbacks of Predictive Coding

While predictive coding has many benefits, it also has some drawbacks.

1. Cost

Although predictive coding can be a cheaper solution than human review, it is not for all cases due to the relatively high upfront cost. As a general rule, it is not cost effective to employ predictive coding for cases having fewer than 200,000 documents needed to be reviewed.

2. Not suitable for all document types

Predictive coding is not conducive for cases that involve documents having large quantities of graphics, spreadsheets, non-textual materials, and/or materials in foreign languages. This is because current predictive coding software does not perform well in identifying those types of documents, but AI type of machine learning software may be a potential solution.

3. Skilled specialist required

The success of predictive coding often depends on a team of people that can validate and verify the accuracy of the predictive coding search technology. Skilled e-discovery specialists are required to design a robust predictive coding algorithm. In addition, active involvement of experienced reviewers is also required. For predictive coding to work, the software has to be trained by an experienced attorney who is familiar with the case to recognize and locate relevant documents. The accuracy of the predictive coding software is ultimately dependent on the decisions of the reviewer, from the selection of the seed set to the subsequent coding choices.

4. Seed set disclosure

Many disputes have been centered on how transparent parties have to be with how their seed sets are constructed and coded. It appears that many courts prefer transparency and thus require disclosure with their seed set development. This means that opposing party will be entitled to see the entire seed set, including nonresponsive documents and all documents used to train the predictive coding algorithm (which is not available under a typical manual document review process).

A random seed set does not disclose attorney-work product, while a judgmental seed set would, because it involves the selection of certain documents deemed to be representative of issues in the case. This problem can be eliminated if parties agree to build the seed set collaboratively.

B. Courts' view on TAR

In *Da Silva Moore v. Publicis Groupe*, 287 F.R.D. 182 (S.D.N.Y. 2012), the court approved of the use of TAR of ESI, making it likely the first case to recognize that TAR is an acceptable way to search for relevant ESI in appropriate cases.

DA SILVA MOORE V. PUBLICIS GROUPE
287 F.R.D. 182 (S.D.N.Y. 2012)

PECK, Magistrate Judge

COMPUTER-ASSISTED REVIEW EXPLAINED

My Search, Forward article explained my understanding of computer-assisted review, as follows:

By computer-assisted coding, I mean tools (different vendors use different names) that use sophisticated algorithms to enable the computer to determine relevance based on interaction with (i.e., training by) a human reviewer.

Unlike manual review, where the review is done by the most junior staff, computer-assisted coding involves a senior partner (or [small] team) who review and code a "seed set" of documents. The computer identifies properties of those documents that it uses to code other documents. As the senior reviewer continues to code more sample documents, the computer predicts the reviewer's coding. (Or, the computer codes some documents and asks the senior reviewer for feedback.)

When the system's predictions and the reviewer's coding sufficiently coincide, the system has learned enough to make confident predictions for the remaining documents. Typically, the senior lawyer (or team) needs to review only a few thousand documents to train the computer.

Some systems produce a simple yes/no as to relevance, while others give a relevance score (say, on a 0 to 100 basis) that counsel can use to prioritize review. For example, a score above 50 may produce 97% of the relevant documents, but constitutes only 20% of the entire document set.

Counsel may decide, after sampling and quality control tests, that documents with a score of below 15 are so highly likely to be irrelevant that no further human review is necessary. Counsel can also decide the cost-benefit of manual review of the documents with scores of 15-50.

My article further explained my belief that *Daubert* would not apply to the results of using predictive coding, but that in any challenge to its use, this Judge would be interested in both the process used and the results:

> [I]f the use of predictive coding is challenged in a case before me, I will want to know what was done and why that produced defensible results. I may be less interested in the science behind the "black box" of the vendor's software than in whether it produced responsive documents with reasonably high recall and high precision.
>
> That may mean allowing the requesting party to see the documents that were used to train the computer-assisted coding system. (Counsel would not be required to explain why they coded documents as responsive or non-responsive, just what the coding was.) Proof of a valid "process," including quality control testing, also will be important.

Of course, the best approach to the use of computer-assisted coding is to follow the Sedona Cooperation Proclamation model. Advise opposing counsel that you plan to use computer-assisted coding and seek agreement; if you cannot, consider whether to abandon predictive coding for that case or go to the court for advance approval.

THE ESI DISPUTES IN THIS CASE AND THEIR RESOLUTION

***

Custodians

The first issue regarding the ESI protocol involved the selection of which custodians' emails would be searched. MSL agreed to thirty custodians for a "first phase." MSL's custodian list included the president and other members of MSL's "executive team," most of its HR staff and a number of managing directors.

***

The final issue raised by plaintiffs related to the phasing of custodians and the discovery cutoff dates. MSL proposed finishing phase-one discovery completely before considering what to do about a second phase. Plaintiffs expressed concern that there would not be time for two separate phases, essentially seeking to move the phase-two custodians back into phase one. The Court found MSL's separate phase approach to be more sensible and noted that if necessary, the Court would extend the discovery cutoff to allow the parties to pursue discovery in phases.

Sources of ESI

The parties agreed on certain ESI sources, including the "EMC SourceOne [Email] Archive," the "PeopleSoft" human resources information management system and certain other sources including certain HR "shared" folders. As to other "shared" folders, neither side was able to explain whether the folders merely contained forms and templates or collaborative working documents; the Court therefore left those shared folders for phase two unless the parties promptly provided information about likely contents.

The Court noted that because the named plaintiffs worked for MSL, plaintiffs should have some idea what additional ESI sources, if any, likely had relevant information; since the Court needed to consider proportionality pursuant to Rule 26(b)(2)(C), plaintiffs needed to provide more information to the Court than they were doing if they wanted to add additional data sources into phase one. The Court also noted that where plaintiffs were getting factual information from one source (e.g., pay information, promotions, etc.), "there has to be a limit to redundancy" to comply with Rule 26(b)(2)(C).

The Predictive Coding Protocol

The parties agreed to use a 95% confidence level (plus or minus two percent) to create a random sample of the entire email collection; that sample of 2,399 documents will be reviewed to determine relevant (and not relevant) documents for a "seed set" to use to train the predictive coding software. An area of disagreement was that MSL reviewed the 2,399 documents before the parties agreed to add two additional concept groups (i.e., issue tags). MSL suggested that since it had agreed to provide all 2,399 documents (and MSL's coding of them) to plaintiffs for their review, plaintiffs can code them for the new issue tags, and MSL will incorporate that coding into the system. Plaintiffs' vendor agreed to that approach.

To further create the seed set to train the predictive coding software, MSL coded certain documents through "judgmental sampling." The remainder of the seed set was created by MSL reviewing "keyword" searches with Boolean connectors (such as "training and Da Silva Moore," or "promotion and Da Silva Moore") and coding the top fifty hits from those searches. MSL agreed to provide all those documents (except privileged ones) to plaintiffs for plaintiffs to review MSL's relevance coding. In addition, plaintiffs provided MSL with certain other keywords, and MSL used the same process with plaintiffs' keywords as with the MSL keywords, reviewing and coding an additional 4,000 documents. All of this review to create the seed set was done by senior attorneys (not paralegals, staff attorneys or junior associates). MSL reconfirmed that "[a]ll of the documents that are reviewed as a function of the seed set, whether [they] are ultimately coded relevant or irrelevant, aside from privilege, will be turned over to" plaintiffs.

The next area of discussion was the iterative rounds to stabilize the training of the software. MSL's vendor's predictive coding software ranks documents on a score of 100 to zero, i.e., from most likely relevant to least likely relevant. MSL proposed using seven iterative rounds; in each round they would review at least 500 documents from different concept clusters to see if the computer is returning new relevant documents. After the seventh round, to determine if the computer is well trained and stable, MSL would review a random sample (of 2,399 documents) from the discards (i.e., documents coded as non-relevant) to make sure the documents determined by the software to not be relevant do not, in fact, contain highly-relevant documents. For each of the seven rounds and the final quality-check random sample, MSL agreed that it would show plaintiffs all the documents it looked at including those deemed not relevant (except for privileged documents).

Plaintiffs' vendor noted that "we don't at this point agree that this is going to work. This is new technology and it has to be proven out." Plaintiffs' vendor agreed, in general, that computer-assisted review works, and works better than most alternatives. Indeed, plaintiffs' vendor noted that "it is fair to say [that] we are big proponents of it." The Court reminded the parties that computer-assisted review "works better than most of the alternatives, if not all of the [present] alternatives. So the idea is not to make this perfect, it's not going to be perfect. The idea is to make it significantly better than the alternatives without nearly as much cost."

The Court accepted MSL's proposal for the seven iterative reviews, but with the following caveat:

> But if you get to the seventh round and [plaintiffs] are saying that the computer is still doing weird things, it's not stabilized, etc., we need to do another round or two, either you will agree to that or you will both come in with the appropriate QC information and everything else and [may be ordered to] do another round or two or five or 500 or whatever it takes to stabilize the system.

***

FURTHER ANALYSIS AND LESSONS FOR THE FUTURE

The decision to allow computer-assisted review in this case was relatively easy — the parties agreed to its use (although disagreed about how best to implement such review). The Court recognizes that computer-assisted review is not a magic, Staples-Easy-Button, solution appropriate for all cases. The technology exists and should be used where appropriate, but it is not an ease of machine replacing humans: it is the process used and the interaction of man and machine that the courts needs to examine.

The objective of review in ediscovery is to identify as many relevant documents as possible, while reviewing as few non-relevant documents as possible. Recall is the fraction of relevant documents identified during a review; precision is the fraction of identified documents that are relevant. Thus, recall is a measure of completeness, while precision is a measure of accuracy or correctness. The goal is for the review method to result in higher recall and higher precision than another review method, at a cost proportionate to the "value" of the case.

The slightly more difficult case would be where the producing party wants to use computer-assisted review and the requesting party objects. The question to ask in that situation is what methodology would the requesting party suggest instead? Linear manual review is simply too expensive where, as here, there are over three million emails to review. Moreover, while some lawyers still consider manual review to be the "gold standard," that is a myth, as statistics clearly show that computerized searches are at least as accurate, if not more so, than manual review. Herb Roitblatt, Anne Kershaw, and Patrick Oot of the Electronic Discovery Institute conducted an empirical assessment to "answer the question of whether there was a benefit to engaging in a traditional human review or whether computer systems could be relied on to produce comparable results," and concluded that "[o]n every measure, the performance of the two computer systems was at least as accurate (measured against the original review) as that of human re-review."

Likewise, Wachtell, Lipton, Rosen & Katz litigation counsel Maura Grossman and University of Waterloo professor Gordon Cormack, studied data from the Text Retrieval Conference Legal Track (TREC) and concluded that: "[T]he myth that exhaustive manual review is the most effective—and therefore the most defensible—approach to document review is strongly refuted. Technology-assisted review can (and does) yield more accurate results than exhaustive manual review, with much lower effort." The technology-assisted reviews in the Grossman-Cormack article also demonstrated significant cost savings over manual review: "The technology-assisted reviews require, on average, human review of only 1.9% of the documents, a fifty-fold savings over exhaustive manual review."

Because of the volume of ESI, lawyers frequently have turned to keyword searches to cull email (or other ESI) down to a more manageable volume for further manual review. Keywords have a place in production of ESI—indeed, the parties here used keyword searches (with Boolean connectors) to find documents for the expanded seed set to train the predictive coding software. In too many cases, however, the way lawyers choose keywords is the equivalent of the child's game of "Go Fish." The requesting party guesses which keywords might produce evidence to support its case without having much, if any, knowledge of the responding party's "cards" (i.e., the terminology used by the responding party's custodians). Indeed, the responding party's counsel often does not know what is in its own client's "cards."

Another problem with keywords is that they often are over-inclusive, that is, they find responsive documents but also large numbers of irrelevant documents. In this case, for example, a keyword search for "training" resulted in 165,208 hits; Da Silva Moore's name resulted in 201,179 hits; "bonus" resulted in 40,756 hits; "compensation" resulted in 55,602 hits; and "diversity" resulted in 38,315 hits. If MSL had to manually review all of the keyword hits, many of which would not be relevant (i.e., would be false positives), it would be quite costly.

Moreover, keyword searches usually are not very effective. In 1985, scholars David Blair and M. Mar≤n collected 40,000 documents from a Bay Area Rapid Transit accident, and instructed experienced attorney and paralegal searchers to use keywords and other review techniques to retrieve at least 75% of the documents relevant to 51 document requests. Searchers believed they met the goals, but their average recall was just 20%. This result has been replicated in the TREC Legal Track studies over the past few years.

Judicial decisions have criticized specific keyword searches. Important early decisions in this area came from two of the leading judicial scholars in ediseovery, Magistrate Judges John Facciola (District of Columbia) and Paul Grimm (Maryland). I followed their lead with William A. Gross Construction Associates, Inc., when I wrote:

> This Opinion should serve as a wake-up call to the Bar in this District about the need for careful thought, quality control, testing, and cooperation with opposing counsel in designing search terms or "keywords" to be used to produce emails or other electronically stored information ("ESI").
>
> Electronic discovery requires cooperation between opposing counsel and transparency in all aspects of preservation and production of ESI. Moreover, where counsels are using keyword searches for retrieval of ESI, they at a minimum must carefully craft the appropriate keywords, with input from the ESI's custodians as to the words and abbreviations they use, and the proposed methodology must be quality control tested to assure accuracy in retrieval and elimination of "false positives." It is time that the Bar—even those lawyers who did not come of age in the computer era — understand this.
>
> Computer-assisted review appears to be better than the available alternatives, and thus should be used in appropriate cases. While this Court recognizes that computer-assisted review is not perfect, the Federal Rules of Civil Procedure do not require perfection. Courts and litigants must be cognizant of the aim of Rule 1, to "secure the just, speedy, and inexpensive determination" of lawsuits. Fed.R.Civ.P. 1. That goal is further reinforced by the proportionality doctrine set forth in Rule 26(b)(2)(C) ***.
>
> In this case, the Court determined that the use of predictive coding was appropriate considering: (1) the parties' agreement, (2) the vast amount of ESI to be reviewed (over three million documents), (3) the superiority of computer-assisted review to the available alternatives (i.e., linear manual review or keyword searches), (4) the need for cost effectiveness and proportionality under Rule 26(b)(2)(C), and (5) the transparent process proposed by MSL.
>
> This Court was one of the early signatories to The Sedona Conference Cooperation Proclamation, and has stated that "the best solution in the entire area of electronic discovery is cooperation among counsel. This Court strongly endorses The Sedona Conference Proclamation (available at www.TheSedona Conference.org). An important aspect of cooperation is transparency in the discovery process. MSL's transparency in its proposed ESI search protocol made it easier for the Court to approve the use of predictive coding. As discussed above on page 10, MSL confirmed that "[a]ll of the documents that are reviewed as a function of the seed set, whether [they] are ultimately coded relevant or irrelevant, aside

from privilege, will be turned over to" plaintiffs. While not all experienced ESI counsel believe it necessary to be as transparent as MSL was willing to be, such transparency allows the opposing counsel (and the Court) to be more comfortable with computer-assisted review, reducing fears about the so-called "black box" of the technology. This Court highly recommends that counsel in future cases be willing to at least discuss, if not agree to, such transparency in the computer-assisted review process.

Several other lessons for the future can be derived from the Court's resolution of the ESI discovery disputes in this case.

First, it is unlikely that courts will be able to determine or approve a party's proposal as to when review and production can stop until the computer-assisted review software has been trained and the results are quality control verified. Only at that point can the parties and the Court see where there is a clear drop off from highly relevant to marginally relevant to not likely to be relevant documents. While cost is a factor under Rule 26(b)(2)(C), it cannot be considered in isolation from the results of the predictive coding process and the amount at issue in the litigation.

Second, staging of discovery by starting with the most likely to be relevant sources (including custodians), without prejudice to the requesting party seeking more after conclusion of that first stage review, is a way to control discovery costs. If staging requires a longer discovery period, most judges should be willing to grant such an extension.

Third, in many cases requesting counsel's client has knowledge of the producing party's records, either because of an employment relationship as here or because of other dealings between the parties (e.g., contractual or other business relationships). It is surprising that in many cases counsels do not appear to have sought and utilized their client's knowledge about the opposing party's custodians and document sources. Similarly, counsel for the producing party often is not sufficiently knowledgeable about their own client's custodians and business terminology. Another way to phrase cooperation is "strategic proactive disclosure of information," i.e., if you are knowledgeable about and tell the other side who your key custodians are and how you propose to search for the requested documents, opposing counsel and the Court are more apt to agree to your approach (at least as phase one without prejudice).

Fourth, the Court found it very helpful that the parties' ediscovery vendors were present and spoke at the court hearings where the ESI Protocol was discussed. Even whereas here counsel is very familiar with ESI issues, it is very helpful to have the parties' ediscovery vendors (or in-house IT personnel or in-house ediscovery counsel) present at court conferences where ESI issues are being discussed. It also is important for the vendors and/or knowledgeable counsel to be able to explain complicated ediscovery concepts in ways that make it easily understandable to judges who may not be tech-savvy.

CONCLUSION

This Opinion appears to be the first in which a Court has approved of the use of computer-assisted review. That does not mean computer-assisted review must be used in all eases, or that the exact ESI protocol approved here will be appropriate in all future cases that utilize computer-assisted review. Nor does this Opinion endorse any vendor, nor any particular computer-assisted review tool. What the Bar should take away from this Opinion is that computer-assisted review is an available tool and should be seriously considered for use in large-data-volume cases where it may save the producing party (or both parties) significant amounts of legal fees in document review. Counsel no longer have to worry about being the "first" or "guinea pig" for judicial acceptance of computer-assisted review. As with keywords or any other technological solution to ediscovery, counsel must design an appropriate process, including use of available technology, with appropriate quality control testing, to review and produce relevant ESI while adhering to Rule 1 and Rule 26(b)(2)(C) proportionality. Computer-assisted review now can be considered judicially-approved for use in appropriate cases.

***

ENTRATA, INC. V. YARDI SYSTEMS, INC.
No. 2:15-cv-00102 (D. Utah 2018)

WADDOUPS, Judge

***

I. Background

On December 21, 2016, the parties submitted a Stipulated Attorneys Planning Meeting Report. This Meeting Report contained a "Discovery Plan." The discovery plan provided, in part, that "[d]iscovery of electronically stored information ("ESI") should be handled as follows: The Parties are negotiating an ESI protocol which they intend to present to the Court by stipulation."

According to Entrata, "[i]n May of 2017," "the parties conferred on multiple occasions regarding the use of TAR." According to Entrata, the parties met telephonically on May 12, 2017 "to negotiate aspects of the parties' document collection and production methodologies, including Entrata's proposed use of TAR." According to Entrata, the parties did the same on May 16, 2017. On May 19, 2017, one of Yardi's attorneys, Jessica Walker, sent Entrata's attorneys "a list of questions ... about the TAR process [Entrata] [was] planning to use." On May 25, 2017, Mary Gilbert, an Entrata attorney, responded "we will be prepared to discuss your questions about the TAR process Entrata is planning to use on our call tomorrow."

According to both parties, on May 26, 2017, the parties met and conferred again regarding TAR. According to Entrata, at this meet and confer, "Entrata's counsel answered questions from Yardi's counsel regarding Entrata's anticipated TAR process, including how Entrata intended to identify seed documents, whether Entrata would be filtering any data before using TAR, and how Entrata would handle documents that could not be categorized by TAR." According to Entrata, "Entrata's counsel also made clear that Entrata was using TAR as a culling mechanism and would be doing a linear review of documents identified by TAR as likely responsive to Yardi's discovery requests."

On May 26, 2017, the same day that the parties met and conferred regarding TAR, Entrata filed a Short-Form Motion for Entry of an Order Governing Discovery of Electronically Stored Information. As an attachment to this Motion, Entrata included a Proposed Order Governing ESI discovery. Entrata's proposed order contained the following provision:

> The parties agree to work together in good faith to identify and negotiate a reasonable set of search terms and/or other search methodology to be used in searches for ESI. If the parties are unable to agree on a reasonable set of search terms or other search methodology within 30 days of the entry of this Order, the parties will submit competing proposals using the short-form discovery motion procedure set forth in DUCivR 37-1(a).

On May 26, 2017, Yardi also filed a Short-Form Motion for Entry of an Order Governing Discovery of Electronically Stored Information. Like Entrata, Yardi also attached a Proposed Order Governing Discovery of Electronically Stored Information. Yardi's proposed order contained the following provision:

> The parties agree to work together in good faith to identify and negotiate a reasonable set of search terms and/or other search methodology to be applied to the parties' searches for ESI responsive to any and all RFPs. If the parties are unable to agree on a reasonable set of search terms or other search methodology within 30 days of the entry of this Order, the parties will submit competing proposals using the short-form discovery motion procedure set forth in DUCivR 37-1(a).

On May 30, 2017, Ms. Walker, one of Yardi's attorneys, wrote to Entrata's attorneys: "we are still conferring with our expert on TAR, and appreciate the information you provided during our call last week." According to Entrata, "Yardi did not pose any further questions" regarding TAR until sometime in October 2017.

On September 20, 2017, the Magistrate Court entered an Order Governing Discovery of Electronically Stored Information. The Order provided, in part:

> [t]he parties are to work together in good faith to identify and negotiate a reasonable set of search terms and/or other search methodology to be used in searches of ESI. If the parties are unable to agree on a reasonable set of search terms or other search

methodology within 30 days of the entry of this Order, the parties will submit competing proposals using the short-form discovery motion procedure set forth in DUCivR 37-1(a).

Neither party submitted a proposal within 30 days of the Magistrate Court's entry of this Order.

As noted in footnote 2, Yardi raised TAR again during an October 2, 2017 meet and confer. According to Entrata, this occurred "after the substantial completion deadline for document productions, after Entrata had relied on TAR to fulfill its discovery obligations, and after Entrata had objected to Yardi's massive [September 29-30] document dump." In an October 16 filing to the Magistrate Court, Yardi stated that it "anticipate[d] bringing a motion to compel Entrata to share its TAR statistics and, if appropriate, to produce all responsive documents that were withheld based on an almost certainly unreliable and therefore insufficient TAR process."

Both parties agree that a meet-and-confer occurred on January 26, 2018. According to Entrata, at this meet-and-confer, "[f]or the first time since October 2017, Yardi demanded ... TAR metrics from Entrata." According to Yardi, at this meet-and-confer, "Entrata's counsel ... took the position that Yardi had waited too long to ask about Entrata's TAR metrics."

On April 4, 2018, Yardi sent Entrata an email. In this email, Yardi demanded that Entrata "provide complete information about its TAR process, including ... its recall results." On April 13, 2018, Entrata responded to Yardi's email, characterizing Yardi's request as "untimely and improper." In this email, Entrata referenced the October 2, 2017 meet and confer. It appears that the parties met and conferred again on April 23, 2018 during a conference call. This meet and confer call was summarized in an April 24, 2018 email. The email reveals that TAR was mentioned at the meet and confer call. On May 13, 2018 the parties exchanged emails regarding a proposal relating to TAR information, but ultimately came to an "impasse."

May 21, 2018 was the last day of fact discovery. On that day, Yardi filed its Short Form Discovery Motion to Compel Production of TAR Information. In that Motion, Yardi "respectfully request[ed] that the Court compel Entrata ... to produce the complete methodology and results of Entrata's Technology Assisted Review (TAR) process." Yardi argued that "[t]his information is necessary to allow Yardi to assess the adequacy of Entrata's document collection and review efforts and the completeness of Entrata's productionsùand fully supported by case law."

On May 29, 2018, Entrata filed its Opposition to Yardi's Motion. Entrata argued that Yardi's motion was "remarkably untimely," in part, because Yardi "wait[ed] until the last day of fact discovery" to file it. Entrata also argued that Yardi's motion "offer[ed] no reason to believe ... that Entrata's TAR process was deficient."

On June 20, 2018, the Magistrate Court entered an Order denying Yardi's Motion. In its Order, the Magistrate Court stated, in part:

> Yardi has not provided any specific examples of deficiencies in Entrata's document production or any specific reason why it questions the adequacy of Entrata's document collection and review. Without more detailed reasons why production of Entrata's TAR information is needed, the court is unwilling to order Entrata to produce such information. Furthermore, it is not lost on the court that Yardi waited until the last day of fact discovery to file this motion. In the court's view, if Yardi had specific concerns about Entrata's TAR process, it should have sought court intervention long ago. For those reasons, this motion is denied.

On July 5, 2018, Yardi filed its Objection to the Magistrate Court's Order. Yardi argued that "the Chief Magistrate incorrectly concluded that Yardi bore the burden to provide specific reasons for questioning the adequacy of Entrata's document collection and review, and, from that erroneous premise, denied Yardi's Motion ...." Yardi also argued that it "has shown that the Federal Rules of Civil Procedure and case law require Entrata, in the first instance, to provide transparent disclosures as a requirement attendant to its use of TAR in its document review."

On August 1, 2018, Entrata filed its Response to Yardi's Objection. Entrata argued that Yardi had identified "no particular factual finding that it contends is clearly erroneous or any legal standard underlying the Magistrate Judge's decision that it contends is contrary to law." Entrata further argued that the Magistrate Court properly exercised its "broad discretion in finding Yardi's Motion untimely" and in "finding no cause to delve into Entrata's TAR process at the close of fact discovery." Entrata also argued that it "is entitled to fees and costs for [Yardi's] frivolous appeal."

On August 8, 2018, Yardi filed its Reply. Yardi argued that the Magistrate Court's Order "is clearly erroneous because it relied on Entrata's factual misrepresentations regarding its TAR information." Yardi also argued that "the Magistrate Judge's Order and Entrata's Opposition ignore established law requiring transparency and cooperation when employing TAR." In support of this argument, Yardi stated: "Entrata fails to provide the court with any evidence supporting its claims that Entrata shared information regarding its TAR process. That is because no such evidence exists."

On August 10, 2018, Entrata filed a Motion for Leave to file Sur-Reply. Entrata filed this Sur-Reply "to correct material misstatements by Yardi ...." More specifically, Entrata argued that Yardi's claim that "no such evidence exists" "is demonstrably false." Entrata's Motion was marked as "Unopposed." On August 13, 2018, the court granted Entrata's Motion for Leave to File Sur-Reply. On that same day, Entrata filed its Sur-Reply. On August 14, 2018, Yardi filed a Request to Submit for Decision Regarding Its Rule 72(a)

Objection relating to TAR. Yardi argued that Entrata's Motion for Leave to file Sur-Reply was improper. Yardi requested oral argument "to both further address the merits of its TAR Objection and to rebut and refute any of [Entrata's] improper argument" regarding Entrata's Motion for Leave to file Sur-Reply. The court heard oral argument on September 25, 2018, taking the matter under submission.

II. Rule 72(a)

Under Federal Rule of Civil Procedure 72(a), a district court is required to "consider timely objections [to a nondispositive order from a magistrate judge] and modify or set aside any part of the order that is clearly erroneous or is contrary to law." Fed. R. Civ. P. 72(a); see also 28 U.S.C. § 636(b)(1)(A) ("A judge of the court may reconsider any pretrial matter under this subparagraph (A) where it has been shown that the magistrate judge's order is clearly erroneous or contrary to law."). "Under Rule 72, a district court is 'required to 'defer to the magistrate judge's ruling unless it is clearly erroneous or contrary to law.'" ***

III. Analysis

Yardi argues that the Magistrate Court's Order was "clearly erroneous and contrary to law." Yardi argues that the "Magistrate Judge's Order is clearly erroneous because it relied on Entrata's misrepresentations regarding its TAR information." Yardi also appears to argue that the Magistrate Court's order was contrary to law because "the Federal Rules of Civil Procedure and case law require Entrata, in the first instance, to provide transparent disclosures as a requirement attendant to its use of TAR in its document review."

Factual Findings

Yardi argues that "[t]he Magistrate Judge's single paragraph Order denied Yardi's Motion due to Entrata's false claim that it cooperated with Yardi and provided Yardi with information regarding its TAR metrics and training procedures. This was simply not the case." But nothing in the Magistrate Court's Order indicates that it relied on Entrata's "false claim." The Magistrate Court denied Yardi's Motion because Yardi did not point to any deficiencies in Entrata's production and because Yardi waited until the last day of fact discovery to file its Motion-not because it made a factual finding relying on any of Entrata's representations. The Magistrate Court's order was not clearly erroneous.

Legal Determinations

Yardi argues that "the Chief Magistrate incorrectly concluded that Yardi bore the burden to provide specific reasons for questioning the adequacy of Entrata's document collection and review, and, from that erroneous premise, denied Yardi's" Motion. Yardi argues that it did not bear the burden to demonstrate deficiencies in Entrata's production. As noted above, Yardi argues that "the Federal Rules of Civil Procedure and case law require Entrata, in the first instance, to provide transparent disclosures as a requirement attendant to its use of TAR in its document review." As Entrata points out, Yardi cites no Federal Rule in support of this argument. The court nevertheless briefly discusses the parties' obligations under the Federal Rules of Civil Procedure.

"The scope of the obligation to search for, and produce, ESI is circumscribed by Federal Rule of Civil Procedure 26(g) ...." Karl Schieneman & Thomas C. Gricks III, The Implications of Rule 26(g) on the Use of Technology-Assisted Review, 7 Fed. Cts. L. Rev. 239, 243 (2013). But "[n]othing in Rule 26(g) obligates counsel to disclose the manner in which documents are collected, reviewed and produced in response to a discovery request." *Id.* at 254. "However, Federal Rule of Civil Procedure 26(f) does require counsel to meet and confer, and prepare a discovery plan, which 'must state ... any issues about disclosure, discovery, or preservation of electronically stored information, including the form or forms in which it should be produced." Id. at 254-55 (quoting Federal Rule of Civil Procedure 26(f)(3)(C)). "The Rule 26(f) discovery conference is not merely a perfunctory exercise." Scheindlin & Daniel J. Capa, Electronic Discovery and Digital Evidence 257 (2015). "Rather, it is an opportunity for the parties to educate themselves and their adversaries, anticipate and resolve electronic discovery disputes before they escalate, expedite the progress of their case, and assess and manage litigation costs." *Id.* (emphasis added); *see also UnitedHealthcare of Fla., Inc. v. Am. Renal Assocs. LLC*, No. 16-CV-81180, 2017 WL 4785457, at *4 (S.D. Fla. Oct. 20, 2017) ("Courts expect that counsel will endeavor to cooperate and reach agreements early in litigation regarding ... the method of search (keyword, TAR, combination) ... and to revisit issues, if necessary, as more facts are discovered or legal theories are refined." (quoting The Federal Judges' Guide to Discovery, Edition 3.0, The Electronic Discovery Institute (2017) at 50)). "The obligation to address electronic discovery at the Rule 26(f) meet and confer rests with the litigants." Scheindlin & Daniel J. Capa, Electronic Discovery and Digital Evidence 258 (2015).

The Federal Rules of Civil Procedure assume cooperation in discovery. Here, the parties never reached an agreement regarding search methodology. In the court's view, the lack of any agreement regarding search methodology is a failure on the part of both parties. Nevertheless, Yardi knew, as early as May of 2017, that Entrata intended to use TAR. The Magistrate Court's September 20, 2017 Order stated, in part, that "[i]f the parties are unable to agree on ... search methodology within 30 days of the entry of this Order, the parties will submit competing proposals ...." Yardi, as early as October 2, 2017, knew that "Entrata [was] refus[ing] to provide" "TAR statistics." In other words, Yardi knew that the parties had not reached an agreement regarding search methodology well before the thirty day window closed. Because Yardi knew that the parties had not reached an agreement on search methodology, it should have filed a proposal with the Magistrate Court. This would have almost certainly aided in resolving this dispute long before it escalated. But neither party filed any proposal with the Magistrate Court within 30 days of entry of its Order. Yardi has not pointed to any Federal Rule of Civil Procedure demonstrating that the Magistrate Court's Order was contrary to law. This court rejects Yardi's argument relating to the Federal Rules of Civil Procedure.

The court now turns to Yardi's argument that case law required Entrata, "in the first instance, to provide transparent disclosures as a requirement attendant to its use of TAR in its document review." In its objection, Yardi cites primarily to three cases in support of its position.

The first is *Progressive Cas. Ins. Co. v. Delaney*, No. 2:11-CV-00678-LRH, 2014 WL 3563467 (D. Nev. July 18, 2014). In that case, "[t]he parties submitted a joint proposed ESI protocol," "and agreed to search terms to run across ESI which [the plaintiff] represented was in its possession ...." *Id.* at *6. After agreeing to that ESI protocol, the plaintiff "began utilizing predictive coding techniques to review ESI without the Defendant's agreement to amend the parties' stipulated ESI protocol Order ... and without seeking leave of the court to amend the ESI Order." *Id.* at *2. The predictive coding the plaintiff sought "would [have] relieve[d] it of the burden of manual review of ESI according to the ESI protocol it [had originally] stipulated to ...." *Id.* at *10. Ultimately, the court did not allow the plaintiff to use predictive coding. See id. at *11. But the court did state that "[h]ad the parties worked with their e-discovery consultants at the onset of [that] case to a predictive coding-based ESI protocol, the court would not hesitate to approve a transparent, mutually agreed upon ESI protocol. However, this is not what happened." *Id.* at *9. Progressive is different from this case because in Progressive the parties "agreed to search terms to run across ESI." *Id.* at *6. Here, as discussed above, the parties never reached any agreement regarding search methodology.

The second case that Yardi cites is *Bridgestone Americas, Inc. v. Int'l Bus. Machines Corp.*, No. 3:13-1196, 2014 WL 4923014 (M.D. Tenn. July 22, 2014). In that case, the plaintiff "request[ed] to use predictive coding in reviewing something over two million documents for responsiveness." *Id.* at *1. The defendant opposed this request, because it considered the "request as being an unwarranted change in the original case management order" and because it argued that "it is unfair to use predictive coding after an initial screening has been done with search terms." *Id.* The court permitted plaintiff to use predictive coding, but noted that it was "allowing [p]laintiff to switch horses midstream." *Id.* The court also noted that "[i]n the final analysis, the uses of predictive coding is a judgment call ...." *Id.* Like *Progressive*, *Bridgestone* is different from this case because Entrata did not switch to TAR "midstream." Again, Entrata and Yardi never reached an agreement regarding search methodology.

The third case Yardi relies on is *Da Silva Moore v. Publicis Groupe*, 287 F.R.D. 182 (S.D.N.Y. 2012). In that case, "the parties had agreed to defendants' use of [predictive coding,] but had disputes over the scope and implementation, which the Court ruled on, thus accepting the use of computer-assisted review in [that] lawsuit." *Id.* at 183 n. 1. Again, this is different than the facts of this case, where the parties never reached an agreement regarding the use of TAR.

But *Da Silva* does support the proposition that Entrata should have received approval from the court before using TAR. In *Da Silva*, the court stated that "the best approach to the use of computer assisted coding is to follow the Sedona Cooperation Proclamation model. Advise opposing counsel that you plan to use computer-assisted coding and seek agreement; if you cannot, consider whether to abandon predictive coding for that case or go to the court for advance approval." *Id.* at 184 (emphases added) (quoting Andrew Peck, Search Forward, L. Tech. News, Oct. 2011, at 25, 29). But the Magistrate Judge in *Da Silva* noted, in a later case, that "[i]n the three years since *Da Silva Moore*, the case law has developed to the point that it is now black letter law that where the producing party wants to utilize TAR for document review, courts will permit it." *Rio Tinto PLC v. Vale S.A.*, 306 F.R.D. 125, 127 (S.D.N.Y. 2015) (emphasis added).

Each of the cases that Yardi primarily relied on involved parties that had come to agreements early in the discovery process. In fact, nearly all the cases cited by both Entrata and Yardi involved parties that had reached some agreement regarding ESI or TAR early in the discovery process. This case is unique because the parties never reached any agreement. Nevertheless, the court is persuaded that because it is "black letter law" that courts will permit a producing party to utilize TAR, Entrata was not required to seek approval from the Magistrate Court to use TAR where there was never an agreement to utilize a different search methodology. The court agrees with the Magistrate Judge that if Yardi had concerns about Entrata's use of TAR, it should have sought intervention long before the last day of fact discovery. Yardi should have filed a proposal within 30 days of the Magistrate Court's September 20, 2017 Order. It did not. The Magistrate Court's June 20, 2018 Order denying Yardi's Motion was not contrary to law.

***

IN RE BROILER CHICKEN ANTITRUST LITIGATION
No. 1:16-cv-08637 2018 WL 1146371 (N.D. Ill. 2018)

GILBERT, Magistrate Judge

This Order Regarding Search Methodology for Electronically Stored Information ("Search Methodology Order") shall govern the Parties in the above-captioned case whether they currently are involved or become so in the future, and any related actions that may later be consolidated with this case (collectively, the "Litigation").

I. DOCUMENT SOURCE DISCLOSURES
A. Transparency:
With the goal of permitting requesting Parties an appropriate level of transparency into a producing Party's electronic search process, without micromanaging how the producing Party meets its discovery obligations and without requiring the disclosure of attorney work product or other privileged information, the Parties will endeavor to be reasonably

transparent regarding the universe of documents subject to targeted collections or culling via search terms and/or TAR/CAL.

B. Pre-Search Deduplication & Culling of Collected Data:

1. De-Duplication: Before running either of the Search Processes below in II, data should be de-duplicated by hash value across all agreed or Court-ordered document custodians.

2. Email Threading: If the producing Party's search software has the capability, then the producing Party may choose to only include inclusive emails in the data set subject to the Keyword and/or TAR/CAL Search Process, including the data set against which keyword searches are tested. A producing Party will disclose whether or not they are testing search terms in a set of data that excludes non-inclusive emails. Non-inclusive emails do not need to be searched, reviewed, or produced in this matter.

3. Email Domains: Should the requesting Party want certain email domains excluded from the data set against which search terms are tested, the requesting Party must provide a list of such domain names to the producing Party ahead of the producing Party's testing of search terms. Likewise, if the producing Party identifies domains that it believes should be eliminated, it will produce a list of those domain names to the requesting Party. Plaintiffs' analysis to date of the Florida AG productions made by certain Defendants indicates there are a large variety of industry email newsletters that can be culled (*i.e.*, excluded from a Defendant's review and production of documents) where there are no internal forwards of such documents after their receipt. Plaintiffs agree to provide a list of these domain names prior to Defendants undertaking a search of their data.

4. Targeted Collections: Only documents a producing Party intends to subject to electronic searching parameters should be included in the data set against which search terms are tested. As an example, a centralized, non-custodial folder of responsive Agri Stats reports that a party intends to produce in its entirety (to the extent not privileged) should not be included in the data set against which search terms are tested.

5. Exception Reporting: For any documents not otherwise identified as system or operating files, the producing Party must disclose processing exceptions that are unresolved at the end of the discovery period, such as documents that cannot be opened due to encryption or other issues.

6. Disclosure of Other Culling Parameters Required: A producing Party is permitted to cull data using the agreed-upon custodial and non-custodial sources, agreed-upon date parameters, and agreed-upon search terms (if applicable), and a producing Party is permitted to remove known system or operating files, such as those that appear on the National Software Reference Library (NSRL) hash list. As such, the Parties may cull entire file directories from computer hard drives that contain Program Files, Program Data,

SWTOOLs, Windows Operating System files, etc. For those excluded directories, the Parties will only conduct searches on user-created content that is reviewable and likely to yield relevant content. To the extent a producing Party elects to use additional culling parameters, those parameters will be disclosed.

II. SEARCH METHODS

The following TAR/CAL and Keyword Search Processes govern how collected data may be electronically culled in this matter.

A. TAR/CAL Search Process:
1. Use of Search Terms with TAR/CAL:
a. No later than December 22, 2017, the requesting Party will propose to a producing Party a limited number of Document Custodians for whom, across their email only, it requests that no search term pre-culling be used prior to applying TAR/CAL during the review process. However, the other data culling parameters described in I(B) may be applied to these Document Custodians, including to their email.

b. No later than January 12, 2018, the Parties will meet and confer on any issues or disputes regarding the requesting Party's proposals.

2. Producing Party TAR/CAL Disclosures:
a. No later than January 19, 2018, a producing Party that elects to use TAR/CAL will disclose the following information regarding its use of a TAR/CAL process: (a) the name of the TAR/CAL software and vendor, (b) a general description of how the producing Party's TAR/CAL process will work, including how it will train the algorithm, such as using exemplars, keyword search strings, or some other method, (c) a general description of the categories or sources of the documents included or excluded from the TAR/CAL process, and (d) what quality control measures will be taken.

3. Requesting Party Response:
a. Within 7 days of receiving a producing Party's TAR/CAL Disclosures, the requesting Party may raise with the producing Party any concerns with the proposed TAR/CAL process or categories of documents that it proposes should be excluded from the TAR/CAL process. A requesting Party may also propose any exemplars it proposes be used to train a TAR/CAL tool or narrow keyword search strings it proposes be used to generate exemplars to train a TAR/CAL tool. A producing Party retains the right to reject and oppose any such requests, subject to resolution by the Special Master and/or the Court. 4. Cooperation: The Parties agree to work together in good faith to resolve any differences that they may have over the producing Party's use of TAR/CAL and its processes, recall, and validation proposals. If an agreement cannot be timely reached, then the Parties agree to raise this issue with the Special Master and to follow her direction absent the showing of good cause to the contrary, and subject to the Parties' rights to petition the Court for review of or relief from any decision or guidance provided by the Special Master.

B. Keyword Search Process:

1. Iterative Process: Developing efficient keyword search terms is an iterative process and will require transparent and cooperative efforts by both the producing and requesting Party; however, it is important to set certain limits in order to effectively and efficiently manage time and expense.

2. Search Software Disclosures: No later than January 12, 2018, the producing Parties will disclose any search software they have decided to use (including version number) and that software's default stop/noise words and search language syntax. Additionally, the Parties should use best efforts to disclose information that answers these questions regarding their search tool:

   a. What stop words have been excluded from the index (if different than the default stop words for the tool)?
   b. Can searches be constrained by upper- and lowercase?
   c. Can numbers and single letters be searched?
   d. Are there characters that cannot be searched or are treated as spaces or ignored?
   e. How are diacritics resolved?
   f. Can searches be run on metadata fields?
   g. Are proximity-limited search terms subject to an evaluation order, *e.g.*, will terms structured X w/5 Y yield hits if the text reads Y w/5 X?
   h. Does the tool offer synonym searching?
   i. How does the tool account for common misspellings?

3. First Phase Search Term Proposals:

   a. Producing Party Proposes an Initial Set of Search Terms: No later than January 19, 2018, the producing Party will propose a set of search terms. The producing Party's proposal will include, to the extent known, semantic synonyms and common spellings of the keywords proposed. Where a producing Party seeks to exclude false positives (aka, "noise hits") by modifying or excluding certain keywords, then it will supply contextual examples of such false positives to explain why they must be excluded.

   b. Requesting Party's Proposed Revisions: Within 12 days of receiving the initial proposed search terms, the requesting Party will provide any proposed revisions to the producing Party's search terms.

   c. Producing Party Provides Information Sufficient to Support Its Objections: Within 8 days of receipt of the requesting Party's proposed revisions, the producing Party will provide information sufficient to support its objections to specific search terms, which could include, for example, estimates of the incremental number of false positive hits and the incremental number of true positive hits introduced by the disputed search terms, as well as examples of the false positive hits.

d. Cooperation: The producing Party and the requesting Party will work together in good faith to reasonably narrow the number of documents returned via search term hits and narrow the number of irrelevant documents captured as a result of the search terms. To the extent any disputes remain concerning the sufficiency of the producing Party's information in support of its objections and/or the use of specific search terms after good faith negotiations have occurred, either Party may request the assistance of the Special Master in resolving such disputes.

4. Second Phase Search Term Proposals:

a. Requesting Party Proposes an Additional Set of Search Terms: The Parties agree that Plaintiffs collectively and Defendants collectively may propose additional search terms to a producing Party one time. No later than May 14, 2018 (60 days after the Court-ordered March 15, 2018 deadline for "Rolling Production of Documents, Prioritizing Custodians as Agreed by the Parties or Ordered by the Court," the requesting Party may propose a set of additional search terms. The requesting Party will explain generally the basis for the additional requested terms, which could include, for example, identifying by Bates number exemplar documents that support the request.

b. Producing Party Provides Information Sufficient to Support Its Objections : No later than 10 days after the requesting Party provides an additional set of proposed search terms, the producing Party will provide information sufficient to support its objections to specific additional search terms, which could include, for example, estimates of the incremental number of false positive hits and the incremental number of true positive hits introduced by the disputed additional search terms, as well as examples of the false positive hits.

c. Requesting Party and Producing Party Will Meet and Confer Regarding Requesting Party's Proposed Additional Search Terms: No later than 15 days after the requesting Party proposes an additional set of search terms, the Parties will meet and confer regarding any disputes or counter-proposals regarding the additional search terms. To the extent any disputes remain concerning the sufficiency of the producing Party's information in support of its objections and/or the use of specific additional search terms after good faith negotiations have occurred, either Party may request the assistance of the Special Master in resolving such disputes.

d. Good Cause Inability of a Party to Meet the Deadlines Imposed in this Order: While it is expected that the Parties shall make their best efforts to comply with the deadlines set forth in this Order, it is conceivable that technical (or other) issues or unanticipated volumes may interfere with a Parties' best efforts to comply.

Should a Party anticipate that for good cause it may be unable to meet a deadline set forth in this Order, the Party shall promptly raise the issue with the other Parties, explain the reason for the inability to timely comply, and negotiate a reasonable extension for compliance. If the Parties are unable to immediately agree upon a revised deadline for compliance, they shall promptly raise the issue with the Special Master or the Court for resolution. This provision shall not be construed as blanket permission for a Party to modify or extend the deadlines agreed to by the Parties and set forth in this Order without good cause, but rather, to recognize that when dealing with search and review of large volumes of electronically stored information, there are sometimes legitimate, unanticipated challenges that may interfere with a Party's best efforts to fulfill its obligations and therefore, to afford the Parties reasonable flexibility and mutual accommodation should such eventuality occur.

III. VALIDATION PROTOCOL

A. The review process should incorporate quality-control and quality-assurance procedures to ensure a reasonable production consistent with the requirements of Federal Rule of Civil Procedure 26(g) . Once a producing Party reasonably believes that it has produced or identified for production substantially all responsive non-privileged documents, it shall conduct validation according to the sampling protocol described below and in Appendix A. This Validation Protocol shall apply to the review process regardless of whether technology-assisted review ("TAR") or exhaustive manual review ("manual review") was used by the producing Party.

B. The Document Collection ("Collection") is defined as including all documents identified for review for responsiveness and/or privilege following the application of keywords or other culling criteria. This Validation Protocol assumes that the completeness or adequacy of the Collection has already been established. For purposes of the three putative plaintiff classes' validation requirements under this Validation Protocol, the Collection refers to the combined set of documents of a particular proposed class of plaintiffs, rather than to each individual named representative of a particular class of plaintiffs.

C. The Collection shall be partitioned into the following two or three Subcollections, for manual review or for TAR processes, respectively:

1. Documents identified by the review as responsive to at least one Request for Production, including any privileged documents, but not including family members

of responsive documents, unless those family members are deemed to be responsive in their own right ("Subcollection C(1)");

2. Documents coded as non-responsive by a human reviewer, regardless of how the documents were selected for review (*e.g.*, by TAR, manual review, or otherwise) ("Subcollection C(2)");

3. Documents excluded from manual review as the result of a TAR process ("Subcollection C(3)"). If the review process involved only manual review and no TAR, the Collection will not include Subcollection C(3).

D. A sample shall be drawn consisting of the following:

1. 500 documents selected at random from Subcollection C(1) ("Subsample D(1)");

2. 500 documents selected at random from Subcollection C(2), if TAR was used, otherwise 2,500 documents selected at random from Subcollection C(2), if manual review was used ("Subsample D(2)");

3. 2,000 documents selected at random from Subcollection 1(c) if TAR was used ("Sample D(3)"). If TAR was not used, there will be no Subsample D(3).

E. Should a producing Party believe that the sample sizes specified in Paragraph III(D) would be disproportionate or unduly burdensome under the circumstances, that Party shall promptly raise the issue with the requesting Party. To the extent a dispute remains concerning the sample sizes to be used after good faith negotiations have occurred, either Party may request the assistance of the Special Master in resolving such dispute.

F. The sample of 3,000 documents comprised of the documents from Subsamples D(1), D(2), and, if TAR was used, D(3), shall be combined into a single Validation Sample, with no indication of the Subcollection from which the documents were derived or how they were previously coded. The Validation Sample shall be reviewed and coded by a subject matter expert ("SME") who is knowledgeable about the subject matter of the litigation. This should be an attorney who is familiar with the RFPs and the issues in the case. During the course of the review of the Validation Sample, the SME shall not be provided with any information concerning the Subcollection or Subsample from which any document was derived or the prior coding of any document.

The intent of this requirement is to ensure that the review of the Validation Sample is blind; it does not preclude a Party from selecting as SMEs attorneys who may have had prior involvement in the original review process.

G. Once the coding in Paragraph III(F) has been completed, the producing Party shall prepare a table listing each of the 3,000 documents in the Validation Sample. For each document, the table shall include:

1. the Bates number of the document (for documents produced), or a control/identification number (for nonproduced documents);

2. the Subsample from which the document came (*i.e.*, D(1), D(2), or, if TAR was used, D(3));

3. the SME's responsiveness coding for the document (*i.e.*, responsive or non-responsive);

4. the SME's privilege coding for the document (*i.e.*, privileged or not privileged). If the document is coded as non-responsive, a privilege determination need not be made. All documents in the Validation Sample coded as privileged shall be included on the producing Party's Privilege Log, as per the requirements set forth in VI of ESI Protocol.

5. for putative class plaintiffs, the named class representative associated with the document.

H. The following items shall be provided to the requesting Party and to the Special Master:

1. the table described in Paragraph III(G);

1. a copy of each responsive, non-privileged document in the Validation Sample that was not previously produced or identified for production to the requesting Party;

3. the statistics and recall estimate detailed in Appendix A to this Order.

I. Once the requesting Party has received and has had an opportunity to review the items described in Paragraph III(H) and Appendix A, the Parties shall meet and confer to determine whether or not the Parties agree that the recall estimate, and the quantity and nature of the responsive documents identified through the sampling process, indicate that the review is substantially complete. If the recall estimateand the samples indicate that Subcollections C(2) and/or C(3) still contain a substantial number of non-marginal, nonduplicative responsive documents as compared to Subcollection C(1), the review and quality assurance process shall continue, and the validation process shall be repeated, as warranted. If the parties are unable to agree on whether the review is substantially complete, or whether the validation process must be repeated, the Special Master shall render a decision, subject to the Parties' rights to petition the Court for review of or relief from any decision or guidance provided by the Special Master.

APPENDIX A

GROSSMAN, Special Master

Method of Recall Estimation

An estimate of recall shall be computed to inform the decision-making process described in III(H) of the Validation Protocol; however, the absolute number in its own right shall not be dispositive of whether or not a review is substantially complete. Also of concern is the novelty and materiality (or conversely, the duplicative or marginal nature) of any responsive documents identified in Subsamples D(2) and/or D(3). The estimate of recall shall be derived as described below, depending on whether or not the review process involved the use of TAR. It should be noted that, when conducted by an SME pursuant to Paragraph III(F) of the Validation Protocol, a recall estimate on the order of 70% to 80% is consistent with, but not the sole indicator of, an adequate (*i.e.*, high-quality) review. A recall estimate somewhat lower than this does not necessarily indicate that a review is inadequate, nor does a recall in this range or higher necessarily indicate that a review is adequate; the final determination also will depend on the quantity and nature of the documents that were missed by the review process.

Recall Estimation Method for a Review Process Involving TAR:

The number of responsive documents found ≈ the size of Subcollection C(1) × the number of responsive docs in Subsample D(1) ÷ 500.

The number of responsive documents coded incorrectly ≈ the size of Subcollection C(2) × the number of responsive documents in Subsample D(2) ÷ 500.

The number of responsive documents not reviewed ≈ size of Subcollection C(3) × the number of responsive documents in Subsample D(3) ÷ 2,000.

Estimated recall ≈ the number of responsive documents found ÷ (the number of responsive documents found + the number of responsive documents coded incorrectly + the number of responsive documents not reviewed).

Recall Estimation Method for a Review Process Involving Manual Review:

The number of responsive documents found ≈ the size of Subcollection C(1) × the number of responsive documents in Subsample D(1) ÷ 500.

The number responsive documents coded incorrectly ≈ the size of Subcollection C(2) × the number of responsive documents in Subsample D(2) ÷ 2,500.

Estimated recall ≈ the number of responsive documents found ÷ (the number of responsive documents found + the number of responsive documents coded incorrectly).

***

CHAPTER 9

PRODUCTION OF ELECTRONICALLY STORED INFORMATION

A. Forms of Production

After ESI has been collected, processed and reviewed, the ESI can be produced. FRCP Rule 34 governs the forms of production. According to the FRCP, parties need to discuss at an initial discovery planning conference the form(s) in which ESI should be produced. A requesting party needs to specify the form(s) of production in document requests or a subpoena. The FRCP rules recognize that different forms of production may be appropriate for different types of ESI, but the responding party need not produce the same ESI in more than one form. If the requesting party fails to request a form of production, or the responding party objects to the form requested, the responding party must state the form(s) the responding party intends to use.

There are generally four forms in which ESI may be produced, namely, native, near-native, image (near-paper), and paper.

1. Native Format

A native format production includes responsive ESI in the form that it is ordinarily maintained on the producing party's systems, and it usually includes the metadata that are associated with the documents.

Metadata are information that reflects characteristics (such as origin, usage, structure, and alteration) of the ESI. For example, metadata can describe how, when, and by whom ESI was created, accessed, and modified. Some metadata, such as file dates and sizes, can easily be seen by users. Other metadata are hidden or embedded and generally unavailable to causal users.

Native format production tends to provide cost and time savings because no conversion of the ESI into images and associated load files is needed.

Drawbacks of a native format production include the inability to number individual pages (*i.e.*, Bates stamp) for document control, the inability to redact for privilege or other reasons, or the inability to label the documents as confidential. In addition, the producing party cannot control or limit the metadata produced. Also, sometimes proprietary or legacy software is required to review ESI produced in native format.

2. Near-Native Format

Some files cannot be reviewed or produced without some form of conversion. For example, emails often are saved in a single text file or database rather than in separate files. Databases and data compilations may include a large number of tables having hundreds and thousands of data fields, which require proprietary software to review in their original form. Thus, email and large databases and data compilations are generally not produced in true native format. These types of ESI are more likely to be produced in a format, such as near-native format, to be more conducive for review than if produced in native form.

In near-native format, files are extracted or converted into another searchable format. For example, emails may be converted to .htm, .msg, or .rtf files. Databases may be converted to .txt or .csv files, or exported to Excel spreadsheet for production. Near-native files include some or all metadata.

Although there is a cost associated with converting files from native to near-native format, near-native conversion is usually less costly and time intensive compare to the total image conversion required in an image production. Near-native format is also readily searchable. Thus, near-native format allows the producing party to have more control over the metadata it produces than with native format. As with native format, however, it is not possible to individually number pages, redact or mark material as confidential in a near-native production.

3. Image (near-paper) Format

ESI can also be produced in an image, or near-paper, format. The ESI is converted (usually to .tiff or .pdf files) so that a "picture" is taken of the ESI as it might exist if it were in paper format or viewed onscreen. Hard copy documents also can be scanned and produced in an image format. The images themselves often cannot be searched or indexed, but they are usually produced with accompanying extracted text and metadata in load files so that they may be viewable and searchable in a review tool. Optical character recognition (OCR) may be used to render scanned hard copy documents searchable.

Image format includes no metadata in the images themselves, but load files containing certain fields of metadata necessary to make the ESI reasonably usable (e.g., searchable) are usually included in the production.

Advantages of an image production include the ability to number, redact and mark documents as confidential, as well as the ability to control the metadata fields that are produced. Imaged files also carry less risk of accidental alteration because they are non-editable. Disadvantages of an image production include the cost and time involved in converting the ESI to images, and potential challenges regarding the sufficiency of the metadata and searchability.

4. Paper Format

Paper documents are physical documents copied from other physical documents or printed from ESI. They share some of the control advantages of near-paper format files (such as numbering, redaction, and labeling). However, a paper production does not include any metadata and cannot be searched or indexed electronically. There may be some instances when printed hard copies may be reasonably usable for purposes of a particular case.

Although the responding party is not required to produce ESI in native format, the option to produce ESI in a reasonably usable form generally does not mean that the responding party may convert ESI to a form that makes it difficult or impossible for the requesting party to use the ESI efficiently in the litigation.

Because different forms of production are often appropriate for different types of ESI, it is common for document productions to involve a combination of forms. One common combination, for example, is for most files to be converted to image format, with the exception of files like spreadsheet, which may not be as usable in image format, and therefore are produced in native or near-native format. Another common combination is for email, databases and proprietary files to be produced in a near-native format; for attachments and loose files to be produced in native format; and for files requiring redaction to be produced in image format.

IN RE SYNGENTA AG MIR 162 CORN LITIGATION, MDL 2591
No. 16-2788-JWL 2018 WL 4609112 (D. Kan. 2018)

O'HARA, Magistrate Judge

By informal letter briefs dated September 24, 2018, the parties have asked the court to resolve a dispute concerning the format of electronic discovery to be produced by Louis Dreyfus Company Grains Merchandising LLC ("LDC"). Specifically, LDC seeks to meet the current document-production deadlines by producing electronic discovery in native format, rather than in TIFF image format as required by the ESI Protocol Order. LDC states its TIFF productions would "follow expeditiously, on a rolling basis." ***

On August 16, 2018, the court ordered LDC to complete its document production by September 6, 2018. On August 31, 2018, LDC sought an extension, asserting that technical complications and infrastructure limitations made it impossible to meet the deadline. There was no mention in LDC's motion or supporting briefs of any difficulty LDC would have producing the documents in TIFF format. The court granted LDC's request and ordered LDC to produce "as many documents as possible (which should be most)" by September 28, 2018; and to produce the remainder of the documents by October 12, 2018. The court set these deadlines so as to "not impact the parties' ability to conduct and complete fact depositions by the current December 14, 2018 deadline."

On September 5 and 11, 2018, LDC produced a large number of documents in native format. LDC states that it did so in order to get the documents to Syngenta as expeditiously as possible, asserting that converting documents to TIFF adds "substantial time to production." Syngenta complained to LDC about the production format on September 11, 2018. Syngenta accurately noted that production of documents in native format—with only the first page of a document numbered, rather than page-by-page bates numbering—creates confusion when a party wishes to reference a particular page of a document during depositions, in court filings, and at trial. Moreover, the ESI Protocol Order requires producing parties to convert ESI from native format to an image file (*e.g.* TIFF) for production.

In its September 24, 2018 letter brief, LDC asks the court, for the first time, to relieve it from the production requirements of the ESI Protocol Order. The ESI Protocol Order contains a provision that if "a Producing Party identifies a particular source or type of responsive Data for which it reasonably believes that application of this Protocol would be unduly burdensome or impractical, the party identifying the source or type of responsive Data shall promptly notify the Requesting Party." If the parties then cannot reach agreement on a modification of the production requirements, the order provides that the producing party "bears the burden of seeking relief from the Court."

LDC's instant request for relief argues that the exception to the ESI production protocol applies because LDC "has been required to produce a huge number of documents under extreme time pressure." LDC recognizes that Syngenta would be prejudiced in depositions because documents produced in native format do not contain a bates stamp on every page, but characterizes this prejudice as a "minor inconvenience."

LDC states it "is converting these files to TIFF format, but Syngenta is unreasonably insisting that all documents be in TIFF before the deadline."

LDC's arguments are unpersuasive. First, there is no dispute that documents in TIFF format are easier to work with and enable depositions and court proceedings to run more smoothly. As recognized by the Sedona Conference, they allow a party to refer to particular portions of a document—perhaps in designating confidentiality or directing a witness to particular language—by page number.

Second, the ESI Protocol Order requires a party seeking to deviate from the image/TIFF-format production to "promptly" notify the requesting party as soon as it identifies a source of data to which the protocol should not apply (because it would be unduly burdensome or impractical). Here, LDC did not notify Syngenta or the court before producing documents in native format. LDC made no mention of its perceived formattingproduction issue in its previous briefs addressing Syngenta's proposed search terms or seeking extensions of the production deadlines.

Third, LDC has offered no evidence to support its "burdensome" and "impracticality" arguments. To the contrary, LDC informed Syngenta on September 14, 2018, that converting the native files in its previous document productions would take approximately two weeks. Thus, the first TIFF production should occur by the September 28, 2018 deadline for the majority of LDCÆs documents. As for documents yet to be produced, LDC does not state how long producing them in the first instance in TIFF format (as opposed to native format with a subsequent conversion) might take its vendor. Accordingly, the court is not convinced that it is impossible for LDC to meet the October 12, 2018 deadline for final production.

Finally, the court is determined to keep this case moving forward. Although the court deemed it necessary to extend the written-discovery deadline, it has continuously declined suggestions to extend the December 14, 2018 fact-deposition deadline (knowing that so doing would inevitably result in the extension of all remaining deadlines). Production of LDC's documents in TIFF format by the October 12, 2018 deadline helps ensure depositions efficiently go forward as scheduled. As noted in the court's September 12, 2018 order, the court will only extend deadlines upon a showing of good cause. Good cause has not been established by LDC under the current record.

For all of these reasons, the court denies LDC's request that it be permitted to complete its document production in native format only by the October 12, 2018 deadline.

***

MITCHELL V. RELIABLE SEC., LLC,
No. 1:15-cv-03814-AJB, 2016 WL 3093040 (N.D. Ga. 2016)

BAVERMAN, Magistrate Judge

This matter is presently before the Court for resolution of a dispute between the parties over the production of electronically stored information ("ESI"), specifically, whether ESI should be produced in native format or PDF format. ***

In the subsequently filed status report, Defendant estimates that the volume of potentially relevant ESI is 3GB. Defendant further represents that it will cost approximately $3,000 more to process and produce 3GB of ESI in native format than it would in PDF format, "comprised of a flat rate of $2,000 for ESI processing and production, plus approximately $1,000 for hourly paralegal time ($150/hour) to manage the production of native emails and Excel spreadsheets."

Defendant also argues that the damages in the case, absent attorneys' fees, "are likely less than $10,000," and that the additional cost for native production of the ESI is therefore unreasonable.

In response, Plaintiff contends that because Defendant asserts that it did not assign her shifts not due to her pregnancy but instead due to lack of shift availability and because the emails and spreadsheets supporting the defense theory are susceptible to post hoc manipulation, the production of emails and Excel spreadsheets in native format, with retention of metadata, is necessary in this case. She also argues that Defendant's statement regarding the estimated additional costs to produce native files rather than PDF files is insufficient because Defendant did not explain how it arrived at the estimated cost it provided, did not provide an actual estimate from an ESI expert or vendor, and did not explain its contention that production of emails and spreadsheets in native format would require more paralegal time to manage the production of native emails; because defense counsel's own marketing communications suggest that it employs discovery management software commonly used to streamline ESI production; because there are other free or low-cost means of production of the native files; and because Plaintiff's counsel has offered to assist in downloading emails in electronic format to minimize costs and avoid the retention of an expert or vendor to do the same. Plaintiff also contends that Plaintiff's compensatory and punitive damages could range from $50,000 to $300,000, plus lost wages and benefits and reasonable attorneys' fees and costs.

On Friday, May 20, 2016, Plaintiff's counsel, representing that she was acting with consent of Defendant's counsel, contacted the Court to ask the status of the Court's decision regarding the dispute. When asked, Plaintiff's counsel further represented that neither party sought to file additional briefing.

With briefing complete, the Court has considered the oral arguments and the supplement briefs, and it finds in favor of Plaintiff. The Federal Rules of Civil Procedure allow for the Court to limit ESI discovery under certain conditions:

> A party need not provide discovery of electronically stored information from sources that the party identifies as not reasonably accessible because of undue burden or cost. On motion to compel discovery or for a protective order, the party from whom the discovery is sought must show that the information is not reasonably accessible because of undue burden or cost. If that showing is made, the court may nonetheless order discovery from such sources if the requesting party shows good cause ...

Fed. R. Civ. P. 26(b)(2)(B). Here, Defendant has simply asserted that production of the files in native format rather than PDF format will require an additional expenditure of $2,000 for ESI processing and production, plus approximately $1,000 for hourly paralegal time, but it has not explained the reason for the additional costs.

Consequently, the Court remains *** at a loss to understand why the production of native documents is more costly than production of PDF files. The Court therefore finds that Defendant has not made an adequate showing that production of the native files is cost prohibitive.

Additionally, the Court finds that even had Defendant made a showing that it costs $3,000 more to produce the native files than to produce the PDF files, Plaintiff has shown good cause for the Court to order the production. While there has been no specific reason so far to believe that the emails and scheduling spreadsheets would have been modified since the time period at issue in the suit, it is not at all unreasonable for Plaintiff to wish to verify herself whether the emails or spreadsheets had been subsequently manipulated, modified, altered, or changed. Moreover, while it does appear that Plaintiff's suit is unlikely to be of an especially high dollar value, the Court finds that the public value of allowing a civil-rights plaintiff opportunity to access information relevant and quite possibly necessary to her pregnancy-discrimination suit far outweighs the asserted $3,000 cost.

For these reasons, it is hereby ORDERED that Defendant produce the requested ESI in its native format with FOURTEEN (14) DAYS of the date of this Order.

***

VENTURE CORP. V. BARRETT
No. 5:13-cv-03384 (N.D. Cal. 2014)

GREWAL, Magistrate Judge

Most lawyers (and hopefully judges) would be forgiven if they could not recite on demand some of the more obscure of the Federal Rules of Civil Procedure. Rule 80 (Stenographic Transcript as Evidence) and Rule 64 (Seizing a Person or Property) come to mind. But Rule 34 (Producing Documents, Electronically Stored Information, and Tangible Things) is about as basic to any civil case as it gets. And yet, over and over again, the undersigned is confronted with misapprehension of its standards and elements by even experienced counsel. Unfortunately, this case presents yet another example.

After Defendant James P. Barrett served initial document requests and Plaintiffs Venture Corporation Ltd. and Venture Design Services, Inc. responded, the parties met and conferred about how the Ventures would produce documents. So far, so good. But despite their best efforts, the parties could not agree. Barrett wanted the documents organized and labeled to identify the requests to which they were responsive. The Ventures demurred at such an obligation. What followed was a production of approximately 41,000 pages, even though there was nothing close to a meeting of the minds. Because this production did not square with the requirements of either Rule 34(b)(2)(E)(i) or (ii), the Ventures shall try again, as explained below.

I.

Even in the days of paper measured by the carton and large, cold-storage warehouses, the document dump was recognized for what it was: at best inefficient and at worst a tactic to work over the requesting party. Rule 34 aims to prevent such a scenario with two specific and separate requirements. First, "[a] party must produce documents as they are kept in the ordinary course of business or must organize and label them to correspond to the categories in the request." Second, "[i]f a request does not specify a form for producing electronically stored information, a party must produce it in a form or forms in which it is ordinarily maintained or in a reasonably usable form or forms. A party need not produce the same electronically stored information in more than one form."

Barrett is the owner of three patents on an air monitor and gas scrubber component. The Ventures say those patents belong to them, and filed this suit to confirm their ownership. Barrett countersued, saying the Ventures welched on commitments they made to induce Barrett to assign the patents.

After the initial case management conference and the filing of a scheduling order, Barrett began serving document requests together with other discovery. After the Ventures served objections, but no documents, the parties met by telephone. What happened during that call is hotly contested. The Ventures say Barrett agreed to accept documents in bulk and in PDF or native format despite initially insisting on an identification of which documents correspond to each request. Barrett denies this, saying that he only agreed to review whatever the Ventures would produce while reserving the right to later demand identification by request.

What is not contested is that the Ventures proceeded to produce, on flash drive and by email, approximately 41,000 pages. The drive and email contained no custodial index, no table, no information at all—just folders of the files themselves. After Barrett took various depositions, he followed up on what he understood the original deal to be by serving interrogatories requesting identification of what documents responded to various categories. Barrett served the follow-up interrogatories by email pursuant to Fed. Civ. P. 5(b)(2)(E), just 30 days before the discovery cutoff set out in the court's scheduling order.

The Ventures balked at what they claim were untimely requests and more generally unwarranted demands calling for document and ESI production other than as they are kept in the usual course of business. Barrett then moved to compel answers to the interrogatories and requests for production and sanctions in the form of attorney's fees and costs.

***

III.

Rule 34(b)(2)(E)(i) is plain: if documents are not organized and labeled to correspond to the categories in the request, they must be produced as they are kept in the usual course of business. The Ventures did not do this.

First, there is no real dispute that the Ventures did not organize and label their production. Not even the Ventures claim this.

Second, the Ventures have submitted no evidence that in the ordinary course of business they keep documents and ESI in folders as they were produced. "A party selecting the alternative method of production bears the burden of demonstrating that the documents made available were in fact produced consistent with that mandate.... To carry this burden, a party must do more than merely represent to the court and the requesting party that the documents have been produced as they are maintained." At a minimum, the court would expect to see the documents and ESI kept by the name of the employee from whom the documents were obtained or at least which Venture entity had produced the documents. But here, there was nothing in the way of any such source information.

Once again, the Ventures do not dispute that their documents and ESI are kept in some more hierarchical scheme. Instead they claim that while they offered to produce the files together with load files and an index, Barrett told them he would accept production in PDF and native form. As an initial matter, the Ventures' proof of this is thin at best. The Ventures tender neither a contemporaneous letter nor any email following up the call between counsel. All that Venture musters is an attorney declaration prepared many months after the call and only once Barrett brought his motion. The only such contemporaneous communication is from Barrett, in which his counsel makes clear she was not agreeing to much of anything. More fundamentally, even if there was such an agreement, an agreement on form relieves a responding party of any further form obligations under subsection (ii) of Rule 34(b)(2)(E). It does nothing to relieve such a party of its obligation under subsection (i) to produce the documents and ESI as they are kept in the ordinary course of business.

This distinction matters. Form under subsection (ii) is about whether the production should be native, near-native, imaged as PDF (or more commonly, as TIFFs accompanied by load files containing searchable text and metadata) or in paper (printed out). Providing information about how documents and ESI are kept under subsection (i) "[a]t a minimum ... mean[s] that the disclosing party should provide information about each document which ideally would include, in some fashion, the identity of the custodian or person from whom the documents were obtained, an indication of whether they are retained in hard copy or digital format, assurance that the documents have been produced in the order in which they are maintained, and a general description of the filing system from which they were recovered."

Third, because there was not even an agreement on form, Venture had an obligation under subsection (ii) to show that the production was in which "it is ordinarily maintained or in a reasonably usable form or forms." Once again, there is no serious question that a grab-bag of PDF and native files is neither how the Ventures ordinarily maintained the documents and ESI nor is "in a reasonably usuable form."

IV.

This leaves only the question of remedy. While Barrett wants the production organized and labeled, as he has all along, the court sees no reason to limit the remedy to only what Barrett wants. After all, during the meet and confer, and even at the hearing on this matter, Barrett kept insisting that organization and labeling is always required--never mind the disjunctive structure of subsection (i)'s language. And so to remedy this situation, the Ventures shall do three things: (1) either organize and label each document it has produced or it shall provide custodial and other organizational information along the lines outlined above and (2) produce load files for its production containing searchable text and metadata.

As for Barrett's requested fees and costs, this request is denied. Barrett's unwillingness to accept the disjunctive nature or subsection (i), insistence on organization and labeling and delay in bringing this motion only contributed to the unfortunate situation at hand.

***

D'ONOFRIO V. SFX SPORTS GRP., INC.
247 F.R.D. 43 (D. D.C. 2008)

FACCIOLA, Magistrate Judge

***

I. Background

This lawsuit involves claims by plaintiff, Audrey (Shebby) D'Onofrio, that she received disparate treatment from her employer, SFX Sports Group, Inc. ("SFX"), based upon her gender. Plaintiff also alleges that she was subjected to a hostile work environment and was terminated in retaliation for her protected activities. She brings this lawsuit under the District of Columbia Human Rights Act ("DCHRA"), the Equal Pay Act, and the District of Columbia Family Medical Leave Act.

***

III. Electronically Stored Information

Many of the discovery disputes at issue in the Motion relate to electronically stored information. In particular, plaintiff: (a) asks the court to compel the production of the Business Plan in its original electronic format, with accompanying metadata; (b) asks the court to compel the production of defendants' e-mails in an original format with accompanying metadata; and (c) claims that defendants have deliberately caused the spoliation of electronic records and have purposely failed to produce many e-mails and documents.

A. Business Plan

***

Plaintiff argues that Rule 34 permits the production of documents outside of their original format only "if necessary," and, in this case, no such necessity exists. Defendants respond that: (a) plaintiff did not request that the Business Plan or any other documents be produced in a specific format; (b) production in original electronic format with metadata is not required by the Federal Rules of Civil Procedure or in the absence of a clear agreement or court order, neither of which are present here; and (c) plaintiff has not made any attempt to demonstrate the relevance of the metadata.

***

Metadata has been defined as "information about a particular data set which describes how, when, and by whom it was collected, created, accessed, or modified and how it was formatted."

1. Rule 34-"If Necessary"

As an initial matter, plaintiff argues that Rule 34 of the Federal Rules of Civil Procedure permits the production of documents other than in their original format only "if necessary." Rule 34(a) states, in relevant part:

(a) In General. A party may serve on any other party a request ...:

   (1) to produce and permit the requesting party or its representative to inspect, copy, test, or sample the following items in the responding party's possession, custody, or control:

      (A) any designated documents or electronically stored information-including writings, drawings, graphs, charts, photographs, sound recordings, images, and other data or data compilations-stored in any medium from which information can be obtained either directly or, if necessary, after translation by the responding party into a reasonably usable form.

Rule 34(a) does not set forth constraints on the manner of production, but instead establishes the permissible scope of a request. ("A party may serve on any other party a request ..."). Consequently, the "if necessary" clause seized upon by plaintiff is actually a constraint on the requesting party rather than the responding party. In other words, electronic data is subject to discovery if it is stored in a directly obtainable medium. If, however, it is not stored in a directly obtainable medium, a request may be made of the responding party to translate the electronic data into a "reasonably usable form." Because the step of translating this type of electronic data adds an extra burden on the responding party, the request may only seek for it to be done "if [the translation is] necessary." It is not the case that this clause requires the responding party to produce data in its original form unless "necessary" to do otherwise.

2. Request for Specific Form of Production

This does not end the analysis of whether a responding party might be required to produce electronic data in its original form with metadata. To the contrary, Rule 34(b) states that a discovery request "may specify the form or forms in which electronically stored information is to be produced." Fed.R.Civ.P. 34(b)(1)(C). In this case, plaintiff argues that she so specified in Instruction No. 4 of Plaintiff's Requests for the Production of Documents (the "Instruction"):

> [F]or any documents that are stored or maintained in files in the normal course of business, such documents shall be produced in such files, or in such a manner as to preserve and identify the file from which such documents were taken.

It is apparent that this language, when first written, was not meant to encompass electronic data. Instead it addresses a common concern of paper discovery: the identification of a document's custodian and origination. It is for this reason that the Instruction applies to documents "stored or maintained in files," and why it seeks to" preserve and identify" the identity of that file. Indeed, the Instruction makes perfect sense when one presumes "file" to refer to a physical file cabinet or folder.

***

Of course, "file" can also mean electronic data stored on an electronic medium. Using this definition, the Instruction can be strained to provide the responding party with two options for producing electronic documents: (a) produce the electronic file containing the document (i.e. a .PDF or .XLS file), or (b) produce the document in such a manner as to "preserve and identify the file from which" it was taken. The inclusion of the word "preserve" makes it very difficult to understand how the Instruction could apply to electronic documents; after all, how can the production of a document without the electronic file encompass the "preserv[ation]" of that electronic file? A more credible reading of the second option is that a document need not be produced as an electronic file if the alternate production "preserve[s the] identi[ty of] the file from which" it was taken. In practice this would likely refer to a "trailer" at the bottom of a printed electronic document containing its location on electronic storage media (i.e. an electronic spreadsheet could be printed on a piece of paper with the trailer "c: accounting harry FY07 charts.xls"). I do not know if defendants provided such a trailer because plaintiff did not attach the Business Plan to its Motion or provide any other detail concerning its format, other than to state that it was not in its original form with accompanying metadata. Nevertheless, it is clear that the Instruction, if applicable to electronic files, permits production of the Business Plan in a non-native form without accompanying metadata.

***

Ultimately, then, it does not matter whether the Instruction referred to paper or electronic files-a plain reading leads to the conclusion that plaintiff did not make a request that the Business Plan be produced solely in its original format with accompanying metadata. *** Because no such request has been made concerning the Business Plan, the Court will not compel the defendant to produce it in its original form with accompanying metadata.

***

B. Compel Production

SANTANA V. MKA2 ENTERPRISES, INC.
No. 18-2094-DDC-TJJ 2019 WL 130286 (D. Kan. 2019)

JAMES, Magistrate Judge

This is an employment discrimination case. Plaintiff alleges he was discriminated against, retaliated against, and terminated because of his race, in violation of Title VII of the Civil Rights Act and 42 U.S.C. § 1981.

Defendant has filed a Motion to Compel Discovery Requests Plaintiff opposes the motion For the reasons set forth below, the Court denies the motion.

On June 26, 2018, Defendant served its First Request for Production of Documents on Plaintiff. On August 8, 2018, Plaintiff served his responses and objections on Defendant. After conferring, the parties were unable to resolve their disputes as to Request for Production No. 21. That request states:

> Produce all cellular telephones used by you from the date your employment with Defendant started to the present for purposes of inspection and copying.

Plaintiff's response states:

> Plaintiff objects because this request seeks irrelevant information and is not proportional to the needs of this case. The request is unduly burdensome and invasive in light of the nature of the case-Defendant has shown no need for the production of Plaintiff's cell phone. Further, the majority, if not all, of the information contained on said device is entirely irrelevant to the present cause of action and any request for relevant nonprivileged information can be made through less invasive means.

Although not the subject of the motion to compel, Defendant also requested that Plaintiff "produce a full and complete copy of all text messages between (Plaintiff) and Defendant and between (Plaintiff) and current or former employees of Defendant." Plaintiff's response stated "Plaintiff objects to the extent this request seeks irrelevant information and is not proportional to the needs of this case. Subject to and without waiving said objections, see SANTANA 000007-000010."

The parties agree that the relevancy of a discovery request is governed by Fed. R. Civ. P. 26(b). That rule states "[p]arties may obtain discovery regarding any nonprivileged matter that is relevant to any party's claim or defense and proportional to the needs of the case ..." The rule goes on to say that the Court must limit discovery if it determines that the discovery sought is unreasonably cumulative or duplicative; can be obtained from a more convenient, less burdensome, or less expensive source; or is outside the scope permitted by Fed. R. Civ. P. 26(b)(1).

Defendant argues its request is relevant on its face because Plaintiff's cell phone contains information relevant to his claims and Defendant's defenses, specifically in the form of "texts, other messages, and phone calls to co-workers, former co-workers, and current employees of Defendant." Plaintiff argues that even if
the request is relevant, Defendant's motion to compel should be denied pursuant to Fed. R. Civ. P. 26(b)(2) because the request is unduly burdensome and invasive and is not proportional to the needs of this case.

The Court agrees.

Defendant's RFP No. 21 is broad in scope, requesting production of all Plaintiff's cell phones for inspection and copying, without any limitation on the data ultimately to be produced from the copy or image of the phone(s). Defendant in its briefing attempts to limit the request to "texts, other messages, and phone calls to co-workers, former co-workers, and current employees of Defendant." But, on its face the request is not so limited and Defendant sets out no protocol or process through which the data it deems responsive would be culled from the copy or image of the phone(s) and any unresponsive and/or privileged data removed or protected.

In any event, Plaintiff's cell phone likely contains a tremendous volume of information, including possibly text messages, email messages, phone logs, and photographs that are not at all relevant to the claims or defenses in this case. Even many or most of those texts and messages between Plaintiff and his co-workers or former co-workers may have no relevance to the claims and defenses in this case. Further, Defendant does not define what it means by "other messages," or explain how phone calls are relevant. It is not readily apparent how the mere fact that a phone call to a co-worker, former co-worker, or current employee of Defendant was made could be relevant to this employment discrimination case. Even if Plaintiff did call a coworker, there would be no way to tell what was discussed, or whether the phone call had anything to do with Plaintiff's allegations. Any relevant information concerning phone calls Plaintiff made to or received from coworkers and former co-workers could be more easily and less invasively obtained by asking Plaintiff about the calls during his deposition.

As noted in the Advisory Committee Notes to Fed. R. Civ. P. 34(a):

Inspection or testing of certain types of electronically stored information or of a responding party's electronic information system may raise issues of confidentiality or privacy. The addition of testing and sampling to Rule 34(a) with regard to documents and electronically stored information is not meant to create a routine right of direct access to a party's electronic information system, although such access might be justified in some circumstances. Courts should guard against undue intrusiveness resulting from inspecting or testing such systems.

Defendant cites no cases involving the imaging of a cell phone and only one case in which a computer inspection and imaging was ordered. However, in Jacobson, the Court noted that it was "unusual" to order production of a computer for inspection, but that it did so because the record in that case reflected a history of Starbucks providing incomplete and inconsistent responses to Jacobson's production requests (Starbucks had failed to have three key employees search their computers for documents responsive to plaintiff's discovery requests). As will be discussed in greater detail below, there is no evidence of such a history on the part of Plaintiff in this case. Defendant has never explained why it is necessary for it to conduct a physical inspection and copying of Plaintiff's cell phone(s), and its mere skepticism regarding whether Plaintiff has produced complete copies of all responsive text messages from the phone(s) does not warrant such a "drastic discovery measure."

The Court finds that Defendant's RFP No. 21 is overly broad, unduly burdensome and not proportional to the needs and issues of this case. Defendant's separate request for the narrowed scope of text messages also illustrates that Defendant has the ability to obtain relevant cell phone data through less invasive means. In accordance with Rule 34(a), the Court must guard against the undue intrusiveness that would result from the requested inspection and copying of Plaintiff's cell phone(s). The Court will therefore sustain Plaintiff's objections to RFP No. 21.

Defendant requested text messages in another request, which Plaintiff provided. Defendant contends Plaintiff produced an incomplete copy of one of his text conversations, so there could be other missing information that is relevant and discoverable, as justification for its request to image and copy Plaintiff's cell phone.

Defendant attached the incomplete text conversation to its motion to compel. But Plaintiff claims when Defendant raised this issue, Plaintiff realized he had mistakenly failed to produce the entire conversation and then remedied the issue by producing the entire conversation, which is attached to Plaintiff's response. Defendant fails to address Plaintiff's statement that he remedied the issue or explain whether there is another conversation produced with which Defendant has concerns. From the briefing and evidence provided, it does not appear there is any history of Plaintiff failing to provide discovery responses in good faith. To the extent, if any, that there are any problems with incomplete production of text messages by Plaintiff to date, those deficiencies will be corrected and resolved by the Court's order, below.

Although not raised by Defendant, to the extent Plaintiff has failed to fully respond to RFP No. 41, Plaintiff is directed to supplement his answer. That request asks for a complete copy of all text messages between Plaintiff and Defendant and between Plaintiff and current or former employees of Defendant. Plaintiff's objection states: "Plaintiff objects to the extent this request seeks irrelevant information and is not proportional to the needs of this case. Subject to and without waiving said objections, see SANTANA 000007-000010."

This is a conditional objection. "Conditional objections occur when `a party asserts objections, but then provides a response `subject to' or `without waiving' the stated objections.'" It is well settled in this district that "conditional answers are invalid and unsustainable." Therefore, Plaintiff is ordered to produce complete copies of all responsive text messages to the extent they have not already been produced. This will address Defendant's concerns regarding Plaintiff's alleged incomplete production of responsive text messages without the need for imaging Plaintiff's cell phone. If Plaintiff has provided all responsive text messages, Plaintiff shall supplement his answer to so state.

IT IS THEREFORE ORDERED BY THE COURT that Defendant's Motion to Compel Discovery Requests is denied.

IT IS FURTHER ORDERED that Plaintiff shall, prior to Plaintiff's deposition, supplement his response to Request for Production No. 41 and produce complete copies of all responsive text messages to the extent they have not already been produced.

IT IS SO ORDERED.

***

WASHINGTON V. GEO GROUP, INC.
No. 17-5806 RJB 2019 WL 2743390 (W.D. Wash. 2019)

BRYAN, District Judge

This matter comes before the Court on Defendant GEO Group Inc.'s ("GEO") Motion to Compel Production of Documents and Metadata. The Court has considered the pleadings filed in support of and in opposition to the motion and the file herein. This case arises out of GEO's alleged failure to compensate immigration detainees at the Northwest Detention Center ("NDC"), a private detention center, in accord with the Washington Minimum Wage Act ("MWA").

I. RELEVANT FACTS AND PROCEDURAL HISTORY
A. FACTS

GEO is a private corporation that has owned and operated the NWDC, a 1,575-bed detention facility in Tacoma, Washington, since 2005. GEO operates the NWDC based on a contract with U.S. Immigration and Customs Enforcement ("ICE"). Under this contract,

GEO provides "detention management services including the facility, detention officers, management personnel, supervision, manpower, training certifications, licenses ... equipment, and supplies" for immigration detainees awaiting resolution of immigration matters.

GEO is also required by the contract to manage a Voluntary Work Program ("VWP"). Detainees who participate in the VWP collect and distribute laundry, prepare and serve food, clean, paint interior walls, and use electric sheers to cut hair. GEO pays detainees who participate in the VWP at $1 per day. In accord with the contract with ICE, GEO agreed to comply with "[a]pplicable federal, state and local labor laws and codes."

B. PROCEDURAL HISTORY

On September 20, 2017, the State filed this case in Pierce County, Washington Superior Court. The Complaint maintains that the GEO-ICE Contract at least allows for, if not requires, GEO to compensate detainees working in the VWP commensurate with the State MWA. The State alleges that GEO has been unjustly enriched by compensating detainees below that required by state law. In its "quasi-sovereign interest," the State makes a claim against GEO for unjust enrichment, and seeks: (1) an order requiring GEO to disgorge its unjust enrichment from compensating detainees below the minimum wage, (2) declaratory relief that GEO is an "employer" subject to the MWA when managing detainee employees, and (3) injunctive relief for GEO to be enjoined from paying detainees less than the minimum wage.

In its Answer, GEO makes a counterclaim for unjust enrichment, seeks declaratory and injunctive relief, and asserts thirteen affirmative defenses.

On February 28, 2018, GEO's counterclaim for unjust enrichment was dismissed. Further, State's motion to strike the affirmative defenses of laches, unclean hands, failure to join necessary parties (Washington Department of Labor and Industries ("L & I") and ICE), and ripeness, justiciability, and a portion of the offset defense, was denied without prejudice; no finding was made as to the affirmative defense of preemption. The remaining affirmative defenses were stricken.

On August 30, 2018, GEO filed a motion for an order compelling the State to produce information from various State agencies related to State work programs, maintaining that the information was "extremely relevant to GEO's affirmative defenses of unclean hands and laches." The State opposed the motion, arguing that the State Agencies were not parties to the case and that the State agencies were better positioned to respond themselves.

On October 2, 2018, GEO's motion to compel was granted. Dkt. 133. The State was ordered to produce "all relevant, responsive, non-privileged information held by all divisions of the [Attorney General's Office ("AGO")] and agencies of the State." The order provided that it made "no findings as to the merits of specific discovery requests." The

October 2, 2018 order further ordered that as to "all discovery from AGO divisions, the State should produce metadata in native format, without summarizing or otherwise manipulating the information."

On May 13, 2019, GEO's affirmative defenses of laches, unclean hands and failure to join L & I and ICE were dismissed.

C. PENDING MOTION

GEO now moves for an order compelling the State to produce:

(1) relevant information from all agencies for (a) the State's use of work programs at its correctional or rehabilitation facilities, including why it pays some (but not all) work program participants market wages, whether the participants are volunteers, the hours worked, duties performed, and pay rates for participants, and the State's use of contractors to assist in the operation of work programs and (b) the State's assessment of federal and/or state law as it relates to the operation of work program;

(2) accurate and complete metadata for all of its productions, including custodian and author information, dates of creation and modification, and file path without modification; and

(3) logged documents on the common interest privilege log that are missing date, author, sender, recipient, or subject matter information and communications between third parties for which no basis for common interest privilege exists.

It argues that the information sought is relevant to the State's unjust enrichment claim and to GEO's preemption claim. Id. GEO maintains that the State has not produced metadata as ordered by the Court on October 2, 2018 and asserts that it should be ordered to do so. As it relates to the State's common interest privilege log, GEO asserts that it includes unknown third parties and fails to provide basic information that is necessary for GEO to assess the validity of the log. GEO argues that either the State should be ordered to produce an updated privilege log or produce each of the documents for which the State has failed to meet its burden.

The State opposes the motion. In regard to documents related to work programs, the State maintains that it has turned over documents responsive to GEO's requests for production. The State argues that GEO's motion fails to identify any particular request for production to which the State did not respond. In regard to the metadata, the State asserts that it has turned over the metadata it has, when it was available. It further maintains that it organized the documents in a "form ... in which it is ordinarily maintained [and is] reasonable useable." The State argues that the motion to compel regarding the privilege log should be denied because it produced a new updated privilege log. GEO has filed a reply and the motion is ripe for decision.

II. DISCUSSION
A. DISCOVERY GENERALLY AND MOTION TO COMPEL STANDARD
Fed. R. Civ. P. 26(b)(1) provides:

> Unless otherwise limited by court order, the scope of discovery is as follows: Parties may obtain discovery regarding any nonprivileged matter that is relevant to any party's claim or defense and proportional to the needs of the case, considering the importance of the issues at stake in the action, the amount in controversy, the parties' relative access to relevant information, the parties' resources, the importance of the discovery in resolving the issues, and whether the burden or expense of the proposed discovery outweighs its likely benefit. Information within this scope of discovery need not be admissible in evidence to be discoverable.

"The court should and ordinarily does interpret `relevant' very broadly to mean matter that is relevant to anything that is or may become an issue in the litigation." *Oppenheimer Fund, Inc. v. Sanders*, 437 U.S. 340, 351, n.12 (1978)(quoting 4 J. Moore, Federal Practice 26.56 [1], p. 26-131 n. 34 (2d ed. 1976)). Rule 37(a)(1) provides:

> On notice to other parties and all affected persons, a party may move for an order compelling disclosure or discovery. The motion must include a certification that the movant has in good faith conferred or attempted to confer with the person or party failing to make disclosure or discovery in an effort to obtain it without court action.

B. MOTION TO COMPEL DOCUMENTS REGARDING WORK PROGRAMS
GEO's motion to compel documents regarding the work programs should be denied.

The State argues that it reviewed thousands of pages of discovery from five agencies and produced hundreds of pages responsive to the requests for production. GEO fails to identify a specific response for production to which the State did not respond. In its reply, it identifies "discovery categories" and then collectively cites 17 requests for production that it asserts applies. This is not sufficient and the motion should be denied.

Moreover, while analysis under Rule 26(b)(1) is difficult when it is not entirely clear which request for production the State allegedly has not complied with, GEO has generally failed to demonstrate that further information regarding the State's work program is relevant and proportional to the needs of the case. This is particularly true "considering the importance of the issues at stake in the action, the amount in controversy, the parties' relative access to relevant information, the parties' resources, the importance of the discovery in resolving the issues, and whether the burden or expense of the proposed discovery outweighs its likely benefit." The motion to compel further documentation on the State's work programs should be denied.

C. MOTION TO COMPEL ACCURATE METADATA

GEO's motion for an order compelling the State to produce accurate metadata should be denied. The State indicates that it has complied with the October 2, 2018 Order to the extent that it was able, particularly as it relates to the custodians. Further, GEO has not shown that the information is relevant and proportional to the needs of the case.

D. MOTION TO COMPEL RELATED TO COMMON PRIVILEGE LOG

"Common interest is a long-recognized extension of the traditional common law doctrine of attorney-client privilege, which was pioneered by the Ninth Circuit to protect the confidentiality of communications passing from one party to the attorney for another party where the parties have undertaken a joint defense effort." *** "[A] shared desire to see the same outcome in a legal matter is insufficient to bring a communication between two parties" within the common interest rule. *** "Instead, the parties must make the communication in pursuit of a joint strategy in accordance with some form of agreement—whether written or unwritten."

GEO's motion to compel either an updated common privilege log or the documents for which the State has failed to meet its burden should be denied. The State has now produced an updated log. Moreover, it appears that the parties have not met and conferred as to this recent log as required under Fed. R. Civ. P. 37(a)(1). GEO's motion should be denied.

III. ORDER

Therefore, it is hereby ORDERED that: GEO's Motion to Compel Production of Documents and Metadata IS DENIED.

***

COREL SOFTWARE, LLC V. MICROSOFT CORP.
No. 2:15-cv-00528-JNP-PMW (D. Utah 2018)

WARNER, Chief Magistrate Judge

*** Before the court are Defendant Microsoft Corporation's ("Microsoft") short form discovery motion for protective order and Plaintiff Corel Software, LLC's ("Corel") short form motion to compel. ***

In its motion, Microsoft seeks a protective order barring further retention and production of its telemetry data ("Telemetry Data"). Microsoft admits that it has already produced some Telemetry Data to Corel, but contends that producing all Telemetry Data is infeasible because of its size. Microsoft asserts that locating the portion of Telemetry Data that relates to the Live Preview feature, which is the feature accused of infringement in this case, is highly burdensome. Microsoft further maintains that retaining Telemetry Data "raises tension with Microsoft's obligations under the European General Data Protection Regulation 2016/679 ["GDPR")], which regulates (among other things) telemetry data and would require additional burdensome steps to anonymize the data." For those reasons, Microsoft argues that continued retention and production of Telemetry Data is "technically challenging and cost prohibitive," cumulative in nature, unlikely to add any probative value, and disproportional to the needs of this case.

In response, Corel argues that Telemetry Data is relevant to infringement, damages, and validity, and, therefore, it should be retained and produced by Microsoft. Corel also contends that Microsoft has failed to establish that retention and production of Telemetry Data would result in undue burden or expense because Microsoft has not presented any support for its contentions concerning the alleged burden of isolating the Live Preview data or the alleged tension with GDPR. Corel further asserts that the Telemetry Data it now seeks is not cumulative because it relates to a time period distinct from the time period for which Microsoft already produced Telemetry Data. Finally, Corel argues that its request for additional Telemetry Data is proportional to the needs of the case because it is seeking only Telemetry Data that is relevant to showing usage of Live Preview, as opposed to all Telemetry Data.

Corel's motion to compel also relates to Telemetry Data. In its motion, Corel seeks compelled production of all Telemetry Data relating to the usage of the Live Preview feature, along with documents sufficient to identify the extent of any deleted Telemetry Data. Corel also requests compelled production of documents describing Microsoft's telemetry systems and decoding of Telemetry Data, as well as the deposition of knowledgeable witness regarding the Telemetry Data, Microsoft's telemetry systems, Microsoft's deletion schedule for Telemetry Data, and methods of decoding Telemetry Data. In support of its motion, Corel presents substantially the same arguments it raised in opposing Microsoft's motion for protective order.

In response to Corel's motion, Microsoft presents substantially the same arguments it asserted in support of its motion for protective order. Microsoft also contends that Corel's requests for compelled production of documents describing Microsoft's telemetry systems and the Corel's request for a deposition should be denied because the fact discovery deadline in this case has passed. As for Corel's other two requests, Microsoft urges the court to deny them, but does not argue that they are improper because the discovery deadline has expired.

With one exception, the court is not persuaded by Microsoft's arguments. With respect to the sole exception, the court concludes that Corel is not entitled to compelled production of documents describing Microsoft's telemetry systems or production of a Microsoft deponent because the fact discovery deadline has passed.

As for Corel's two remaining requests, the court concludes that Corel is entitled to discovery of Telemetry Data related to usage of Live Preview and information regarding its deletion. With respect to Microsoft's request for a protective order, the court concludes that Microsoft must continue to retain and produce Telemetry Data related to usage of Live Preview. The court has reached those conclusions for two primary reasons.

First, the court is persuaded that Telemetry Data related to usage of Live Preview and information regarding its deletion are directly relevant to the claims and defenses in this case. Specifically, the court agrees with Corel's argument that such information is directly relevant to infringement, damages, and validity. Importantly, Microsoft has not disputed the relevance of either Telemetry Data or information concerning its deletion and, based upon Microsoft's prior production of some Telemetry Data, Microsoft essentially concedes its relevance.

Second, the court concludes that production of Telemetry Data and information about its deletion is proportional to the needs of this case. In reaching that conclusion, the court has weighed the relevant factors set forth in Rule 26(b)(1). The court has determined that the information sought by Corel is important to and will help resolve the issues at stake in this case, as that information is directly relevant to the parties' claims and defenses. The court has also considered Microsoft's resources and has determined that those resources weigh against a finding that production of the information sought by Corel is unduly expensive. Additionally, the court is not persuaded by Microsoft's arguments concerning undue burden. Contrary to those arguments, the court concludes that, for many of the reasons already stated, the benefit of producing the information sought by Corel outweighs the burden and expense imposed upon Microsoft. Finally, the court is unpersuaded by Microsoft's argument that the information sought by Corel is cumulative in nature and unlikely to add any probative value. The court agrees with Corel's argument that the information it seeks is from a distinct time period and, therefore, will add probative value.

In summary, IT IS HEREBY ORDERED:

1. Microsoft's short form discovery motion for a protective order is DENIED.

2. Microsoft shall continue to retain and produce Telemetry Data related to the usage of Live Preview.

***

Baker v. Santa Clara University
No. 17-cv-02213-EJD (VKD) 2018 WL 3629838 (N.D. Cal. 2018)

DEMARCHI, Magistrate Judge

Plaintiff LaVonne Baker asks for an order requiring defendant Santa Clara University ("SCU") to produce all responsive, electronically stored information in native format. The parties jointly submitted a discovery letter brief on July 27, 2018. Resolution of this dispute does not require a hearing.

***

Ms. Baker served 54 requests for the production of documents on May 31, 2018. Her document requests included a single request that purports to cover the format of production for all documents responsive to the other 53 requests. Request for Production No. 54 states:

> With respect to each request, produce all documents in native format, including electronically stored information, metadata, and all metadata fields. Do not do anything that strips, removes, changes, limits, or otherwise alters the actual electronically stored information and metadata fields of any document that exists in an electronic format. Ensure that all such evidence remains intact, undisturbed, and is produced with each and every electronic document.

SCU produced over 2,500 pages of documents in response to Ms. Baker's document requests. SCU objected to Request No. 54, and produced all documents in .pdf format without metadata. SCU does not contend that the documents it produced are maintained in .pdf format in the usual course of its business.

Ms. Baker's primary argument for the re-production of SCU's electronically stored documents appears to be that having these documents (particularly email) in native format "is very useful in identifying missing `parent emails'[,] `child emails'[,] hidden attachments[,] altered electronic records[,] and other electronic activity having the usefulness of establishing the existence of electronic records that have not been produced." Essentially, Ms. Baker contends that having these documents in native format will allow her to more easily discover if SCU has omitted responsive documents from its production.

SCU states, without contradiction, that it attempted to engage Ms. Baker's counsel in a discussion of the search and production of electronically stored information more than a year ago in connection with the parties' obligations under Rule 26(f), and that Ms. Baker's counsel did not meaningfully engage in the required discussion. SCU points out that Ms. Baker delayed her demand for production in native format until late in the fact discovery period. SCU objects that producing responsive documents now in native format with metadata will be "time consuming, burdensome, and expensive." SCU does not elaborate beyond this conclusory statement regarding the nature or extent of the undue burden it claims.

Neither party has complied with the rules and guidelines that govern the production of electronically stored information. Rule 34(b)(2) requires a party responding to document requests to object to a requested form of production for electronically stored information, and to state the form or forms of production it intends to use. Fed. R. Civ. P. 34(b)(2)(D). Absent agreement or Court order regarding the form of production, the responding party must produce documents as they are kept in the usual course of business, or it must organize and label its production to correspond to the categories of documents sought in the requests. Fed. R. Civ. P. 34(b)(2)(E)(i). Here, while SCU objected to the form of production demanded by Ms. Baker in response to Request No. 54, it did not specify the form of production it intended to use, and it apparently did not organize and label its production to correspond to the categories in Ms. Baker's requests.

For her part, Ms. Baker appears to have utterly failed to comply with the requirements of Rule 26(f) and this Court's Guidelines for the Discovery of Electronically Stored Information by refusing to meaningfully engage in any discussions early in the case about the search and production of documents stored in electronic format.

The parties now find themselves in a dispute two weeks before the close of fact discovery that might have been avoided had they both complied with their respective and mutual discovery obligations. The Court's resolution of this dispute is guided by the dual requirements of relevance and proportionality in Rule 26(b)(1). Ms. Baker's primary argument for demanding production of documents in native format is that such production might reveal that SCU has not produced all of the documents it should have. SCU's document production is not particularly voluminous, and Ms. Baker has had nearly a month to review it. Absent a specific, articulable basis for believing SCU has not complied with its discovery obligations, Ms. Baker does not have a compelling reason for demanding that SCU re-produce its entire responsive document production in native format simply because she might find something missing. At the same time, SCU has not made any showing that re-producing some or all of its production in native format would be unduly burdensome.

Accordingly, at this time the Court will not require SCU to re-produce in native format the documents it has already produced in .pdf format. The Court's denial of Ms. Baker's present request is without prejudice. If Ms. Baker identifies particular documents or specific categories of documents for which she requires metadata or production in native format, she should make a request for re-production of those documents to SCU, together with an explanation of why re-production is necessary, as SCU has invited her to do already. If the parties cannot agree on whether or to what extent re-production may be necessary or justified, they may bring their dispute before the Court pursuant to the Court's Standing Order for Civil Cases.

***

C. Privacy

HENSON V. TURN, INC.
No. 15-cv-01497-JSW (N.D. Cal. 2018)

BEELER, Magistrate Judge

INTRODUCTION

Plaintiffs Anthony Henson and William Cintron, subscribers to Verizon's cellular and data services, bring this data-privacy class action against defendant Turn, Inc. The plaintiffs' allegations center around "cookies": lines of software code that monitor and gather information about users' browsing and app use. Web browsers, computers, and mobile devices have settings that allow users to block or delete cookies from their devices. The plaintiffs allege Turn engaged in a practice of placing so-called "zombie cookies" on users' devices: cookies that users either cannot delete or block or that, when users try to delete them, "respawn" to continue tracking users across the web. The plaintiffs, both New York residents, bring claims for (1) violations of New York General Business Law, which makes unlawful "[d]eceptive acts or practices in the conduct of any business, trade or commerce or in the furnishing of any service in [New York]," and (2) trespass to chattels.

Turn issued a number of discovery requests for production ("RFPs") to the plaintiffs. Among other things, Turn requested that the plaintiffs (1) produce their mobile devices for inspection or produce complete forensic images of their devices (RFP 1), (2) produce their full web browsing history from their devices (RFP 32), and (3) produce all cookies stored on or deleted from their devices (RFP 33). The plaintiffs argue that Turn's requests are overbroad and invade their privacy rights. The plaintiffs propose instead that they produce (1) their web browsing history and cookies associated with Turn partner websites (contingent on Turn's identifying such sites) and (2) the date fields (but not the content) of all other cookies on their mobile devices. The plaintiffs oppose allowing Turn to inspect their devices or producing complete forensic images of their devices.

STATEMENT

1. The Plaintiffs' Allegations

Users increasingly use a single mobile device—a smartphone or a tablet—for their online activities, including web browsing, reading the news, listening to radio content, accessing their banking information and managing their finances, shopping online, using GPS for directions and traffic updates, communicating over email and social networks, and reading sites like WebMD to assess their medical condition. Marketing companies like Turn have developed ways to place "tracking beacons" on these devices—lines of code called "cookies"—through web browsers or other smartphone apps. Cookies monitor and gather information about a user's website browsing and app use, which includes personal information regarding the user's daily routines. The resulting data is analyzed and used to target advertisements that match the user's profile.

Consumers have expressed discomfort at the idea of an unknown third party surreptitiously monitoring their online activity for commercial purposes. As one academic study reported:

> Web browsing history is inextricably linked to personal information. The pages a user visits can reveal her location, interests, purchases, employment status, sexual orientation, financial challenges, medical conditions, and more. Examining individual page loads is often adequate to draw many conclusions about a user; analyzing patterns of activity allows yet more inferences.... In mid-2011, we discovered that an advertising network, Epic Marketplace, had publicly exposed its interest segment data, offering a rare glimpse of what third-party trackers seek to learn about users. User segments included menopause, getting pregnant, repairing bad credit, and debt relief. Several months later we found that the free online dating website OkCupid was sending to the data provider Lotame how often a user drinks, smokes, and does drugs. When Krishnamurthy et al. tested search queries on ten popular health websites, they found a third party learned of the user's query on nine of them.

In a 2013 white paper issued in conjunction with Forbes, Turn surveyed Americans' attitudes about online tracking, marketing, and privacy. The survey found that, among other things, 69% of participants deleted cookies in order to "shield their online privacy," 56% of participants "are generally uncomfortable with the amount of information companies know about them or could learn about them through their activities," and 54% of participants felt that "their privacy concerns outweigh[ed] any benefits derived from sharing information with businesses" In light of privacy concerns, manufacturers and software companies developed functions for clearing and blocking cookies, which have long been standard features on all smartphones, tablets, computers, and web browsers.

Turn developed a method that allegedly made an "end-run" around users' cookie-blocking-and-deleting technologies. Turn allegedly did so through a Verizon function that created a persistent, unique identifier header ("UIDH" or "X-UIDH") for Verizon subscribers. Each Verizon customer had a unique X-UIDH value. Verizon embedded that unique X-UIDH value into the header of every HTTP request that its customers made from their mobile devices. Turn monitored the web traffic of its partner websites, searching for HTTP requests from Verizon customers (and the attendant X-UIDH values embedded in the requests). Upon receiving an HTTP request, Turn would check the X-UIDH value in the request against a database of values that it had stored from previous cookies. If there was a match, Turn would place a new cookie on the user's device that contained all of the values from the old cookies in its database that were associated with the same X-UIDH -- even if the user had previously deleted cookies from her device in an effort to not be tracked. Turn refers to this as "respawning," which led security experts to refer to these cookies as "zombie cookies" because they have the ability to regenerate and continue to track users despite users' attempts to not be tracked.

The plaintiffs alleged the following example of this process at work, citing in part an analysis conducted by Stanford professor Jeremy Mayer. Without a Verizon X-UIDH, when a user visits a Turn partner website, the website might place a cookie in her browser with a certain ID number (the example ID number used in the complaint of the cookie placed in the user's browser was 24152307171135370700).

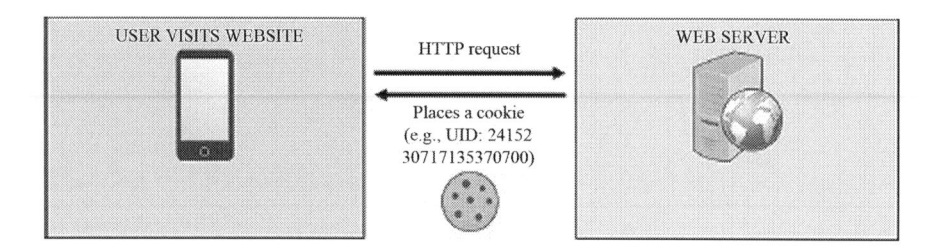

As long as the cookie remains in the browser, it allegedly transmits the user's browsing history back to the third party that first generated the cookie.

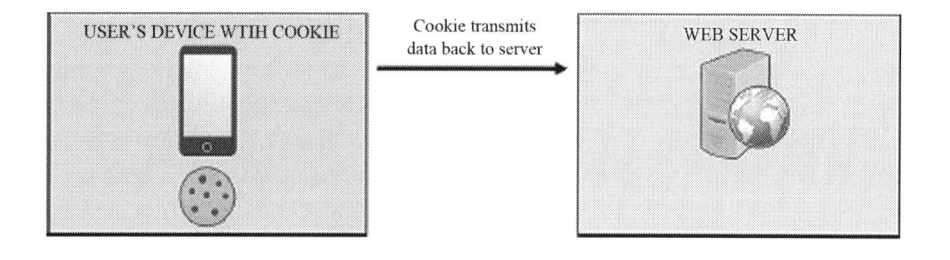

If the user then deletes her cookies:

and then visits another Turn partner website, the website would place a new cookie in her browser with a new ID number (the new example ID number used in the complaint was 4425321986559530189).

With a Verizon X-UIDH, however, when a user visits a Turn partner website, the website might place a cookie in her browser with a certain ID number (the example X-UIDH used in the complaint was "OTgxNT...," and the example ID number of the cookie placed in the user's browser was 4012847891611109688).

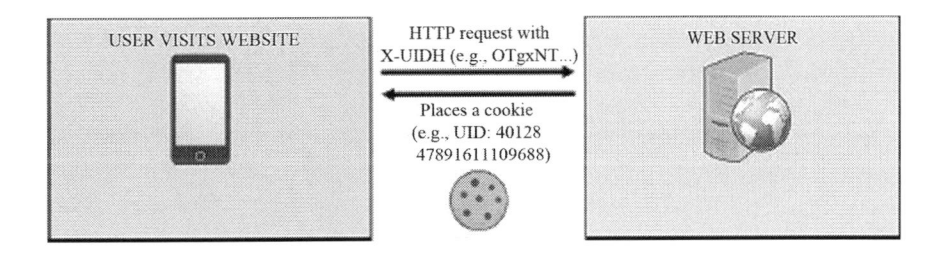

If the user then deletes her cookies:

and visits another Turn partner website, the website recognizes the Verizon X-UIDH and places a cookie in her browser with the same ID as before and all of the values from the user's old cookie that Turn stored within its database.

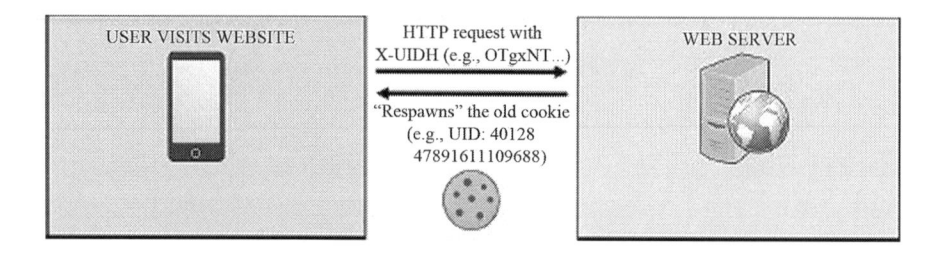

2. The Parties' Discovery Dispute

The parties raise disputes with respect to three of Turn's requests for production: RFP 1, RFP 32, and RFP 33. RFP 1 is a request for the plaintiffs to produce "[a]ll mobile devices with which You accessed the internet via the Verizon network during the alleged Class Period" (or complete forensic images of the devices). RFP 32 is a request for the plaintiffs to produce "[a]ll data from each Mobile Device reflecting or regarding the user's web browsing history, including web pages viewed either through a dedicated browser application or an 'in-app' browser embedded in another type of application." RFP 33 is a request for the plaintiffs to produce "[a]ll data from each Mobile Device reflecting or regarding any cookies stored on and/or deleted from the device, including the filenames, contents, and creation/modification/deletion dates of each cookie."

2.1 RFP 1: Inspection or Complete Forensic Images of the Plaintiffs' Mobile Devices

Turn argues that the plaintiffs' mobile devices "are at the very heart of this case." Specifically, with respect to the plaintiffs' New York unfair-business-practices claim, Turn argues that the claim "is wholly dependent on allegations about the content of Plaintiffs' phones, including whether Turn placed (and replaced) cookies on the phones, what kind of cookies Turn placed on the phones (if any) and when, whether Plaintiffs regularly deleted cookies and their browsing history from their phones, whether Turn 'circumvented device settings' on the phones, and what information (if any) was gathered from the phones." With respect to the plaintiffs' trespass-to-chattels claim, Turn argues that "the phones are the very 'chattels' that Plaintiffs allege Turn 'trespassed[.]'" Turn argues that "[i]t's hard to imagine a closer connection between plaintiffs' claims and their phones to justify allowing Turn's digital forensics experts to analyze them directly."

The plaintiffs respond that allowing Turn to inspect their devices or producing a complete forensic image would allow Turn to "access to Plaintiffs' entire phones and thus access to their private text messages, emails, contact lists, photographs and web browsing histories unrelated to Turn." The plaintiffs represent that they objected to RFP 1 and invited Turn to make requests for specific information, which prompted Turn to issue a second, more specific set of requests—RFPs 27-35—for which (aside from RFPs 32 and 33) the plaintiffs have produced responsive information. The plaintiffs argue that Turn's request for the full contents of their devices "flies in the face of Rule 26(b)'s relevancy and proportionality requirements."

2.2 RFP 32: Production of the Web Browsing History on the Plaintiffs' Devices

Turn argues that it is entitled to review the plaintiffs' complete browsing history "[(1)] to investigate whether and to what extent Plaintiffs even visited websites that worked with Turn cookies; [(2)] to test Plaintiffs' claim that they regularly deleted their browsing history in order to protect their privacy; and [(3)] to show that it does not constitute personally identifiable information implicating a protected privacy interest in any event." Turn also argues that the plaintiffs alleged that its cookies "transmit [] a user's web-browsing history back to the third party that generated the cookie, thus allowing the third party to glean valuable information about the user and her (presumed) interests" and that it "is entitled to discovery into all evidence that would provide those allegations untrue."

The plaintiffs respond that producing their full web browser history is overbroad, irrelevant, and invasive of their privacy interests. They argue that "people often browse the Internet for private reasons, such as health, dating, finances, and personal interests." In response to Turn's first argument, the plaintiffs state that they are willing to produce all browsing history associated with Turn partner websites, contingent on Turn's identifying its partner websites. In response to Turn's second argument, the plaintiffs state that (1) their web browsing history does not speak to the zombie-cookie scheme they allege, and that (2) in any event, Turn can discover whether the plaintiffs regularly deleted their browsing history by asking for the date ranges of the history on their devices, without the contents of the history. In response to Turn's third point, the plaintiffs argue that they "need not disclose the contents of every website ever visited in order to allege that Turn's surreptitious tracking of their web browsing violates Plaintiffs' privacy" and that "whether the information Turn catalogued implicates PII [personally identifiable information] is best determined by evaluating the information Turn has or had in its possession." The plaintiffs also argue that "Turn ignores that it obtains web browsing information by establishing relationships with Turn partner websites, and using cookies to track users as they visit those websites over time. And yet Turn's request is not limited to browsing history related to Turn's partner websites—it seeks everything."

2.3 RFP 33: Production of Cookies on the Plaintiffs' Devices

Turn argues that it is entitled to review all cookies stored on the plaintiffs' mobile devices "to technically examine what Turn cookies (if any) are on Plaintiffs' devices and compare them to standard browser cookies—including other non-Turn cookies that Plaintiffs permitted on their devices." Turn argues that "if Plaintiffs have numerous cookies on their devices over a wide range of installation dates, that information would prove their claim [that they regularly deleted cookies] to be false." Turn also argues that "if the devices have cookies dated after the complaint, it suggests a failure to preserve key evidence in its original condition."

The plaintiffs respond that their cookies implicate the same privacy interests as their web browsing history. The plaintiffs state that they are willing to produce cookie data related to any Turn partner website, to identify the date fields (but not the contents) of all other cookies, and to meet and confer to consider requests for specific cookies.

ANALYSIS

1. Inspection or Complete Forensic Images of the Plaintiffs' Mobile Devices

The undersigned denies Turn's request to require the plaintiffs to produce their mobile devices for Turn's inspection or, in the alternative, to produce complete forensic images of their mobile devices. Federal Rule of Civil Procedure 26(b)(1) limits discovery to matters that are (1) "relevant to any party's claim or defense" and (2) "proportional to the needs of the case[.]" Turn's request to inspect the plaintiffs' mobile devices or for complete forensic images call for information that is not relevant and is disproportional to the needs of the case.

With respect to relevance, as the plaintiffs correctly point out (and as Turn does not address), Turn's request to directly inspect the plaintiffs' mobile devices or for complete forensic images of the devices threatens to sweep in documents and information that are not relevant to the issues in this case, such as the plaintiffs' private text messages, emails, contact lists, and photographs. Just as a hypothetical request from the plaintiffs for Turn to allow them to directly inspect its emails servers (or produce complete forensic image of its servers) would likely sweep in numerous emails that are not relevant to this action, Turn's request for the plaintiffs to allow it to directly inspect their mobile devices (or produce complete forensic images of their devices) would likely sweep in numerous irrelevant documents as well. *See John B. v. Goetz*, 531 F.3d 448, 457-58 (6th Cir. 2008) (noting that "imaging of these computers and devices will result in the duplication of confidential and private information unrelated to the [] litigation"); *Salazar v. Bocanegra*, No. 12cv0053 MV/LAM, 2012 WL 12893938, at *2 (D.N.M. July 27, 2012) (noting that forensic images, due to their broad nature, may include information irrelevant to the parties' claims or defenses); *Sony BMG Music Entm't v. Arellanes*, No. 4:05-CV-328, 2006 WL 8201075, at *1 (E.D. Tex. Oct. 27, 2006) (finding meritorious responding party's argument that a full forensic image of her computer hard drive would sweep in irrelevant documents).

Turn's request might sweep in privileged documents as well, such as emails the plaintiffs might have sent their attorneys that may be stored in email applications on their mobile devices.

With respect to proportionality, Turn's request for the plaintiffs to allow it to inspect their mobile devices (or produce complete forensic images of their devices) is disproportional to the needs of the case. While questions of proportionality often arise in the context of disputes about the expense of discovery, proportionality is not limited to such financial considerations. Courts and commentators have recognized that privacy interests can be a consideration in evaluating proportionality, particularly in the context of a request to inspect personal electronic devices. *Tingle v. Hebert*, No. 15-626-JWD-EWD, 2018 WL 1726667, at *7-8 (M.D. La. Apr. 10, 2018) (finding that "Defendants have also made no showing that the requested forensic examination of Plaintiff's personal cell phone and personal email accounts are proportional to the needs of this case" and holding that "'[t]he utility of permitting a forensic examination of personal cell phones must be weighed against inherent privacy concerns'") (quoting *John Crane Grp. Corp. v. Energy Devices of Tex., Inc.*, No. 6:14-CV-178, 2015 WL 11112540, at *2 (E.D. Tex. Oct. 30, 2015)); *Crabtree v. Angie's List, Inc.*, No. 1:16-cv-00877-SEB-MJD, 2017 WL 413242, at *3 (S.D. Ind. Jan. 31, 2017) (denying request to forensically examine plaintiff's personal cell phones and holding that the forensic examination "is not proportional to the needs of the case because any benefit the data might provide is outweighed by Plaintiffs' significant privacy and confidentiality interests"); *Hespe v. City of Chicago*, No. 13 C 7998, at *3 (N.D. Ill. Dec. 15, 2016) (affirming order denying request to inspect plaintiff's personal computer and cell phone because, among other things, inspection "is not 'proportional to the needs of this case' because any benefit the inspection might provide is 'outweighed by plaintiff's privacy and confidentiality interests'"); *Areizaga v. ADW Corp.*, No. 3:14-cv-2899-B, 2016 WL 9526396, at *3 (N.D. Tex. Aug. 1, 2016) (denying request to inspect plaintiff's personal computer, smart phone, and other electronic devices because the request "is not proportional to the needs of the case at this time, when weighing [defendant]'s explanation and showing as to the information that it believes might be obtainable and might be relevant against the significant privacy and confidentiality concerns implicated by [defendant]'s request"); *In re Anthem, Inc. Data Breach Litig.*, No. 15-md-02617 LHK (NC), 2016 WL 11505231, at *1-2 (N.D. Cal. Apr. 8, 2016) (denying request to inspect or forensically image plaintiffs' computers, tablets, and smartphones as "invad[ing] plaintiffs' privacy interests" and "disproportional to the needs of the case"); *Agnieszka A. McPeak*, Social Media, Smartphones, and Proportional Privacy in Civil Discovery, 64 U. Kan. L. Rev. 235, 288-91 (2015) (arguing that courts should consider privacy burdens in evaluating proportionality under Rule 26(b)(1)); *see John B.*, 531 F.3d at 460 (issuing writ of mandamus to set aside orders for forensic imaging of state-owned and privately-owned employee computers because, among other things, "[t]he district court's compelled forensic imaging orders here fail to account properly for the significant privacy and confidentiality concerns present in this case"); *see also Johnson v. Nyack Hosp.*, 169 F.R.D. 550, 562 (S.D.N.Y. 1996) (holding that Rule 26 allows courts to limit discovery on account of burden, including "where the burden is not measured in the time or expense required to respond to requested discovery, but lies instead in the adverse consequences of the disclosure of sensitive, albeit unprivileged, material," and that courts should consider "the burdens imposed on the [responding parties]' privacy and other interests").

Rule 26(b)(1) expressly provides that "whether the burden or expense of the proposed discovery outweighs its likely benefit" is a consideration in evaluating proportionality.

As the Supreme Court has recognized, "[m]odern cell phones are not just another technological convenience. With all they contain and all they may reveal, they hold for many Americans 'the privacies of life.'" *Riley v. California*, 134 S. Ct. 2473, 2494-95 (2014) (citation omitted). As the Court observed:

> Even the most basic phones that sell for less than $20 might hold photographs, picture messages, text messages, Internet browsing history, a calendar, a thousand-entry phone book, and so on....
> ....
>
> .... [I]t is no exaggeration to say that many of the more than 90% of American adults who own a cell phone keep on their person a digital record of nearly every aspect of their lives—from the mundane to the intimate....
>
> .... An Internet search and browsing history, for example, can be found on an Internet-enabled phone and could reveal an individual's private interests or concerns ù perhaps a search for certain symptoms of disease, coupled with frequent visits to WebMD. Data on a cell phone can also reveal where a person has been. Historic location information is a standard feature on many smart phones and can reconstruct someone's specific movements down to the minute, not only around town but also within a particular building....
>
> Mobile application software on a cell phone, or "apps," offer a range of tools for managing detailed information about all aspects of a person's life. There are apps for Democratic Party news and Republican Party news; apps for alcohol, drug, and gambling addictions; apps for sharing prayer requests;

> apps for tracking pregnancy symptoms; apps for planning your budget; apps for every conceivable hobby or pastime; apps for improving your romantic life. There are popular apps for buying or selling just about anything, and the records of such transactions may be accessible on the phone indefinitely. There are over a million apps available in each of the two major app stores; the phrase "there's an app for that" is now part of the popular lexicon. The average smart phone user has installed 33 apps, which together can form a revealing montage of the user's life.

Id. at 2489-90 (citations omitted); accord *McPeak*, 64 U. Kan. L. Rev. at 244-45 (discussing how a smartphone can contain information about its owner and her emails, text messages, phone calls, calendars, social-media accounts, photographs, videos, what books she reads, what music she listens to, where she goes, when she sleeps, what she buys, and whom she dates—"[q]uite simply, her [smartp]hone is a portal to a complete, intimate portrait of her entire life"). While *Riley* was a criminal case, courts have applied its observations about the privacy concerns implicated by modern cell phones in the context of civil discovery as well. *See Bakhit v. Safety Mktg., Inc.*, No. 3:13CV1049 (JCH), 2014 WL 2916490, at *3 (D. Conn. June 26, 2014) (citing *Riley* in denying civil-discovery request to inspect personal cell phones).

Turn cites no authorities to support its request that the plaintiffs allow it to directly inspect their mobile devices (or produce complete forensic images of their devices). Turn cites to several cases where courts have ordered a party responding to a discovery request to forensically image its devices—in situations where there was a "sufficient nexus" between the party's devices and the claims or defenses at issue. But forensic imaging itself is not the issue here. The plaintiffs represent that they have already forensically imaged their devices and are producing information from those images. What Turn raises is the separate issue of its being allowed to directly access its opponents' devices or forensic images. None of the cases it cites supports that proposition.

Turn's first case, *Calyon v. Mizuho Securities USA, Inc.*, No. 07CIV02241RODF, 2007 WL 1468889 (S.D.N.Y. May 18, 2007), undercuts its request for direct access to the plaintiffs' devices or forensic images. That case, like this one, involved a discovery request for the responding parties (there, the defendants) to produce forensic images of their personal devices. There, as here, the responding parties created forensic images of their devices and offered to search the images (or to have a neutral third-party expert search the images) and produce responsive information. There, as here, the requesting party demanded that it be allowed to directly inspect the entirety of the responding parties' forensic images. ("At bottom, [the requesting party] maintains that only its expert—as opposed to the [responding parties]' expert or an independent third-party expert—would possess the requisite incentive to search exhaustively for evidence, and that only [its] expert would be able to confer with [its] counsel on an on-going basis to refine search methods."). The court denied the requesting party's request, finding that the requesting party had not made a showing as to why it would be entitled to such "extraordinary" access. Turn's other cases likewise do not support its position. In each of them, the responding party or a neutral third-party expert accessed and produced information from the responding party's forensic images. In none of them did the requesting party directly access its opponent's devices or forensic images ***.

Turn also cites *Austin v. Foodliner*, Inc., No. 16-cv-07185-HSG (DMR), 2018 WL 1168694 (N.D. Cal. Mar. 6, 2018), to argue that the protective order in this case "is more than sufficient to protect Plaintiffs' privacy concerns." But the information at issue in Austin was just phone-number contact information, and the court there specifically distinguished such contact information from "the disclosure of medical or financial information" or information that "implicates special privacy concerns or threatens 'undue intrusion into one's personal life.'"

The parties appear to have in place a protocol for producing information from the plaintiffs' devices or forensic images. Turn has issued nine RFPs (RFPs 27-35) for specific information from the plaintiffs' devices. The plaintiffs represent (and Turn does not deny) that they have produced information from their devices responsive to all of these requests (other than with respect to RFPs 32 and 33 regarding the browsing-history and cookie disputes the parties raise in their joint letter brief, which the undersigned addresses below). Given this, and in light of the fact that the plaintiffs' devices likely contain information not relevant to this case, may contain privileged information, and implicate significant privacy concerns, Turn's request for the plaintiffs to allow it to directly inspect their devices (or produce complete forensic images of their devices) is not relevant or proportional to the needs of this case.

2. Full Web Browsing History and Cookies

The plaintiffs have produced or have offered to produce (1) their web browsing history and cookies associated with Turn partner websites (contingent on Turn's identifying such sites) and (2) the date fields (but not the content) of all other cookies on their mobile devices. The plaintiffs also represent that they offered to meet and confer with Turn to consider requests for specific cookies. The undersigned finds the plaintiffs' position and proposals to be reasonable and proportional, with a slight modification ù the plaintiffs should produce the dates (but not the content) of the entries in their browsing history (as they are doing for their cookies).

The undersigned denies Turn's request to require the plaintiffs to produce their full web browsing history and cookie data. As discussed above, requiring the plaintiffs to produce their full browsing history presents significant privacy concerns. *See Riley*, 134 S. Ct. at 2490 ("An Internet search and browsing history, for example, can be found on an Internet-enabled phone and could reveal an individual's private interests or concerns ù perhaps a search for certain symptoms of disease, coupled with frequent visits to

WebMD."). Cookies, which the plaintiffs assert (and Turn does not deny) are closely associated with websites, raise similar privacy concerns. Turn has not shown that its request for the plaintiffs' full browsing history and cookies as they relate to websites other than Turn partner websites is relevant or proportional to the needs of this case.

Turn claims that it needs to examine what Turn cookies are on the plaintiffs' devices, but the plaintiffs have agreed to produce those cookies, so there is no dispute there. Turn claims it needs web browsing history to determine whether the plaintiffs visited websites that worked with Turn cookies in the first place, but the plaintiffs have agreed to produce their browsing history and cookies for those sites, so again there is no dispute there. Turn claims it needs to compare its cookies to standard browser cookies, but it does not need all of the cookies on the plaintiffs' devices to run that comparison. Turn claims that it needs to determine whether the plaintiffs regularly deleted their cookies or browsing histories as they allege, but it can do so through the date fields of the plaintiffs' cookies and browsing histories and does not need the full content of the cookies and histories to do so. Turn claims that the plaintiffs argued that Turn's cookies transmit a user's web-browsing history back to Turn, but Turn has not shown why it needs the plaintiffs' full browsing history to determine what information was or was not transmitted back to Turn (information that is presumably within Turn's possession, custody, or control). Given all this, and in light of the significant privacy concerns present here, Turn has not shown that its request for plaintiffs' full browsing history or cookies is relevant or proportional to the needs of this case.

* * *

As another court in this district noted in the context of a data-breach case, "[t]here is an Orwellian irony to the proposition that in order to get relief for a theft of one's personal information, a person has to disclose even more personal information, including an inspection of all his or her devices that connect to the internet. If the Court were to grant [that] request, it would further invade plaintiffs' privacy interests and deter current and future data theft victims from pursuing relief." *In re Anthem Data Breach*, 2016 WL 11505231, at *1. The same holds true here. There is an Orwellian irony to the proposition that in order to get relief for a company's alleged surreptitious monitoring of users' mobile device and web activity, a person has to allow the company unfettered access to inspect his mobile device or his web browsing history. Allowing this discovery would further invade the plaintiffs' privacy interests and may deter current and future plaintiffs from pursuing similar relief. *Cf. Rivera v. NIBCO, Inc.*, 364 F.3d 1057, 1065 (9th Cir. 2004) (affirming district court's refusal to allow discovery into certain private information of plaintiffs in a Title VII employment case because, among other things, "[t]he chilling effect such discovery could have on the bringing of civil rights actions unacceptably burdens the public interest").

The undersigned does not mean to imply that there could never be an instance where a request to directly inspect a litigant's electronic devices or forensic images, or a request that a litigant produce his complete web browsing history or cookies, would be relevant and proportional. There may be situations where such a request would be proper, and this order is without prejudice to Turn's renewing its request should such a situation arise. But that situation has not presented itself here. Turn's request for the plaintiffs to allow it to directly inspect their mobile devices (or produce complete forensic images of their devices) and for the plaintiffs to produce their complete browsing history and cookies, is denied.

CONCLUSION

The court adopts the plaintiffs' proposals, with the slight modification that the plaintiffs should also produce the dates of the entries in their browsing history.

***

RODRIGUEZ-RUIZ V. MICROSOFT OPERATIONS P.R., L.L.C.
No. 18-1806 (PG) (D. P.R. 2020)

PEREZ-GIMENEZ, Senior District Judge

I. Background

Plaintiff Luis Noel Rodriguez Ruiz ("Plaintiff" or "Rodriguez") filed the above-captioned claim on October 26, 2018. Plaintiff alleges that defendant Microsoft Operations Puerto Rico, L.L.C. ("Microsoft" or "Defendant") discriminated against him and denied him reasonable accommodation in violation of the Americans with Disabilities Act 42 U.S.C. § 12117 *et seq.* ("ADA"), and wrongfully terminated him pursuant to Law No. 80 of May 30, 1976, as amended, 29 P.R. LAWS ANN., tit. 29, § 185a *et seq.* ("Law 80"). Plaintiff states that he suffers from cerebral palsy, a major disabling motor disorder that causes him to have a limp and difficulty walking, among other things. Plaintiff also avers that he suffers from severe headaches and back pain after severe and permanent cervical damage suffered in a non-work-related automobile accident.

Pursuant to the allegations in the complaint, on December 5, 2005, Plaintiff commenced his employment with Microsoft as an engineer. According to Plaintiff, on or about the end of the year 2011, his new supervisor Hector Baez began a campaign of discrimination and harassment against him because of his disabilities. Rodriguez alleges that Baez created a hostile work environment, ordered disadvantageous transfers, gave him poor performance reviews, denied reasonable accommodations and made disparaging comments about Plaintiff's impediments. He was eventually discharged on August 19, 2016. Plaintiff now requests to be indemnified for his wrongful termination and for the damages suffered. He seeks reinstatement, damages for pain and suffering and economic harm, punitive damages, front and back pay in lieu of reinstatement, as well as attorney fees.

Defendant answered the complaint on December 21, 2018 and discovery proceedings ensued. The court held two conferences with parties' attorneys and granted an extension of time to conduct discovery until December 31, 2019. On the last possible day, Defendant filed a Motion to Compel complaining about Plaintiff's insufficient responses to both its interrogatories and requests for production. The Plaintiff responded arguing that some discovery disputes had already been resolved, and were thus moot, and that some interrogatories and discovery requests were overly broad, burdensome, and/or in violation of Plaintiff's privacy rights.

On February 6, 2020, the court held a status conference in this case to discuss the pending motion. After the conclusion of the conference, the only pending matter in the motion to compel to be adjudged was whether Plaintiff should respond to Interrogatory No. 17 and Requests for Production of Documents Nos. 17 and 18, regarding the production of Plaintiff's Facebook or social media profile(s). As such, the court deems MOOT all other issues raised in the motion to compel and will limit the discussion *infra* to Microsoft's request for the content of Plaintiff's social media account on Facebook.

II. Discussion

A. General Legal Principles

Rule 26(b)(1) of the Federal Rules of Civil Procedure states that, "[u]nless otherwise limited by court order, the scope of discovery is as follows: Parties may obtain discovery regarding any nonprivileged matter that is relevant to any party's claim or defense and proportional to the needs of the case ... Information within this scope of discovery need not be admissible in evidence to be discoverable." Fed. R. Civ. P. 26(b)(1). "Rule 26 promotes fairness both in the discovery process and at trial." *** That is because "[m]utual knowledge of all the relevant facts gathered by both parties is essential to proper litigation." ***

Rule 26 is to be "construed broadly to encompass any matter that bears on, or that reasonably could lead to other matter that could bear on, any issue that is or may be in the case." *** Nevertheless, "[t]he proportionality provision was added to Fed. R. Civ. P. 26 (b)(1) in December 2015 to emphasize that there are intended to be limits on the breadth of discovery to which a party is entitled." ***

If a discovery dispute arises, a party seeking discovery may file a motion to compel discovery pursuant to Rule 37 of the Federal Rules of Civil Procedure. *** "The party seeking information in discovery has the burden of showing its relevance." *** On the other hand, "[w]hen a party resists the production of evidence, it 'bears the burden of establishing lack of relevancy or undue burden.'" ***

B. Parties' Discovery Motions

Pursuant to the motion to compel, Microsoft's Interrogatory No. 17 requests that Plaintiff identify all social media profiles he manages, and Request for Production of Document No. 17 states as follows:

As to any social media account you may have, produce the following:

a. Complete copy of your profile, including, without limitation, all messages, posts, status updates, comments on your wall or page, causes and/or groups to which you have joined, which are in your account and which were published or posted between January 2010 and the present, related or referring to any emotions, feelings, mental status, or mood status.

b. Copy of all communications from you, whether through private messages in your profile or messages on your wall or page, which may provide context to the communication mentioned in the previous sub-section.

c. Any and all photos taken and/or uploaded to your account between January 2010 and the present.

On the other hand, Request for Production of Documents No. 18 states the following:

Regarding any Facebook account you have or may have had, the information requested in subsections a - c, may be obtained by following these steps: (1) enter your Facebook profile; (2) go to the "account" section; (3) go to "account settings"; (4) select the option of "download your information"; (5) select "download."

In its motion, Defendant opposes Plaintiff's objections to these requests. Specifically, Plaintiff objected the requests are not "related in any way to the case, are overbroad, burdensome, offensive and a violation of plaintiff's right to privacy."

C. Electronic Discovery of Social Media

Microsoft moves the court to order Plaintiff to provide the requested content of Plaintiff's social media profile because it is relevant to its defenses and, therefore, discoverable. See Docket No. 15 at pages 14-18. Microsoft asserts that the information stemming from his social media profile(a) is also relevant to Plaintiff's mental and emotional state regarding his emotional damages. Microsoft cited a string of cases in support of its contentions that Plaintiff has no right of privacy over the evidence requested and that Plaintiff is required to produce this evidence. See Docket No. 15 at pages 14-18.

In his response, Plaintiff merely states that he has given Defendant authorizations to access his income tax returns, as well as his medical and psychological records, and "that should be enough ... ."

For starters, the court is persuaded that Plaintiff lacks a right to privacy with regards to the content of his social media profile(s). Various courts have held that "[i]nformation posted on a private individual's social media 'is generally not privileged, nor is it protected by common law or civil law notions of privacy.'" *** Therefore, Plaintiff's reluctance to produce the content of his social media page(s) on account of a claim to a right of privacy is unfounded.

Having agreed with our sister courts that the posted or published content in a social networking site, such as a Facebook profile, is devoid of a right of privacy, the court must then determine whether the request for production is relevant to the claims being litigated. "Courts have ... found social media, diaries, and journals generally discoverable provided that they are relevant to a plaintiff's claims." ***

More specifically, several courts have found that the contents of a plaintiff-employee's social media profile, postings, or messages (including status updates, wall comments, causes joined, groups joined, activity streams, blog entries during a relevant time period) are relevant and discoverable in employment cases which include claims of emotional distress, when they "reveal, refer, or relate to events that could reasonably be expected to produce a significant emotion, feeling, or mental state." *** In fact, a fellow judge in this district court has already deemed this type of evidence - to wit, a plaintiff's Facebook profile - discoverable in the context of an employment litigation. ***

Though courts have concluded that information posted or published on a party's social media page may be relevant, courts generally do not "endorse an extremely broad request for all social media site content." *** "[A] party does not have 'a generalized right to rummage at will through information that [an opposing party] has limited from public view.'" ***

With those principles in mind, courts have held that "a plaintiff's entire social networking account is not necessarily relevant simply because he or she is seeking emotional distress damages.'" *** The fact that a plaintiff's mental or emotional state is at issue does not "automatically justify sweeping discovery of social media content." *** Therefore, "[t]he production of a social media account's contents in full will therefore rarely be appropriate." ***

Here, Defendant has adequately demonstrated the relevance of the content of Plaintiff's social media account, and Plaintiff's boilerplate and generalized objections to this request for production are not enough to carry the day. "[G]eneralized objections to an opponent's discovery requests are insufficient." *** Hence, the court finds that some discovery of Plaintiff's social media profile(s) is appropriate here.

The court must now define the permissible scope of this type of discovery in cases like the above-captioned since "[i]t is reasonable to expect severe emotional or mental injury to manifest itself in some [social networking site] content ... ." *** To that effect, the court agrees with other district courts' conclusion that social media content that is reflective of a person's emotional state is relevant and discoverable when the same has been placed at issue. For example:

[P]osts specifically referencing the emotional distress plaintiff claims to have suffered or treatment plaintiff received in connection with the incidents alleged in [his] complaint and posts referencing an alternative potential source of cause of plaintiff's emotional distress are discoverable. ... In addition, posts regarding plaintiff's social activities may be relevant to plaintiff's claims of emotional distress and loss of enjoyment of life.

Pursuant to the foregoing, Microsoft's request for production is hereby granted, but only in part. First, the Plaintiff shall respond to Microsoft's interrogatory requesting he identify all the social media platforms in which he has an account or profile. However, the court will not allow Defendant to have unrestricted access to Plaintiff's social media account(s). Instead, Plaintiff's counsel shall review all of Plaintiff's social media content during the requested period (from January 2010 to the present) and produce any and all content, posts or comments referencing Plaintiff's "emotions, feelings, mental status, or mood status," (as requested), including any photographs which may have accompanied such posts or comments. The same test shall be applied to the request for Plaintiff's uploaded photos insofar as "pictures of the claimant taken during the relevant time period and posted on a claimant's profile will generally be discoverable because the context of the picture and the claimant's appearance may reveal the claimant's emotional or mental status." *** "The Court trusts that plaintiff's counsel, as an officer of the Court, will review social media content and communications and produce any relevant information." ***

Finally, Microsoft may "challenge the production if it believes the production falls short of the requirements of this order. Nothing in this Order is intended to foreclose such follow-up procedures." *** During the course of this exercise, the parties are encouraged to review the cited caselaw for illustration and may file a motion for clarification as to any specific issue of law that arises.

III. Conclusion

Pursuant to the foregoing, the court hereby GRANTS IN PART the single pending issue in Microsoft's motion to compel regarding the complete production of Plaintiff's social media account(s) and/or profile(s) ***.

DENSON V. CORP. OF PRESIDENT OF CHURCH OF JESUS CHRIST OF LATTER-DAY SAINTS

No. 2:18-cv-00284 (D. Utah 2020)

PEAD, Chief Magistrate Judge

***

FACTUAL BACKGROUND

In April 2018, Plaintiff McKenna Denson (Denson) initiated this action. Denson claims Defendant COP had knowledge that Defendant Joseph L. Bishop (Bishop) is or was a sexual predator, yet made representations that he was a safe and respectable person. Despite an alleged history of questionable sexual behavior, Bishop was called to serve as President of a Missionary Training Center (MTC) where he had authority over thousands of young men and young women. Plaintiff alleges she had a traumatic and challenging adolescence that included past physical and sexual abuse. Denson received special permission to serve a mission for her church and entered the MTC in January 1984.

While in the MTC, Denson avers she was singled out by Bishop and after several meetings where others were present, she then met alone with Bishop in his office per his request. Eventually Bishop allegedly sexually assaulted Denson in a basement room. A few years later in approximately 1987 or early 1988, Denson revealed the details of the sexual assault to church leaders. Elder Carlos Asay, a general authority and member of the First Quorum of the Seventy at the time, interviewed Denson and told her he would investigate the incident and let her know the outcome. Elder Asay never contacted her about the incident again.

PROCEDURAL BACKGROUND

***

Following a series of status conferences and court orders staying this case for a time to allow Denson opportunities to find new counsel, Denson represented to the court that she intended to pursue a dismissal of the case. Shortly thereafter however, Denson changed course and entered a notice of *pro se* appearance. The court then held a hearing on COP's short form discovery motion to compel the recording of Plaintiff's visit with Ronald Leavitt. During the hearing Denson represented to the court that certain items pertaining to this case, including the recording, have gone missing. The court ordered Denson to file a sworn affidavit concerning the missing items within 30 days. In an order following the hearing the court stated:

As discussed at the hearing, Ms. Denson is to provide the necessary level of detail concerning the missing items, including the date on which she had possession of these items, how they were stored, the date upon which they were removed from storage and the approximate date that they were no longer in her actual or constructive possession.

The court also granted Denson's request for mediation. To date, the COVID-19 global pandemic has postponed the mediation. Denson filed a sealed affidavit on March 20, 2020. Five days later Defendant COP filed a Sealed Motion for Additional Information requesting the court order Plaintiff to supplement her affidavit regarding the evidence she claims has gone missing. Denson did not respond to the motion and the court entered an order to show cause directing her to respond. In response to the court's order to show cause, Denson provided that she gave a trusted friend the recorder, which held the "original recording of my conversation with Joseph Bishop and Ron Leavitt in April of 2019 to hold for safe keeping." Plaintiff did not have a "safe deposit box" but her friend had a lock box at her residence, where she kept the recorder. Denson also provided correspondence from two individuals, Kathryn Sisney, who had the lock box with the recorder and recording, and Michael Bratcher, a friend of 11 or 12 years.

Most recently, Defendant filed a Sealed Motion for Preservation of Electronic Evidence. COP seeks a court order allowing a third-party forensic technology specialist to collect data from Denson's electronic devices and cloud-based accounts. In support COP points to the lost evidence in this case and the representations Denson has made concerning evidence. Plaintiff has opposed this motion and it is now ripe for decision as COP has filed their reply.

DISCUSSION

Federal Rule of Civil Procedure 26(b)(1), which governs discovery disputes such as this, provides that

> Parties may obtain discovery regarding any nonprivileged matter that is relevant to any party's claim or defense and proportional to the needs of the case, considering the importance of the issues at stake in the action, the amount in controversy, the parties' relative access to relevant information, the parties' resources, the importance of the discovery in resolving the issues, and whether the burden or expense of the proposed discovery outweighs its likely benefit. Information within this scope of discovery need not be admissible in evidence to be discoverable. F.R.C.P. 26(b)(1).

Denson is acting *pro se* in this case, so her pleadings are entitled to a liberal construction and she is held to a less stringent standard than other litigants. *** Yet, *pro se* litigants "are subject to the same rules of procedure that govern other litigants." *** This includes complying with discovery obligations as set forth in Rule 26. ***

(i) The recording of Plaintiff's conversation with Ronald Leavitt and the court order affidavit

The recording sought by Defendant is relevant to this case under Rule 26 and is subject to Defendant's prior discovery request seeking "All edited and unedited video and audio files regarding the allegations in the Complaint or this lawsuit." COP's RFP 21. Denson did not object to this request and she should have provided the recording. The court, therefore, will grant COP's Motion to Compel production of the recording. Denson is ordered to perform a new extensive and thorough search for the recording and if found it is to be produced within thirty (30) days from the date of this order.

The problem, however, is it appears the recording along with other items, have gone missing according to Plaintiff. To help remedy this the court ordered Denson to provide a detailed affidavit concerning the missing items. This was to include "the date on which she had possession of these items, how they were stored, the date upon which they were removed from storage and the approximate date that they were no longer in her actual or constructive possession." Denson has failed to comply with this requirement. The court will therefore order Plaintiff to file a supplemental affidavit that specifically lists each and every single item that is missing, a detailed description of each item, the dates Plaintiff had possession of each item, the date it went missing and precisely where each item has been stored. The supplemental affidavit is to be signed by Plaintiff. A letter from a friend or others that is not in the form of a sworn affidavit will not suffice.

The court is very concerned by the shifting representations made by Plaintiff. At the hearing held on February 20, 2020, Denson represented that the recording "was in a safe deposit box, but I took it out because I was handing it over to the Utah Bar." Denson provided that she could look through her records to determine when it was removed. Nonetheless, in her affidavit Plaintiff did not identify a bank or safe deposit box where the recording and other evidence was stored. Plaintiff now represents, in a filing before the court, that she does not "nor have ever had a safe deposit box." Instead, the recorder and recording was stored at a friend's house in a lock box. This new representation is now accompanied by completely unsupported assertions made regarding the theft of the items possibly by individuals in this case, which border on absurd and irrational. The court will grant COP's Motion for Additional Information. Plaintiff has thirty (30) days from the date of this order to file a supplemental affidavit that provides explicit details regarding the evidence she claims has gone missing.

(ii) Defendant's request for a third party forensic specialist to preserve evidence

Most recently, COP seeks a court order allowing a third-party forensic technology specialist to collect all data from Denson's electronic devices and cloud-based accounts. COP argues this is necessary because 1) Plaintiff has abused the discovery process; 2) improperly withheld and concealed evidence; and 3) made misrepresentations. Specifically, COP points to Plaintiff's denial under oath of not having any Reddit account, and then later admitting that she not only had one, but also used it regularly to write about this case; Plaintiff's testimony that she is writing a book about her allegations, followed by a response to a document request that the manuscript consists of only a one-page outline; and, the ever shifting representations concerning the now missing evidence as noted above.

COP cites to Federal Rule 34(a) and offers two cases in support of its motion, *Jacobsen v. Starbucks Coffee Co.*, 2006 WL 3146349 (D. Kan. 2006) (unpublished) and *Talon Transaction Tech. Inc. v. Stoneeagle Services, Inc.*, 2013 WL 12172924 (N.D. Tex. 2013) (unpublished). Rule 34 of the Federal Rules of Civil Procedure provides that a party my request another party to "produce and permit the requesting party or its representative to inspect, copy, test, or sample the following items ...: any designated documents or electronically stored information-including ... images, and other data or data compilations-stored in any medium ...." Fed. R. Civ. P. 34(a). The advisory committee notes to the 2006 amendment of Rule 24 provide that the term "electronically stored information" is broad and the court finds it can encompass the request sought by COP.

A sister court in this district, the District of Kansas, decided Jacobsen. In that case, the plaintiff brought employment discrimination claims and sought to compel the production of certain items. Because of "questionable discovery responses" the plaintiff also sought production of her supervisor's computer, or a mirror image of the computer. The court granted the request pointing to the circumstances in the case that warranted it. "The record before the court reflects a history of incomplete and inconsistent responses to plaintiff's production requests" the court said, and, "Defendant's belated search using four terms and it offer to conduct additional searches is simply 'too little, too late.'" The defendant's objections that the computer contained irrelevant, proprietary and confidential business data, was not enough to overcome the circumstances that warranted its production.

Similarly, the Northern District of Texas in *Talon v. Stoneeagle Services*, discussed the value of electronic evidence and the need and duty to preserve it. "To ensure that evidence has been properly preserved in cases involving electronic evidence, courts have permitted the taking of a "mirror images" of a party's relevant computer equipment." That court then cited to examples of cases where this was done, including one from this circuit *Balboa Threadworks, Inc. v. Stucky*, 2006 WL 763668, at * 4 (D. Kan. Mar. 24, 2006), where the court ordered that all of the defendants' computers and peripheral equipment, such as ZIP Drives, shall be made available for mirror imaging. ***

Denson opposes the request for access to her electronic devices and cloud based accounts arguing that it is "not only unnecessary but it is also invasive and an absolute invasion of my privacy." Denson points to her prior productions asserting she has produced emails and or messages. Plaintiff also offers the password to her Facebook account and to her "Reddit account entitled nopotofgold." Finally, Denson asserts the draft of her book entitled "The Rape Room" was included with the flash drives that went missing and in any event, it is unimportant because the parties are heading into settlement negotiations.

The cases cited to by Defendant are not controlling, but the court finds the principles set forth in them persuasive. The Federal Rules require a party to conduct a reasonable search for responsive information. *** Denson, although now proceeding *pro se*, is not exempt from the discovery requirements of the Federal Rules. Having reviewed the history of the discovery in this case, the court finds Denson has failed to meet her discovery obligations. This is evident in her failure to produce items that are relevant and responsive to Defendant's discovery requests.

Based upon the circumstances in this case, which includes the loss of evidence, the changing stories of Plaintiff concerning this evidence and how it was stored, the conflicting nature of reports Plaintiff has offered concerning an individual outside her home, and the alleged attacks upon her, the court finds the circumstances here warrant access to her electronic devices and cloud based accounts to create a mirrored image. This will preserve any evidence and perhaps discover evidence that has been lost. Denson's offer of her password to certain social media accounts is insufficient to address the concerns cited above. Plus, even with access, there is nothing to prevent an attempt at destruction of evidence. The court presumes parties appearing before it will act in good faith, yet Plaintiff's actions here have left the court with significant reservations.

Denson argues allowing access to her devices will be an invasion of her privacy. The court acknowledges there will be some private items on her devices and cloud accounts that will be irrelevant to this case and need not be turned over to Defendants. Defendant proposes that an independent third-party, Xact Data Discvoery, Inc. (XDD) a nationwide discovery and forensic service provider, not counsel, image her devices and collect the data. The court adopts this proposal. Counsel for Defendant will not have any access to the data collected until after the court approves a review plan. The court finds this will adequately protect Plaintiff's privacy interests. Once the data is collected and a report generated, the parties may propose a review process to account for documents and information that is privileged or irrelevant.

Defendant "is willing to pay the costs associated with XDD's services at this time" subject to seeking sanctions and fees against Plaintiff if necessary. The court orders Defendant to engage XDD and begin the process. If necessary, the court will determine how the final costs for the services will be split or paid for at a later time. Plaintiff is ordered to not destroy any evidence or electronic devices. Plaintiff's devices shall be turned over to XDD for imaging within a reasonable time frame from the date of this order. Plaintiff is also to turn over passwords to all her cloud based accounts to XDD for imaging. The court is mindful that the COVID-19 pandemic may create some challenges to mirroring, but the court expects that the process will begin no later than sixty (60) days from the date of this order. Accordingly, Defendant's Motion for Preservation of Electronic Evidence shall be GRANTED.

***

Chapter 10

Privilege Concerns in Electronic Discovery

Federal Rules of Evidence (FRE) Rule 502(b) provides a three-part test that allows the producing party to avoid waiver when:

(1) the disclosure is inadvertent;
(2) the holder of the privilege or protection took reasonable steps to prevent disclosure; and
(3) the holder promptly took reasonable steps to rectify the error, including (if applicable) following FRCP Rule 26(b)(5)(B).

A. Burden of Proving Inadvertent Disclosure

FRE Rule 502 does not assign the burden of proving inadvertence, but courts consistently assign that burden to the party seeking clawback of the privileged documents. Also, FRE Rule 502(b) does not define "inadvertent," most courts apply the first prong of the test permissively, asking only whether the disclosure was intended or mistaken.

Coburn Group, LLC v. Whitecap Advisors LLC
640 F. Supp. 2d 1032 (N.D. Ill. 2009)

BROWN, Magistrate Judge

Before the court is Defendant Whitecap Advisor LLC's Motion to Compel Return of Documents and to Strike Deposition Testimony. For the reasons set out below, to the extent that it was not resolved at previous hearings, the motion is granted.

BACKGROUND

Coburn Group, LLC, ("Coburn") claims in this lawsuit that Whitecap Advisors, LLC, ("Whitecap") breached an oral contract to pay Coburn fees for referring investors to Whitecap. In the present motion, Whitecap originally requested an order requiring Coburn to return two documents totaling 16 pages that it claims are privileged and were inadvertently produced in its document production of approximately 40,000 pages. Whitecap also asked that the court strike any deposition testimony related to the documents and bar Coburn from using any information obtained from the documents. Coburn refused

Whitecap's request to return the documents and opposes the motion. The parties submitted a number of briefs. Several hearings were held, at which almost all of the issues were resolved. The sole remaining issue is a half-page long e-mail that Whitecap employee Brian Broesder sent to Whitecap principal Eric Kamisher on September 26, 2007 (hereinafter, "the e-mail").

***

Whitecap claims that the e-mail is protected work product and was produced inadvertently despite the efforts of Whitecap and its counsel. Michael Hultquist, one of Whitecap's attorneys, states that, in order to respond to Coburn's discovery requests, Whitecap provided him with computer hard drives containing approximately 72,000 pages of potentially responsive documents. He assigned two experienced paralegals to review the documents and to separate them into categories for production or assertion of privilege, including attorney-client and work-product material. That review took five weeks. On March 6, 2008, Whitecap produced approximately 40,000 responsive documents to Coburn in hard-copy form. A CD with electronic copies of those documents was sent to Coburn in June 2008.

Mr. Hultquist states that he first realized that the e-mail had been produced to Coburn when Coburn's counsel began questioning Mr. Broesder about it at his deposition on July 14, 2008. Mr. Hultquist objected. The next day, at Mr. Kamisher's deposition, Mr. Hultquist told Coburn's counsel that the e-mail was privileged and work-product protected, and requested its return. Two days after Mr. Kamisher's deposition, Mr. Hultquist again requested the return of the e-mail. Whitecap agreed that Coburn could have some time to research the issues about the e-mail and the other then-disputed document based on Coburn's attorneys' representation that they would "quarantine" the documents and not use or disseminate them while doing the research. Notably, Coburn's counsel agreed that it would not raise any delay by Whitecap in bringing a motion about the documents as evidence that Whitecap did not consider the documents protected. On August 5, 2008, Coburn's counsel wrote to Whitecap's counsel refusing to return the documents. In that letter, Coburn's counsel asked whether Whitecap intended to present the issue to the court, agreed to keep the documents secured until the court's decision, and requested that the parties try to work out an agreed briefing schedule in light of the lawyers' schedules. Whitecap filed its motion on September 5, 2008.

It was unclear initially whether Whitecap is asserting both attorney-client privilege and work-product protection for the e-mail. In its Reply, Whitecap clarified that it is asserting only work-product protection, not attorney-client privilege. In opposition to Whitecap's motion, Coburn argues: first, that the e-mail is not protected work product; second, that Whitecap's inadvertent production waived any protection; third, that Coburn is entitled to the e-mail because it reveals that Whitecap mislead the court on an earlier motion; and, relatedly, that "Illinois' ethics rules not only allow Coburn Group's attorneys to use these documents in this litigation but arguably demand that they do."

ANALYSIS

I. Work-product protection

***

The court's in camera review shows that the e-mail is work product. The e-mail was sent on September 26, 2007, more than four months after this lawsuit was filed. The subject line of the e-mail is "Requests on Coburn Filing." In it, Mr. Broesder provides Mr. Kamisher with information he gathered about Whitecap's dealings with Coburn, in order to respond to requests by attorneys who were already representing Whitecap.

Coburn argues that the e-mail is not work product because it contains only "underlying facts regarding the residences of certain Whitecap investors." That is not completely accurate. The e-mail is not opinion work product—there is no disclosure of an attorney's mental impressions, conclusions, opinions or theories—but it is still work product. The e-mail communicates Mr. Broesder's responses to questions posed by Mr. Kamisher for the attorneys regarding the "Coburn Filing." In order to formulate those responses, Mr. Broesder collected, selected and organized certain information. The facts regarding the residences of Whitecap investors are not protected from discovery, but the work done by Mr. Broesder in preparing the responses is protected. ***

Thus, the e-mail is protected against disclosure unless Whitecap has waived the protection or Coburn has made the showing of "substantial need" required by Rule 26(b)(3)(A)(ii).

II. Waiver

Fed.R.Evid. 502, which became effective September 19, 2008, creates a new framework for managing disclosure issues in a cost effective manner in the age of large electronic document productions. Before Rule 502 was adopted, courts considering whether the unintended disclosure of a privileged document resulted in a waiver of privilege looked at the circumstances surrounding the disclosure and followed a "balancing approach" considering a number of factors. Rule 502 organizes those considerations into three steps:

> When made in a Federal proceeding or to a Federal office or agency, the disclosure [of a communication or information covered by the attorney-client privilege or work-product protection] does not operate as a waiver in a Federal or State proceeding if:
>
> (1) the disclosure is inadvertent;
> (2) the holder of the privilege or protection took reasonable steps to prevent disclosure; and
> (3) the holder promptly took reasonable steps to rectify the error, including (if applicable) following Federal Rule of Civil Procedure 26(b)(5)(B).

A. Inadvertent disclosure

Rule 502 does not define "inadvertent." Under the prior case law, reaching the conclusion that a document had been "inadvertently produced" required analysis of the circumstances surrounding the production, including the number of documents produced in discovery and the care with which the pre-production document review was performed. See Judson Atkinson, 529 F.3d at 388. If the production was found to be inadvertent, the court used a "balancing approach" to determine whether the inadvertent disclosure waived the privilege. In that step, many of the same factors, such as scope of discovery and reasonableness of precautions taken, were reviewed again.

Some opinions determining the question of "inadvertent disclosure" under subpart (b)(1) of Rule 502 repeat the prior case law's process. *See e.g. Heriot v. Byrne*, 257 F.R.D. 645, 2009 WL 742769 at *11 (N.D. Ill. March 20, 2009). In *Heriot*, for example, to determine whether the disclosure was inadvertent, the court considered "factors such as the total number of documents reviewed, the procedures used to review the documents before they were produced, and the actions of producing party after discovering that the documents had been produced." The court also applied the first two of these factors to the analysis under subpart (b)(2), considering whether the producing party took reasonable steps to prevent disclosure.

In this court's view, the structure of Rule 502 suggests that the analysis under subpart (b)(1) is intended to be much simpler, essentially asking whether the party intended a privileged or work-product protected document to be produced or whether the production was a mistake. To start, the parallel structure of subparts (a)(1) and (b)(1) of Rule 502 contrasts a waiver that is intentional with a disclosure that is inadvertent. More importantly, subparts (b)(2) and (b)(3) separately address the reasonableness of the privilege holder's steps to prevent disclosure and to rectify the error. That they are set out as separate subparts distinct from the question of inadvertent disclosure strongly suggests that the drafters did not intend the court to consider for subpart (b)(1) facts such as the number of documents produced only to repeat the consideration of those same facts for subparts (b)(2) and (b)(3).

Here, there is no real dispute that Whitecap did not intend to produce a work-product protected e-mail, and that producing the e-mail was a mistake. The court finds that the production of the e-mail was inadvertent.

B. Reasonable steps to prevent disclosure

The factors used in prior case law are helpful in determining what are "reasonable steps to avoid disclosure" under subpart (b)(2) of Rule 502. According to the Judicial Conference Rules Committee, the rule "is really a set of non-determinative guidelines that vary from case to case.... [C]onsiderations bearing on the reasonableness of a producing party's efforts include the number of documents to be reviewed and the time constraints for production." Rule 502 comm. explanatory n. (2007).

The scope of discovery is a logical starting point in many cases because "[w]here discovery is extensive, mistakes are inevitable and claims of inadvertence are properly honored so long as appropriate precautions are taken." As discussed above, Whitecap gave its attorneys computer hard drives containing approximately 72,000 pages of potentially responsive documents, from which 40,000 pages of documents were produced to Coburn. Those numbers substantially exceed the number of documents that have been characterized as "large." *See Heriot*, 2009 WL 742769 at * 12 (collecting cases where production characterized as "large" ranged from 7864 to 25,000 documents).

Mr. Hultquist, one of Whitecap's lead counsel for this case, supervised the document production and submitted an affidavit about the document review process. He states that he implemented a protocol for two experienced paralegals with 17 and 16 years' experience, respectively, to follow in reviewing the documents received from Whitecap for production to Coburn. The protocol to govern the document review included the following parameters:

(a) identify responsive documents by date;
(b) identify and mark for my review any correspondence between Whitecap's general counsel and any employee at Whitecap;
(c) identify and mark as privileged any correspondence between Whitecap's employees and Whitecap's outside counsel;
(d) identify and mark as privileged documents prepared by any employee of Whitecap in anticipation of or in preparation for litigation pursuant to request by Whitecap's outside counsel;
(e) pursuant to a protective order entered on November 16, 2007, mark responsive documents relating to customers as "confidential material" or "attorneys only;" and
(f) segregate non-responsive documents, including documents relating to "Offshore II."

The review took five weeks, during which Mr. Hultquist reviewed many documents that were marked as privileged, and other documents that the paralegals presented to him with questions.

Coburn criticizes Whitecap's use of paralegals for the document review. Although the experience and training of the persons who conducted the review is certainly relevant to the reasonableness of the review, this court joins with Heriot in declining to hold that the use of paralegals or non-lawyers for document review is unreasonable in every case. In light of the large number of documents to be reviewed, Whitecap's use of experienced paralegals who were given specific direction and supervision by a lawyer who is lead counsel in the case was not unreasonable.

Coburn also claims that the protocol described by Mr. Hultquist did not teach the paralegals what to look for in determining whether a document was "prepared in anticipation of litigation." Coburn argues that it is unreasonable to expect the paralegals to identify the e-mail at issue here as work product because it is not apparent on its face that it is work product and therefore the procedure was unreasonable.

Unquestionably, reviewing documents for work product can be challenging because sometimes there are subtleties to the determination. As Coburn points out, whether a document is work product can rest on facts not apparent from the face of the document, as in this case. Here, although there are clues on the face of the e-mail, the fact that it was prepared to provide information to Whitecap's attorneys is not apparent from the document itself. But the document review cannot be deemed unreasonable solely because a document slipped through which in close examination and with additional information turns out to be privileged or work product. If that were the standard, Rule 502(b) would have no purpose; the starting point of the Rule 502(b) analysis is that a privileged or protected document was, in fact, turned over.

Notably, as far as has been presented to this court, only three documents that Whitecap claimed as privileged or protected slipped through the review of 72,000 pages and production of 40,000 pages, and all three of those were e-mails. *Cf. Heriot*, 2009 WL 742769 at *12 (196 privileged documents were inadvertently produced out of a total production of 1499 documents).

Coburn cites *Relion, Inc. v. Hydra Fuel Cell Corp.*, 2008 WL 5122828 at *3 (D. Or. Dec. 4, 2008), in which the court found that the producing party waived attorney-client privilege for two e-mails. The e-mails were part of 40 feet of documents that were produced to the requesting party after review by the producing party's attorneys and support staff. Id. The requesting party selected and copied certain documents for its own use, and made both paper and electronic copies of those selected documents for the producing party. Id. The court held that because the producing party had not reviewed either of those two sets of the selected and copied documents, it had failed to take "all reasonable means" to preserve the confidentiality of the documents.

This court respectfully disagrees with the *Relion* decision. The standard of Rule 502(b)(2) is not "all reasonable means," it is "reasonable steps to prevent disclosure." Furthermore, the decision appears to be contrary to the view of the Judicial Conference Rules Committee that Rule 502 "does not require the producing party to engage in a post-production review to determine whether any protected communication or information has been produced by mistake."

The court finds that Whitecap took reasonable steps to prevent disclosure. That Whitecap made a mistake in producing the e-mail despite those steps is not fatal to its claim for protection.

C. Reasonable steps to rectify the error

Coburn cites two time periods as demonstrating that Whitecap failed to promptly take reasonable steps to rectify the error: the four month delay between the document production in March 2008 and Whitecap's counsel's discovery at the depositions in July 2008 that the e-mails had been produced, and the five weeks between Coburn's final refusal to return the documents on August 5, 2008 and Whitecap's filing the present motion.

Prior to Rule 502, courts in this circuit looked to the time between a party's learning of the disclosure and that party's taking action to remedy it, rather than the time that elapsed since the document was placed in the hands of the other party. The Committee's comment that Rule 502 does not require a post-production review supports this view that the relevant time under subpart (b)(3) is how long it took the producing party to act after it learned that the privileged or protected document had been produced.

In this case, there is no dispute that Whitecap was unaware that the e-mail had been produced until Coburn's counsel asked Mr. Broesder about it, and that Whitecap's counsel immediately objected to its use. The next day Whitecap's counsel requested its return and followed that up with a written request. There was no delay on Whitecap's part in trying to rectify the error once it was discovered.

As for the delay in filing the motion, the facts recited above show that counsel for both sides acted reasonably and civilly in dealing with the disputed documents and the associated deposition transcripts. The lawyers for both sides needed time to investigate the facts and law surrounding the documents, and the issues turned out to have some complexity. In light of the fact that Whitecap accommodated Coburn's counsel's request for additional time to formulate Coburn's position, and that Coburn agreed to "quarantine" the documents until the dispute was resolved, the time Whitecap took to file the actual motion was not unreasonable.

The court finds, pursuant to Rule 502, that Whitecap did not waive work-product protection for the e-mail.

III. Substantial need

The finding that the e-mail is protected work product and that Whitecap has not waived that protection does not end the inquiry. Coburn may still retain the e-mail if it demonstrates that it has "substantial need for the materials to prepare its case and cannot, without undue hardship, obtain their substantial equivalent by other means." Fed.R.Civ.P. 26(b)(3)(A)(ii).

Coburn argues that it should be able to retain the e-mail because, in its view, paragraph 4 in the e-mail (relating to Whitecap's Illinois investors and whether any were brought to Whitecap by Coburn) contradicts statements Whitecap made in 2007 when it moved to dismiss Coburn's complaint for lack of personal jurisdiction. Importantly, Coburn does not argue that it has not be able to get discovery about Whitecap's Illinois investors. Rather, it is the e-mail itself that Coburn wants, to seek sanctions and "show at trial a pattern of untruthfulness by Kamisher...."

***

Finally, relying on a 1999 advisory opinion by the Illinois State Bar Association, Coburn's attorneys argue that they have a right, indeed, perhaps a duty, to retain the e-mail in order to represent their client zealously. The advisory opinion concluded that a lawyer who, without notice of the inadvertent transmission, receives and reviews an opposing party's confidential materials through the error or inadvertence of opposing counsel, may use the information in such materials.

The advisory opinion did not purport to address a situation where, as here, the court has found that the document retains work-product protection. Rule 502 prevents inadvertent disclosure from waiving the assertion of privilege or protection if the privilege holder has acted reasonably. That rule applies in federal court even if state law provides the rule of decision. Rule 502(f). Additionally, the advisory opinion did not have the force of law even when it was issued and the continuing validity of its conclusion is doubtful in light of the evolution of the law in the past decade. The recently revised Illinois Rules of Professional Conduct added a new subsection requiring a lawyer who receives a document that the lawyer knows was inadvertently sent to notify the sender promptly. Ill. Rule of Prof. Conduct 4.4(b) (effective Jan. 1, 2010). The commentary states that the purpose of the notification is to allow the sender to take protective measures, although whether the privileged status of the document has been waived is beyond the scope of the rule. Requiring the receiving lawyer to notify the sending lawyer is clearly at odds with any purported duty on the part of the receiving lawyer to use the information for the benefit of his or her client.

Under Rule 502, Whitecap may assert work-product protection for the e-mail notwithstanding the inadvertent disclosure. Coburn's counsel is not under a duty to use the e-mail and, indeed, is not permitted to use the e-mail.

CONCLUSION

For the foregoing reasons, to the extent that it was not previously resolved, Defendant Whitecap Advisor LLC's Motion to Compel Return of Documents and to Strike Deposition Testimony is granted. Plaintiff Coburn Group, LLC and its counsel shall return the e-mail (document bates stamped WHITECAP 0039877), including any copies in any format, to Whitecap's counsel immediately and shall not use that document for any purpose.

***

B. Reasonable Steps to Prevent Disclosure

After meeting the threshold of inadvertence, the producing party must show that it took "reasonable steps to prevent disclosure" of privileged documents. In deciding whether preproduction review was reasonable, courts will consider the methods used by the producing party in searching for and segregating privileged documents, including the extent of the disclosure relative to the entire production, the time constraints for production, and the experience of and supervision over the reviewers.

For example, Courts will compare the percentage of inadvertently produced documents to the size of the overall production. If production is extensive or includes large volumes of ESI, even the inadvertent production of many privileged documents will not necessarily mean waiver of privilege. Inadvertent production of a relatively low proportion of documents in a large production under a short timetable due to mistake is usually excused. However, as the number and proportion of inadvertently produced documents increases, courts are less likely to find that the producing party took reasonable precautions.

Because the producing party has the burden of showing inadvertent disclosure, the producing party must give the court details about the preproduction review in order to show reasonable precautions were taken. Courts expect specific details such as how many pages were produced in total, how many privileged pages were produced, what keywords were used in ESI searches, who defined the keywords and the expertise of the search designer, whether the keyword searches were tested before production, whether attorneys or paralegals completed the manual review after ESI searches, whether the review protocol was specific enough to alert the reviewers, whether a quality control review was completed, and whether the producing party completed a timely and thorough privilege log.

Courts may consider facts other than the preproduction review in deciding whether counsel took measures adequate to protect privileged documents. For example, if a privileged document is produced more than once, especially if by more than one mechanism, a court is likely to find the disclosure so careless as to waive the privilege.

If a party does not give sufficient specific evidence about the review or does not produce an adequate or timely privilege log, courts often find they have not met their burden to show reasonable precautions to prevent disclosure.

KELLY V. CSE SAFEGUARD INSURANCE CO.
No. 2:08-cv-88-KJD-RJJ 2011 WL 3494235 (D. Nev. 2011)

JOHNSTON, Magistrate Judge

BACKGROUND

This is an insurance bad faith (refusal to settle) case that stems from an automobile collision, in which Plaintiff, James Kelly, was injured. The discovery dispute currently before the Court centers around the deposition of John Phelps, an employee of Mosher Administrative Services (Mosher). Mosher was hired by CSE Safeguard Insurance Company (CSE) to handle claims adjustment duties during the time the underlying incident occurred, March 2001. However, CSE and Mosher ended their relationship in 2003. At that time, CSE began handling all claims, including Kelly's claim, under CSE policies. All previously generated claim files were supposedly turned over to CSE. Seven years later, Plaintiff took Phelps' deposition regarding the handling of Kelly's claim by Mosher and other related topics.

Without CSE's knowledge, Phelps printed out Mosher's claim file log notes that were still contained in Mosher's computer system, and brought them to the deposition. These files were marked as "Exhibit 10" to the deposition. Shortly after the documents were marked, CSE and Mosher's counsel took a short break. After the break, Mosher informed Kelly that the claim file logs printed out by Phelps had already been produced during discovery, but in a redacted form. Further, counsel stated that some of the information contained in the documents was subject to the attorney-client privilege held between CSE and CSE's counsel. CSE and Mosher then requested that the claim log notes be redacted to conform with the copy already produced. Plaintiff's counsel refused to allow any redaction of the documents. The documents remained in the custody of the court reporter until the transcript was produced and distributed on May 5, 2011. The transcript included an unredacted copy of the documents as Exhibit 10.

CSE asserts that Exhibit 10 was sealed and should not have been viewed or used by Plaintiff's counsel. As a result, CSE seeks sanctions. Plaintiff argues that no improper behavior took place because Exhibit 10 was not sealed or protected and that any privilege that may have protected the documents was waived.

CSE seeks an order instructing Plaintiff to return the unredacted copy to Mosher, that any unredacted copies in Plaintiff's possession be destroyed, and that Plaintiff be prohibited from referencing or referring to the redacted portions of Exhibit 10. Kelly opposes the motion, arguing that the documents have been properly disclosed and that any and all privileges or protections have been waived.

DISCUSSION

I. Whether Exhibit 10 is Privileged and Should be Protected

CSE argues that the documents should be protected because they have already been produced in a redacted form in order to protect attorney-client and work product protection. Plaintiff asserts that there is no attorney-client privilege because the documents were on Mosher's computer system, and that even if there was a privilege, CSE waived it by not objecting to the exhibit before it was marked at the deposition.

The Court may, for good cause, issue an order protecting a party from annoyance, oppression, or undue burden or expense by forbidding discovery or preventing discovery of certain matters. The party seeking a protective order bears the burden of demonstrating good cause by "showing that specific prejudice or harm will result if no protective order is granted."

When a disclosure is made during a Federal proceeding the disclosure does not operate as a waiver if: 1) the disclosure is inadvertent; 2) the holder of the privilege or protection took reasonable steps to prevent disclosure; and 3) the holder promptly took reasonable steps to rectify the error, including (if applicable) following Federal Rule of Civil Procedure 26(b)(5)(B). FED. R. EVID. 502.

A disclosure is inadvertent when it is a mistaken, unintended disclosure. Here, the disclosure was not intentional. CSE did not know that Mosher had kept CSE claim log notes on its computer system. CSE did not know that Phelps had printed out the claim log and brought it with him to the deposition. Further, CSE had already produced a redacted copy of the claim log. CSE did not realize that Phelps had unredacted copies of the claim log until the deposition had already commenced and the documents had been marked. The disclosure of the unredacted copy was inadvertent.

Next, Rule 502 requires that CSE take reasonable steps to prevent disclosure. In 2003, CSE physically took back all of its claim files, with the understanding that Mosher no longer possessed any documents related to claims on CSE insurance policies. CSE also contacted Mosher before the deposition in order to ensure that Mosher no longer possessed any documents, including computer claim logs, responsive to the subpoena. Despite these precautions, CSE was unable to prevent Phelps from printing out and bringing the documents in question to the deposition. Though CSE could have taken the additional step of reviewing any documents in Phelps' possession before the deposition began, the steps CSE took were reasonably designed to prevent disclosure. This is especially so, given the fact that Mosher and CSE terminated their relationship in 2003, and the deposition was conducted in 2011. Such a long time period, combined with Mosher's statements that it no longer possessed documents, would have made it difficult for CSE to predict that Phelps would still have access to the electronic claim log over seven years after the termination of the relationship between Mosher and CSE. CSE took reasonable steps to prevent disclosure of the claim log.

Finally, Rule 502 requires that the disclosing party promptly take reasonable steps to rectify the error. When the privilege holder objects immediately upon discovery of the inadvertent disclosure, Rule 502(b)(3) is satisfied. CSE addressed the inadvertent disclosure shortly after the documents were marked at the deposition. As soon as CSE became aware that the marked exhibit contained privileged material, CSE requested that the privileged material be set aside for redaction or that the parties enter into a stipulation allowing the exhibit to be redacted. Plaintiff refused. CSE promptly took reasonable steps to rectify the inadvertent disclosure. The fact that the exhibit was already marked is of no consequence.

Plaintiff's argument that the privilege is waived because the claim log was in Mosher's possession must also fail. Voluntary disclosure of the content of a privileged attorney communication constitutes waiver of the privilege. Here, however, CSE never disclosed the claim log to Mosher as a third party. The only reason Mosher possessed the privileged information was because Mosher was formerly an authorized agent of CSE. Mosher simply possessed the claim log because it never returned or erased the electronic file when its relationship with CSE was terminated in 2003. There is nothing to suggest that Mosher ever had the authority to waive CSE's attorney-client privilege. It still would be unable to do so, even after termination of its relationship with CSE. Kelly also argues that disclosure of Exhibit 10 to the court reporter qualifies as disclosure of privileged material to a third party and constitutes waiver. However, Kelly cites no authority to support such an assertion, and it is rejected.

Because Exhibit 10 was inadvertently disclosed and because CSE took reasonable steps to prevent the disclosure and rectify the error, the attorney-client privilege protecting the redacted portions of Exhibit 10 is not waived. Good cause exists to support the issuance of a protective order. Kelly must return all unredacted copies of Exhibit 10 to CSE and destroy any unredacted electronic copies. Kelly is prohibited from using unredacted portions in any manner.

***

SIDNEY I. V. FOCUSED RETAIL PROPERTY I, LLC
274 F.R.D. 212 (N.D. Ill. 2011)

DENLOW, Magistrate Judge

This case comes before the Court on Plaintiffs' motion for return of privileged documents and Defendants' joint motion to determine waiver of claimed privilege. *** Plaintiffs claim the documents remain privileged despite their production, while Defendants assert Plaintiffs waived the privilege by disclosing the documents and failing to object to their use at the deposition. ***

I. BACKGROUND FACTS

These motions arise from a discovery dispute in a case involving Plaintiffs' investment in certain of Defendants' shopping centers. Plaintiffs claim Defendants fraudulently induced them to invest in shopping centers in Ohio, Georgia, and North Carolina and that the Defendants failed to make certain payments to Plaintiffs' Trust. Plaintiffs are represented by attorneys in California ("California counsel") and Chicago ("Chicago counsel"). In the course of discovery, Plaintiffs' Chicago counsel produced to Defendants a number of privileged communications between Plaintiff Sidney Pilot ("Pilot") and California counsel. At Pilot's deposition, defense counsel introduced two of these documents. Plaintiffs' counsel did not object to Defendants' use of the privileged correspondence at the deposition, but Chicago counsel later sent Defendants a letter demanding that Defendants return them and the other privileged correspondence. The present motions present the issue of whether and to what extent Plaintiffs waived the attorney-client privilege.

A. Plaintiffs Disclose Privileged Communications in their Rule 26 Disclosures.

Plaintiffs disclosed the documents in question to Defendants as part of their initial disclosures produced pursuant to Federal Rule of Civil Procedure 26(a)(1)(A)(ii). On April 22, 2010, Plaintiffs produced 588 pages of documents in their initial disclosures. Among those documents were eight letters totaling eleven pages between Pilot and California counsel. Plaintiffs' Chicago counsel sent a transmittal letter along with the initial disclosure, but did not include a privilege log. Plaintiffs' counsel did not mark the disclosed documents for identification with Bates stamping or page numbers. Between the initial disclosure and Pilot's deposition, Plaintiffs' counsel did not request the return of any documents produced to Defendants' counsel.

Plaintiffs' Chicago counsel states that he did not mean to include the privileged documents in the Rule 26 production. He had received documents related to the case from California counsel. By February 2010, he reviewed the documents, segregating privileged correspondence from the remainder of the documents. He forgot, however, that his file also contained a duplicate set of these documents, with the privileged and unprivileged material still intermixed. In April 2010, Chicago counsel instructed his assistant to copy the documents related to this case and send them to opposing counsel. Counsel did not inspect the documents that his assistant assembled for production and does not mention giving his assistant any instructions related to screening privileged documents. Apparently, his assistant copied the set of documents that contained the privileged material, rather than the set from which privileged correspondence had been segregated.

B. Defendants Use the Privileged Materials in Plaintiff Sidney Pilot's Deposition.

On January 6 and 7, 2011, Defendants deposed Pilot in California. During the deposition, Defendants' counsel introduced two of the privileged documents that had been disclosed. The first was a one-page fax cover sheet on California counsel's letterhead with a message from California counsel to Pilot, dated December 19, 2006. The fax as it was used at the deposition had attached a letter from Pilot to a third party, but Plaintiffs assert that the attachment was not included with the fax in its original form, and they do not claim a privilege as to it. At the deposition, defense counsel presented Pilot with the cover sheet and attachment as a single exhibit but questioned Pilot only about the attachment. The second privileged document used at the deposition was a two-page letter from California counsel to Pilot dated June 5, 2008. Defense counsel read this letter into the record and questioned Pilot about it. Defense counsel also entered both documents as exhibits, tendering them to the court reporter at the conclusion of the deposition. Plaintiffs' counsel did not object to any of this during the deposition, even though the same lawyer who had authored both privileged documents was defending the deposition. Pilot, himself an attorney, also did not object, though the parties disagree whether a stroke has affected his mental capacity.

On Monday, January 10, 2011, the next business day, Plaintiffs' Chicago counsel sent Defendants a letter demanding the return of the privileged correspondence used at Pilot's deposition. Plaintiffs claimed the letters were protected by the attorney-client privilege and demanded Defendants return the original letters and any copies pursuant to Federal Rule of Civil Procedure 26(b)(5)(B). Plaintiffs also identified the remaining privileged documents, asserted the attorney-client privilege, and demanded their return. Defendants refused, arguing that Plaintiffs waived the attorney-client privilege by producing the documents and not objecting to their use at the deposition.

The parties agree that the attorney-client communications at issue were privileged. Both sides filed motions to determine whether the privilege was waived. Oral argument was held on March 24, 2011.

II. DISCUSSION

A. Federal Law Governs the Waiver of Attorney-Client Privilege.

Federal Rule of Evidence 502 addresses waiver of attorney-client privilege, and Rule 502(b) sets forth a test for whether inadvertent disclosures "made in a Federal proceeding" operate as a waiver of privilege. But Plaintiffs argue that state law should govern the issue of waiver, because this is a diversity case. They rely on Rule 501, which directs courts to apply state privilege law where state law provides the rule of decision. Rule 502, however, operates as an exception to Rule 501's choice of state privilege law for diversity cases. Rule 502(f) says as much: "[N]otwithstanding Rule 501, this rule applies even if State law provides the rule of decision." In other words, even though state law governs the attachment of attorney-client privilege in this diversity case, Rule 502 governs waiver of the privilege.

Plaintiffs also argue that Rule 502 is unconstitutional, but their argument lacks merit. Rule 502(f) applies the rule's waiver standards even to state proceedings, and Plaintiffs argue that this portion of the rule exceeds Congress's Commerce Clause power. As the rule applies to this action, however, it governs a federal proceeding and thus rests on Congress's power to regulate the federal courts.

B. Plaintiffs Have Waived the Attorney-Client Privilege Regarding the Disputed Materials.

When deciding whether a disclosure has waived the attorney-client privilege, a court must first determine whether the disclosed documents are privileged and then apply the elements of Rule 502(b) to determine whether the disclosure waives the privilege. Since the parties here agree that the disclosed documents were privileged, the Court begins with the Rule 502(b) analysis. Under Rule 502(b), a disclosure of information covered by the attorney-client privilege does not operate as a waiver of that privilege if (1) the disclosure was inadvertent; (2) the holder of the privilege or protection took reasonable steps to prevent the disclosure; and (3) the holder promptly took reasonable steps to rectify the error, including (if applicable) following Federal Rule of Civil Procedure 26(b)(5)(B). The party asserting privilege has the burden of proving he has satisfied the requirements of Rule 502(b).

Before Congress enacted Rule 502 in 2008, courts applied a list of factors to determine whether an inadvertent disclosure waived privilege. Rule 502 does not explicitly codify these factors but "is flexible enough to accommodate" them, as they represent "a set of non-determinative guidelines that vary from case to case." Fed.R.Evid. 502(b) advisory committee's note. As a result, older cases applying these factors remain relevant to the Rule 502(b) inquiry. The factors include the reasonableness of precautions taken; the time taken to rectify the error; the scope of discovery; the extent of disclosure; and the overriding issue of fairness.

For the reasons explained below, Plaintiffs have established the first element but have failed to establish the second or third elements of the Rule 502(b) test. Accordingly, they have waived their privilege regarding the eight documents in question.

1. The Disclosure Was Inadvertent.

To show they did not waive the attorney-client privilege, Plaintiffs must first prove the disclosure was inadvertent. Fed.R.Evid. 502(b)(1). Rule 502 does not define "inadvertent disclosure," and the courts in this district have offered two different tests for determining whether a disclosure is inadvertent. One method looks to factors developed in pre-Rule 502 case law, such as "the total number of documents reviewed, the procedures used to review the documents before they were produced, and the actions of producing party after discovering that the documents had been produced." The other method concludes that Rule 502 simplified this first step of the analysis, and "essentially ask[s] whether the party intended a privileged or work-product protected document to be produced or whether the production was a mistake." This Court agrees with the simpler method, because Rule 502(b)(1) poses a straightforward question of intent. Meanwhile, the multi-factor approach is redundant of the later analysis. In fact, two of *Heriot*'s "inadvertence" factors simply restate the inquiries spelled out in Rule 502(b)(2) and (3). Under either approach, however, the disclosure here was inadvertent.

Under the simple intent-based approach, Chicago counsel's affidavit establishes that the disclosure was a mistake. Chicago counsel states that he initially separated the privileged documents from all other documents, and did not intend to disclose the privileged material.

The multi-factor approach likewise suggests inadvertence. First, the Court considers the size of the disclosure viewed against the overall production. Plaintiffs' Chicago counsel reviewed and produced 588 pages of documents, of which eleven pages--or about two percent of the total production--were privileged. A production of 588 documents is relatively small. A ratio this small does not suggest intentional disclosure.

As for the other factors, Plaintiffs' actions before production and after discovering the disclosure support a finding that the disclosure was inadvertent. Upon receiving the case materials from California counsel, Plaintiffs' Chicago counsel initially separated the privileged material from the other 577 pages of documents in preparation for initial disclosures. Later, after learning that Defendants used privileged documents in Pilot's deposition, Chicago counsel sent a letter the next business day demanding a return of the privileged documents. While these actions may not establish either reasonable steps to prevent disclosure or reasonable steps to rectify the error, they do suggest that Plaintiffs' disclosure was inadvertent. Thus, under either method, the Court finds that the disclosure was inadvertent.

Because the disclosure was inadvertent, the Court need not consider whether any waiver should extend to undisclosed materials. Pursuant to Rule 502(a)(1), waiver extends to undisclosed communications only if it was intentional. The Court denies Defendants' request that any waiver extend to the subject matter of Plaintiffs' Rule 26 production.

2. Plaintiffs Did Not Take Reasonable Steps to Prevent the Disclosure.

After establishing the disclosure was inadvertent, Plaintiffs must next show they took reasonable steps to prevent the disclosure. Fed.R.Evid. 502(b)(2). The most logical place to start is the procedure Plaintiffs followed to prevent disclosure of the privileged material. Plaintiffs argue that Chicago counsel's initial review for privileged documents was enough to prevent waiver. The Court disagrees. In *Kmart*, for instance, the disclosing party's attorney personally reviewed documents in preparation for production, specifically looking for "attorney-client or work-product privilege issues." Even so, the court found insufficient steps to prevent disclosure, stressing that the disclosing party did not mention any software, records management system, or other facts to demonstrate that a "sufficient screening process was used."

Here, Plaintiffs failed to demonstrate any screening process at the time of production. Plaintiffs' Chicago counsel admits in his affidavit that he did not review the April production before sending the documents to Defendants. Nor does he mention instructing his assistant to screen for privileged documents. Counsel protests that he had previously reviewed the file for privileged documents and merely forgot that a duplicate set of documents existed. But this argument only illustrates that he should have either used an organized screening procedure or reviewed the actual production, lest such a mistake occur. Counsel's review of the documents he originally received did not make up for his total failure to review the production itself.

The Court also weighs the scope of discovery and the extent of disclosure in concluding Plaintiffs did not take reasonable steps to prevent the disclosure. Plaintiffs disclosed the privileged material as part of their Rule 26 initial disclosures. Rule 26 productions are narrow in scope and only apply to documents a party "may use to support its position." Fed.R.Civ.P. 26(a) advisory committee's note (2000 Amendment). Inadvertent disclosures of privileged documents occur more commonly when responding to broad requests to produce, which often cover thousands of documents. The production here was only 588 pages, and this small size weighs in favor of waiver. Likewise, the number of privileged documents disclosed suggests waiver, especially since they were obviously privileged. Although the privileged documents made up less than two percent of the production's pages, producing eight privileged letters, several on firm letterhead, is significant in such a small total production.

Lastly, time constraints on the discovery did not prevent a waiver. Plaintiffs' Chicago counsel emphasizes his busy schedule around the time of production and argues that he took reasonable steps to review the production given his other commitments. During April 2010, he tried three cases and was participating in discovery for another case. But the relevant time constraints are those relating to this discovery, not an attorney's schedule. Here, Plaintiffs had two months to review less than 600 pages, more than enough to accomplish the necessary review. Thus, the Court finds that Plaintiffs did not take reasonable steps to avoid disclosing the privileged documents.

3. Plaintiffs Did Not Take Reasonable Steps to Rectify Their Error.

With regard to the two documents introduced at Pilot's deposition, Plaintiffs also waived the privilege by failing to take reasonable steps to rectify their error. For this Rule 502(b)(3) inquiry, courts focus on the producing party's response after it realizes that it has disclosed privileged material. Most importantly here, Plaintiffs' counsel failed to assert a privilege at the deposition. Attorneys commonly discover an inadvertent disclosure at a deposition, and objecting to the use of privileged material represents an important step toward preserving the privilege.

Here, Plaintiffs waived the privilege when, despite ample opportunity, they failed to raise a privilege objection at Pilot's deposition. Defense counsel read privileged material into the record; questioned Pilot about it; and tendered the privileged documents to the court reporter. This all occurred without objection from Plaintiffs' counsel, even though both documents were obviously privileged. Both appeared on California counsel's letterhead, and they represented communications between the deponent and one of the lawyers defending the deposition. The Court can scarcely imagine stronger facts to support a waiver. Under these circumstances, a demand letter could not substitute for objecting at the deposition, even if Plaintiffs' counsel sent it the next business day.

Regarding the privileged documents disclosed to Defendants but not used at Pilot's deposition, a closer calls exists as to whether Plaintiffs took reasonable steps to rectify their error. But the Court has already held that Plaintiffs waived their privilege to these documents under Rule 502(b)(2), and therefore has no need to address them under Rule 502(b)(3).

III. CONCLUSION

Plaintiffs have waived attorney-client privilege regarding the eight documents at issue. For the reasons set forth in this opinion, the Court grants in part and denies in part Defendants' joint motion to determine waiver of privilege and denies Plaintiffs' motion for return of privileged documents.

C. Reasonable Steps to Rectify Error

In addition to preproduction review, FRE Rule 502(b) requires the privilege-holder to promptly take "reasonable steps to rectify the error" in production. The relevant time period is how long it took the producing party to act after it learned that the privileged or protected document had been produced.

While FRE Rule 502(b)(3) requires prompt action to prevent waiver, the length of the permissible delay varies according to the facts of the case. Since attorneys commonly discover inadvertent disclosures at depositions, attorneys should object to the use of the document at the deposition and prevent further questioning on that document. If an attorney objects at the deposition and then takes some time to investigate the facts of the disclosure or if both sides confer in an attempt to solve the problem informally, courts will generally accept a few weeks between notice and filing a motion. In *Coburn Group, LLC v. Whitecap Advisors LLC*, 640 F.Supp.2d 1032 (N.D. Ill. 2009), the court held that three weeks of investigation before filing motion was not waiver.

The best course of action is to demand the return or destruction of the document the day of or day after discovering the inadvertent disclosure. If, however, a party fails to quickly demand return or fails to follow up on its initial demand for return of a document, courts are far more likely to find waiver. In *Williams v. Wendy Spencer Chief Exec. Officer Corp.*, 806 F. Supp. 2d 246 (D.D.C. 2011), the court found waiver where producing party did not follow up on its initial demand for two years and nine months. In *Clarke v. J.P. Morgan Chase Co.*, WL 970940, at *6 (S.D.N.Y.2009), the court found waiver where privilege was asserted two months after discovering production. In *Rhoads Industries, Inc. v. Building Materials Corp. of America*, 254 F.R.D. 216 (E.D. Pa. 2008), the court found waiver where producing party did not produce privilege log for inadvertently disclosed documents until four months after notice.

A party that inadvertently produces privileged documents will most likely prevent waiver under FRE Rule 502(b) if actions are taken quickly.

Bellamy v. Wal-Mart Stores, Texas, LLC
No. SA-18-CV-60-XR (W.D. Tex. 2019)

RODRIGUEZ, District Judge

Background

This is a slip and fall case. Plaintiff alleges that on November 11, 2016, she was shopping at the Wal-Mart located at 1515 N Loop 1604 E in San Antonio, Texas. She tripped over a pallet while walking through sliding doors into the garden center. Plaintiff alleges that she sustained severe injuries to her knees and ankles. On November 22, 2017, Plaintiff had surgery on her right knee. Plaintiff filed her lawsuit on January 4, 2018 in state court and the case was removed based on diversity jurisdiction.

There have been several discovery disputes that have arisen in this case. The Magistrate Judge presided over the first round of disputes and eventually ordered that the Plaintiff's [First] Motion for Sanctions be dismissed without prejudice to allow for the deposition of a Wal-Mart employee who may have been responsible for leaving the pallet unattended. The Magistrate Judge further ordered that Defendant supplement its disclosures and discovery responses, amend its objections, and provide Plaintiff with a privilege log as to any withheld documents.

This latest round of disputes centers on what happened next. In responding to the Magistrate Judge's Order, a paralegal in counsel for Defendant's office inadvertently produced documents that Defendant claims are privileged under the attorney-client privilege or work product. Plaintiff responds that some documents are not privileged. With regard to documents that are privileged, Plaintiff argues that these documents nonetheless demonstrate that Defendant's counsel has acted in bad faith and engaged in discovery abuse.

Analysis

A. FED. R. EVID. 502(d)

This Court encourages parties to enter into a Rule 502(d) Order, which states: "A federal court may order that the privilege or protection is not waived by disclosure connected with the litigation pending before the court." FED. R. EVID. 502(d). Despite this Court's encouragement, the Defendant did not request such an Order. This was the first of many mistakes by Defendant's counsel in this case. In the absence of a 502(d) Order, the Court then turns to an analysis under Rule 502(b).

B. FED. R. EVID. 502(b)

The following provisions apply, in the circumstances set out, to disclosure of a communication or information covered by the attorney-client privilege or work-product protection.

***

(b) Inadvertent Disclosure. When made in a federal proceeding or to a federal office or agency, the disclosure does not operate as a waiver in a federal or state proceeding if:

(1) the disclosure is inadvertent;
(2) the holder of the privilege or protection took reasonable steps to prevent disclosure; and
(3) the holder promptly took reasonable steps to rectify the error, including (if applicable) following Federal Rule of Civil Procedure 26(b)(5)(B).

1. What documents are covered by the attorney-client privilege or work-product protection?

Defendant contends that documents Bates Nos. 345-399, 400-406 and 436-480 are privileged because they are emails between Defendant and its employees and counsel. The Court has reviewed these documents in camera.

Because Plaintiff concedes the documents are privileged, the Court will not dwell on this issue. However, the Court notes that despite being given a "do over" by the Magistrate Judge, the privilege log that was tendered is deficient.

"The proponent of the attorney-client privilege bears the burden of showing the applicability of the privilege to the particular information in question." *Hernandez v. Frazier*, No. SA-11-CA-9-FB, 2012 WL 12895537, at *5 (W.D. Tex. 2012). "[C]ursory descriptions are not sufficient to support a claim of privilege." "[W]hen practicable, the privilege log should generally include a document number (`Bates number'), author or source, recipient, persons receiving copies, date, document title, document type, number of pages, and any other relevant nonprivileged information."

In this case the privilege log was woefully deficient. Specifically, the Court is unable to ascertain the identities of various recipients of the emails in question. "Because the privilege protects only confidential communications, the presence of a third person while such communications are made or the disclosure of an otherwise privileged communication to a third person eliminates the intent for confidentiality on which the privilege rests. The privilege is not, however, waived if a privileged communication is shared with a third person who has a common legal interest with respect to the subject matter of the communication." *Hodges, Grant & Kaufmann v. U.S. Gov't, Dep't of the Treasury, I.R.S.*, 768 F.2d 719, 721 (5th Cir. 1985).

But as stated above, because Plaintiff concedes that the documents are privileged, the Court will not disturb the concession that the documents are covered by the attorney-client privilege.

2. Was the disclosure inadvertent?

On April 8, 2019, counsel for Defendant's paralegal sent supplemental responses to Plaintiff's discovery requests as ordered by the Magistrate Judge. The paralegal mistakenly sent a folder labeled "Privilege Log Docs" along with the supplemental responses. The disclosure was inadvertent.

3. Did Defendant take reasonable steps to prevent disclosure?

Defendant explains that attorney Bryan Puente separated the privileged documents from the materials to be produced. Rather than producing the privilege log, a paralegal, now no longer employed at the firm, inadvertently sent the "Privilege Log Docs." Reasonable steps were taken to prevent the disclosure.

4. Did the Defendant promptly take reasonable steps to rectify the error?

Defendant states that it became aware of the inadvertent disclosure when Plaintiff filed its motion for sanctions on July 10, 2019. Thereafter, the next day, attorney Paul Garcia sent an email to Plaintiff's counsel requesting a "claw back" of the documents. The Defendant took prompt, reasonable steps to rectify the error.

Accordingly, pursuant to Fed. R. Evid. 502(b) and Fed. R. Civ. P. 26(b)(5)(B), Defendant is entitled to "claw back" the documents it inadvertently produced. But that is not the end of this analysis. Although Plaintiff may not further use these documents in this case, preventing their use in analyzing the pending motion for sanctions would result in a perverse result, upending the rules of civil procedure and encouraging discovery abuse.

C. Plaintiff's Motion for Sanctions

In reviewing the inadvertently produced emails, Plaintiff's counsel became aware of the following: (1) As early as July 23, 2018, Defendant's counsel knew of the identity of the store manager who interviewed Plaintiff shortly after her accident; (2) As early as July 23, 2018, Defendant's counsel knew of the identity of the employee who left the pallet unattended; (3) By August 6, 2018, counsel for Defendant knew of the addresses and phone numbers for these two persons; and (4) By February 9, 2019, counsel for Defendant knew the identity of the asset protection manager that was supposed to obtain the surveillance footage.

With regard to the above individuals, Defendant failed to list them in its Fed. R. Civ. P. 26(a)(1) initial disclosures and failed to timely list them in answers to interrogatories. It is apparent from a reading of the materials submitted either Defendant's counsel was grossly negligent in fulfilling their discovery obligations or they realized they had an uncooperative manager who was refusing to assist in their investigation, and they did not want to disclose the identities of potentially "bad" witnesses. Counsel for Defendant attempts to shift some of this blame by stating that Plaintiff was already aware of the manager and garden center employee because of her prior employment with Wal-Mart. This shifting is unpersuasive. Defendant's counsel had obligations to provide this information and it unreasonably and untimely did not.

In reviewing the inadvertently produced emails, Plaintiff's counsel also became aware of the following: (5) On November 21, 2016, the manager completed a Document Preservation Directive[5] requesting that surveillance video be collected, along with photos taken at the scene and the statement from the customer; (6) By January 16, 2018, Defendant was aware that the store lost the video and that the store manager was refusing to provide any statement; (7) Wal-Mart's outside claim investigation agency reported that exposure on this claim was probable and suggested that the claim be "compromise[d] to avoid spoliation potential"; and (8) on June 29, 2018, one of Defendant's outside counsel wrote an email to "Travis Rodmon-Legal" indicating that the claim file notes video from the scene was saved; "however, the Walmart discovery sources have not been able to provide a video to date."

Counsel for Defendant never disclosed to Plaintiff's counsel that at one time video may have existed that was now lost. Rather, counsel merely kept repeating that video does not exist.

Finally, Plaintiff's counsel discovered in the inadvertently produced emails that: (9) Defendant hired an investigator to conduct a full social media/background check on the Plaintiff on June 20, 2018; and (10) outside counsel for Defendant notified "Travis Rodmon-Legal" that surveillance had been completed on the Plaintiff and "it is debatable if the footage will be beneficial.... The investigator informs me that she moves very slowly, gingerly and hobbles a bit."

Counsel for Defendant never disclosed that it possessed video of the Plaintiff. Defendant was under an obligation to disclose any such video as a request for production had been made to that effect. Likewise, Wal-Mart had obtained numerous statements from the Plaintiff prior to her obtaining representation. These statements were requested in requests for production, but not timely disclosed. Counsel for Defendant attributes this failure to the fact that one attorney working this file left the firm and the file was reassigned and the new attorney was unaware of the video's existence. Although this suggests no "bad faith", at the time Wal-Mart sent its responses to requests for production and stated that it had no video of the Plaintiff it violated Rule 26(g).

Plaintiff requests that Defendant be sanctioned for failing to disclose that store surveillance video at one point existed and at some point became "lost." Plaintiff also seeks sanctions because the Wal-Mart manager testified at her deposition that she took multiple photos (including of the pallet) and these photos have never been produced. Likewise, the manager testified that she obtained a statement from the employee who left the pallet unattended and that statement has never been produced. Plaintiff also seeks sanctions because Wal-Mart did not preserve the pallet in question. Finally, Plaintiff requests sanctions generally for Defendant's failure to honor its discovery obligations. Plaintiff also requests that the Court provide an adverse inference instruction to the jury regarding the missing information.

Plaintiff seeks these various sanctions citing generally to Fed. R. Civ. P. 37 and the court's "inherent authority." The Court will now analyze what relief Plaintiff may be able to secure under each of the applicable sections.

1. Rule 37(a)(3)(A), (a)(4), and (c)(1)

Because Defendant failed to timely disclose individuals with knowledge of relevant facts and attempted to hide these persons from Plaintiff, Defendant is sanctioned as follows: Defendant is ORDERED to reimburse Plaintiff for all attorney's fees associated with the filing of Plaintiff's motion to compel and Plaintiff's motion. Defendant is further ORDERED to reimburse Plaintiff any court reporter fees associated with the depositions of Nick Kouchoukos, the employee who left the pallet unattended, and Marcie Errisuriz, the store manager at the time of this incident.

Although not raised by the Plaintiff, the Court notes that Defendant lodged "boilerplate" objections to virtually all of the requests for production in violation of Fed. R. Civ. P. 34(b)(2).

In addition, counsel for Defendant initially produced a "Claim Form" related to the incident, but then later produced a slightly different version on a later date with no explanation.

2. Loss of the video and Rule 37(e)

The loss of electronically stored information is governed by Rule 37(e), which provides:

> If electronically stored information that should have been preserved in the anticipation or conduct of litigation is lost because a party failed to take reasonable steps to preserve it, and it cannot be restored or replaced through additional discovery, the court:
> (1) upon finding prejudice to another party from loss of the information, may order measures no greater than necessary to cure the prejudice; or

(2) only upon finding that the party acted with the intent to deprive another party of the information's use in the litigation may:
   (A) presume that the lost information was unfavorable to the party;
   (B) instruct the jury that it may or must presume the information was unfavorable to the party; or
   (C) dismiss the action or enter a default judgment.

a. When did the duty to preserve the video arise?

Generally, federal courts have stated that the "obligation to preserve evidence arises when the party has notice that the evidence is relevant to litigation or when a party should have known that the evidence may be relevant to future litigation." *Zubulake v. UBS Warburg LLC*, 220 F.R.D. 212, 216 (S.D.N.Y. 2003). *** Not every slip and fall places a premises owner on notice that litigation is imminent. In this case, however, by December 28, 2016, the Plaintiff told Wal-Mart's claims manager that she intended to pursue a claim. Plaintiff's counsel argues that the trigger date for preservation occurred even earlier based upon internal company policies that Wal-Mart maintains to investigate customer accidents. At one point in this case counsel for Defendant appeared to agree with this articulation. The Court refuses to accept this date as the trigger date. For companies of any size, this would impose preservation obligations for countless claims where litigation is neither threatened nor reasonably anticipated. Any argument now being raised by Wal-Mart that the trigger date for preservation arose at a later date than December 28, 2016 is belied by the claim file that clearly notes Plaintiff was now threatening she was going to pursue a claim. Although Plaintiff's counsel did not inform Wal-Mart until November 11, 2017 of their representation of Plaintiff, the trigger date in this case arose when Plaintiff herself clearly expressed that she was going to pursue litigation. Indeed, at one point Wal-Mart was taking the position that its entire claims file was privileged because it was under anticipation of litigation. A defendant cannot take the inconsistent position that it was under anticipation of litigation for privilege purposes and then simultaneously deny that it had any duty to preserve relevant and proportional documents and ESI.

b. Loss of the video because Wal-Mart failed to take reasonable steps to preserve

A note in Defendant's file indicates that on November 24, 2016 there was a FedEx tracking number for evidence obtained in the store, but it is not clear whether the video was sent in this package. On January 10, 2017, another CMI entry states that it appears that the video has been lost. It is uncertain whether the video was lost after the preservation trigger of December 28, 2016. Nonetheless, CMI is recommending by January 11, 2017 to "compromise" the claim to "avoid spoliation potential." Wal-Mart failed to take reasonable steps to preserve the video.

c. The video cannot be restored or replaced through additional discovery

It is undisputed that the video cannot be restored or replaced. Likewise, because any photographs taken by the manager on the day of the incident have been lost, such photos cannot serve as alternative evidence in this case.

d. Rule 37(e)(2) is not applicable because Plaintiff has failed to establish that Wal-Mart acted with the intent to deprive her of the video

Although not citing to Rule 37(e)(2), Plaintiff states that an adverse inference instruction or dismissal based on spoliation is proper here because Defendant and or its attorneys have acted in "bad faith" and all of the discovery abuse listed above suffices to establish sufficient circumstantial evidence of "bad faith." The Court disagrees. The claims file indicates that the store manager requested that the footage of the scene be preserved, and it appears that was done and sent to either CMI or some other Wal-Mart affiliated entity. Reasonable efforts were made to attempt to locate the video without success. Defendant's and its counsel's mistakes were failing to be upfront with the loss of the video.

e. Plaintiff has established prejudice under Rule 37(e)(1)

Having found that Rule 37(e)(2) does not apply, the court does agree that Plaintiff has been prejudiced by the loss of the video and Rule 37(e)(1) is applicable. "Texas requires an invitee to prove four elements on a premises-liability claim: that `(1) the property owner had actual or constructive knowledge of the condition causing the injury; (2) the condition posed an unreasonable risk of harm; (3) the property owner failed to take reasonable care to reduce or eliminate the risk; and (4) ... the risk was the proximate cause of injuries to the invitee.'" *Garcia v. Wal-Mart Stores Texas, L.L.C.*, 893 F.3d 278, 279 (5th Cir. 2018) (citing *Henkel v. Norman*, 441 S.W.3d 249, 251-52 (Tex. 2014)). "[T]he Texas Supreme Court explained that a plaintiff can prove knowledge, the first element, by showing that (a) the defendant placed the substance on the floor; (b) the defendant actually knew that the substance was on the floor; or (c) it is more likely than not that the condition existed long enough to give the premises owner a reasonable opportunity to discover it. To prove any of these three propositions, plaintiffs may rely upon either direct or circumstantial evidence."

Given the loss of the video, Plaintiff is prejudiced by not being able to establish that the pallet was placed unattended on the customer floor space for an extended period of time to provide the premises owner a reasonable opportunity to correct the condition.

Further, Defendant has raised a contributory negligence defense in this case. Although unclear, it appears that Defendant is arguing that Plaintiff failed to keep an adequate lookout and that the danger was open and obvious. Although it appears that all parties agree that the Plaintiff tripped over a 4'x4' pallet, there is contradictory evidence as to whether the pallet was painted blue or was merely unpainted wood. Apparently, Wal-Mart is trying to argue that it should have been obvious to the Plaintiff that an obstacle was on the floor because of its color. The appropriate curative measure in this case is to disallow the Defendant from asserting or arguing any comparative negligence in this case.

f. Loss of photos and statements and the pallet

The issue of whether Rule 37(e) also applies to non-ESI spoliation claims involving tangible documents and evidence is unresolved in the Fifth Circuit. Other district courts have applied the Court's inherent authority to deal with the spoliation of non-ESI. In a pre-2015 rule change case, the Tenth Circuit applied the same Rule 37 analysis to non-ESI spoliation issues. According to the 2015 Advisory Committee Note to Rule 37, the rule applies only to electronically stored information.

Although it is not yet clear, it appears that in the Fifth Circuit a court may use its inherent authority to sanction a party for the loss or destruction of non-ESI, but sanctions can only be assessed upon a showing of "bad faith" or "bad conduct." *See Guzman v. Jones*, 804 F.3d 707, 713 (5th Cir. 2015) ("We permit an adverse inference against the spoliator or sanctions against the spoliator only upon a showing of `bad faith' or `bad conduct.'"). Again, counsel for Wal-Mart was less than candid about the loss of photos and statements in this case. Indeed, it appears that it actually believes that its own manager may be lying about what she did in interviewing the Plaintiff because Wal-Mart believes she may have not followed company policies in investigating the accident. If the photos and statements were actually taken by the store manager and placed in an envelope for mailing to CMI, the only thing that has been established it that package was lost inadvertently. With regard to the pallet, there was no duty to preserve the pallet because a preservation obligation had not yet arisen, and the pallet was likely moved or discarded the day of the accident. Plaintiff fails to establish "bad faith" in the loss of this evidence. Counsel for Defendant's lack of candor to opposing counsel has been rectified by the sanctions imposed above.

D. Duty of Candor, Cooperation and FED. R. CIV. P. 1

Counsel for Defendant wisely opened its Response brief with the following: "Defendant's counsel acknowledges and accepts it made mistakes during the discovery of this matter. It accepts that consequences may come from the Court as it considers Plaintiff's Motions before the Court."

It is apparent that at the time of the accident, Defendant considered this a low-value or nuisance case. It did not contemplate the severity of the Plaintiff's injuries and medical treatment. But once Plaintiff placed Defendant on notice that she was going to pursue litigation, reasonable and proportionate preservation obligations were required to be met. Likewise, defense counsel may be on billing constraints, but discovery obligations and adherence to the rules of civil procedure must be met.

Federal Rules of Civil Procedure 1 and 26(f) contemplate that the parties meet in good faith to discuss the case and facilitate resolution of the case and discovery issues because the parties have an obligation "to secure the just, speedy, and inexpensive determination of every action." Rather than complying with the rules, defense counsel delayed the production of adverse material and the identity of witnesses and the extent of the inappropriate acts only fully became revealed after an inadvertent production of emails was made (after intervention by the Magistrate Judge).

A reading of the file in this case makes apparent that Wal-Mart has known early on that it is responsible for the pallet being left unattended for some period of time in an area frequented by customers. Many counsel for defendants argue that the burden is on a plaintiff to establish all elements of their causes of action. That is true. But if that is going to be the Defendant's strategy (even when knowing they will likely suffer defeat), this Court is not sympathetic to complaints that litigation is too expensive. In this case, rather than focusing on the extent of Plaintiff's damages, Wal-Mart has now expended significant time and fees on the liability issue its own claims investigator conceded a long time ago.

Conclusion

Defendant's Motion to Abate or Strike Plaintiff's Second Motion for Sanctions is DENIED, but as stated above Plaintiff may not use the inadvertently produced documents for any other purpose and counsel must return any documents still in Plaintiff's possession, if any, to Defendant. Plaintiffs' Motion for Sanctions is GRANTED as stated above. Defendant may not assert any comparative negligence defense in this case, including arguing that the danger was open and obvious.

***

D. Clawback Agreements

Even though FRE Rule 502(b) may prevent an inadvertent disclosure from operating as a waiver by establishing (1) disclosure is inadvertent, (2) holder of the privilege document took reasonable step to prevent disclosure, and (3) holder promptly took reasonable steps to rectify the error, but it should be easier to overcome the problem of an inadvertent disclosure if a clawback agreement is already in place.

A clawback agreement, pursuant to FRE Rules 502(d) and (e), is intended to avoid waiver of privileges without having to resort to proof under FRE Rule 502(b). It enables parties in a case to agree, in advance, that if privileged documents are inadvertently produced during e-discovery, the privilege on those documents will not be waived. A clawback agreement should:

1. establish that inadvertent disclosure is NOT a waiver;
2. establish separate procedures for invoking clawback; and
3. avoid unnecessary disputes regarding reasonable steps.

However, even with a clawback agreement in place, some courts may not be willing to enforce a generally stated agreement unless it explicitly speaks to the Rule 502(b) standard. Thus, it is important to develop and implement comprehensive and defensible search and review protocols for ESI during e-discovery. Such protocols will ensure that privileged documents are properly recognized and designated, and demonstrating that reasonable steps were taken to avoid an inadvertent production.

IRTH SOLUTIONS, LLC v. WINDSTREAM COMM., LLC
No: 2:16-cv-219 2018 WL 575911 (S.D. Ohio 2018)

GRAHAM, District Judge

This matter is before the Court on the motion of defendant Windstream Communications, LLC for reconsideration of the magistrate judge's August 2, 2017 Opinion and Order, 2017 WL 3276021. The magistrate judge found that Windstream had waived its attorney-client privilege with respect to 43 documents which it twice produced to plaintiff irth Solutions, LLC. The Court may reconsider any part of the magistrate judge's order that is shown to be clearly erroneous or contrary to law. 28 U.S.C. § 636(b)(1); Fed. R. Civ. P. 72(a).

I.

The factual background of this dispute is thoroughly described in the magistrate judge's order and need not be fully recited here. Notably, four weeks after the deadline for production of documents, defendant electronically produced 2200 pages of documents, of which only 1400 pages were in a readable format. Included in the readable documents were 43 documents (totaling 146 pages) that defense counsel, Jacqueline Matthews, later recognized as privileged when she was preparing a privilege log about 12 days after their production. The privileged nature of the 43 documents was initially missed because Ms. Matthews's co-counsel, Marissa Black, who reviewed the documents for privilege, was not familiar with the name of Windstream's in-house counsel. This occurred even though, as the magistrate judge observed, in-house counsel's name and position were displayed prominently on several of the 43 documents. Ms. Matthews's pre-production check of Ms. Black's review did not catch the privileged documents either.

Upon discovering that she had produced privileged documents, Ms. Matthews contacted plaintiff's counsel and requested a clawback of the 43 documents. Counsel had previously agreed that an inadvertent disclosure (a term not defined in the agreement) would not waive the attorney-client privilege. Plaintiff's counsel sequestered the 43 documents and did not show them to his client, but he challenged the assertion that the clawback agreement applied because he believed the disclosure resulted from more than mere inadvertence.

Two months after the first production, and "in the midst of arguing to this Court that it should protect Defendant's attorney-client communications and award it fees and costs, ... defense counsel again produced the privileged documents." Aug. 2, 2017 Magistrate Judge Order, 2017 WL 3276021 at *4. Defense counsel, who was responding to a request from plaintiff's counsel to make the produced documents text-searchable, instructed litigation support staff to perform the task of converting the documents. Ms. Matthews created an electronic folder of the documents that needed to be converted; the 43 privileged documents were not in the folder. The litigation support staff, however, drew from a different folder, which did contain the 43 documents. After the documents were converted, Ms. Matthews performed a spot check but did not notice the inclusion of the 43 privileged documents. Upon receiving the production, plaintiff's counsel noticed the 43 documents and again sequestered them.

II.

Counsel jointly notified the magistrate judge of their dispute over defendant's claims of privilege and non-waiver regarding the 43 documents. The magistrate judge conducted a hearing in which the parties were given the opportunity to submit evidence. In addition, the parties submitted pre- and post-hearing briefs. The documents at issue were provided to the magistrate judge for in camera review.

The magistrate first found that the 43 documents are privileged under Ohio law—a finding that is not challenged and is hereby adopted by the Court.

Turning to the issue of waiver, the magistrate applied Federal Rule of Evidence 502, which governs disclosures of privileged documents in a federal proceeding. Rule 502 provides in part:

> (a) Disclosure Made in a Federal Proceeding or to a Federal Office or Agency; Scope of a Waiver. When the disclosure is made in a federal proceeding or to a federal office or agency and waives the attorney-client privilege or work-product protection, the waiver extends to an undisclosed communication or information in a federal or state proceeding only if:
>
> (1) the waiver is intentional;
>
> (2) the disclosed and undisclosed communications or information concern the same subject matter; and
>
> (3) they ought in fairness to be considered together.
>
> (b) Inadvertent Disclosure. When made in a federal proceeding or to a federal office or agency, the disclosure does not operate as a waiver in a federal or state proceeding if:
>
> (1) the disclosure is inadvertent;
>
> (2) the holder of the privilege or protection took reasonable steps to prevent disclosure; and
>
> (3) the holder promptly took reasonable steps to rectify the error, including (if applicable) following Federal Rule of Civil Procedure 26(b)(5)(B).

Fed. R. Evid. 502(a) and (b).

The magistrate judge found that Rule 502 presents a "binary choice" for classifying a disclosure: intentional or inadvertent (a term not defined by the Rule). Aug. 2, 2017 Mag. J. Order, 2017 WL 3276021 at *8. Where a party intended for privileged documents to be produced, Rule 502(a) governs the scope of the waiver. Where a party did not intend for privileged documents to be produced, but they were produced through mistake, negligence or recklessness, then Rule 502(b) governs whether there has been a waiver of the privilege. *** The magistrate assumed that the two productions were inadvertent because the record developed here did not contain concrete evidence showing that defendant intended to produce privileged documents.

Before applying the remaining two elements of Rule 502(b)'s three-part test for waiver, the magistrate judge addressed the interplay between Rule 502(b) and the parties' clawback agreement. Under Rule 502(e), parties may agree on the effect of disclosure in a federal proceeding, and courts have recognized the ability of parties to contract away from Rule 502(b)'s test for waiver. The magistrate reviewed the three different approaches that courts have taken on the matter: (1) "that a clawback arrangement (no matter how cursory) requires the return of inadvertently produced documents, regardless of the care taken by the producing party"; (2) "that where there is a protective order with a clawback provision, inadvertent production of a document does not constitute waiver unless the document production process itself was completely reckless"; and (3) that "the requirements of Rule 502(b) can be superseded by a clawback agreement only to the extent such an order or agreement provides concrete directives regarding each prong of Rule 502(b) i.e., (1) what constitutes inadvertence; (2) what precautionary measures are required; and (3) what the privilege holder's post-production responsibilities are to escape waiver." ***

Noting that the Sixth Circuit has not yet addressed the issue, the magistrate rejected the first approach because allowing attorneys to agree to a clawback irrespective of the care they took during production "would undermine the lawyer's responsibility to protect the sanctity of the attorney-client privilege." *** She further found that, in any event, the clawback agreement in this case did not contain language that would have eliminated the duty of pre-production review or provided for non-waiver regardless of the care taken by the producing party.

The magistrate found that waiver had occurred under both the second and third approaches; thus, she did not find it necessary to choose one approach over the other. She found under the second approach that defense counsel was completely reckless because, among other things: Ms. Black failed to become familiarized with the identity of in-house counsel; "the documents contain obviously privileged material on their face"; the privileged documents were not a needle-in-the-haystack but comprised "more than 10% of the entire production" of 1400 readable pages; and counsel "produced the exact same documents again—while simultaneously asking this Court to protect its privilege." ***

Under the third approach, the magistrate found that the parties' clawback agreement was "cursory" because the agreement, while stating that inadvertent disclosure would not waive the privilege, did not define what constitutes inadvertence or state what precautionary measures, if any, should be taken to prevent disclosure. *** This meant that the duty under Rule 502(b)(2) to take "reasonable steps to prevent disclosure" was not displaced. The magistrate found that defense counsel did not take reasonable steps to prevent disclosure for the same reasons that she found counsel's conduct to be completely reckless. ***

Having concluded that defendant waived its attorney-client privilege, the magistrate determined that the waiver was limited to the 43 documents and did not constitute a full-subject matter waiver.

Finally, the magistrate rejected defendant's motion to sanction plaintiff for not destroying or returning the 43 documents. The magistrate observed that plaintiff's counsel had sequestered the documents and that under Fed. R. Civ. P. 26(b)(5)(B) a party must "return, sequester, or destroy" documents which are subject to a claim of privilege. Though defense counsel argued that the clawback agreement limited those options to "destroy or return," the magistrate was satisfied that plaintiff's counsel acted appropriately "in the midst of confusion regarding if and how the clawback agreement applied." ***

III.

Defendant's objection to the magistrate judge's order concerns whether the parties' clawback agreement should supersede Rule 502(b). The clawback agreement was memorialized in an email exchange between counsel as three bullet points:

- If a producing party discovers that it has inadvertently produced a document that is privileged, the producing party will promptly notify the receiving party of the inadvertent production.

- The receiving party will promptly destroy or return all copies of the inadvertently-produced document.

- Inadvertent production of privileged documents does not operate as a waiver of that privilege.

Defendant argues that the "plain terms" of the clawback agreement "as written" provided that the parties had no duty of care to prevent disclosure. The clawback agreement, however, does not so provide in express or plain terms. Defendant's position thus depends upon interpreting the agreement's silence regarding precautionary measures as meaning that the parties had no duty prevent inadvertent disclosure.

The Court notes that in order for defendant to prevail on its objection, the first approach identified by the magistrate judge— where even a cursory clawback agreement requires the return of inadvertently produced documents, regardless of the care taken by the disclosing party—must be adopted. Defendant's objection does not relate to the second or third approaches. That is, defendant does not object to the magistrate's finding that defense counsel was "completely reckless" in disclosing the 43 documents. Nor does defendant object to the magistrate's findings that the clawback agreement lacked concrete directives regarding each prong of Rule 502(b) and that defense counsel failed to take reasonable steps to prevent disclosure.

The magistrate judge cited several unpublished cases which have adopted the first approach. These cases reason that because Rule 502 permits an agreement or court order on the effect of disclosure, a clawback agreement "defeat[s] the default operation of Rule 502(b)" and eliminates the duty to take reasonable steps in pre-production privilege review. This approach has the advantage of curbing the costs of pre-production review for privilege and work product.

The magistrate rejected the position that Rule 502(b)'s standard is displaced by a clawback agreement which is silent on the issue of what precautionary measures, if any, parties should take to prevent inadvertent disclosure. She found as follows:

> To be clear, the Court acknowledges that clawback agreements are powerful. They are one tool (among many), which Rule 502 affords to attorneys to protect the sanctity of the attorney-client privilege. If drafted thoughtfully and then followed, clawback agreements effectuate the dual purposes of Rule 502—providing a predictable, uniform set of standards under which parties can determine the consequences of a disclosure, while simultaneously reducing discovery costs. For example, the predictability is achieved when the parties draft an agreement that is explicit in stating that Rule 502(b)'s reasonableness prong is irrelevant. *** And discovery costs are reduced when clawback agreements outline discovery mechanisms that may not pass muster under Rule 502, such as eliminating the need for any pre-production review or enabling lawyers and parties to use computer-based analytical methods to search for and identify privileged and protected information. ***
>
> But for clawback agreements to serve these purposes, lawyers must draft them with care. Indeed, the advisory committee's note states parties "may provide for return of documents without wavier irrespective of the care taken by the disclosing party." Fed. R. Evid. 502(d) advisory committee's note (emphasis added). Further, the Court notes that these arrangements are enforceable, even if inconsistent with Rule 502. ***
>
> All of this is to say that the Court reads Rule 502 as providing lawyers a variety of mechanisms by which to protect the attorney-client privilege. Considering Rule 502's text and purpose, the parties' agreement, and counsel's actions, the Court

rejects the first approach in this case. To find otherwise would undermine the lawyer's responsibility to protect the sanctity of the attorney-client privilege. ***

Aug. 2, 2017 Magistrate Judge Order, 2017 WL 3276021 at *12.

The Court finds that defendant has not demonstrated that the magistrate judge's rejection of the first approach is clearly erroneous or contrary to law. Indeed, the Court agrees fully with the magistrate judge's analysis and adopts it as its own. The Court finds that Rule 502(b)(2) provides an important safeguard of the attorney-client privilege and that if parties wish to remove that safeguard, their agreement must reflect such an understanding. As the magistrate noted, the clawback agreement here lacked any language to support a finding that the parties came to an understanding that there would be no pre-production review. *** Moreover, the email memorializing the parties' clawback agreement also contained a provision requiring the parties to provide privilege logs for all documents withheld on the basis of attorney-client privilege or other protection—showing that the parties did in fact contemplate meaningful pre-production privilege review.

Finally, the Court rejects defendant's objection to the magistrate's refusal to sanction plaintiff's counsel. The magistrate's finding that counsel's decision to sequester the documents was not inappropriate under the circumstances is not clearly erroneous or contrary to law.

IV.

Accordingly, defendant's objections to the magistrate judge's August 2, 2017 Opinion and Order are overruled.

***

CHAPTER 11

COST SHIFTING AND COST SHARING

Under the American Rule, the presumption is that each party bears its own litigation costs in the absence of statutory authorization or a contractual agreement stating otherwise. Thus, the party seeking cost-shifting or cost-sharing bears the burden of overcoming that presumption.

A. Cost Shifting under Statues

Under FRCP

The Federal Rules provide mechanisms in the discovery phase that allow parties to shift discovery costs. A court has discretion under FRCP Rule 26(c)(3) or Rule 37(a)(5) to cost-shift or condition discovery on the requesting party's payment of the costs of the discovery.

FRCP Rule 37. Failure to Make Disclosures or to Cooperate in Discovery; Sanctions

(a) Motion for an Order Compelling Disclosure or Discovery.
...
    (5) Payment of Expenses; Protective Orders.

      (A) If the Motion Is Granted (or Disclosure or Discovery Is Provided After Filing). If the motion is granted, or if the disclosure or requested discovery is provided after the motion was filed, the court must, after giving an opportunity to be heard, require the party or deponent whose conduct necessitated the motion, the party or attorney advising that conduct, or both to pay the movant's reasonable expenses incurred in making the motion, including attorney's fees. But the court must not order this payment if:

        (i) the movant filed the motion before attempting in good faith to obtain the disclosure or discovery without court action;
        (ii) the opposing party's nondisclosure, response, or objection was substantially justified; or
        (iii) other circumstances make an award of expenses unjust.

The FRCP does not set forth factors for a cost-shifting or cost-sharing analysis. However, the Advisory Committee's notes to the 2006 amendments of FRCP Rule 26(b)(2)(C) do suggest certain factors for a court to consider concerning whether "good cause" exists for production of ESI from not reasonably accessible sources. Such factors include:

(1) the specificity of the discovery request;
(2) the quantity of information available from other and more easily accessed sources;
(3) the failure to produce relevant information that seems likely to have existed but is no longer available on more easily accessed sources;
(4) the likelihood of finding relevant, responsive information that cannot be obtained from other, more easily accessed sources;
(5) predictions as to the importance and usefulness of the further information;
(6) the importance of the issues at stake in the litigation; and
(7) the parties' resources.

Under 28 U.S.C. § 1920

FRCP Rule 54(d) permits a prevailing party to obtain costs. A court has wide latitude to award costs as long as the costs are enumerated in 28 U.S.C. § 1920. However, there is a considerable difference in opinions among courts as to what ESI costs may be recovered.

---

28 U.S.C. § 1920. Taxation of costs

A judge or clerk of any court of the United States may tax as costs the following:

(1) Fees of the clerk and marshal;
(2) Fees for printed or electronically recorded transcripts necessarily obtained for use in the case;
(3) Fees and disbursements for printing and witnesses;
(4) Fees for exemplification and the costs of making copies of any materials where the copies are necessarily obtained for use in the case;
(5) Docket fees under section 1923 of this title;
(6) Compensation of court appointed experts, compensation of interpreters, and salaries, fees, expenses, and costs of special interpretation services under section 1828 of this title.

JARDIN V. DATALLEGRO, INC.
No: 08-CV-1462-IEG (WVG) (S.D. Cal. 2011)

GONZALEZ, Chief District Judge

BACKGROUND

At the outset of this litigation, Plaintiff alleged certain products manufactured and sold by Defendant DATAllegro infringed U.S. Patent No. 7,177,874 (the "'874 patent"). Defendant Frost founded DATAllegro. Microsoft Corporation acquired the company in 2008, and DATAllegro remains a wholly-owned subsidiary of Microsoft. Microsoft, however, is not a party to this action.

***

Following the Clerk's entry of judgment, Defendants each submitted a Bill of Costs to the Clerk, seeking taxation of costs allowed under Federal Rule of Civil Procedure 54, 28 U.S.C. § 1920, and Civil Local Rule 54.1. After conducting a telephonic hearing and receiving supplemental submissions from the parties, the Clerk taxed $55,726.49 in costs for DATAllegro and $78,448.34 for Frost. In this motion, Jardin challenges the Clerk's award of costs, arguing that (1) no award of costs is appropriate in this case; (2) if an award of costs is appropriate, then the award granted by the Clerk should be substantially reduced; and (3) if an award of costs is appropriate, it should be stayed pending Jardin's appeal before the Federal Circuit.

LEGAL STANDARD

"'Under the well-established Rule 54(d)(1) case law, the district court is charged with making a *de novo* review of the clerk's determination of the costs issue.'" "Unless a federal statute, these rules, or a court order provides otherwise, costs—other than attorney's fees—should be allowed to the prevailing party." Fed.R.Civ.P. 54(d)(1). "Rule 54(d) creates a presumption in favor of awarding costs to prevailing parties, and it is incumbent upon the losing party to demonstrate why the costs should not be awarded." ***

Rule 54(d) does not, however, authorize a court to award costs beyond those authorized by statute or contract. Thus, the court's discretion in awarding costs under Rule 54(d) is limited to awarding costs that are within the scope of 28 U.S.C. § 1920. Section 1920 lists the following as taxable costs:

(1) Fees of the clerk and marshal;
(2) Fees for printed or electronically recorded transcripts necessarily obtained for use in the case;
(3) Fees and disbursements for printing and witnesses;
(4) Fees for exemplification and the costs of making copies of any materials where the copies are necessarily obtained for use in the case;

(5) Docket fees under section 1923 of this title;

(6) Compensation of court appointed experts, compensation of interpreters, and salaries, fees, expenses, and costs of special interpretation services under section 1828 of this title.

"`Once it is established that an item falls within 28 U.S.C. § 1920, the prevailing party is presumed to be entitled to recover costs, and the burden is on the losing party to show impropriety of an allowance.'" Because of Rule 54(d)'s presumption in favor of awarding costs to a prevailing party, "a district court need not give affirmative reasons for awarding costs; instead, it need only find that the reasons for denying costs are not sufficiently persuasive to overcome the presumption in favor of an award."*** "The presumption itself provides all the reason a court needs for awarding costs, and when a district court states no reason for awarding costs, [the Ninth Circuit] will assume it acted based on that presumption."

A court that declines to award costs, however, must justify its decision by explaining "why a case is not `ordinary' and why, in the circumstances, it would be inappropriate or inequitable to award costs." "Proper grounds for denying costs include (1) a losing party's limited financial resources; (2) misconduct by the prevailing party; and (3) the chilling effect of imposing ... high costs on future civil rights litigants, as well as (4) whether the issues in the case were close and difficult; (5) whether the prevailing party's recovery was nominal or partial; (6) whether the losing party litigated in good faith; and (7) whether the case presented a landmark issue of national importance." ***.

DISCUSSION

I. Whether Costs Should Be Denied Entirely

Jardin argues costs should be denied because (1) he litigated this action in good faith, (2) the issues in this case were close and difficult, and (3) there is a significant economic disparity between Microsoft and him. Even assuming all three of the factors to which Jardin points weigh in his favor, Jardin has not sufficiently rebutted Rule 54's presumption in favor of awarding costs.

No party has substantively asserted that Jardin did not pursue this action in good faith. But if this were sufficient to overcome Rule 54's presumption in favor of awarding costs, the "good faith" exception would swallow Rule 54's presumption.

In arguing that this action involved issues that were "close and difficult," Jardin makes much of a statement by the Court during the hearing on Defendants' motion for summary judgment of noninfringement, in which the Court acknowledged that understanding the technology at issue in this case required significant effort. Unlike this case, however, the cases on which Jardin relies for this argument were not decided on summary judgment but involved long and complicated trials, and often turned on determinations of credibility related to conflicting testimony at trial. ***

Finally, the economic disparity between Microsoft and Jardin does not justify denial of costs. First, Microsoft is not a party to this action. While DATAllegro is a wholly-owned subsidiary of Microsoft, Jardin has not provided a single authority suggesting that the Court should consider a nonparty parent company's finances when assessing costs in an action in which only a subsidiary company is a party. Nor does Jardin make a substantial effort to show that Microsoft's financial assets are particularly relevant in this case. Jardin merely points to the fact that Microsoft owns DATAllegro, and argues that DATAllegro's e-discovery invoices were addressed to Microsoft and that Microsoft Corporation "has a market cap of $226.17 billion." At oral argument, however, Frost's counsel clarified that the costs of discovery in this case were not paid by Microsoft, but out of an escrow account established when Microsoft acquired DATAllegro. Given the level of independence-financial and otherwise-many subsidiaries have from their parent corporations, Jardin has not sufficiently established that the Court should consider a nonparty parent corporation's finances.

Second, while a few courts assessing costs under Rule 54 have noted disparities between the financial resources available to opposing parties, they have done so in cases involving a party of limited financial resources. *** Therefore, to the extent a financial disparity among parties is a valid consideration, it appears to be so only where the party seeking to avoid costs has limited financial resources and thus payment of costs would present a significant hardship. ***.

Here, Jardin has not argued paying the costs in this case would be a financial hardship. To the contrary, he has painted himself as a "highly successful database architecture inventor" who "founded IPivot, Inc., a networking company, which was eventually sold to Intel for approximately $500 million." ***

Given the strong presumption in favor of awarding costs, Jardin has not established that this case was sufficiently extraordinary to justify denying costs entirely. Accordingly, Jardin's motion to deny costs is DENIED.

II. Whether the Court Should Reduce the Costs Taxed by the Clerk

The Clerk awarded a total of $134,174.83 in taxed costs to Defendants: $55,726.49 for DATAllegro, and $78,448.34 for Frost. Jardin challenges the validity of three sets of costs: (1) costs associated with converting large amounts of variously formatted electronic data ("e-data") into the .TIFF format, taxed under the umbrella of "exemplification costs" and awarded to both Defendants ($5,477.98 to DATAllegro, and $58,817.98 to Frost); (2) costs of $5,950.00 awarded to DATAllegro for project management of its e-discovery; and (3)

$1,200.20 of the $3,179.89 awarded to Frost for service costs. Jardin has failed to show that any of the costs taxed by the Clerk are improper.

A. Costs for Converting Data to the .TIFF Format Are Recoverable

.TIFF images are electronic copies of paper or electronic documents that were originally produced in other formats—*e.g.*, Microsoft Word, WordPerfect, Excel, PowerPoint, PDF, or various email formats. Defendants explain that converting such files to .TIFF prevents the receiving side from altering the documents, enables Bates stamping, and protects the confidentiality of metadata associated with e-data. ".TIFF is also the format most commonly used by document review software and was employed for Jardin's convenience."

Jardin argues that 28 U.S.C. § 1920 authorizes taxation of costs for "hard copies made and for making digital images of hard copies to be produced," but does not authorize "the conversion of [electronic] documents from one format to another." Defendants, Jardin argues, could have produced e-data in its original format without incurring the conversion costs.

Under 28 U.S.C. § 1920(4), a prevailing party can recover "[f]ees for exemplification and the costs of making copies." "`The terms "exemplification" and "copying" originated in and were developed in the world of paper.'" Notably, however, and ostensibly in recognition of the growing dependency on electronic discovery in federal courts, Congress amended the text of § 1920(4) in 2008 from "[a] judge or clerk of any court of the United States may tax as costs the following: ... fees for exemplifications and copies of papers" to "fees for exemplification and the costs of making copies of any materials." Since that amendment, "no court has categorically excluded e-discovery costs from allowable costs." And even before the amendment, "courts in many jurisdictions had come to recognize that `exemplification,' in the modern era, includes electronic copying."

While § 1920 does not categorically exclude costs associated with e-discovery, federal courts are divided over whether converting e-data from one format into another is a valid exemplification cost. *** "There is a division of opinion as to whether these costs are recoverable under 28 U.S.C. § 1920." The thrust of the debate is whether courts should view the conversion as something akin to "the 21st Century equivalent of making copies" or something more like "assembling records for production." ***

"We are well past the day when all copies are basic photocopies." *** The Federal Rules of Civil Procedure require parties to produce electronically stored information unless they can "show that the information is not reasonably accessible because of undue burden or cost." Because e-data may be created and stored in many different formats—often incompatible with one another or requiring individual licenses to access data—converting data into a format that all parties can utilize not only allows for more efficient and less expensive discovery, but is often necessary for any meaningful discovery at all. The processes required to properly preserve, restore, retrieve, or convert e-data so that it may be produced in discovery are "highly technical" and substantially different from "the types of services that attorneys or paralegals are trained for or are capable of providing." *See also Tibble*, 2011 WL 3759927, *7 (holding costs for an e-discovery experts were "necessarily incurred in responding to plaintiffs' discovery requests," where, inter alia, the plaintiffs "aggressively sought electronic files, whether active, deleted, fragmented, or stored on electronic media or network drives"). Thus, a categorical rule prohibiting costs for converting data into an accessible, readable, and searchable format would ignore the practical realities of discovery in modern litigation. Therefore, where the circumstances of a particular case necessitate converting e-data from various native formats to the .TIFF or another format accessible to all parties, costs stemming from the process of that conversion are taxable exemplification costs under 28 U.S.C. § 1920(4). ***

Converting data to the .TIFF format was a necessary part of discovery in this case. The information sought in discovery included massive amounts of e-data stored in various digital formats, including email files, attached documents, and data in several formats that require special software and proprietary licenses in order to gain access. *** Additionally, Defendants did not seek duplicative costs for conventional photocopying; rather, the "electronic conversion was `in lieu of making conventional copies.'" Furthermore, as Jardin's counsel stated during the hearing on this motion, the parties agreed to produce documents electronically in the .TIFF format because the .TIFF conversion made discovery easier, more efficient, and less expensive for all parties. *** Finally, Defendants seek only those costs stemming from the conversion process itself; neither DATAllegro nor Frost seeks "reimbursement for any legal fees charged by the attorneys and/or paralegals who reviewed documents to determine responsiveness, privilege, and confidentiality designations for the processed documents."

Thus, Jardin's motion to re-tax costs awarded to Defendants for converting data to the .TIFF format is DENIED.

B. DATAllegro's Costs for "Project Management" of the .TIFF Conversion Are Recoverable

Of the $38,722.58 the Clerk awarded DATAllegro for exemplification fees, $20,576.00 was awarded for time billed for technicians to work on DATAllegro's e-discovery; and $5,950.00 was awarded for management of its e-discovery projects. Jardin argues costs associated with a "project manager" are not taxable because they relate to the "intellectual effort involved in [document] production," and are thus not recoverable. DATAllegro argues the project manager's duties related exclusively to the process of converting data to the .TIFF format.

Under § 1920(4), "fees are permitted only for the physical preparation and duplication of documents, not the intellectual effort involved in their production." The distinction between the "physical production" versus "intellectual effort" is that costs associated with physically replicating or producing documents or data are recoverable under § 1920(4), while costs arising out of discovery-related activities tied to strategic, confidentiality, or other types of concerns typically entrusted to lawyers involve intellectual effort and are not recoverable. ***

In arguing that the project management costs here are not recoverable, Jardin relies heavily on Gabriel Technologies. In Gabriel Technologies, the district court held that a consultant hired at a fee of $1.5 million to "review and manage Defendants' electronic documents to respond to Plaintiffs' broad discovery requests" engaged in intellectual effort related to discovery. Thus, the costs of the consultant in Gabriel Technologies, who performed discovery-related tasks usually performed by lawyers, were not recoverable. *** But where, unlike *Gabriel*, a third-party technician is engaged to perform duties limited to technical issues related to the physical production of information, related costs are recoverable under § 1920. ***

Here, the project manager did not review documents or contribute to any strategic decision-making; he oversaw the process of converting data to the .TIFF format to prevent inconsistent or duplicative processing. Because the project manager's duties were limited to the physical production of data, the related costs are recoverable. Accordingly, the Court DENIES Jardin's motion to re-tax costs awarded to DATAllegro for its e-discovery project manager.

***

B. Cost Shifting under Judicial Rules

Cost Shifting with inaccessibility being a factor

The 2003 *Zubulake* decision set forth a related but slightly different set of factors specifically for cost-shifting. The *Zubulake* factors include:

(1) the degree to which the request for information is designed to discover germane information,
(2) the availability of the same information from different sources,
(3) the cost of production as compared to the amount in controversy,
(4) the cost of production as compared to the resources of each party,
(5) the parties' relative abilities to control discovery costs and their incentives to control costs,
(6) the degree of importance of the issues being decided in the litigation, and
(7) the relative benefits to each of the parties in obtaining the information at issue.

SURPLUS SOURCE GROUP, LLC v. MID AMERICA ENGINE
No. 4:08-cv-049 2009 WL 961207 (E.D. Tex. 2009)

SCHELL, District Judge

***

This lawsuit involves the Defendants' alleged failure to split profits from a number of sales of industrial equipment in accordance with the details of a purported joint venture with the Plaintiffs. On July 8, 2008, the Plaintiffs served document requests on the Defendants. The Defendants responded on August 7, 2008. Over the next several months, the Defendants produced approximately 4,000 pages of documents, but the Plaintiffs claimed that the productions were incomplete. In addition, the Defendants have conducted two rounds of searches into their electronically stored information ("ESI") and produced responsive documents uncovered pursuant thereto. The second search was conducted in late January and early February of 2009.

On December 10, 2008, defense counsel requested additional information from the Plaintiffs so that the second ESI search could be conducted. On January 20, 2009, Plaintiffs' counsel sent an email to defense counsel summarizing supposed shortcomings of the original ESI search gleaned from a conversation between Plaintiffs' counsel and the outside search firm that conducted the Defendants' original ESI search. Later that day, Mid America's in-house counsel responded by email, again requesting additional search terms so that a more comprehensive ESI search could be conducted. On February 5, 2009, Plaintiffs' counsel for the first time submitted a list of proposed search terms to conduct a second ESI search. By this time, however, the second search had been conducted, apparently utilizing some of the parameters set forth in Plaintiffs' counsel's January 20 email. Responsive documents from that search have been produced to the Plaintiffs.

At issue is the production of financial documents related to the nine transactions for which the Plaintiffs seek remuneration for their role in the purported joint venture. These documents, the Plaintiffs contend, will allow them to calculate their alleged portion of the profits. The Defendants have maintained that their discovery responses are complete, and they persist in that position.

Federal Rule of Civil Procedure 26(b)(1) provides that discovery may be obtained "regarding any nonprivileged matter that is relevant to any party's claim or defense ..." The discovery rules are accorded a broad and liberal treatment to affect their purpose of adequately informing litigants in civil trials. It is generally the rule that the responding party must bear the expense of complying with discovery requests. *Oppenheimer Fund, Inc. v. Sanders*, 437 U.S. 340, 358 (1978). The court may, however, shift the costs to the requesting party where doing so would protect the responding party from "undue burden or expense."

At issue, then, are two competing interests: the "needs of broad discovery and manageable costs." *Zubulake v. UBS Warburg LLC*, 217 F.R.D. 309, 311 (S.D.N.Y. 2003). The Defendants have not complained that the documents sought by the Plaintiffs are irrelevant, and the court's review of the record indicates that, if found, they would be relevant. The documents are discoverable under Rule 34. The presumption, then, is that the Defendants should bear the cost of obtaining them.

Yet, the Defendants have shown a persistent willingness to aide the Plaintiffs in crafting an ESI search that would yield the documents if they do, in fact, exist. Going back to December of 2008, the Defendants have requested from the Plaintiffs the desired search terms that the Plaintiffs did not disclose until February 5, 2009, after the second ESI search was conducted. It is apparent to the court that, had the Plaintiffs provided the search terms included in their email of February 5, 2009 when first requested, the second search would have been conducted on those terms rather than on the terms upon which it was actually conducted. In other words, the second ESI search was only conducted because of the Plaintiffs' delay in forwarding to the Defendants the search parameters desired by the Plaintiffs.

Because the records sought by the Plaintiffs are indeed critical to the resolution of material issues in this case, their discovery should be allowed. Therefore, the court finds that a third ESI search should be conducted, and that search should be based on the parameters contained in Plaintiffs' counsel's email of February 5, 2008. However, the cost of searching for these records is likely to far exceed what it would have had the Plaintiffs been more diligent in communicating their search terms to the Defendants because three searches will have been conducted rather than two. The search is conditioned on the Plaintiffs' willingness to pay the costs of the third ESI search up to the amount spent by the Defendants in conducting the second ESI search. If the third ESI search costs more than the second ESI search, the Defendants shall pay those expenses.

This approach comports with the Court's teaching in *Oppenheimer* that the responding party should typically incur the costs of responding but that costs may be shifted by the court in appropriate circumstances. The Defendants will end up paying the amount of the third ESI search, and the Plaintiffs will bear the costs of the second ESI search that would not have taken place but for their delay in communicating what the parameters of that search should have been. The court is, therefore, of the opinion that the Plaintiffs' Motion to Compel should be, and hereby is, GRANTED IN PART and DENIED IN PART insofar as it requests that a third ESI search be conducted. It is therefore

***

ORDERED that said ESI search shall be contingent on the Plaintiffs' willingness to bear the costs of the search up to and in the amount of the second ESI search that was conducted by the Defendants in January and February of 2009. It is further

ORDERED that the Defendants shall bear any expenses incurred in conducting the third ESI search that exceed the cost of the second ESI search.

***

BAILEY V. BROOKDALE UNIV. HOSP. MED. CTR.
No. 2:16-cv-02195-ADS-AKT (E.D.N.Y. 2017)

TOMLINSON, Magistrate Judge:

I. BACKGROUND

On May 3, 2016, Plaintiff Lloyd Bailey ("Plaintiff" or "Bailey") commenced the instant action against Brookdale University Medical Center ("Brookdale") and Carlos Ortiz ("Ortiz") (collectively, the "Defendants") seeking damages based upon Defendants' violation of Title VII of the Civil Rights Act of 1964 ("Title VII"), 42 U.S.C. §§ 2000e *et seq.*, 42 U.S.C. § 1983, the Age Discrimination in Employment Act ("ADEA"), 29 U.S.C. § 621 *et seq.*, the New York State Human Rights Law ("NYSHRL"), New York Executive Law §§ 290 *et seq.* and the New York City Human Rights Law ("NYCHRL"). See generally Complaint ("Compl.")

The Court conducted an Initial Conference with the parties in accordance with Rule 26(f) of the Federal Rules of Civil Procedure on August 18, 2016. Specifically, the Court pointed out that

[t]he parties have met and conferred and have defined the parameters of the electronically stored information ("ESI") which may be relevant in this case. I am now directing counsel to have a further meet-and-confer to reach an agreement on the method by which electronically stored information ("ESI") shall be produced in this case. The Court expects that discussion to include issues such as the custodians who should be included, what search terms are to be utilized if necessary, etc. Under Rule 26, requesting party has the right to demand the manner in which the production takes place. For example, if the requesting party wishes to have the materials produced in the traditional manner in hardcopy, that is fine. If the requesting party wants the material produced on a disc in some type of searchable software format (*e.g.*, .tiff, .pst, .pdf, native format, etc.), that is fine as well. However the parties are directed to reduce their agreement to a writing, with specific details as to the manner of production for all parties. Counsel are to file their letter agreement, executed by all counsel, on ECF no later than September 30, 2016 advising me of what agreement/ procedure has been put in place, and the specific details of such agreement.

Thereafter, on September 30, 2016, the parties submitted a fully executed ESI Agreement for the Court's review. DE 23. The Court "so ordered" the parties' ESI Agreement on October 4, 2016.

On January 13, 2017, the parties took part in the Court's required Discovery Status Conference. DE 31. During that conference, an issue arose concerning the parties' ESI Agreement. Specifically, the Court stated that

[n]otwithstanding the fact that the parties previously entered into an ESI agreement, which the Court "so ordered" on October 4, 2016, plaintiff's counsel now seeks to "undo" various provisions of that agreement. Attorney Gabor argued that it would be "unduly burdensome and costly for the sole plaintiff ... To produce the ESI in the manner as set forth in the Order."

The Court pointed out that the ESI agreement had been freely negotiated over a more than reasonable time frame given by the Court. Those provisions, negotiated by Attorney Tand, who was also in the courtroom, had not changed in any way. Mr. Tand had ample opportunity to discuss and negotiate those terms with opposing counsel before freely signing the agreement and submitting it to the Court. A case of buyer's remorse on the part of the plaintiff at this juncture is unpersuasive.

However, the Court directed plaintiff's counsel to review the parameters of the ESI agreement with an outside vendor and obtain a written estimate of the cost involved in making the production. Likewise, if plaintiff is claiming this is an economic hardship, then he must provide an affidavit detailing the reasons for asserting a claim of economic hardship. Defendants' counsel offered to contact their ESI vendor which might provide Plaintiff with the benefit of the same discounted rate that Defendants have arranged with this vendor. The Court recommended that the parties speak further about this prospect, noting that it is entirely up to Plaintiff's attorneys whether they wish to pursue this gesture. In any event, Plaintiff is to directed to provide the estimate and/or the affidavit to the Court within ten (10) days.

In accordance with the Court's Order, on January 20, 2017, Plaintiff submitted an Affidavit of Economic Hardship. The Affidavit states, in relevant part, that: (1) "ESI discovery will cost approximately $2,000.00 to $3,000.00;" and (2) the expense would cause Plaintiff to experience "severe financial hardship" since he is "the only working member of [his] family." Plaintiff added that although he earns "roughly $90,000 per year," he has expenses (including child support, daycare, mortgage payment and transportation expenses) which leave him "with approximately $1650 per month to provide for my wife and three children."

On January 26, 2017, Defendants filed opposition to the relief sought in the Bailey Affidavit. Specifically, Defendants assert that: (1) "[t]he law is clear, that the producing party (Plaintiff) should bear the cost of his ESI production" (citing cases); (2) the estimate of $2,000 to $3,000 that "Plaintiff received from [the] outside discovery vendor LDiscovery ... is very reasonable;" (3) "Plaintiff is not economically disadvantaged'" since "his affidavit [states] that he is earning a salary of roughly $90,000" and therefore he "can pay this reasonable cost;" (4) "Plaintiff commenced the lawsuit [and therefore] he should produce the ESI that has been put in issue due to his own claims;" and (5) the cost should not be shifted to Defendants in light of the fact that "Brookdale [is a] non-profit hospital operating in a low income neighborhood [and it] has already had to bear its own costs here."

In response, Plaintiff reiterates that his affidavit "clearly sets forth that for him to expend between $2,000.00 and $3,000.00 for the production of ESI discovery for his emails would most certainly pose an extreme hardship" since, although Plaintiff "earns approximately $90,000.00 per annum, [he] is the sole support for his family." In addition, Plaintiff maintains that "it is highly offensive that Defendants refer to the cost of the ESI ... as æminimal' and ævery reasonable'" since such a position concerns "a subjective matter."

II. APPLICABLE LAW

Rule 34(a) of the Federal Rules of Civil Procedure delineates the type of items that a requesting party may "inspect, copy, test or sample" when such items are in the "responding party's possession, custody, or control[.]" Fed. R. Civ. P. 34(a). The overall scope of Rule 34 is broad and includes "information that is fixed in a tangible form and to information that is stored in a medium from which it can be retrieved and examined. At the same time, a Rule 34 request for production of ædocuments' should be understood to encompass, and the response should include, electronically stored information ...." Fed. R. Civ. P. 34 (Advisory Committee Notes to 2006 Amendments). Rule 34(b)(2)(E) governs the manner in which production of documents or electronically stored information ("ESI") must be made. The Rule states as follows:

> (E) Producing the Documents or Electronically Stored Information. Unless otherwise stipulated or ordered by the court, these procedures apply to producing documents or electronically stored information:
>
> (i) A party must produce documents as they are kept in the usual course of business or must organize and label them to correspond to the categories in the request;
>
> (ii) If a request does not specify a form for producing electronically stored information, a party must produce it in a form or forms in which it is ordinarily maintained or in a reasonably usable form or forms; and
>
> (iii) A party need not produce the same electronically stored information in more than one form.

Fed. R. Civ. P. 34(b)(2)(E). By it terms, Rule 34(b)(2)(E)(i) and (ii), concerning the production of documents or ESI respectively, permits the producing party, unless otherwise ordered by the Court, to choose which method to produce the items sought by the requesting party. See Rule 34(b)(2)(E)(i) ("A party must produce documents as they are kept in the usual course of business or must organize and label them to correspond to the categories in the request.") (emphasis added); Rule 34(b)(2)(E)(ii) ("a party must produce [ESI] in a form or forms in which it is ordinarily maintained or in a reasonably usable form or forms") (emphasis added). Thus, "under the provisions of Rule 34(b)(2), a responding party clearly controls the manner in which production will occur, and specifically which of the two prescribed methods of production will be employed." ***

With regard to the cost of production, the general rule is that the responding party bears all such costs. ***

Notwithstanding operation of the general rule, a court may, under limited circumstances, consider "cost-shifting" of such production expenses to the requesting party. *** However, such a deviation "should be considered only when electronic discovery imposes an 'undue burden or expense' on the responding party." *** Generally, "[d]ata that is 'accessible' is stored in a readily usable format that 'does need to be restored or otherwise manipulated to be usable.' Conversely, data that is 'inaccessible' is not readily useable and must be restored to an accessible state before the data is usable." *** In the event a threshold determination is made that the electronic data sought is "relatively inaccessible," the court in *Zubulake* set forth the following factors which should be considered:

1. The extent to which the request is specifically tailored to discover relevant information;
2. The availability of such information from other sources;
3. The total cost of production, compared to the amount in controversy;
4. The total cost of production, compared to the resources available to each party;
5. The relative ability of each party to control costs and its incentive to do so;
6. The importance of the issues at stake in the litigation; and
7. The relative benefits to the parties of obtaining the information.

III. DISCUSSION

Initially, the Court points out that the record does not contain any facts indicating that the ESI being sought is "inaccessible." Indeed, the Bailey Affidavit states only that the $2,000 to $3,000 estimated cost of ESI production — based upon the methods set forth in the parties' ESI Agreement — would "create a severe financial hardship" in light of the fact that Plaintiff is the "sole source of revenue for [his] family" and is responsible for all monthly expenses. However, as stated above, whether ESI production is unduly burdensome or expensive so as to justify cost-shifting generally turns directly upon the accessibility or inaccessibility of the data being sought. *** Here, the Court has not been presented with any facts to conclude that the ESI being sought by Defendants is inaccessible. Thus, it necessarily follows that such production would not be so unduly burdensome or expensive to justify deviating from the general rule requiring the producing party to bear the expense of production. ***

Notwithstanding the above, this is not the end of the inquiry in light of the specifics facts and circumstances of this case. Indeed, the scope and parameters of ESI "should be a party-driven process." *** Therefore, "[d]iscussions about ESI should begin early in the case. Rule 26(f) requires that the parties meet and confer to develop a discovery plan that discusses æany issues about disclosure or discovery of [ESI], including the form or forms in which it should be produced.'" *** Such "[c]ooperation ... requires ... that counsel adequately prepare prior to conferring with opposing counsel to identify custodians and likely sources of relevant ESI, and the steps and costs required to access that information. It requires disclosure and dialogue on the parameters of preservation." *** It follows that cooperative efforts "between counsel regarding the production of electronically stored information allows the parties to save money, maintain greater control over the dispersal of information, maintain goodwill with courts, and generally get to the litigation's merits at the earliest practicable time." *** To be sure, such cooperation in generating and reviewing ESI discovery parameters is therefore of paramount importance since it is the "parties, not [the] courts, [who must] [] make the tough choices [concerning the scope of ESI] that fit[s] the particular discovery needs of a case." ***

Despite this guidance, it is clear that the above procedures were not adequately followed in this case. Although the parties did present a fully executed ESI Agreement to the Court, which the Court reviewed and ultimately "so ordered," the Agreement itself, although undoubtedly thorough, appears to have been drawn for use in corporate settings as opposed to the single plaintiff employment discrimination case at issue here. After engaging in a further review as to the scope and depth of the ESI Agreement, the Court can reach no other conclusion except that Plaintiff's counsel did not engage in meaningful discussions with his client regarding the terms of the proposed agreement and what costs might be incurred by producing the information in the format Defendants sought. Likewise, it further appears that Plaintiff's counsel did not engage in a meaningful meet-and-confer session with opposing counsel concerning this Agreement nor did he thoroughly review the Agreement (or consider its ramifications) prior to signing it. Indeed, as is the case in many ESI disputes which come before the Court, the provisions concerning the overall scope and methods of Plaintiff's ESI production would likely have been the subject of zealous negotiation and compromise had Plaintiff's counsel undertaken a more substantive review. As it stands, Plaintiff's counsel has placed his client in the position of having to abide by an Agreement, which, in the current context, appears overly complex in light of the straightforward subject matter and claims involved here.

The Court points out that "[a] party who voluntarily chose [an] attorney as his representative in [an] action ... cannot ... avoid the consequences of the acts or omissions of this freely selected agent." *** However, this principle must be balanced against the Court's over-arching responsibility "to ensure a level playing field for both sides." *** Here, Defendants drafted and presented an ESI Agreement which is typically utilized in a more complex litigation involving multiple parties and corporate entities rather than a single plaintiff employment discrimination action. The manner and means of ESI production is set forth in largely technical and precise terms ù which clearly has an impact on the overall costs of the production of such information. In addition, there is no indication in the record that Defendants are amenable to considering an alternative format for the production which could prove less expensive. The Court understands that Defendants would like to have the materials presented in a manner which makes their search capabilities easier and perhaps more efficient. That is a rational goal. But the Defendants' aspirations are not the only issue the Court must consider.

The Court does not find that sufficient grounds exist to rescind the Agreement. However, to the extent the Defendants continue to insist on the production being made to the letter of the requirements/formatting they set forth in the Agreement, the Court finds that employing a measure of partial cost-shifting is appropriate here. *** Specifically, the Court directs that 40% of the production costs for Plaintiff's ESI shall be borne by Defendants while 60% shall be assessed to Plaintiff. Given the circumstances set forth in this Memorandum, the Court finds that fairness dictates the Plaintiff's costs should be borne by Plaintiff's counsel rather than Plaintiff himself.

IV. CONCLUSION

For the foregoing reasons, the costs of Plaintiff's ESI production will be allocated as follows: 40% to Defendants and 60% to Plaintiff. The production is to be completed forthwith.

***

Cost Shifting in the form of sanctions

After *Zubulake*, some courts began to expand cost-shifting to ESI beyond inaccessibility. Some courts have held that cost-shifting may take the form of sanctions when a party has abused the discovery process. Discovery sanctions serve three purposes:

(1) to ensure that a violating party does not benefit from its own failure to comply with discovery;
(2) to serve as a specific deterrent to achieve compliance with the particular discovery order at issue; and
(3) to serve as a general deterrent in the case at hand and in other litigation, provided that the party against whom sanctions are imposed was in some sense at fault.

THE ESTATE OF LARRY SHAW V. EDIE SHAW MARCUS
No. 14 Civ. 3849 (S.D.N.Y. 2017)

McCARTHY, Magistrate Judge

With this Order, the Court addresses a pattern of delinquent conduct by Joseph H. Adams ("Mr. Adams"), former counsel to Plaintiffs Estate of Larry Shaw and Susan Shaw (jointly "Plaintiff"), in connection with his complete disregard for the Court's Orders and lack of respect for the Court and opposing counsel.

On May 2, 2016, Defendants in Action 1, Sam Shaw, Inc., Meta Stevens, Edith Marcus, Melissa Stevens and David Marcus, Esq. (the "Shaw Family") filed a letter motion for sanctions relating to Plaintiff's failure to comply with the Court's Discovery Orders, and for cost-shifting relating to the forensic review of Plaintiff Susan Shaw's laptop computer (the "Sanctions Motion"). Plaintiff filed its opposition on May 23, 2016 and May 24, 2016.

The Shaw Family filed a second motion for sanctions (the "Omnibus Sanctions Motion") on June 13, 2016. On August 12, 2016 and August 19, 2016, Plaintiff filed incomplete versions of its opposition to the Omnibus Sanctions Motion on this Court's Electronic Case Filing ("ECF") system, and served the Court with a courtesy copy of one of the versions of these submissions. The Court continued to receive letters from Plaintiff seeking extensions of time to file the complete and corrected opposition, with certain exhibits filed under seal. On August 22, 2016, Plaintiff filed the final version of its opposition to the Omnibus Sanctions Motion, with Exhibits I, J, and K filed under seal, and served the Court with a courtesy copy of the submission. Plaintiff's earlier submissions in opposition to the Omnibus Sanctions Motion were subsequently marked deficient by the Clerk's Office. Accordingly, on September 20, 2016 the Court returned the courtesy copy of those deficient submissions to counsel for Plaintiff. The Court has retained the courtesy copy of Docket No. 380, as well as the Shaw Family's reply and has deemed the motion fully submitted.

***

I. BASES FOR SANCTIONS

By way of their Sanctions Motion and Omnibus Sanctions Motion, the Shaw Family argues that the Court should impose sanctions as follows: (i) Plaintiff and Mr. Adams should bear the costs relating to the Shaw Family's forensic review of Susan Shaw's laptop computer (the "Computer"); (ii) Plaintiff's and Mr. Adams' conduct requires monetary sanctions and the dismissal of Plaintiff's Second Amended Complaint (the "Complaint") and Plaintiff's Answer to the Shaw Family's Amended Complaint (the "Answer") pursuant to Federal Rules of Civil Procedure Rule 16(f) ("Rule 16"); (iii) Plaintiff's and Mr. Adams' failure to comply with the Court's Discovery Orders require monetary sanctions and dismissal of the Complaint and the Answer pursuant to Federal Rules of Civil Procedure Rule 37 ("Rule 37"); (iv) Plaintiff's and Mr. Adams' conduct warrants sanctions pursuant to the Court's inherent power; (v) Mr. Adams' conduct warrants sanctions pursuant to 28 U.S.C. § 1927; and (vi) the Court should report Mr. Adams' conduct to the grievance committee.

The Shaw Family bases its request for sanctions on the following instances of misconduct, which occurred throughout the pendency of this case and over the course of nine discovery conferences before the undersigned, often ranging from two to three hours each: (i) Mr. Adams and Plaintiff Susan Shaw failed to preserve relevant material on the Computer, which now requires a forensic examination; (ii) Mr. Adams failed to comply with Court Orders relating to the production of the Computer; (iii) Mr. Adams failed to comply with the Court's April 15, 2015, December 23, 2015, April 19, 2016, May 19, 2016, and July 28, 2016 Discovery Orders; (iv) Mr. Adams invited a third party to eavesdrop on the January 7, 2016 telephonic meet-and-confer, which included sensitive and confidential information; and (v) Mr. Adams behaved unprofessionally and disrespected opposing counsel and the Court at hearings before the undersigned.

II. APPLICABLE LAW
A. Cost-Shifting Pursuant to *Zubulake*

Rule 26(b) of the Federal Rules of Civil Procedure states that parties may "obtain discovery regarding any matter, not privileged, that is relevant to the claim or defense of any party," except where, *inter alia*, "the burden or expense of the proposed discovery outweighs its likely benefit, taking into account the needs of the case, the amount in controversy, the parties' resources, the importance of the issues at stake in the litigation, and the importance of the proposed discovery in resolving the issues." Fed. R. Civ. P. 26(b).

There is a presumption that "the responding party must bear the expense of complying with discovery requests." *** However, pursuant to the Federal Rules of Civil Procedure Rule 26(c) ("Rule 26(c)"), a district court may issue an order protecting the responding party from undue burden or expense by "conditioning discovery on the requesting party's payment of the costs of discovery." *** Such an order may be granted only on the motion of the responding party and "for good cause shown." Fed. R. Civ. P. 26(c). Further, "the responding party has the burden of proof on a motion for cost-shifting." ***

In *Zubulake v. UBS Warburg LLC*, the court set forth an analytical framework for determining whether it is appropriate to shift the costs of electronic discovery. 217 F.R.D. 309, 322 (S.D.N.Y. 2003) ("*Zubulake I*"). In that case, the plaintiff claimed that key evidence was located in e-mails that were contained only in backup tapes and sought an order compelling the defendant, UBS Warburg LLC ("UBS"), to produce the e-mails at its own expense. Id. at 311-312. After UBS was ordered to produce the e-mails, the *Zubulake I* court considered whether cost-shifting was appropriate.

As an initial matter, the *Zubulake I* court stated that "cost-shifting should be considered only when electronic discovery imposes an `undue burden or expense' on the responding party." *** "[W]hether production of documents is unduly burdensome or expensive turns primarily on whether it is kept in an accessible or inaccessible format (a distinction that corresponds closely to the expense of production)." "Accessible" data is stored in a readily usable format that "does not need to be restored or otherwise manipulated to be usable." On the other hand, data that is "inaccessible" is not readily usable and must be restored to an accessible state before the data is usable.

If the responding party is producing data from inaccessible sources, the *Zubulake I* court identified seven factors to be considered in determining whether shifting the cost of production is appropriate: (i) the extent to which the request is specifically tailored to discover relevant information; (ii) the availability of such information from other sources; (iii) the total costs of production, compared to the amount in controversy; (iv) the total costs of production, compared to the resources available to each party; (v) the relative ability of each party to control costs and its incentive to do so; (vi) the importance of the issues at stake in the litigation; and (vii) the relative benefits to the parties of obtaining the information. The *Zubulake I* court weighed the factors, with the first being the most important consideration and the seventh being the least.

B. Sanctions Pursuant to Rule 16

Rule 16 authorizes a court to order sanctions if an attorney "fails to appear at a scheduling or other pretrial conference" or "fails to obey a scheduling or other pretrial order." Fed. R. Civ. P. 16(f)(1). Specifically, it provides that the court "must order the [violating] party, its attorney, or both to pay reasonable expenses ù including attorney's fees ù incurred because of any noncompliance with this rule, unless the noncompliance was substantially justified or other circumstances make an award unjust." Fed. R. Civ. P. 16(f)(2). "In deciding whether a sanction is merited, the court need not find that a party acted in bad faith. The fact that a pretrial order was violated is sufficient to allow some sanction." Charles Alan Wright, Arthur R. Miller, Mary Kay Kane & Richard L. Marcus, 6A Federal Practice and Procedure ° 1531 (3d ed. 2010) (footnote omitted). The imposition of sanctions pursuant to Rule 16 is within the sound discretion of the court. *** The sanctions provided by Rule 16(f) are the same as those provided by Rule 37(b)(2)(B), (C) and (D). *** In determining whether sanctions pursuant to Rule 16(f) are appropriate, courts apply the same standards developed with respect to Rule 37(b)(2) sanctions. *See* Fed. R. Civ. P. 16 Advisory Committee Notes, 1983 Amendment ("Rule 16(f) incorporates portions of Rule 37(b)(2), which prescribes sanctions for failing to make discovery. This should facilitate application of Rule 16(f), since courts and lawyers already are familiar with the Rule 37 standards."); see also infra Part II.C.

Pursuant to Rule 16(f)(2), both a party and its counsel may be held liable for the expenses, including attorneys' fees and costs, resulting from the violation of either a scheduling order or Rule 26(a). Rule 16(f)(2) mandates the award of attorneys' fees for an unjustified violation of a scheduling or pretrial order: "[i]nstead of or in addition to any other sanction, the court must order the [violating] party, its attorney, or both to pay the reasonable expenses ù including attorney's fees ù incurred because of any noncompliance with this rule, unless the noncompliance was substantially justified or other circumstances make an award of expenses unjust." Fed. R. Civ. P. 16(f)(2) (emphasis added). Rule 16(f) also authorizes the Court to impose sanctions such as striking a party's pleadings. ***

C. Sanctions Pursuant to Rule 37

Rule 37 sets forth the Court's procedures for enforcing discovery and sanctioning misconduct. Where "a party ... fails to obey an order to provide or permit discovery ... the court where the action is pending may issue further just orders." Fed. R. Civ. P. 37(b)(2)(A). Such orders may include: (i) directing that matters in the litigation be taken as established by the prevailing party; (ii) prohibiting the sanctioned party from supporting or opposing claims or defenses or from introducing evidence; (iii) striking pleadings in whole or in part; (iv) staying further proceedings until the order is obeyed; (v) dismissing the action or proceeding; (vi) entering a default judgment against the disobedient party; or (vii) treating as contempt of court the failure to obey any order except an order to submit to a physical or mental examination. Fed. R. Civ. P. 37(b)(2)(A); ***. Reasonable expenses, including attorneys' fees, also may be awarded against the party and/or the attorney failing to act, unless a court finds that the failure "was substantially justified, or that other circumstances make an award of expenses unjust." Fed. R. Civ. P. 37(b)(2)(C).

Numerous factors are relevant to a district court's exercise of its broad discretion to order sanctions under Rule 37, including: (i) the willfulness of the non-compliant party or the reason for the noncompliance; (ii) the efficacy of lesser sanctions; (iii) the duration of the period of noncompliance; and (iv) whether the non-compliant party had been warned of the consequences of his non-compliance. See Bambu Sales, Inc. v. Ozak Trading Inc., 58 F.3d 849, 852-54 (2d Cir. 1995). In addition, an award of sanctions under Rule 37 should effectuate its three purposes: (i) obtaining compliance with discovery orders; (ii) ensuring the disobedient party does not benefit from non-compliance; and (iii) providing a general deterrent in the particular case and litigation in general. *** A court may consider the full record in the case in order to select the appropriate sanction. ***

The sanctions of striking pleadings and dismissal are the most extreme sanctions available. *** Dismissal is appropriate "only where the noncompliance is due to willfulness, bad faith, fault or gross negligence rather than inability to comply or mere oversight." *** Non-compliance may be deemed willful "when the court's orders have been clear, when the party has understood them, and when the party's non-compliance is not due to factors beyond the party's control." *** In addition, "a party's persistent refusal to comply with a discovery order" presents sufficient evidence of willfulness, bad faith or fault. ***

D. Sanctions Pursuant to 28 U.S.C. § 1927

Another vehicle by which a court may issue sanctions is Section 1927 of Title 28 of the United States Code ("28 U.S.C. § 1927" or "§ 1927"). 28 U.S.C. § 1927 authorizes the courts to sanction an attorney "who so multiplies the proceedings in any case unreasonably and vexatiously." 28 U.S.C. § 1927. To impose sanctions under § 1927, the court must make a finding of "conduct constituting or akin to bad faith." *** "Unlike [other] sanctions which focus on particular papers, the inquiry under § 1927 is on a course of conduct." ***

E. Sanctions Pursuant to the Court's Inherent Authority

Courts also possess the "inherent power to sanction parties and their attorneys, a power born of the practical necessity that courts be able to manage their own affairs so as to achieve the orderly and expeditious disposition of cases." *** However, "when there is bad-faith conduct in the course of litigation that could be adequately sanctioned under the [Federal Rules of Civil Procedure or a specific statute], the court ordinarily should rely on the Rules rather than the inherent power." *** Furthermore, "because the inherent power is considered so potent, courts must be restrained in exercising it." ***

III. THE SANCTIONS MOTION

The Shaw Family argues that the cost associated with the forensic examination of the Computer, which contains material relevant to this litigation, should be shifted to Plaintiff and/or Mr. Adams. The Shaw Family further contends that Mr. Adams should be sanctioned for failing to comply with Court Orders relating to the production of the Computer.

A. Cost-Shifting for the Forensic Examination of the Computer

The Shaw Family contends that, pursuant to the framework set forth in *Zubulake I*, the costs it will incur in examining the Computer should be shifted to Plaintiff and/or Mr. Adams. The Court finds that a portion of the forensic examination cost, which is designed to yield the discovery of inaccessible electronically stored information, should be shifted to Plaintiff.

With respect to the first *Zubulake I* consideration, the request was narrowly tailored to seek relevant e-mails contained on the Computer that demonstrate that Susan Shaw was not shut out of the Shaw Family Archives, Ltd. ("SFA") governance and go to the claims against Plaintiff for self-dealing, interference with SFA and copyright infringement. In fact, this Court ordered the production of the Computer given that it was alleged to contain relevant material. This factor weighs in favor of cost-shifting. The second *Zubulake I* factor also weighs in favor of cost-shifting, as the Shaw Family had no means of accessing this information other than by way of the forensic examination. Further to this point, Mr. Adams admitted that his client discarded one computer and the other crashed, and none of the e-mails were saved even when litigation was anticipated. Third, the total cost of the forensic examination is likely to be far less than the total amount in controversy. This weighs in favor of cost-shifting. The fourth factor is neutral, given that the parties' financial positions are not fully apparent. Fifth, given Mr. Adams' repeated discovery-related misconduct, the Shaw Family was the appropriate party to coordinate the discovery and control costs. This weighs in favor of cost-shifting. The sixth issue, the importance and novelty of the issues in this case, is neutral. Seventh, the e-mails contained on the Computer are important to the informed litigation of this case and essential to both parties' claims. Thus, this factor is neutral.

Given that a majority of the factors, including the first two — and most important ù considerations, weigh in favor of the Shaw Family's claims, the Court finds that cost-shifting is appropriate. "It is beyond cavil that the precise allocation [of how much of the cost should be shifted] is a matter of judgment and fairness rather than a mathematical consequence of the seven factors discussed above. Nonetheless, the analysis of those factors does inform the exercise of discretion." *** Since a majority of the factors weigh in favor of shifting the cost onto Plaintiff, the Court orders that Plaintiff pay for seventy percent of the forensic examination costs and that the Shaw Family pay for thirty percent. "As a general rule, where cost-shifting is appropriate, only the costs of restoration and searching should be shifted." Thus, Plaintiff's seventy-percent share only includes costs for restoration and searching, and not, as the Shaw Family requests, any expenses incurred in the course of review. ***

B. Monetary Sanctions for Violation of Orders Relating to the Discovery of the Computer

The Shaw Family requests attorneys' fees for the time its counsel expended in compelling Mr. Adams' compliance with the Court's Orders to turn over the Computer.

Rule 37 provides that if a motion to compel is granted, "or if the disclosure or requested discovery is provided after the motion was filed — the court must ... award reasonable motion expenses incurred in making the motion." Fed. R. Civ. P. 37(a)(5)(A) (emphasis added). Thus, the Rule sets forth a rebuttable presumption in favor of awarding sanctions against a party that complies with discovery demands after the filing of a motion to compel. *** The Court may not award reasonable expenses, however, if the nondisclosure was "substantially justified" or "other circumstances make an award of expenses unjust." Fed. R. Civ. P. 37(a)(5)(A)(ii), (iii).

Whether a party was substantially justified in resisting discovery is determined by "an objective standard of reasonableness and does not require that he acted in good faith." Instead, conduct is substantially justified if there was a "genuine dispute" or if "reasonable people could differ" as to the appropriateness of the contested action. *** Plaintiff's actions here fail to satisfy this standard. Mr. Adams ignored repeated Court Orders to produce the Computer despite the undersigned's numerous admonitions, and thus cannot establish that the nondisclosure was substantially justified.

Accordingly, the Court agrees that, pursuant to Rule 37(a)(5)(A), Mr. Adams is required to pay attorneys' fees in connection with the Shaw Family's oral motion on April 8, 2016; the letter dated April 15, 2016; and the letter dated April 18, 2016 that were granted and resulted in the Court's April 19, 2016 Order compelling the production of the Computer.

IV. THE OMNIBUS SANCTIONS MOTION

In its Omnibus Sanctions Motion, the Shaw Family requests that the Court impose sanctions on the following five grounds: (i) Plaintiff's and Mr. Adams' conduct requires monetary sanctions and the dismissal of the Complaint and the Answer pursuant to Rule 16; (ii) Plaintiff's and Mr. Adams' failure to comply with the Court's Discovery Orders require monetary sanctions and dismissal of the Complaint and the Answer pursuant to Rule 37; (iii) Plaintiff's and Mr. Adams' conduct warrants sanctions pursuant to the Court's inherent power; (iv) Mr. Adams' conduct warrants sanctions pursuant to 28 U.S.C. § 1927; and (v) the Court should report Mr. Adams' conduct to the grievance committee. As discussed above, see supra n.4, due in part to the parties' verbose and unfocused submissions, the Court only analyzes the following specific instances of misconduct that it deems worthy of note and sanctionable: (i) Mr. Adams' failure to comply with the Court's April 15, 2015, December 23, 2015, February 29, 2016, April 19, 2016, May 19, 2016, and July 28, 2016 Orders; (ii) Mr. Adams' invitation to a third party to surreptitiously sit in on the January 7, 2016 telephonic meet-and-confer, which included sensitive and confidential discussions; and (iii) Mr. Adams' systematic misconduct at various hearings before the undersigned.

A. Monetary Sanctions Pursuant to Rules 16, 37 and 28 U.S.C. § 1927

Rules 16, 37 and 28 U.S.C. § 1927 enable, but do not require, this Court to impose sanctions. *** A review of the record and Mr. Adams' conduct before this Court, however, leaves no doubt that Mr. Adams' violations of Rules 16, 37 and 28 U.S.C. § 1927 warrant sanctions.

i. Discovery Order Violations

On February 29, 2016, after hearing oral argument from the parties, the Court entered an Order directing Mr. Adams to, inter alia, Bates stamp his document production; produce responsive documents requested in the Shaw Family's Second Document Requests dated January 6, 2016; and respond to the Second Set of Interrogatories dated January 4, 2016. Mr. Adams systematically violated this Order, in defiance of this Court's repeated admonitions directing him to comply, which resulted in delayed discovery, a protracted subsequent Court appearance on April 8, 2016 and needless additional legal fees. This is a clear violation of Rule 37 for which Mr. Adams has not demonstrated any substantial justification. *** Accordingly, Mr. Adams is directed to pay for the costs associated with the Shaw Family's counsel's preparation for and attendance at the April 8, 2016 conference.

As discussed *supra*, the Court issued Discovery Orders dated April 15, 2015, April 19, 2016, and May 19, 2016 setting forth correspondence page limits, an Order dated December 23, 2015 directing Mr. Adams to temporarily suspend his correspondence to the Court, and another dated July 28, 2016 ordering Mr. Adams to, *inter alia*, comply with previous discovery directives. Mr. Adams systematically violated each of these Orders and directives, which resulted in protracted conferences before the undersigned on January 11, 2016, and May 19, 2016. Specifically, despite the clear directives in the December 23, 2015

Order, for example, Mr. Adams continued to barrage the Court with his correspondence, including two letters on January 5, 2016.

Thereafter, at the January 11, 2016 conference, the undersigned repeated the Court's admonition to Mr. Adams that he was "violating [the Court's] rules" by, *inter alia*, attaching letters as exhibits to letters and refusing to request page extensions, as required by the Court. Further, in defiance of the directives set forth in the April 15, 2015, April 19, 2016, and May 19, 2016 Orders, Mr. Adams continued to exceed the compulsory pages limits. This pattern of violative conduct warrants sanctions pursuant to Rule 16. ***

Accordingly, Mr. Adams is directed to pay the Shaw Family's attorneys' fees in connection with the January 11, 2016 conference, in addition to the Shaw Family's counsel's time spent reviewing and responding to his two explicitly unauthorized letters filed January 5, 2016.

ii. Improper Conduct at the January 7, 2016 Meet-and-Confer

Next, the Court finds that Mr. Adams should be sanctioned pursuant to 28 U.S.C. § 1927 for inviting a third party to surreptitiously listen to the January 7, 2016 meet-and-confer, which included sensitive and confidential information. In a bizarre effort to relay the tone of the parties' meet-and-confers to this Court, Mr. Adams invited a local merchant, Seth Gopin ("Mr. Gopin"), to eavesdrop on the telephonic meet-and-confer, without informing opposing counsel. Subsequently, Mr. Gopin submitted an affidavit to the Court confirming his clandestine presence at the meet-and-confer. The Court finds that such conduct is sanctionable pursuant to 28 U.S.C. § 1927, as it "multiplie[d] the proceedings ... unreasonably and vexatiously." *** As a result of this conduct, the Court and the parties expended otherwise unnecessary time and effort reviewing the impropriety of this behavior at the May 19, 2016 conference. Further, Mr. Adams' bad faith is clear and egregious, since his actions were "so completely without merit as to require the conclusion that they must have been undertaken for some improper purpose ...." ***

Accordingly, the Court orders Mr. Adams to pay for the Shaw Family's counsel's fees in preparing for and attending the May 19, 2016 conference, at which the Court and counsel expended unnecessary time and effort discussing the impropriety of Mr. Adams' actions.

iii. Attorneys' Fees Associated with the Sanctions Motion and Omnibus Sanctions Motion

The Court also finds that, pursuant to Rule 16, Mr. Adams must compensate the Shaw Family for attorneys' fees and costs associated with bringing the Sanctions Motion and the Omnibus Sanctions Motion. ***

B. Striking Pleadings Pursuant to Rules 16 and 37

The Shaw Family requests that, as a result of Mr. Adams' pattern of sanctionable conduct, the Court should impose the drastic remedy of striking his client's pleadings. Specifically, the Shaw Family contends that it would be proper for the Court to strike the Complaint and the Answer pursuant to Rules 16 and 37. I disagree.

Dismissal of pleadings is considered an "extreme sanction[], to be deployed only in rare situations." *** Using its broad discretion, the Court does not consider Mr. Adams' conduct of the type that would warrant dismissal of his client's Complaint and Answer. *** Further, Mr. Adams has been relieved as counsel and new attorneys have been retained to prosecute this case. Accordingly, using the broad discretion afforded to it, the Court declines to recommend that the Shaw Family's requested remedy of striking the Complaint and the Answer pursuant to Rules 16 and 37 be granted.

C. Report to the Grievance Committee

The Court declines to report Mr. Adams' conduct to a grievance committee. The instant imposition of sanctions, coupled with Mr. Adams' withdrawal as counsel from this case, obviates the need for a report to a grievance committee. However, the Court finds that Mr. Adams' conduct at the December 9, 2015 and January 11, 2016 conferences before the undersigned warrants special note in this Order. Mr. Adams yelled, threw his pen, and sighed loudly while others were talking during these Court conferences. *** While the Court will not impose a judgment of sanctions on Mr. Adams or report him to a grievance committee on account of this behavior, it reiterates its strong condemnation of this unprofessional conduct.

D. Sanctions Pursuant to the Court's Inherent Authority

Given that the Court is able to sanction Mr. Adams on the above statutory grounds, it will not use its inherent authority as a source of sanctioning power. ***

CHAPTER 12

ELECTRONICALLY STORED INFORMATION

FRCP Rule 34(a)(1)(A) allows a party to request another party to produce:

> any designated documents or electronically stored information—including writings, drawings, graphs, charts, photographs, sound recordings, images, and other data or data compilations—stored in any medium from which information can be obtained either directly or, if necessary, after translation by the responding party into a reasonably usable form.

Electronically stored information (ESI) is any information that is created and/or stored electronically. In contrast, paper documents are not considered as ESI. E-discovery specifically refers to the discovery of ESI.

Even though the term ESI seems to be relatively modern, but ESI has been around for a long time. For example, long before the so-called digital age, sound recordings were electronically created and stored in phonographs and magnetic tapes.

A. Analog and Digital ESI

Information (data) can be represented by analog signals and/or digital signals. Generally speaking, an analog signal is a time-varying continuous signal that can be either periodic or non-periodic. The output form of an analog signal resembles a curve or wave. On the other hand, digital signals are discrete signals that represent data as a sequence of individual numerical values.

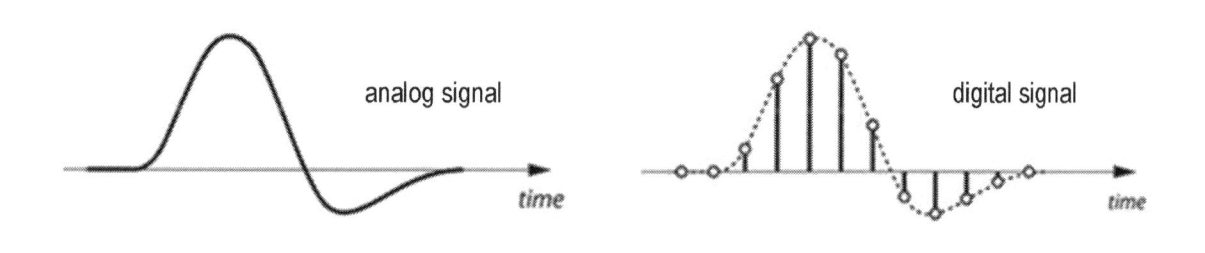

Both analog signals and digital signals can be electronically stored in a storage medium. Some ESI can be stored in an analog form, and some EST can be stored in a digital form.

Storing ESI in Analog Form

Sound recording, for example, can be stored in an analog form. With a tape recording machine, sound can be recorded on a magnetic tape (which is a plastic film coated with tiny magnetic particles on one side) moving pass a record head (which includes a magnet) for converting audio signals into magnetic energy. Specifically, the record head generates a fluctuating magnetic field in response to the changing audio signal inputs. As the magnetic tape passes by, the magnetic pulses from the fluctuating magnetic field align the tiny magnetic particles into patterns that correspond to the sound being recorded. Thus, the pattern sequences of magnetic particles on the magnetic tape represent a sound recording in an analog form.

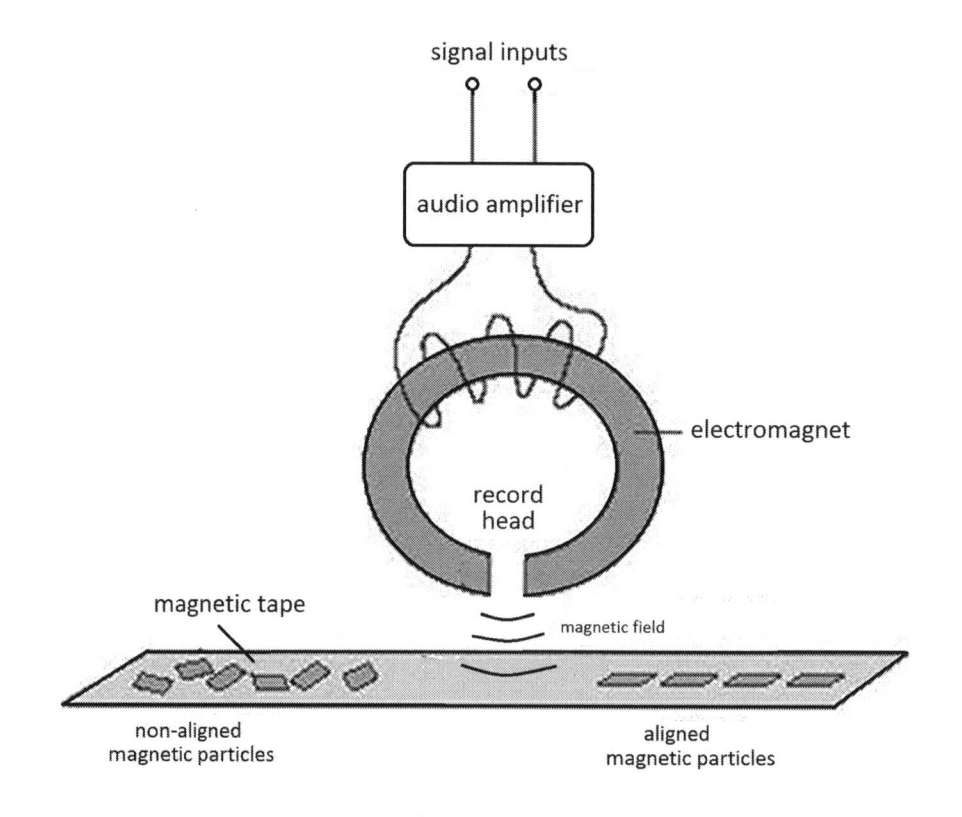

Storing ESI in Digital Form

Instead of storing in an analog form, sound recordings can also be made and stored in a digital form. In order to perform digital recording, sound waves are initially sampled via a sample-and-hold circuit at discrete time intervals, and the sound samples are then individually quantized by an analog-to-digital converter to produce a sequence of discrete numbers that represent various magnitudes of the sound waves. This sequence of discrete numbers can be stored in any medium that is capable of storing digital numbers. For example, a magnetic tape, a compact disc (CD), a digital video disc (DVD), etc. can be utilized to store a sound recording in a digital form as discrete numbers.

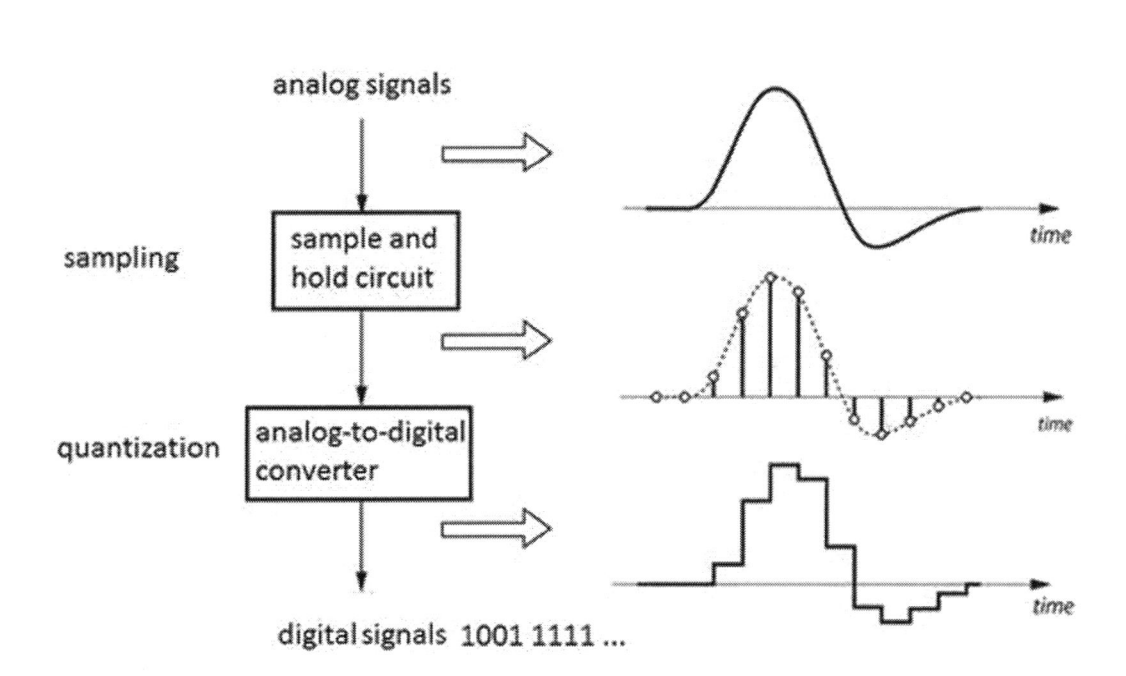

When comes time to play back the sound recording from a storage medium, a digital-to-analog converter and a smoothing filter are employed to convert the sequence of discrete numbers back to analog sound waves for human consumption.

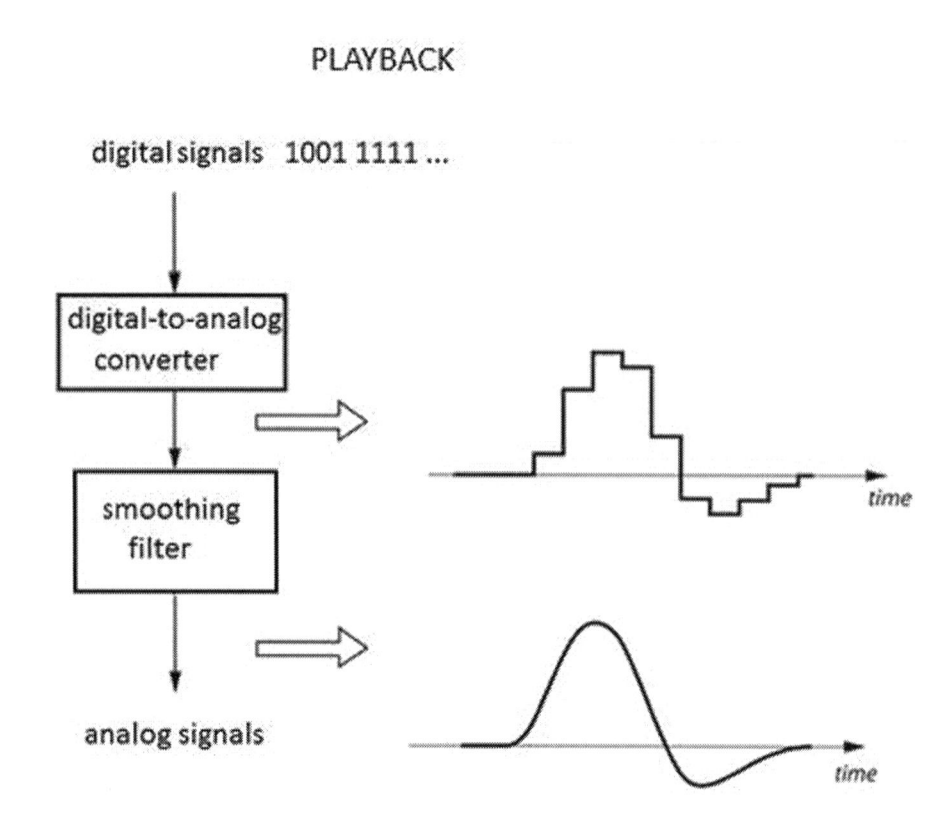

PLAYBACK

digital signals 1001 1111 ...

↓

[digital-to-analog converter] ⇒

↓

[smoothing filter] ⇒

↓

analog signals

Even though digital signals can be easier to process and transmit than analog signals, it took many years for the digital revolution to arrive because of the various limitations on the hardware for producing digital data and for performing digital processing. After the advent of modern digital computers and digital cameras, "writings, drawings, graphs, charts, and photographs" can also be digitally produced and processed. As the speed and functions of digital processing hardware have improved, digital processing became the preferred method of signal processing, which leads to the rapid expansion of ESI in its digital form.

Today, digital ESI can be stored in various medium such as magnetic tapes, electromagnetic hard drives, solid-state drives, thumb drives, CDs, DVDs, Subscriber Identity Module (SIM) cards, etc.

B. Numbering Systems

When comes to numbering systems, human beings have a predilection for a base-10 system probably because of having ten fingers. A base-10 system means that when the count in a unit position reaches a tenth count, then the count in the unit position resets back to zero, and a count in the position adjacent to the unit position (known as the tenth position) is incremented by one to denote a ten (*see* the transition from nine to ten in the base-10 system table). When the count is more than ten, then the count in the unit position begins with one again (*see* the transition from ten to eleven in the base-10 system table).

base-10 system

zero	0	six	6
one	1	seven	7
two	2	eight	8
three	3	nine	9
four	4	ten	10
five	5	eleven	11

It is very likely that cartoon characters, such as Mickey Mouse, would prefer a base-8 system because many of the cartoon characters have eight fingers. A base-8 system means that when the count in a unit position reaches an eighth count, then the count in the unit position resets back to zero, and a count in the position adjacent to the unit position (known as the eighth position) is incremented by one to denote an eight (*see* the transition from seven to eight in the base-8 system table). When the count is more than eight, then the count in the unit position begins with one again (*see* the transition from eight to nine in the base-8 system table).

base-8 system

zero	0	six	6
one	1	seven	7
two	2	eight	10
three	3	nine	11
four	4	ten	12
five	5	eleven	13

In the base-10 system, "10" means ten, but in the base-8 system, "10" means eight. To avoid any confusion, addition notation can be used to signify a base of a number, such as 8_{10} for base-10 and 10_8 for base-8. Since the base-10 system is in common use around the world, the notation for base-10 is generally omitted. The base-10 system is also known as the *decimal* system, and the base-8 system is also known as the *octal* system.

Human beings prefer the base-10 system and cartoon characters may prefer the base-8 system, but digital computers operate in a base-2 system. This is because a digital computer includes many switches, and each switch has two states (*i.e.*, an ON state and an OFF state). Base-2 system means that when the count in an unit position reaches a second count, then the count in the unit position resets back to zero, and a count in the position adjacent to the unit position is incremented by one to denote a two (*see* the transition from one to two in the base-2 system table). When the count is more than two, then the count in the unit position begins with one again (*see* the transition from two to three in the base-2 system table).

base-2 system

zero	0	six	110
one	1	seven	111
two	10	eight	1000
three	11	nine	1001
four	100	ten	1010
five	101	eleven	1011

The base-2 system is also known as the *binary* system because there are only two choices, namely, 1 or 0. In a digital computer, each position in a base-2 number can be handled by a switch, so at least four switches are needed to show number eleven in base-2, *i.e.*, 1011_2. In computer parlance, each of those four positions is known as a *binary digit* or commonly abbreviated as *bit*. In other words, a digital computer needs to use at least four bits to represent the number eleven.

C. Encoding Schemes

In addition to represent numbers by their numeric values under the base-2 system, bits can also be utilized to represent characters within digital computers, audio data within a CD, or video data within a DVD. This is done by way of various encoding schemes.

<u>Encoding Characters</u>

American Standard Code for Information Interchange (ASCII) is one of the encoding schemes for encoding characters such as numbers, letters and symbols that are used in digital computers, digital communication equipment, and other digital electronic devices. ASCII is a 7-bit character set, which means it can encode $2^7 = 128$ different characters. Some of the 128 characters include numbers from 0 to 9, upper and lower case English letters from A to Z, and symbolic characters such as $, #, @, etc. The following is a list of uppercase letters A-Z and lowercase letters a-z and their respective encoded binary representation under the ASCII encoding scheme.

character	encoded binary representation	character	encoded binary representation
A	1000001	a	1100001
B	1000010	b	1100010
C	1000011	c	1100011
D	1000100	d	1100100
E	1000101	e	1100101
F	1000110	f	1100110
G	1000111	g	1100111
H	1001000	h	1101000
I	1001001	i	1101001
J	1001010	j	1101010
K	1001011	k	1101011
L	1001100	l	1101100
M	1001101	m	1101101
N	1001110	n	1101110
O	1001111	o	1101111
P	1010000	p	1110000
Q	1010001	q	1110001
R	1010010	r	1110010
S	1010011	s	1110011
T	1010100	t	1110100
U	1010101	u	1110101
V	1010110	v	1110110
W	1010111	w	1110111
X	1011000	x	1111000
Y	1011001	y	1111001
Z	1011010	z	1111010

An information processing machine, such as a digital computer, that employs the ASCII encoding scheme will represent the word "Cat" as 1000011 1100001 1110100, and the word "Dog" as 1000100 1101111 1100111. The 1s and 0s may seem like a foreign language for humans, but for digital computers, 1s and 0s are their native language, which is sometimes called *machine language*.

Encoding Audio

As mentioned above, sound recording in its digital form can be represented by a sequence of numbers. These numbers can also be encoded into their corresponding binary representations and stored as a file in an appropriate storage medium such as a CD. In order to provide CD quality audio, 16 bits (which can encode $2^{16} = 65,536$ different sound levels) are required.

Encoding Video

Similarly, images and videos data in their digital form can be encoded into their binary representations and stored in an appropriate medium such as a DVD. For example, at least 24 bits (which can encode $2^{24} = 16,777,216$ different video levels) are typically utilized to encode uncompressed video:

As such, in their digital form, the text of a Shakespeare sonnet in a text file, the sound of Beethoven's 5th symphony in an audio file and an image of Mona Lisa in an image file will look very similar to each other because they are just groups of 1s and 0s.

D. File Extensions

Many types of files can be stored in a digital computer, and they are typically known by the type of information they hold. Broadly speaking, a document file contains text information, an image file contains image information, a sound file contains audio information, and a video file contains video information. Many times, the type of file is signified by its file extension that is separated from the filename by a dot. The following is a list of some common file extensions.

file extension	description
.txt	text file
.rtf	rich text format file
.doc	Microsoft Word document file
.docx	Microsoft Word Open XML document file
.xls	Microsoft Excel spreadsheet file
.xlsx	Microsoft Excel Open XML spreadsheet file
.ppt	Microsoft PowerPoint presentation file
.pptx	Microsoft PowerPoint Open XML presentation file
.bmp	bitmap image file
.gif	graphical interchange format file
.tif	tagged image file
.png	portable network graphic file
.jpg	image file in Joint Photographic Expert Group format
.psd	Adobe Photoshop file
.pdf	Adobe portable document format file
.mp3	audio file in MP3 coding format
.wav	audio file in WAVE coding format
.wma	Microsoft Windows Media audio file

E. Metadata

In epistemology, "meta" means "about." So *metadata* is a set of data that provides information about one or more aspects of the other data. Simply put, metadata is "data about data."

Metadata can be embedded in many digital files, along with the actual contents of the files. Although metadata embedded in digital files have marginal value for everyday use, in e-discovery, metadata can be very important and must be included with the collected ESI. The following are different types of metadata that are relevant to e-discovery:

> Application metadata: It is included in a file and contains information generated by application software that creates the file. Application metadata moves with a file when copied, though copying may alter its contents.

> Email metadata: This metadata about an email may not be immediately apparent within the email application that generated it. The amount of email metadata available varies depending on the email system utilized.

> Embedded metadata: Embedded metadata is usually hidden. Examples of embedded metadata include edit history or notes in a Microsoft Presentation file. These may only be viewable in the original, native file since it is not always extracted during processing and conversion to an image format.

> File system metadata: Data generated by a file system to track key statistics about the file, such as name, size, etc., which is usually stored externally from the file itself.

> User-added metadata: Data generated by a user while working with, reviewing, or copying a file.

> Vendor-added metadata: Data generated and maintained by an e-discovery vendor during processing of the native document.

CHAPTER 13

INFORMATION PROCESSING MACHINES

In the beginning, computers were analog in nature, with some being mechanical while others electrical. Over time, analog computers were displaced by digital computers.

These days, digital computers come in many flavors, such as desktop computers, laptops, tablets, etc. Even though many people do not always think of them as computers, but smart phones, smart televisions, fitness trackers, game consoles can also be considered as digital computers as well. Basically, all of them can be collectively called information processing machines.

Regardless of their actual name, information processing machines are electronic devices that can store, retrieve, and process data and information. An information processing machine generally includes hardware such as a processor, memory devices, and input/output devices. In addition, an information processing machine requires software to control the hardware.

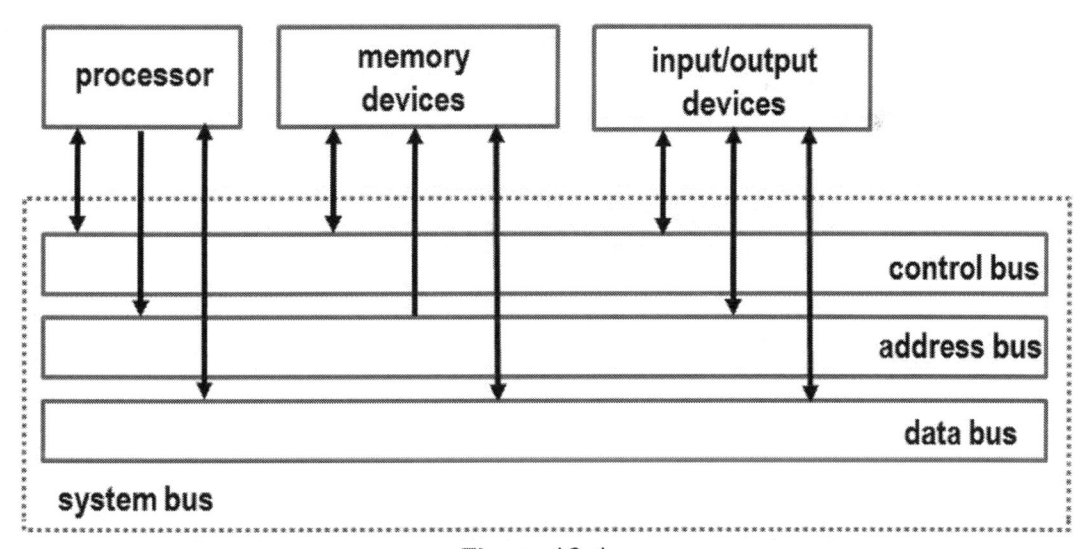

Figure 13.1

A. Hardware

Within an information processing machine, as shown in Figure 13.1, a processor, which is also known as a central processing unit (CPU), is connected to a set of memory devices and some input/output devices via a system bus that is formed by a group of electrical wires.

Processor

A processor includes millions of digital transistors for performing various computations and logic functions according to the instructions from software. Unlike analog transistors that are capable of outputting a series of values, a digital transistor can only output two values that correspond to its being ON or OFF, respectively. In many ways, a digital transistor is similar to a light switch: current runs through the digital transistor when it is turned ON, and no current runs through the digital transistor when it is turned OFF. Conventionally, a numerical "1" is associated with a digital transistor being turned ON to provide an ON output, and a numerical "0" is associated with a digital transistor being turned OFF to provide an OFF output.

When comes performing computations, since a processor can only use 1s and 0s, instead of viewing a processor as a mathematical genius, one can think of the processor as a simpleton doing arithmetic with pebbles and rocks but at lightning speed. Thus, in the end, a processor can still provide computation results drastically faster than any regular human being can do.

Memory devices

There are two types of memory devices, namely, volatile memories and non-volatile memories. The information stored in volatile memories disappear when the power to the volatile memories is turned off. In contrast, non-volatile memories can retain their information absence of power.

Both volatile and non-volatile memories have memory cells (or memory locations) for storing information in the form of electrical charges. These memory cells are made of digital transistors. Since non-volatile memories require more digital transistors to construct, the size of each non-volatile memory cell tends to be bigger than its volatile counterpart. Conventionally, a memory cell having electrical charges stored within signifies a numerical "1," and a memory cell without any electrical charges stored within signifies a numerical "0."

In a digital computer, the non-volatile memory is commonly known as a read-only memory (ROM), and the volatile memory is commonly known a random-access memory

(RAM). The storage capabilities of both volatile and non-volatile memories in a computer, and any information processing machine alike, are relatively small. Thus, external memories are typically added to the computer to store software and data. These external memories, which are also non-volatile in nature, can be a hard drive, a solid-state drive, a memory card, etc.

Input and Output devices

Input devices allow a user to input information to an information processing machine. An input device can be a keyboard, a keypad, a touchpad, a mouse, a trackball, a stylus pen, etc. Output devices allow the user to receive information from the information processing machine. An output device can be a display, a speaker, a printer, etc. Some devices, such as a touchscreen, can serve as both an input as well as an output device.

System bus

A system bus allows data and information to travel among the processor, the memory devices, and the input and output devices. As shown in Figure 13.1, a system bus includes a control bus, an address bus and a data bus, each carrying different types of data and information.

The contents stored within each memory location can be accessed based on its *memory address* accordingly. For example, a processor can read contents from a memory location (or place contents into a memory location) by sending a memory address of the memory location to a memory controller via the address bus, and the contents of the memory location will be delivered to the processor via the data bus. Whether the processor intends to read or store contents to a memory location can be signified by a control signal sent to the memory controller via the control bus. A common address size is known as a *byte* that includes 8 bits. The maximum number of memory locations that can be addressed by 8 bits are $2^8 = 256$.

The maximum number of address locations that can be accessed by a processor is mathematically limited by an address width of an operating system. For example, the maximum number of addressable memory locations for a 32-bit operating system is $2^{32} = 4,294,967,296$ or more commonly referred to as 4 gigabytes. In other words, a 32-bit operating system can only access 4 gigabyte memory locations even when more than 4 gigabytes of memories are installed. Similarly, the maximum number of addressable memory locations for a 64-bit operating system is $2^{64} = 18,446,744,073,709,551,616$.

B. Software

Without software, an information processing machine is simply one big glorify paperweight, much like a body without a soul. Many types of software are required for the operation of an information processing machine, but they can generally be classified into two broad categories: system software and application software.

System software

System software is an interface between hardware and application software. System software "talks" to the hardware of an information processing machine, and handles various housekeeping tasks for the application software. The most important system software is an operating system. Windows, iOS, Linux, and Android are examples of operating system.

Other system software includes the Basic Input/Output System (BIOS), the boot program, device drives, etc.

The BIOS, which is stored in a non-volatile memory of a personal computer, is a small program that starts the personal computer after it has been turned on. The BIOS also manages the data flow between an operating system and input/output devices such as a keyboard, a mouse, etc. After the BIOS has gotten the personal computer started, the boot program loads the operating system into the volatile memory of the personal computer.

Many input/output devices, such as keyboard, mouse, display, etc., require a device driver to operate. A driver enables operating systems and other software to access hardware functions without needing to know the precise details of the hardware being accessed. In other words, a device driver converts the input/output instructions of the operating system to messages that the input/output device can understand.

Application software

Application software (or Apps) performs certain function(s) directly for an end user or, in some cases, for another application. Examples of application software include word processing programs, database programs, web browsers, image editors, etc.

Application software, such as Microsoft Word, are considered proprietary application software and end users typically need to purchase a license in order to use them. End user are not allowed to make modifications to the application software. In contrast, Open Source application software, such as WordPress, provides the source code for end users and developers to use and modify via a generic or public license, such as GNU.

In general, application software is initially written (or coded) in high-level programming languages such as C++, Python, Javascript, that are considered more human friendly. The application software in high-level programming language is then converted into machine language (*i.e.*, 1s and 0s) that is native to digital information processing machines.

Chapter 14

Mobile Devices

In the world of e-discovery, there is some level of consensus regarding the types of ESI that need to be preserved on a regular basis. Quite often, defensible and repeatable procedures have been established for preserving and collecting emails, photographs, videos, and productivity files such as text documents, spreadsheets, presentations, etc. residing on computers and servers. In contrast, there is typically no formal process related to the preservation and collection of ESI residing on mobile devices such as tablets and smartphones.

Like computers and servers, mobile devices can also generate and store emails, photographs, videos, and productivity files such as text documents, spreadsheets, presentations, etc. These ESI can be relevant to e-discovery.

The following are the types of information routinely found on a mobile device.

1. Text Messages

It is very common to have thousands of messages stored in a mobile device such as a smartphone. This is because the default text message retention setting for a text messaging app on a smartphone is to keep messages "forever," unless a user elects to change it to a limited time.

Some text messages are tied to one person and some text messages are tied to multiple persons within a group message, which means one person can show up in different groups of text messages (group chats). This does not present a problem for collection, but it will make the review process more challenging.

Text messages can be exported as text files or portable document format (PDF) files, but this will severely limit the utility of the data in terms of reordering the contents of columns for sender, date, etc. Thus, it is better to export text messages in delimited formats like CSV that can be viewed in a spreadsheet.

Attachments to text messages can also be exported, but the exporting tools may not be able to associate the attachments with its corresponding messages. Emojis may render as cryptic characters unless the encoding is changed to Unicode UTF-8.

Another challenge to exporting text messages is the variety of messaging apps other than the native messaging app that comes with the smartphone. Some common proprietary cross-platform messaging apps include Snapchat, WhatsApp, Facebook Messenger, WeChat, etc.

2. Phone Call History

In the context of e-discovery, phone call histories are not routinely collected just because they are there. They are only collected and produced when the call record was pertinent to a claim or defense in the case. Accordingly, mobile phone call history records are likely to be scrutinized unless a specific request and a plausible nexus between the data and the issues are presented.

Mobile phone call history can be exported in a delimited file, and it should include information such as callers, phone numbers, call times, call directions (incoming/outgoing) and call durations. Mobile phone call history can also be obtained by logging into a mobile phone provider's website to download a call history.

3. Voice Mail

Voice mail can be exported as a delimited CSV file showing time of call, duration, caller, phone number, and maybe a transcript of the voice message. The audio files for each voice message can also be exported in the .amr audio format. The review process can be tedious because there is usually no hyperlink for each audio file within the CSV file.

4. Photographs and Videos

A mobile device typically holds many photographs and videos. Some of these photographs are in full-resolution while some may be just thumbnail-size version because a user decides to save space on the mobile phone by electing to store photographs in the cloud.

Also, the locations of photographs taken by a mobile device are usually embedded in the metadata of the photographs.

5. Browser History and Bookmarks

Browser history and bookmarks can be exported from a phone backup. They are usually not relevant enough to require routine collection.

6. Calendar

Calendar entries for any selected interval can be exported to a CSV file. The mobile calendar data is also easier to redact.

7. Contacts

Contacts can be exported as a CSV file or as individual VCards.

8. Geolocation Data

Under Federal laws, any mobile phone capable of making or receiving calls must broadcast its location in order to support 911 emergency response services. Thus, by default, a mobile phone closely tracks a user's movements for a length of time, recording locations visited and the times and durations of visits in a "Significant Locations" database.

Geolocation data can be relevant and even dispositive in some cases. However, geolocation data are relatively difficult to collect even though they are readily accessible to a user via a few screen taps on a mobile phone.

CHAPTER 15

ENCRYPTION AND HASHING

Encoding is a process for converting data into a format designed for information processing without requiring any key. Encoding can be reversed by using the same algorithm that encoded the content. ASCII is an example of encoding, as mentioned in Chapter 12. Encryption and hashing are more than encoding.

A. Encryption

Encryption is a process for locking up data in order to maintain data confidentiality. Encryption requires the usage of a key that is kept secret. Encryption is a two-way function, meaning what is encrypted can be decrypted with a proper key.

Symmetric encryption

Symmetric encryption uses the same one secret key to encrypt (cipher) and decrypt (decipher) information. The secret key needs to be shared among the people who need to send and/or receive messages using symmetric encryption. By using a symmetric encryption algorithm along with a secret key, plain data can be converted into encrypted data, as shown in Figure 15.1.

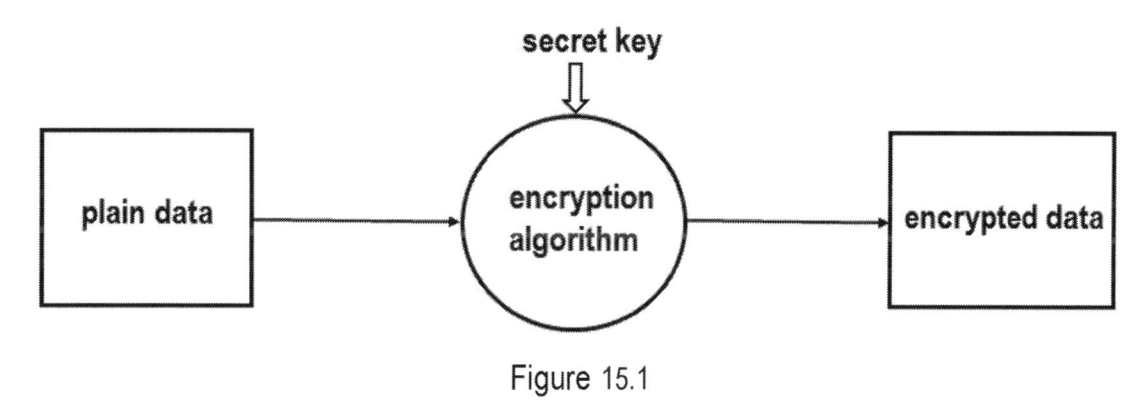

Figure 15.1

Conversely, encrypted data can be reverted back to plain data by using the symmetric encryption algorithm along with the same secret key, as shown in Figure 15.2.

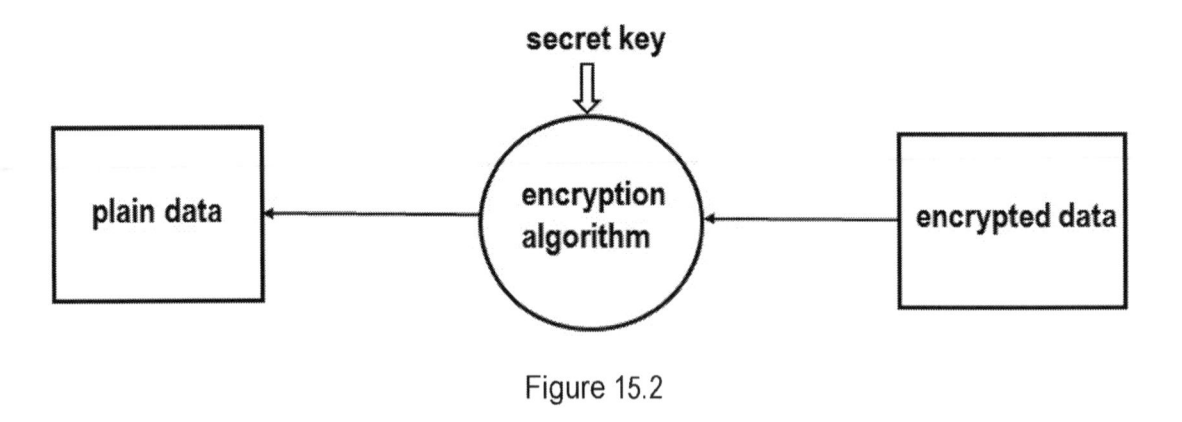

Figure 15.2

The secret key can be a number, a word or a string of random letters. Some commonly used symmetric encryption algorithm includes AES-128, AES-192, and AES-256.

Asymmetric encryption

Asymmetrical encryption, also known as public key cryptography, uses a public key and a private key to encrypt and to decrypt information, respectively. The public key is made freely available to anyone who wants to send messages via asymmetric encryption, but the private key is reserved for only those who need to decrypt the previously encrypted messages. By using an asymmetric encryption algorithm along with a public key, plain data can be converted into encrypted data, as shown in Figure 15.3.

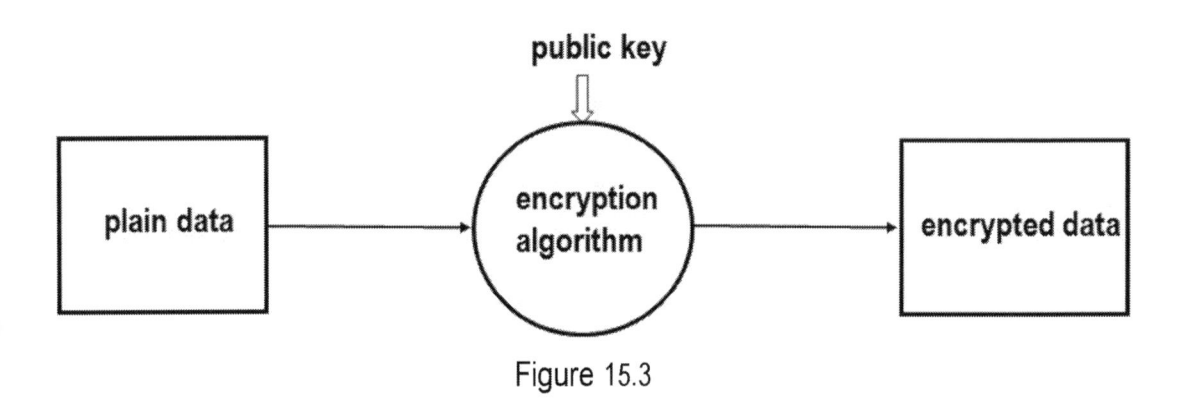

Figure 15.3

Conversely, encrypted data can be reverted back to plain data by using the asymmetric encryption algorithm along with a private key, as shown in Figure 15.4.

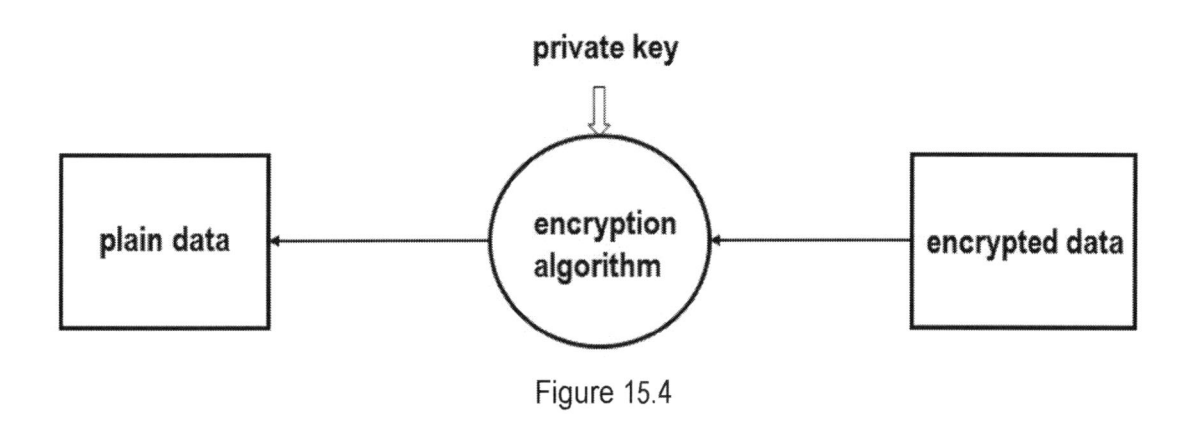

Figure 15.4

A message encrypted using a public key can only be decrypted by using a private key, but a message encrypted using a private key can also be decrypted by using a public key. Security of the public key is not required because it is publicly available. Popular asymmetric encryption algorithm includes RSA, DSA, PKCS, ElGamal, and Elliptic curve techniques.

B. Hashing

Hashing is a mathematical algorithm that scrambles plain data to produce a digest of the plain data in the form of a *hash value*. By using a hashing algorithm, plain data can be reduced into a hash value, as shown in Figure 15.5.

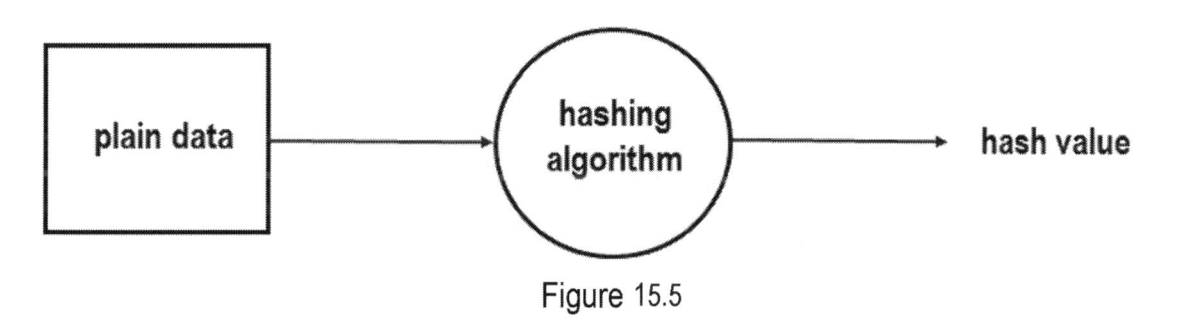

Figure 15.5

While encryption is a two-way function (*i.e.*, encrypt and decrypt), hashing is a one-way function. In other words, the hashing process cannot be reversed, and there is no way to reveal the original plain data by using the hash value.

Specifically, a hash value is a unique number calculated by a hash algorithm during the hashing process. The hash value is usually displayed in the form of an alphanumeric code because the number is expressed in a base-16 numbering system. As an extension to the base-10 numbering system (*see* Chapter 12), the numbers of a base-16 numbering system include numbers 0 to 9 and alphabets A-F, which are commonly known as *alphanumeric characters*.

base-16 system

zero	0	nine	9
one	1	ten	A
two	2	eleven	B
three	3	twelve	C
four	4	thirteen	D
five	5	fourteen	E
six	6	fifteen	F
seven	7	sixteen	10
eight	8	seventeen	11

In the context of e-discovery, a hash value is a computed numerical value that represents a digest of the contents within a document. If and only if two documents are identical to the letter will they return the same hash value from a hashing algorithm. Thus, a hash value can be used as part of a digital signature (or digital fingerprint) to compare document contents.

One hashing algorithm that is commonly used today for e-discovery is the Message-Digest 5 (MD5) algorithm. Invented by Professor Ronald Rivest of Massachusetts Institute of Technology, MD5 algorithm 5 is a hash function with a 128-bit hash value. An MD5 hash value is typically expressed as a 32-digit hexadecimal number.

Another hashing algorithm that is commonly used for e-discovery is SHA-1 that seemingly used MD5 as the model since SHA-1 and MD5 share many common features.

After processing a file, a hashing algorithm, such MD5 or SHA-1, can produce a 32-digit hash value that may look like this:

55A298C8B838E7CA75AB954FA69A2AD9

The hashing algorithm will produce the same hash value every time for the same file as long as the contents within the file have not been altered. A change in the file name will not affect its hash value. The same hash value means that the file is defensibly collected and processed during e-discovery. But if even one character has been modified or deleted from the file, the hashing algorithm will produce a new hash value that is completely different from the one shown above when the file is processed through the hashing algorithm again.

In addition to tamper-proofing, hashing can also be used to eliminate the number of the collected ESI before the document review stage via deduplication, near deduplication, and/or deNISTing.

Deduplication

Deduplication is the elimination of duplicate files in the collected ESI by comparing hash values of files to remove copies of the files having identical hash values.

Near deduplication

Hashing can be performed after identical fields or segments in a document, such as the contents of an email without headers and such, have been isolated and extracted in order to eliminate duplicate files in the collected ESI.

DeNISTing

Hash values permit the identification and removal of system files (files with file extensions such as .exe, .dll, etc.) from the collected ESI. Thus, the hash values in the collected ESI can be compared against the Reference Data Set, which is part of the National Software Reference Library, compiled by the National Institute of Standards and Technology (NIST). The Reference Data Set contains more than 28 million file signatures.

Glossary

A

Archive: A long term repository for storing files.

Assisted Review: A semi-automated method of document review by utilizing advance machine learning, such as predictive coding, to apply a reviewer's coding decisions to a large amount of data.

Attachment: A document that is associated with another document.

B

Backup tape: A portable medium utilized for storing copies of original data as a precaution against the loss or damage of the original data.

Big Data: Large datasets that are difficult to be processed via traditional data processing applications.

Batch Processing: The processing of a large amount of electronically stored information in a single step.

Boolean Search: A technique to connect individual keywords or phrases with a document or file query. Typical Boolean logic connectors are AND, OR, and NOT.

C

Chain-of-Custody: The processing, tracking and recording the movement, handling and location of electronic evidence chronologically from collection to production. It is used to verify the authenticity of the electronic evidence.

Checksum: a numerical method used in hashing.

Concept Search: A method of searching for files not based on keywords, but on the subject matter of the document, paragraph, or sentence.

Container File: A single file containing multiple documents and/or files, usually in a compressed format.

Custodian: An individual who has electronically stored information relevant to a pending litigation, but the individual does not necessarily have to be the author of the information.

D

Data Extraction: The process of parsing data from electronic documents to identify their metadata and body contents.

Data Mapping: The process of identifying and recording the location and types of electronically stored information within an organization's network, and policies and procedures related to that electronically stored information.

De-duplication or De-duping: The process of comparing the characteristics of electronic documents to identify and/or remove duplicate records in order to reduce review time and increase coding consistency.

De-NIST: The process of separating documents generated by a computer system from those created by a user. This automated process utilized a list of file extensions developed by the National Institute of Standards and Technology.

E

e-Disclosure: The e-discovery process as it is practiced in the European Union.

Early Case Assessment: A variety of tools or methods for investigating and quickly learning about document collection for the purposes of estimating the risks, costs, and time spent pursuing a particular legal course of action.

Electronic evidence: Information that is stored in an electronic format.

F

Filtering: The process of applying specific parameters to remove groups of documents that do not fit those parameters, in order to reduce the volume of the data set.

Forensics: The handling of electronically stored information including collection, examination and analysis, in a manner that ensures its authenticity, so as to provide for its admission as evidence in a court of law.

H

Hashing: An algorithm that generates a unique value for each document. It is referred to as a digital fingerprint and is used to authenticate documents and to identify duplicate documents.

Harvesting: It is also referred to as the collection of electronically stored information. Harvesting is the method of gathering electronic data for future use in an investigation or lawsuit, preferable while maintaining file and system metadata.

I

Image Drive: To make an identical copy (mirror image) of a physical hard drive including its empty space.

Image File: To make a picture copy of a document. The most common image formats in e-discovery are TIFF and PDF.

L

Legacy Data: Data whose format has become obsolete.

Load File: A file used to import data into an e-discovery system. It defines document parameters for imaged documents and often contains metadata for all electronically stored information it relates to.

M

Media: The device used to store electronic information

Metadata: The information that describes the characteristics of electronically stored information.

N

Native Format: A file that is maintained in the format in which it was created. This format preserves metadata and details about the data that might be lost if the documents were to be converted to another format.

Near-duplicate: Two or more files that contain a specified percentage of similarity. Also, the process used to identify those nearly-identical files.

Normalization: Reformatting data so that it is stored in a standardized format.

O

OCR: An acronym for Optical Character Recognition, which is the process of converting images of printed pages into electronic text.

P

Parent Document: A document to which other documents/files are attached.

Personal Storage Table: A file format used to store copies of messages, calendar events, and other items within Microsoft software (*e.g.*, Microsoft Outlook, Microsoft Exchange Client, and Windows Messaging) or in the most basic of terms.

Predictive Coding: A document categorization process that extrapolates the tagging decisions of an expert reviewer across a dataset. It is an iterative process for performing document review.

Precision: In a search results analysis, precision is the measure of the level of relevance to the query in the results set of documents.

Processing: The e-discovery workflow that ingests data, extracts text and metadata, and normalizes the data. Some systems include the data indexing and deduplication in the processing workflow.

Production: The delivery, to the requesting party, of documents and electronically stored information that meets the criteria of the discovery request.

PST: a file format for wrapping up huge numbers of emails and attachments in a way that preserves their ability to be searched.

R

Recall: In a search results analysis, recall is the measure of the percentage of total number of relevant documents in the corpus returned in the results set.

Redact: To intentionally conceal, usually via an overlay, portions of a document considered privileged, proprietary or confidential.

S

Search: The process of looking within a dataset using specific criteria (a query). There are several types of search, ranging from simple keyword to concept searches that identify documents related to the query even when the query term is not present in the document.

Slack space: The unused portion of a hard drive disk that exists when the data does not completely fill the space allotted for it. This space can be examined for otherwise unavailable data.

Structured data: Data stored in a structured format such as a database.

System Files: An electronic file that is part of the operating system or other control program. Some system files are created by the operating system, not the user of the computer. Examples of system files for a Windows operating system include msdos.sys, io.sys, ntdetect.com and ntldr.

T

Tagging: The process of assigning classifications, such as by relevance or privilege, to one or more documents.

TIFF: An acronym for Tagged Image File Format, and is a common graphic file format for storing bit map images.

U

Unallocated space: Most often, this is space created on a hard drive when a file is marked for deletion. This space is no longer allocated to a specific file. Until it is overwritten, it still contains the previous data and can often be retrieved.

Unicode: The code standard that provides for uniform representation of character sets for all languages. It is also referred to as double-byte language.

Unstructured Data: Refers to information that does not exist in the usual row-column database. These text and multimedia data files, such as webpages, videos, audio files or videos, lack the ability to be organized effectively within a database.

```
    (\
     \ \ '\
      \ \ '\              _____
       /  '|           ()_____)
       \ '/            \ ~~~~~~~ \
        \\              \ ~~~~~~  \
       (==)             \___~~___\
       (__)          ()_____)
```

About the Author

Antony P. Ng is a registered patent attorney practicing in Austin, Texas. Mr. Ng was a judicial intern for Honorable Judge David Hittner, Southern District of Texas, and Honorable Justice Michol O'Connor, First Court of Appeals of Texas. Mr. Ng has a bachelor's degree in electrical engineering from Texas A&M University and a master's degree in electrical engineering from Rice University. Mr. Ng also graduated from South Texas College of Law where he served as an assistant editor for the *South Texas Law Review*.

Made in the USA
Monee, IL
21 July 2021

327d3964-08ba-4b34-8564-acd71bce41d4R01